NOTEWORTHY

A COLLECTION OF RECIPES FROM THE RAVINIA FESTIVAL

*Additional copies of NOTEWORTHY may be
obtained by writing:*

NOTEWORTHY Publications
1575 Oakwood Avenue
Highland Park, Illinois 60035
Telephone 708/433-8800

All proceeds from the sale of NOTEWORTHY
will support the Young Artists Institute
of Ravinia Festival

First Edition, First Printing: May, 1986
Second Printing: August, 1986
Third Printing: October, 1986
Fourth Printing: April, 1988
Fifth Printing: May, 1989
Sixth Printing: January, 1991

Printed in the United States of America
The Lakeside Press,
R.R. Donnelley & Sons Company

This book is dedicated to the Ravinia Festival, a summer place
that warms our hearts through all of the seasons.

Editor:
Joan Freehling

Co-Editor:
Parsla Mason

Production Editor:
Dorothy Haber

Food Editor:
Jan Weil

Collection Chairman:
Lois Steans

Testing Chairman:
Gloria Gottlieb

Marketing Chairman:
Mary Kay Eyerman

Retail Chairman:
Nancy Woulfe

Wholesale Chairmen:
Alison Good
Jeannie James

Office Chairmen:
Martha Tardy
Sallie Scott

Special Events:
Mary Frey

Treasurers:
Ann McDermott
Boots Pedersen

Design:
Diane Kavelaras

Photography:
William Sladcik

Food Stylist:
Bonnie Rabert

Prop Stylist:
Wendy Marx

Editing Consultant:
Margo Goldsmith

Ravinia Liaison:
Charlis McMillan

Typesetter:
JDtype

CONTENTS

Ravinia's proud history began in 1904 when its gates first opened to a kaleidoscope of music, dance, and theater. In the spectacular era of the '20's, Ravinia became known as the summer opera capital of the world.

Today the Ravinia Festival enjoys its well-deserved reputation as a major American festival of the arts. Hundreds of thousands come each summer to share in the joys of the classical and popular concerts, the recitals, the chamber music, the ballet, and the theater performances. Sprawling over thirty-six wooded acres, the grounds have been carefully landscaped to best display the many varieties of trees and flowers as well as the notable outdoor sculpture. The park is further enhanced by an architecturally outstanding open-air pavilion and a charming vintage theater.

It is in this incomparable natural setting that the Festival bursts forth each summer for a twelve to fourteen week season. Located in suburban Highland Park, twenty-three miles from Chicago, Ravinia engages the Chicago Symphony Orchestra for an annual eight week residency. The brilliant conductor, fine pianist, and chamber musician James Levine is in his fourteenth season as Music Director. Visiting orchestras, eminent guest conductors, and celebrated soloists from around the world perform at the Festival each season. Twenty-four dance companies have appeared at Ravinia since 1947. At the completion of its fiftieth season Ravinia had recorded an attendance of ten million visitors.

The Ravinia experience, however, far transcends facts and figures. It involves the mind, the emotions, the senses. It is an umbrella of trees etched against a golden sunset; the scent of the hydrangeas; a thousand twinkling lights under a fan-shaped roof that floats in the night; a velvet-green carpet of lawn speckled with warm summer colors; picnic baskets, candlelight; and radiant faces as far as the eye can see, engrossed in the unique pleasure of a Ravinia evening.

This book has been made possible by the support of the many who have shared the Ravinia experience. It is our hope that it will help to ensure the Festival's bright and ever-broadening future.

APPETIZERS

Ravinia Notes

It was at the turn of the century that Ravinia first opened its gates as an amusement park. Among the early attractions were a merry-go-round and a baseball diamond. A little-known fact is that baseball endures at Ravinia. The NOTEWORTHY annual event is a highly competitive game played between the Chicago Symphony Orchestra and Ravinia's Trustees and Sustaining Fund Committee. The score to date: the well-practiced orchestra members have emerged victorious eleven times and the Ravinia players twice!

MARINATED SHRIMP WITH ORANGE

Serves 12

3 pounds large shrimp, uncooked, shelled, deveined
4 oranges, peeled, sectioned
4 medium white onions, sliced
1½ cups cider vinegar
1 cup vegetable oil
⅔ cup fresh lemon juice
½ cup ketchup
¼ cup sugar
2 tablespoons drained capers
2 tablespoons minced parsley
2 teaspoons salt
2 teaspoons mustard seeds
1 teaspoon celery seed
¼ teaspoon pepper
2 cloves garlic, crushed
lettuce, optional

In boiling water cook shrimp 2 minutes only. Rinse with cold water until thoroughly chilled. Drain.

Combine shrimp, oranges, and onions in large bowl. Mix remaining ingredients, except lettuce, and pour over shrimp mixture. Cover and refrigerate 8 hours or overnight, stirring occasionally. Serve in individual shells or on a bed of lettuce.

May also be served as a luncheon dish.

See photo page 223.

SHRIMP IN GREEN SAUCE

Serves 8

A vigorous, pesto-like sauce.

2   slices white bread, crusts removed
½   cup red wine vinegar
3   cups packed parsley, stems removed
3   tablespoons drained, rinsed capers
3   cloves garlic, crushed
4   anchovy fillets
¾   cup olive oil
2   pounds large or jumbo shrimp, cooked, shelled, deveined, halved
    Bibb or Boston lettuce, optional
    sliced tomatoes, optional

Soak bread in vinegar 10 minutes in shallow dish. Squeeze dry. In food processor or blender combine bread, parsley, capers, garlic, and anchovies. Purée. With motor running, gradually add olive oil. Blend well. Pour sauce over shrimp. Toss until well coated. If desired, serve on Bibb or Boston lettuce leaf topped with sliced tomato.

WORLD FAMOUS SHRIMP REMOULADE

Serves 12 to 14

¾   cup mayonnaise
¾   cup chili sauce
6   tablespoons horseradish
¾   cup sour cream
3   tablespoons dried chives
6   teaspoons dried parsley
3   teaspoons Beau Monde
1   medium onion, very thinly sliced
3   tablespoons drained capers, optional
3   pounds cooked, shelled, deveined shrimp
    lettuce

Combine all ingredients except lettuce, adding shrimp last. Mix well. Refrigerate overnight. Serve on bed of lettuce.

May also be served as a luncheon salad.

SHRIMP ON A STICK

Serves 8

2 pounds uncooked, shelled, deveined jumbo shrimp
6 cups water
2 cups dry white wine
¼ cup white wine vinegar
1 onion, sliced
1 carrot, sliced
4 parsley sprigs
2 cloves garlic
1 rib celery, sliced
2 bay leaves
1 tablespoon salt
½ teaspoon thyme

Dill Butter:
½ pound butter, softened
1 tablespoon minced fresh dill or 2 teaspoons dried dill weed
1 teaspoon lemon juice
dash Tabasco
fresh dill

Thread each shrimp lengthwise on long bamboo skewer. Refrigerate. In large kettle, combine water, wine, vinegar, vegetables, and seasonings. Bring to boil. Reduce heat and simmer 30 minutes. Strain.

Combine all dill butter ingredients; whip until creamy. Divide into small individual dishes.

When ready to serve, transfer hot bouillon to fondue pot. Serve skewered shrimp on bed of fresh dill. Each guest does his own cooking.

OLD FAVORITE SHRIMP

Serves 8 to 10

3 pounds large shrimp, cooked, shelled, deveined
⅓ cup lemon juice
1 pint Miracle Whip (no substitution)
2 red onions, thinly sliced
1-2 tablespoons sugar
1 tablespoon dried dill weed

Combine all ingredients. Mix well. Chill 24 hours before serving.

SHRIMP-ARTICHOKE APPETIZER

Serves 8

10-12 ounces broccoli or cauliflower, in bite-size pieces
½ cup vegetable oil
½ cup olive oil
½ cup white vinegar
1 tablespoon sugar
1 tablespoon lemon juice
2 cloves garlic, minced
1 teaspoon salt
¼ teaspoon dry mustard
⅛ teaspoon white pepper
1 pound shrimp, cooked, shelled, deveined
14 ounces canned artichoke hearts, quartered
chopped parsley
pimiento strips

Slightly undercook broccoli or cauliflower. Drain. In food processor or blender combine oils, vinegar, sugar, lemon juice, garlic, salt, mustard, and pepper. Blend. In large bowl combine shrimp, artichokes, and broccoli or cauliflower. Add dressing and mix well. Cover and chill overnight. Drain well. Garnish with chopped parsley and pimiento strips. Serve with toothpicks.

SEVICHE IN AVOCADO

Serves 6 to 8

1 pound bay scallops
¾ cup fresh lime juice
salt to taste
pepper to taste
3 mild canned green chilies, chopped
2 medium tomatoes, peeled, chopped
1 large onion, chopped
1 tablespoon drained capers
4 tablespoons olive oil
2 tablespoons dry white wine
1 teaspoon oregano
3-4 avocados
leaf lettuce or parsley

Cover scallops with lime juice. Combine salt, pepper, chilies, tomatoes, onion, capers, olive oil, wine, and oregano. Mix well. Add to scallops. Marinate overnight, stirring occasionally. Just before serving, peel and halve avocados. Fill with scallop mixture. Serve on lettuce or garnish with parsley.

CLAUDIO ABBADO'S CRAB CAPONATA

Serves 6 to 8

¼ cup olive oil
¼ cup vegetable oil
2 medium eggplants, cubed
2 celery hearts, cubed
½ cup ketchup
2 tablespoons sugar
6 ounces red wine vinegar
1 small pepperoni (about 4 inches long), diced
1 small cucumber, diced
8 ounces cooked crab meat
1 tablespoon drained capers
3 ounces pimiento-stuffed Spanish olives, sliced, optional

In large skillet combine oils. Sauté eggplant and celery in oil over medium heat. Remove. Add ketchup, sugar, and vinegar to oil in skillet. Simmer 5 minutes. Add pepperoni and continue to cook 5 minutes. Return eggplant and celery to skillet. Add remaining ingredients; combine well. Remove from heat. Refrigerate until chilled.

Medium shrimp may be substituted for the crab meat.

SCALLOPS IN MUSTARD-DILL SAUCE

Serves 8

2½ pounds uncooked bay scallops
½ cup Dijon mustard
4 teaspoons dry mustard
4 tablespoons sugar
¼ cup white wine vinegar
⅔ cup vegetable oil
½ cup chopped fresh dill
   salt to taste
   lettuce
4 avocados, optional

Poach scallops in simmering water until just opaque. Do not overcook. Rinse under cold water to stop cooking process. Drain and refrigerate. Combine Dijon mustard, dry mustard, and sugar. Stir in vinegar. Gradually add oil, stirring constantly. Add dill and salt to taste. Refrigerate. Combine chilled sauce with scallops. Serve on lettuce-lined plates, in small coquille shells or avocado half. Accompany with toast points or crackers.

MUSSELS IN JACKETS

Yield: 20-24

1 quart mussels, well scrubbed
⅔ cup water
⅛ pound butter, melted
garlic powder to taste
10-12 small new potatoes
1 small onion, finely chopped
grated sharp Cheddar cheese

In deep kettle or saucepan bring water to boil. Add mussels. Cover and steam until mussel shells open, approximately 10 minutes. Discard any mussels that do not open. Use a knife to remove mussels from shells. Place mussels in small bowl. Cover with melted butter and garlic powder. Stir.

Boil potatoes just until tender. Cool. Cut in half and scoop out a portion of each center. Place in baking dish. Sprinkle onion over potatoes. Place 1 mussel with a small portion of garlic-butter in each potato half. Top with cheese. Bake in preheated 350° oven 10 minutes or until cheese is melted and bubbly.

May be assembled and refrigerated several hours before baking.

HERRING SALAD

Serves 6 to 8

⅔ cup sour cream
⅓ cup mayonnaise
1 tablespoon plus 1 teaspoon milk
2 tablespoons lemon juice
1 tablespoon celery seed
2 teaspoons sugar
1 large green pepper, diced
2 small onions, finely chopped
2 carrots, peeled, grated
4 ounces chopped olives
1 teaspoon dried dill weed
12 ounces herring fillets in wine sauce, drained, in bite-size strips
parsley

Combine all ingredients except herring and parsley. Mix well. Add herring. Serve salad in bowl; garnish with parsley. Surround with cocktail rye, thin pumpernickel, or crackers.

CLAM POT

Yield: 4 to 5 cups

19½ ounces canned minced clams, drained
 ½ cup drained clam juice
16 ounces cream cheese
 2 tablespoons chopped scallions
 1 tablespoon Worcestershire sauce
 1 tablespoon lemon juice
 1 teaspoon minced parsley
 ½ teaspoon salt
6-8 drops Tabasco
 1 2-pound round loaf sourdough bread

In food processor combine all ingredients except bread. Blend until smooth. Cut off top of bread, creating a lid. Hollow out center of bread, creating a cavity. Reserve scooped-out bread.

Fill bread cavity with clam mixture. Cover with "lid". Wrap tightly in foil. Bake in preheated 250° oven 3 hours. Wrap scooped-out bread in foil. Bake in 250° oven 1½ hours and use for dipping into baked clam pot.

CHÈVRES TOMATO PUFFS

Yield: 14 to 18

1 frozen puff pastry sheet, thawed no longer than 30 minutes
1 large shallot, chopped
8 ounces cream cheese
1 ounce medium sharp Chèvres cheese
1 tablespoon anchovy paste
1 tablespoon sour cream
4 plum tomatoes, peeled, thinly sliced

Roll out pastry to increase size by half. Using 2-inch cookie cutter, cut pastry into rounds. Place on cookie sheet. Bake in preheated 400° oven 12 to 15 minutes. In food processor or blender combine shallot, cheeses, anchovy paste, and sour cream. Process until smooth. Place 1 tomato slice on each pastry round. Mound cheese mixture over tomato. Broil 2 to 3 minutes or until cheese browns slightly. Serve immediately.

CRAB AND CHÈVRES IN FILO

Yield: 20 to 24

1 pound filo leaves
4 ounces Chèvres cheese
1 egg
2 tablespoons crème fraîche
1 teaspoon Dijon mustard
1 clove garlic, minced
1 teaspoon chopped parsley
⅛ teaspoon salt, or to taste
  freshly ground pepper, or to taste
1 teaspoon fresh thyme or ½ teaspoon dried thyme
6 ounces canned lump crab meat, drained
½ pound butter, melted

Thaw filo leaves according to package directions. In food processor or with electric mixer combine cheese, egg, crème fraîche, mustard, garlic, parsley, and seasonings. Stir in crab meat carefully by hand.

Cut filo in 13- by 7-inch strips. Working with 2 strips at a time, brush with melted butter. Fold in half lengthwise; brush with butter again. Place heaping tablespoon of filling on corner of filo and fold over diagonally. Brush with butter again and continue to fold diagonally, applying melted butter after each fold. Continue procedure with remaining dough and filling.

Place triangles on cookie sheet. Brush each with melted butter. Bake in preheated 400° oven 10 to 12 minutes or until puffed and golden brown.

SMALL COCKTAIL QUICHE

Yield: 4 to 5 dozen

3 eggs
1 pound small curd cottage cheese
3 tablespoons sour cream or sour half and half
4 ounces sharp Cheddar cheese, grated
½ cup Bisquick
¼ teaspoon salt
  pepper to taste
4 tablespoons melted butter or margarine

In large bowl combine all ingredients. Blend just until mixed. Spray miniature muffin tins liberally with vegetable spray or use teflon tins. Fill each cup seven-eighths full. Bake in preheated 375° oven 25 to 30 minutes. Cool in pans 5 minutes before removing.

May be frozen. Reheat 10 minutes before serving.

MUSHROOM TARTS

Yield: 48

Store in freezer for unexpected guests.

Tart:
10 tablespoons butter, in pieces
2½ cups sifted flour
½ teaspoon salt
⅓ cup sour cream
1 egg, slightly beaten

Filling:
4 tablespoons butter
3 tablespoons finely chopped shallots
½ pound finely chopped mushrooms
2 tablespoons flour
1 cup whipping cream
1 tablespoon finely chopped chives
½ teaspoon salt
⅛ teaspoon cayenne pepper
½ teaspoon lemon juice
  parsley sprigs, optional

In food processor combine butter, flour, and salt. Process just until butter breaks into small pieces. Do not overmix. Add sour cream and egg. Mix well. Wrap in wax paper and chill. Press into 48 miniature muffin cups. Bake in preheated 400° oven 12 to 15 minutes or until golden.

In heavy skillet melt butter. Add shallots. Cook 4 minutes, stirring constantly. Shallots should not brown. Blend in mushrooms. Cook until all moisture evaporates, about 10 to 15 minutes. Sprinkle flour over mixture. Mix well. Stirring constantly, add cream and bring to boil. When mixture thickens, reduce heat and simmer 1 to 2 minutes. Remove from heat. Stir in remaining ingredients; cool.

Fill each tart with mixture. Bake in preheated 350° oven 10 minutes. Garnish with small sprigs of parsley, if desired. Serve immediately.

Tarts may be filled, frozen, and baked frozen in preheated 400° oven 12 minutes.

Yield: 24

Shortcut method for tart:
24 slices soft commercial white bread, rolled to flatten
4 tablespoons unsalted butter, softened

Cut 3-inch rounds from each slice of bread. Butter bread generously on both sides. Carefully fit into miniature muffin tins. Fill "cups" with mushroom filling. Bake in preheated 350° oven 10 minutes. Broil 1 minute to crisp. Serve immediately.

Baked tarts may be frozen. Bake frozen in preheated 400° oven 12 minutes.

CHEESE PIROSHKY

Yield: 40

Pastry:
1¾ cups sifted flour
½ teaspoon baking powder
½ teaspoon salt
¼ pound unsalted butter
1 egg, beaten
½ cup sour cream

Filling:
7½ ounces whole milk farmers cheese, softened
4 ounces cream cheese, softened
¾ cup grated Jarlsberg cheese
2 eggs
1 egg beaten

Combine flour, baking powder and salt. Cut in butter until mixture resembles coarse crumbs. Mix egg with sour cream. Stir into flour mixture until dough almost cleans side of bowl. Knead dough 1 minute on lightly floured surface. Refrigerate covered 30 minutes or overnight.

Combine cheeses in large bowl. Beat until smooth. Add 2 eggs, 1 at a time, mixing well. On lightly floured surface roll dough into ⅛-inch-thick rectangle. Cut into 3-inch squares. Beat remaining egg and brush over edges of squares. Place 2 teaspoons of cheese mixture in center of each square. Fold squares on diagonal to form a triangle. Press edges with fork to seal, taking care that no cheese mixture is in seam. Brush triangles lightly with beaten egg. Pierce top of each pastry once with toothpick. Place on floured, greased baking sheet. Bake in preheated 400° oven 15 minutes or until golden brown. Remove to rack to cool. Serve warm or at room temperature.

See photo page 222.

M85'S

Yield: 3 to 4 cups

¼ teaspoon lemon pepper
¼ teaspoon dried dill weed
¼ teaspoon garlic salt
1 ounce package dry Hidden Valley buttermilk dressing
24 ounces oyster crackers, miniature preferred
1 cup vegetable oil

Combine lemon pepper, dill weed, garlic salt, and dressing. Mix well. Place crackers in double brown paper bag. Sprinkle mixture over crackers. Pour oil over all. Shake well. Serve in bowl.

GRAZERS

Yield: about 160

For the yuppie generation and beyond.

1   **loaf whole wheat bread, sliced**
13   **ounces creamy peanut butter**
½   **cup vegetable oil**
2   **tablespoons sugar**

Remove crusts from bread. Halve slices horizontally. Cut each half into 4 pieces vertically. (This is easier if bread is frozen.) Bake sticks and crusts in preheated 250° oven until light brown, 45 to 60 minutes. Crush crusts in plastic bag using rolling pin.

Heat peanut butter, oil, and sugar in top of double boiler. Mix well. Dip bread sticks, a few at a time, into mixture. Roll peanut butter sticks in crumbs. (Use commercial unseasoned bread crumbs to supplement if necessary.) Stack on narrow side to dry.

Grazers freeze well.

ROBIN'S CHEESE CRISPS

Choice of bulk cheese:
     Monterey Jack
     Aged Parmesan
     Aged Swiss
     Colby
     Herkimer
     or other
     Do not use Muenster

Optional seasonings:
     garlic salt
     sesame seed
     jalapeño peppers

Cut cheese in amount desired into *carefully* measured ½-inch cubes. Place on teflon pan (no other type), allowing space between pieces for expansion during cooking. Bake in preheated 375° oven approximately 7 minutes or until crisp. Remove from pan and drain on paper towel. Sprinkle with 1 of optional seasonings, if desired. Cool and serve with cocktails.

This recipe is versatile and works with whatever amount of cheese is on hand.

CHEESE STRAWS

Yield: 24

¼ pound butter
2 cups flour
2 teaspoons baking powder
1 teaspoon salt
½ teaspoon ground red pepper
1 pound extra sharp Cheddar cheese, grated

In food processor or with electric mixer blend butter, flour, baking powder, salt, and pepper. Add cheese gradually, blending into butter-flour mixture. Place in small metal cookie press. Using star design, make 5- to 6-inch "straws". Bake in preheated 375° oven 10 to 12 minutes.

May be made without using cookie press. On lightly floured surface, roll pieces of dough into pencil shapes, about 3½ to 4 inches long each. Bake as above.

SESAME COCKTAIL WAFERS

Yield: 7 dozen

2 cups flour
1 teaspoon salt
  pinch cayenne pepper
¾ cup shortening
¼ cup ice water
1 cup sesame seed, toasted
  salt to taste

Mix flour, 1 teaspoon salt, and cayenne. Cut in shortening. Add ice water as needed to reach pie crust consistency. Add sesame seeds. Roll out dough ¼ to ⅛ inch thick. Cut into 1½-inch round wafers. Place on unbuttered cookie sheet. Bake in preheated 300° oven until lightly browned, about 15 minutes. Sprinkle with additional salt while hot.

May be made ahead and stored in airtight container. To crisp, reheat in 300° oven for 5 minutes.

HERBED PECANS

Yield: 4 cups

6 tablespoons butter
4 teaspoons dried rosemary
⅛ teaspoon dried basil
1 tablespoon salt
½ teaspoon cayenne pepper
4 cups pecan halves

In large saucepan melt butter. Add seasonings and stir. Remove from heat. Add pecans and toss to coat well. Do not break nuts.

Arrange nuts in single layer in jelly-roll pan. Scrape any remaining herb mixture over nuts. Bake in preheated 325° oven 10 to 12 minutes or until well browned. Stir gently 2 or 3 times. Serve warm or at room temperature.

BACON BITS

bacon
Dijon mustard
brown sugar

Cut bacon strips into thirds. Spread with mustard. Sprinkle generously with brown sugar. Place on broiler pan and bake in preheated 350° oven 15 to 20 minutes or until crisp.

This recipe may be prepared with whatever amount of bacon is available.

APRICOT-BACON APPETIZERS

Yield: 24

A quick, simple, hot hors d'oeuvre.

12 slices bacon, halved horizontally
24 dried apricots
¾ cup soy sauce
¼ cup brown sugar

Partially cook bacon. Wrap one-half slice around single, once-folded apricot. Secure with toothpick. Place on cookie sheet. Bake in preheated 350° oven, turning once, about 20 minutes or until brown and crisp. Drain on paper towel and serve immediately with combined soy sauce and brown sugar for dipping.

BARBECUED BITES

Serves 12 to 14

1 medium onion, chopped
1½ tablespoons butter or margarine
12 ounces Bennett's chili sauce
6 ounces water
½ tablespoon lemon juice or vinegar
4 ounces brown sugar
3 drops Tabasco
1 pound salami, in ⅛-inch slices

Sauté onion in butter until soft. Add chili sauce, water, lemon juice, brown sugar, and Tabasco. Simmer until mixture is reduced and thickened. Arrange salami slices in foil-lined 9- by 13-inch baking dish. Pour sauce over salami and let stand 3 hours. Bake in preheated 300° oven, basting and turning frequently, 2 to 2½ hours or until salami is "candied." Serve with cocktail rye, sauce, and Dijon mustard.

MINIATURE PORK KEBABS

Serves 6

6 tablespoons olive oil
1 tablespoon minced parsley
¾ teaspoon cumin
½ teaspoon thyme
½ teaspoon paprika
½ teaspoon ground red pepper
1 bay leaf, crumbled
  salt to taste
  freshly ground pepper to taste
1 pound lean pork tenderloin, in 1-inch cubes

In large bowl combine all ingredients except pork. Mix well. Add pork cubes to marinade. Cover and refrigerate several hours or, for more flavor, overnight. Stir occasionally. Thread pork cubes onto small skewers. Grill, preferably, or broil until well browned, basting with marinade.

SWEET AND SOUR MEATBALLS

Serves 10

The gingersnaps make the difference.

Meatballs:
2 pounds lean ground beef
1 egg
¼ cup ketchup
½ small onion, finely grated

Sauce:
3 onions, diced
 pinch baking soda
6 ounces tomato paste
4 medium pieces sour salt (citric acid)
1 cup firmly packed brown sugar
6 gingersnaps, very finely crushed

Mix ground beef, egg, ketchup, and onion. In large kettle combine all sauce ingredients. Form meat mixture into small balls. Add to sauce and simmer covered 2 hours. Stir often. Important: prepare early in day, preferably 1 day before serving. Skim off fat. Taste while cooking and adjust by adding more sour salt, brown sugar, and/or gingersnaps depending on your preference.

EGGPLANT CHIPS

Yield: 3 dozen

3 baby eggplants, unpeeled, sliced ⅛-inch thick
¼ cup mayonnaise
⅓ cup crushed saltine crackers
⅓ cup grated Parmesan cheese

Spread both sides of eggplant slices with mayonnaise. Combine crushed crackers and cheese. Mix well. Place in shallow plate. Dip eggplant slices into cracker-cheese mixture, coating well on both sides. Place slices on ungreased cookie sheet. Bake in preheated 450° oven 10 to 15 minutes. Serve hot.

Variation: For *Zucchini Chips* substitute unpeeled 1½-inch diameter zucchini for eggplant.

DILLED GREEN BEANS

Serves 8 to 10

Low-cal cocktail food.

2½ quarts water, divided
3 tablespoons coarse salt (iodized may be substituted)
2 pounds green beans, whole or halved, ends removed
1 teaspoon mustard seed
1 teaspoon dried dill weed
1 teaspoon crushed small, dry chili peppers
1 teaspoon dill seed
4 cloves garlic
2 cups white vinegar
⅔ cup sugar

In large kettle bring 2 quarts water to boil. Add 1 tablespoon salt and beans. Return to boil. Cook covered 5 minutes or until beans are tender-crisp. Drain and cool. Pack beans in storage containers. Mix mustard seed, dill weed, chili peppers, dill seed, and garlic. Pour over beans. In saucepan combine 2 cups water, vinegar, sugar, and 2 tablespoons salt. Add to beans. Cool. Cover and refrigerate 3 hours to 3 days (the longer the beans marinate the hotter they become). Drain before serving.

PEANUT DIP

Yield: 1¾ cups

An Indonesian specialty

⅔ cup crunchy peanut butter
6 tablespoons firmly packed dark brown sugar
½ cup lemon juice
4 tablespoons chili sauce
1 teaspoon soy sauce

Combine all ingredients. Refrigerate at least 24 hours. Serve with celery, carrot, cucumber, and zucchini strips.

BRUSSELS SPROUTS WITH BOMBAY DIP

Serves 8 to 10

2   pounds fresh Brussels sprouts or 30 ounces frozen
       Brussels sprouts
1   cup mayonnaise
2   tablespoons lemon juice
2   teaspoons grated onion
2   teaspoons sugar
1   teaspoon curry powder

Heat 1 inch salt water to boiling. Add Brussels sprouts and cover. Cook 6 to 8 minutes or until tender-crisp. Drain, cool, and refrigerate. In small bowl combine remaining ingredients; mix well. Cover and refrigerate at least 2 hours. To serve, arrange sprouts on dish around dip. Provide toothpicks.

HUMMUS

Yield: 2 cups

15¾   ounces canned garbanzo beans, drained
  ⅔   cup fresh lemon juice
  ¾   cup sesame or tahini paste
  4   cloves garlic, minced
  1   teaspoon salt
  ¼   teaspoon pepper
  2   tablespoons olive oil
     fresh parsley, finely chopped
  1   teaspoon paprika
     pita bread, sliced into 1½-inch strips

In food processor or blender combine beans, lemon juice, sesame or tahini paste, garlic, salt, and pepper. Process until smooth. Add olive oil. Process until smooth. Transfer to serving bowl. Sprinkle loosely with parsley and paprika.

Place bowl in center of large plate and surround with pieces of pita bread for dipping.

May also be served with sliced fresh vegetables.

REUBEN COCKTAIL DIP

Yield: 2 cups

6 ounces cream cheese, room temperature
½ cup plain yogurt
¾ cup grated Swiss cheese
1 clove garlic, finely chopped
½ cup drained, chopped sauerkraut
½ pound lean kosher corned beef, finely chopped
½ teaspoon Spike seasoned salt

Combine cream cheese and yogurt. Mix well. Stir in remaining ingredients. Thoroughly heat in double boiler or preheated 300° oven. Serve with toasted rye bread cut into 2-inch strips or pumpernickel sticks.

EGGPLANT APPETIZER

Serves 16

1 medium eggplant, unpeeled, finely chopped
1 large onion, coarsely chopped
½ cup coarsely chopped mushrooms
⅓ cup chopped green pepper
2 cloves garlic, minced
⅓ cup vegetable oil
½ cup chopped stuffed green olives
¼ cup chopped ripe olives
¼ cup drained capers
3 tablespoons pine nuts
6 ounces tomato paste
⅓ cup water
2 tablespoons red wine vinegar
2 teaspoons sugar
1 teaspoon salt
½ teaspoon pepper
½ teaspoon oregano

In large enamel saucepan combine eggplant, onion, mushrooms, green pepper, garlic, and oil. Simmer covered 10 minutes. Add remaining ingredients; mix well and simmer covered 25 minutes, stirring occasionally. Eggplant should be cooked but not overly soft. Refrigerate overnight (may be frozen). Serve at room temperature with crackers or cocktail pumpernickel.

An excellent first course served on lettuce-lined plates. May also be used as a stuffing for tomatoes to accompany meat dishes.

TARAMOSALATA

Yield: 3 cups

7 slices firm white bread, crusts removed
1 cup water
½ cup tarama (carp roe)
3 tablespoons finely chopped onion
¼ cup lemon juice
1 cup olive oil

Break bread into pieces. Place in bowl. Cover with water. Soak several minutes and squeeze dry very well. In food processor or blender combine bread and tarama. Blend. Add onion and lemon juice. Process until smooth. With motor running, add oil very slowly in thin stream. Process until thick. Refrigerate. May be served in hollowed out round bread loaf or cabbage. Serve with melba toast or crackers.

GARDEN PIZZA

Serves 10

A colorful offering featuring garden-fresh vegetables.

8 ounces refrigerated crescent roll dough
8 ounces cream cheese
½ cup mayonnaise
1½ teaspoons dried dill weed
½ teaspoon seasoned salt
½ teaspoon fines herbes
1½ teaspoons lemon juice
2 drops Tabasco
⅛ teaspoon garlic powder
   freshly ground pepper to taste
   fresh, colorful vegetables of choice: tomatoes, zucchini, mushrooms, cucumbers, green pepper, red pepper, avocado, black olives, radishes, broccoli flowerets (blanched 2 minutes), cauliflower flowerets (blanched 2 minutes), grated carrots.

Pinch seams of rolls together. Flatten and fit into pizza pan or 10-inch round spring-form pan, pressing dough ½-inch up sides. Bake in preheated 375° oven 9 to 10 minutes or until lightly browned. Cool.

Combine cream cheese, mayonnaise, and all seasonings. Spread over cooled crust. Sprinkle chopped vegetables decoratively over top or arrange in groupings. To serve, cut pizza into small wedges.

Recipe may be doubled and made in jelly-roll pan.

See photo page 223.

BRIE FRUIT DIP

Yield: 1 1/2 cups

8 ounces ripe Brie, rind removed, room temperature
8 ounces cream cheese, room temperature
1/2 cup plain yogurt
1/4 cup honey
1/8 teaspoon cinnamon
fresh fruit of choice, in decorative, bite-size pieces

Combine all ingredients except fruit. Mix well. Additional yogurt may be added to thin dip, if desired. Refrigerate. Arrange a decorative pattern of fresh fruit (pineapple, red and green apples, pears, strawberries, oranges) around bowl of dip.

May also be served as a refreshing dessert. Arrange fruit on individual plates. Drizzle mixture over fruit.

OLD SOMBRERO

Serves 12

1/3 head shredded iceberg lettuce, optional
21 ounces canned bean dip, jalapeño or plain
6 ounces frozen hot Mexican avocado dip, thawed
6 ounces frozen regular avocado dip, thawed
1 cup sour cream
1/2 cup mayonnaise
1 1/4 ounces packaged taco seasoning mix
7 scallions with tops, chopped
2 tomatoes, chopped
1/3 cup chopped black olives
8 ounces Monterey Jack cheese, grated

If lettuce is desired, arrange on large platter. Spread bean dip over lettuce or directly onto serving platter. Combine hot and regular avocado dips. Spread over bean dip, leaving a half-inch outer border of bean dip exposed.

Combine sour cream, mayonnaise, and taco mix. Spread over avocado layer, leaving a half-inch outer border of avocado exposed.

Sprinkle remaining ingredients in order given above over sour cream layer. Serve with corn chips.

AVOCADO WITH HOT CHUTNEY SAUCE

Serves 6

An unusual first course, luncheon, or supper salad. Very simple and always popular.

2 tablespoons brown sugar
2 tablespoons butter
2 tablespoons red wine vinegar
2 tablespoons chili sauce
2 tablespoons chutney
1 tablespoon Worcestershire sauce
3 ripe avocados, peeled, halved
  Bibb lettuce or watercress

In saucepan combine all ingredients except avocados and greens. Simmer 3 minutes. Spoon 2 heaping tablespoons hot mixture in center of each avocado half. Garnish with Bibb lettuce or watercress. Serve immediately.

COLD ASPARAGUS WITH HOT CRAB SAUCE

Serves 4 to 6

A beautiful presentation of an original combination.

16 ounces cream cheese
1/4 cup mayonnaise
1/3 cup dry white wine
1 teaspoon confectioners sugar
1 teaspoon prepared mustard
1/2 teaspoon onion juice
1/8 teaspoon garlic salt, or to taste
1/8 teaspoon seasoned salt, or to taste
9 ounces canned crab meat, drained
2 pounds thick fresh asparagus, cooked, chilled
  lettuce leaves
1/4 cup slivered almonds, optional

In top of double boiler blend cream cheese, mayonnaise, wine, sugar, mustard, and seasonings until smooth. Stir in crab, breaking up large chunks. Cook over simmering water until very hot. Divide asparagus into individual servings on lettuce leaves. Spoon hot sauce over each. Sprinkle almonds on top, if desired. Serve immediately. Sauce may be made ahead and reheated.

For more informal serving, use asparagus spears to dip into hot crab sauce.

ARTICHOKES IN TOMATO SAUCE

Serves 6

18 ounces frozen artichoke hearts
2 medium onions, sliced
1 cup beef bouillon
½ cup white wine
1 teaspoon sugar
½ teaspoon salt
⅛ teaspoon freshly ground pepper
⅛ teaspoon thyme
4 parsley sprigs
1 bay leaf
  juice of 1 lemon
2 tablespoons olive oil
2 tablespoons tomato paste
  chopped chives

In large saucepan combine all ingredients except chives. Cook uncovered 30 minutes or until thickened. Remove parsley sprigs and bay leaf. Pour into serving dish; garnish with chives. May be served hot or cold.

May also be served as a meat accompaniment.

ARTICHOKE DELIGHT

Serves 6 to 10

28 ounces canned artichokes, drained, coarsely chopped
1 cup mayonnaise
1½ cups grated Parmesan cheese
1-2 tablespoons chopped chives or scallions
4 tablespoons Marsala wine, optional

In small bowl combine all ingredients. Mix well. Transfer to shallow, greased casserole. Bake in preheated 375° oven 30 minutes or until golden brown. Serve immediately with chips, crackers, vegetables, or toasted party rye.

BRIE-APRICOT APPETIZER

Serves 14 to 18

The appearance and flavor of this appetizer belie its ease of preparation.

2   pounds whole brie
16 ounces apricot preserves
1   sheet of frozen puff pastry, thawed

Place whole brie, with rind, in oven-proof serving dish with shallow sides. Spread preserves over cheese. Stretch puff pastry to cover brie and tuck under sides. Bake in preheated 350° oven 25 minutes. Serve with wheat biscuits or favorite crackers.

CREAMED GOAT CHEESE WITH FRESH HERBS

Serves 8 to 10

1   tablespoon chopped fresh parsley
1   tablespoon chopped fresh tarragon leaves or
        ½ teaspoon dried tarragon
1   tablespoon chopped fresh chives
1   medium scallion, in 1-inch pieces
8   ounces cream cheese, cubed, at room temperature
¼   cup whipping cream
¼   pound goat cheese
⅛   teaspoon pepper
    salt to taste
    parsley sprigs

In food processor combine chopped parsley, tarragon, and chives. Process 20 seconds. Add scallion and process 20 seconds or until minced. Remove mixture and set aside.

In same container combine cream cheese, whipping cream, goat cheese, and pepper. Process with quick on-off turns until mixture is smooth, stopping several times to scrape sides. Adjust seasoning to taste; add salt if desired.

Return herb mixture to container. Process with 4 or 5 quick pulses until well mixed. Transfer mixture to serving bowl; cover. Refrigerate 2 hours or until mixture is of spreading consistency. Garnish with parsley sprigs and serve with thinly sliced pumpernickel bread.

PARTY CHEESE BALL

*Yield: One
8-cup ball*

3 pounds cream cheese, room temperature, divided
½ pound Roquefort cheese
½ pound sharp Cheddar cheese, grated
½ cup chopped fresh chives or scallions
1 clove garlic, minced
3 tablespoons black caviar, drained
3 tablespoons red caviar, drained
3 tablespoons chopped black olives
3 tablespoons chopped scallions
3 tablespoons chopped pimiento
3 tablespoons crisply cooked, crumbled bacon
3 tablespoons minced parsley
3 tablespoons chopped green olives
  parsley sprigs

Mix 1 pound cream cheese with Roquefort cheese. Mix 1 pound cream cheese with Cheddar cheese. Mix 1 pound cream cheese with chives and garlic. Place 3 mixtures together without mixing to form large ball. Smooth top of ball and score into 8 sections. Transfer to serving platter. With flat side of knife, press into each section 1 of 8 remaining ingredients, except parsley sprigs for garnish. Chill. Remove from refrigerator 30 minutes before serving. Garnish with parsley where 8 sections meet at top and around bottom.

At Christmas time, omit 8 toppings and cover entire ball with chopped parsley. Decorate with parsley sprigs and pimiento in holly shape at top. Place on large parsley sprigs and intersperse with occasional cherry tomato to simulate a wreath.

This recipe makes a huge ball. May also make 3 smaller ones and freeze extras. When decorating smaller balls, use no more than 3 toppings.

EAST INDIA CHEESE BALL

Serves 12 to 14

16 ounces cream cheese, softened
½ cup chopped mango chutney
½ cup slivered almonds, toasted
½ teaspoon dry mustard
1½ tablespoons curry powder
2-3 ounces shredded coconut

Combine cream cheese, chutney, almonds, mustard, and curry powder. Mix well. Roll into ball. Roll ball in coconut. Serve with crackers. May be stored in refrigerator for several weeks.

CHEDDAR CHUTNEY SPREAD

Yield: 2½ to 3 cups

8 ounces sharp Cheddar cheese, grated
8 ounces cream cheese
1½ tablespoons chopped onion
3 tablespoons dry sherry
½-1 teaspoon curry powder
  dash Tabasco
¾ cup chutney
2 tablespoons slivered almonds, toasted

In food processor or blender, combine cheeses, onion, sherry, curry, and Tabasco. Blend well. Spread mixture in shallow dish. Cover with chutney. Sprinkle almonds over top. Cover and refrigerate several hours. Serve spread at room temperature with crackers.

Variation:
Blend all ingredients, including almonds, in food processor or blender; increase almonds to ½ cup. Pack into crock and store in refrigerator several hours. Serve at room temperature with crackers.

JEZEBEL

Yield: 20 ounces

9 ounces pineapple preserves
9 ounces apple jelly
2½ ounces horseradish
½ ounce dry mustard
½ teaspoon freshly ground black pepper
8 ounces cream cheese

Combine all ingredients except cream cheese. Mix well and refrigerate. Place cream cheese on serving dish. Spoon half of sauce over cheese. Serve with crackers. Refrigerate remaining half. Keeps well.

May also be served as an accompaniment to ham or turkey.

COUNTRY TERRINE

Serves 15 to 20

1 pound ground veal
1 pound ground round steak
½ pound sweet Italian sausage, casing removed
10 ounces frozen spinach, thawed, drained
1 cup soft bread crumbs
¼ cup milk
1 medium onion, minced
2 eggs, well beaten
1 teaspoon basil
1 teaspoon thyme
½ teaspoon nutmeg
¾ cup pine nuts (pignola)
10 ounces frozen peas, thawed, drained
Kitchen Bouquet

In large bowl combine veal, beef, and sausage. Mix well. Add spinach, bread crumbs, milk, onion, eggs, and seasonings. Blend well. Gently stir in pine nuts and peas. Transfer to standard 1-pound loaf pan. Bake in preheated 350° oven 1½ hours, basting occasionally with Kitchen Bouquet. Cool in pan. To serve, remove to platter and accompany with sliced pickles.

May be frozen.

See photo page 226.

CHICKEN LIVER PÂTÉ

Serves 10 to 12

1 pound chicken livers
¾ pound unsalted butter, divided
½ cup minced onions
2 tablespoons brandy
1 teaspoon allspice
1 teaspoon salt
½ teaspoon cracked black pepper
¼ cup sour cream
1 tablespoon Benedictine
1 tablespoon lemon juice
2 tablespoons black truffles, or ripe olives, chopped, optional

continued

In large skillet, sauté livers quickly in ¼ pound butter. Remove livers from skillet. Sauté onions in drippings. Cook until wilted. Remove from heat. Return livers to skillet. Flame brandy in small saucepan. Add to livers. Stir in allspice, salt, pepper, sour cream, and Benedictine. In blender or food processor purée mixture until smooth. Refrigerate 30 minutes.

Cream remaining ½ pound butter until light. Add to liver mixture. Mix well. Stir in lemon juice and truffles, if desired. Place in oiled 3- to 4-cup mold or bowl, packing down firmly. Cover and refrigerate. Keeps 3 or 4 days in refrigerator. Allow to stand at room temperature 20 minutes before serving. Serve with small toasted rye rounds.

If using truffles, reserve a few to place at bottom of mold before adding pâté. May garnish with finely chopped parsley.

May be frozen for up to 4 weeks.

MIXED PÂTÉ

Serves 10

1¼ pounds boneless cooked chicken, finely ground or chopped
½ pound cooked pork, finely ground or chopped
½ pound cooked ham, finely ground or chopped
2 cloves garlic, crushed
3 scallions, finely chopped
1 medium onion, finely chopped
1 tablespoon finely chopped parsley
1 bay leaf
¼ teaspoon thyme
½ teaspoon salt
 freshly ground pepper to taste
2 eggs, lightly beaten
1 tablespoon flour
¼ pound butter, softened
¼ cup brandy
½ pound bacon
 Bibb or Boston lettuce

Combine chicken, pork, and ham. Add garlic, scallions, onion, parsley, bay leaf, thyme, salt, and pepper. Mix well. Stir in eggs, flour, butter, and brandy. Line standard 1-pound loaf pan with slices of bacon; reserve 4 pieces. Transfer meat mixture to loaf pan and top with reserved bacon. Cover pan well with foil and place in pan of hot water. Bake in preheated 350° oven 1 hour. Remove from oven and cool. Place a weight on top of pâté and refrigerate at least 1 day. Serve thinly sliced on bed of Bibb or Boston lettuce.

SMOKED TROUT MOUSSE

Serves 6 to 8

1 pound smoked trout, skinned, boned
2 tablespoons chopped scallion, white part only
2 teaspoons chopped fresh dill
¼ teaspoon freshly grated nutmeg
¼ teaspoon salt
¼ teaspoon white pepper
1½ teaspoons fresh lemon juice
1 tablespoon unflavored gelatin
1½ cups whipping cream
½ cup plain yogurt
dill sprigs

In food processor or blender purée trout with scallion, dill, nutmeg, salt, pepper, and lemon juice. Soften gelatin in cream. Heat without boiling until gelatin is dissolved. Remove from heat. Combine gelatin and yogurt. Add to trout mixture and process until smooth. Pour mixture into oiled 3-cup mold. Refrigerate until firm, about 4 hours or overnight. Unmold and arrange dill sprigs decoratively over mold. Serve with toast points. May be made in individual molds for use as first course.

Smoked whitefish may be substituted for trout.

MUSHROOM MOUSSE

Serves 10

½ pound butter
2 pounds mushrooms, finely chopped
¾ teaspoon salt
freshly ground pepper to taste
3 egg yolks
1 tablespoon whipping cream

In heavy skillet melt butter. Add mushrooms. Cook over low heat, stirring frequently, until liquid evaporates and mushrooms brown, about 35 minutes. Season with salt and pepper. Remove from heat. In separate bowl mix egg yolks with cream. Add 3 tablespoons of mushroom mixture to yolks. Mix well. Combine yolk mixture with mushrooms in skillet. Cook over low heat 2 to 3 minutes, stirring constantly. Pour into 3-cup decorative mold. Chill until firm. Unmold and serve at room temperature with crackers.

May also be served warm in individual molds as meat accompaniment.

CAVIAR EGG MOLD

Serves 8 to 10

3½ ounces black caviar
1½ tablespoons unflavored gelatin
3 tablespoons lemon juice
9 hard-boiled eggs
½ onion, quartered
1½ cups mayonnaise
1½ teaspoons Diable sauce
1½ teaspoons anchovy paste

Spread caviar on bottom of greased 6-cup mold. In small bowl combine gelatin and lemon juice. Blend remaining ingredients in food processor or blender. Add dissolved gelatin mixture and blend again. Pour into mold. Refrigerate overnight. Invert onto serving plate. Garnish as desired. Serve with cocktail rye.

Golden caviar may be substituted for black caviar.

ZESTY BLUE CHEESE MOLD

Serves 12

A bold accompaniment to cocktails.

1 tablespoon unflavored gelatin
2 tablespoons cold water
3 tablespoons hot milk
3 ounces cream cheese
8 ounces Danish blue cheese
1 tablespoon caraway seed
2 teaspoons Worcestershire sauce
½ teaspoon paprika
½ cup whipping cream, lightly whipped
whole walnuts
parsley

In small saucepan soften gelatin in cold water. Add hot milk. Stir over medium heat until gelatin is dissolved. Remove from heat. Combine cheeses in medium bowl and blend thoroughly. Stir in caraway seed, Worcestershire sauce, and paprika. Add gelatin. Blend well. Fold in whipped cream. Transfer to well-greased 4-cup mold and refrigerate until firm.

Unmold and garnish with walnuts and parsley. Serve with pumpernickel, rye, or melba rounds.

CONFETTI COCKTAIL MOLD

Serves 6 to 8

A pale pink mold, flecked with red and green.

1 tablespoon unflavored gelatin
¼ cup cold water
½ cup hot milk
8 ounces cream cheese
1 cup sour half and half
1 tablespoon Worcestershire sauce
1 teaspoon lemon juice
1 tablespoon dried dill weed
½ teaspoon lemon pepper
¼ teaspoon salt
1 tablespoon horseradish
1 tablespoon chopped parsley
½ cup chopped scallion tops
⅓ pound sliced smoked salmon, coarsely chopped
2 ounces Romanoff red lumpfish caviar
  lettuce
  parsley
  cherry tomatoes

Soften gelatin in cold water. Add hot milk; mix thoroughly. Cool. In food processor or blender mix cream cheese, sour half and half, gelatin mixture, Worcestershire sauce, lemon juice, dill weed, lemon pepper, and salt. Transfer to bowl. Add horseradish, 1 tablespoon parsley, scallion, and salmon. Mix by hand. Carefully fold in caviar so as not to break globules. Pour into well-greased individual decorative molds or 3-cup mold. Chill several hours.

Invert onto lettuce-lined platter and garnish with parsley and cherry tomatoes. Serve with melba toast rounds, cocktail pumpernickel, or rye.

See photo page 222.

SOUPS

Ravinia Notes

Grand opera came to Ravinia in 1919 and thrived for more than a dozen years. Among the great voices projecting from the little stage were those of Lucrezia Bori, Tito Schipa, and Giovanni Martinelli. A NOTEWORTHY innovation at the Festival in recent years has been the presentation of opera in concert form. Audiences have thrilled to the performances of such world-reknowned artists as Renatta Scotto, Leontyne Price, Sherrill Milnes, Tatiana Troyanos, Martina Arroyo, and Beverly Sills.

SUMMER SYMPHONY SOUP

Serves 6

3   medium cucumbers, peeled, seeded
3   cups sour cream
3   cups chicken broth
3   tablespoons cider vinegar
1   clove garlic, minced
2   tablespoons fresh dill
2   teaspoons salt
    toasted sliced almonds
    chopped parsley
    peeled, seeded, chopped tomatoes
    chopped scallions

Grate cucumbers or chop coarsely. Drain and squeeze. Place in large bowl.
Add sour cream, broth, vinegar, garlic, dill, and salt. Mix and chill. To serve,
pass almonds, parsley, tomatoes, and scallions in separate bowls as garnish
accompaniments.

WHITE GAZPACHO

Serves 10 to 12

An auspicious beginning to a Ravinia Festival evening.

1   bunch white hearts of celery, sliced
2   radishes, quartered
3   small zucchini, seeded, sliced
3   medium cucumbers, peeled, seeded, sliced
3   cups chicken broth
1   clove garlic, sliced
2   cups sour cream
3   tablespoons white wine vinegar
½   teaspoon salt, or to taste
1   teaspoon white pepper
    chopped parsley
    thin cucumber slices
    thin radish slices

In food processor or blender combine celery hearts, quartered radishes,
zucchini, sliced cucumbers, broth, and garlic; purée. Transfer to large container.
Stir in sour cream, ½ cup at a time. Add vinegar, salt, and pepper. Mix well.
Refrigerate covered overnight. Garnish with parsley, cucumber, or radish slices.

SPANISH GAZPACHO

Serves 6

Garnish with imagination.

1 quart tomato juice
  juice of 1 lemon
2 medium green peppers, finely chopped
1 small onion, finely chopped
2 tomatoes, seeded, finely chopped
1 small cucumber, seeded, finely chopped
3 cloves garlic, minced
2 tablespoons olive oil
  salt to taste
  Tabasco to taste

In large bowl combine tomato and lemon juices; mix well. Add remaining ingredients. Mix well and chill. If thinner consistency is desired, add cold water.

GAZPACHO ON THE ROCKS

Serves 8 to 12

1 cucumber, seeded, chopped
1 green pepper, chopped
½ cup finely chopped scallion with tops
30 ounces tomato sauce with bits
10½ ounces chicken broth
5 ounces water
2 tablespoons lemon juice
1 teaspoon basil
  dash Tabasco
1 clove garlic, minced, optional

Combine all ingredients; mix well. If thinner consistency is desired, stir in additional chicken broth. Refrigerate covered. May be served over ice.

TOMATO SLUSH

Serves 6

A stylish recipe from a Chicago grande dame, circa 1930.

6   large tomatoes, peeled
1   small onion, grated
1½ teaspoons salt
⅓   teaspoon freshly ground pepper
5   tablespoons mayonnaise
1   tablespoon parsley
1   teaspoon curry powder

Put tomatoes through food grinder using medium knife. Mix tomatoes with onion, salt, and pepper. Transfer to freezer tray. Freeze several hours or until of frosty consistency (do not allow to become solidly frozen). Mix mayonnaise, parsley, and curry powder. Serve frosted soup in cups, spooning mayonnaise mixture over top of each serving.

CHILLED CREAM OF TOMATO SOUP

Serves 4

Quick, delicious, light—and it doubles well.

3   cups Sacramento tomato juice
2   tablespoons tomato paste
4   green onions, minced
    rind of ½ lemon, grated
2   tablespoons lemon juice
    dash of Tabasco
½   teaspoon curry powder
    pinch thyme
    pinch sugar
    salt to taste
1   cup sour cream or sour half and half
4   tablespoons chopped parsley

Combine all ingredients except sour cream and parsley. Mix well and chill. Before serving, blend in sour cream and sprinkle each serving with parsley.

COLD CUCUMBER AND SPINACH SOUP

Serves 8 to 10

3-4 tablespoons butter
2 bunches scallions, chopped
6 cucumbers, divided
6 cups strong chicken stock
1 pound fresh spinach, stems removed, or 10 ounces
    frozen chopped spinach, thawed, drained
1 cup whipping cream
½ cup half and half
1 tablespoon lemon juice
    salt to taste
    freshly ground pepper to taste

In large kettle melt butter. Add scallions and cook slowly until tender. Peel, seed, and dice 5 cucumbers. Add to scallions. Sauté slowly 5 minutes. Add stock. Bring to boil. Reduce heat and simmer until cucumbers are tender, 10 to 20 minutes. Add spinach. Cook 5 minutes. Remove from heat. Stir in cream and half and half; cool. Purée in food processor or blender. Blend in lemon juice, salt, and pepper. Chill 4 hours. To serve, garnish with remaining unpeeled cucumber, thinly sliced.

FIVE-MINUTE CUCUMBER SOUP

Serves 4 to 6

2 medium cucumbers, peeled, seeded, cut into 2-inch pieces
2 scallions with tops, cut into 2-inch pieces
21 ounces canned cream of chicken soup
¾ cup sour cream
¼ cup mayonnaise
1⅓ teaspoons dried dill weed
1 teaspoon salt
    pepper to taste
½ cup half and half, optional
    choice of parsley, watercress, or thinly sliced cucumber

In food processor or blender combine cucumber pieces and scallions. Process until finely chopped. Transfer to large bowl. Add soup, sour cream, mayonnaise, dill, salt, and pepper. Mix well. If thinner consistency is desired, add half and half. Chill. Garnish with parsley, watercress, or thinly sliced cucumber.

CHILLED CUCUMBER SOUP

Serves 6 to 8

1	medium Spanish onion
3	fresh shallots or 1 teaspoon freeze-dried shallots
1	celery rib, finely chopped
10¾	ounces canned cream of chicken soup
1	teaspoon Coleman's English mustard
1	teaspoon Worcestershire sauce
4	dill sprigs or 1 teaspoon dried dill weed
1	teaspoon fresh or freeze-dried chives
1	teaspoon salt
¼	teaspoon white pepper
¼	teaspoon garlic powder
¼	teaspoon Maggi sauce
⅛	teaspoon poultry seasoning
2	cups peeled, seeded, puréed cucumbers
1	cup sour cream
1	cup buttermilk, strained
	finely chopped cucumbers
	chives

In large kettle combine all ingredients except puréed cucumbers, sour cream, buttermilk, chopped cucumbers, and chives. Bring to boil. Remove from heat; cool. Refrigerate until chilled. In food processor or blender, process mixture until smooth. Add puréed cucumbers, sour cream, and buttermilk. Stir well. Serve chilled. Garnish with finely chopped cucumbers and chives.

CHINESE CUCUMBER SOUP

Serves 4 to 5

2	small thin cucumbers or 1 medium cucumber
¼	cup thinly sliced 1-inch pieces cooked pork
2	teaspoons soy sauce
½	teaspoon dry sherry
1	teaspoon cornstarch
4	cups chicken broth
1	teaspoon sesame oil

Peel cucumbers, leaving some green. Slice in half vertically. Hollow out and discard seedy portion. In food processor slice cucumbers thinly (should make 1½ to 2 cups). Combine pork, soy sauce, sherry, and cornstarch; mix well. In saucepan bring chicken broth to boil. Blend in pork mixture until soup boils again. Stir in cucumber. Do not allow cucumber to cook. Remove from heat. Add sesame oil. Serve immediately.

GRAPEFRUIT SOUP

Yield 4 to 6

Try this unusual combination for a new taste treat.

2 tablespoons chopped onion
1 tablespoon butter
3 cups tomato juice
2 cups orange juice
1 bay leaf
  salt to taste
  pepper to taste
2 grapefruit, peeled, sectioned

Sauté onion in butter. Drain. Combine onion with remaining ingredients except grapefruit sections. Let flavors blend at least 1 hour. Remove bay leaf before serving. Place several grapefruit sections in bottom of individual bowls. Pour soup over to cover. Serve hot or cold.

COLD BROCCOLI SOUP

Serves 4 to 6

1½ pounds broccoli, trimmed, or 20 ounces frozen chopped broccoli
4 cups chicken stock
1 medium onion, quartered
2 tablespoons butter
2 teaspoons curry powder
  salt to taste
  dash pepper
2 tablespoons lime juice
  lemon slices
  sour cream
  chives

In large kettle combine broccoli, stock, onion, butter, curry powder, salt, and pepper. Bring to boil; reduce heat. Simmer covered 8 to 12 minutes, until broccoli is tender. In food processor or blender blend half the mixture until smooth. Repeat with remaining mixture. Stir in lime juice. Cover and chill 4 hours. Serve soup with slice of lemon topped with sour cream and chives.

GARDEN FRESH SORREL SOUP

Serves 4

Gardeners, take note. A unique green bounty.

6 tablespoons unsalted butter
1 medium to large onion, chopped
1 clove garlic, minced
½ pound sorrel leaves, stems removed
½ cup celery, chopped
2½ cups chicken broth
1 tablespoon chopped parsley
¼ teaspoon salt
¼ teaspoon freshly ground pepper
¼ teaspoon freshly grated nutmeg

In large kettle melt butter. Sauté onion and add garlic. Cook 5 minutes or until onion is transparent. Add sorrel and celery. Cook 5 minutes or until sorrel is wilted. Add broth, parsley, salt, pepper, and nutmeg. Simmer 20 minutes. Remove from heat and purée in food processor or blender. Transfer to bowl and chill.

CHILLED PUMPKIN SOUP

Serves 8

Serve this in a scooped-out pumpkin on an Indian summer eve.

4 cups clear chicken broth
1 large onion, minced
2 pounds canned pumpkin purée
2 teaspoons Worcestershire sauce
1 tablespoon plus 1 teaspoon brown sugar
  salt to taste
  pepper to taste
1 teaspoon ground ginger
1½ cups half and half
  sour cream
  minced scallions
  paprika

In large kettle combine chicken broth and onion. Bring to boil. Reduce heat and simmer 15 minutes. Remove from heat and gradually stir in pumpkin purée. Add Worcestershire sauce, sugar, salt, pepper, and ginger. In food processor or blender purée mixture in batches. Transfer to large bowl. Cool. Stir in half and half. Chill. Garnish with sour cream, scallions, and paprika.

CARROT VICHYSSOISE

Serves 10 to 12

3   potatoes, peeled, sliced
7   carrots, peeled, divided
2½ leeks, sliced, divided
1   ham bone or ham shank
5   cups chicken broth
1   cup half and half
    salt to taste
    pepper to taste

In large kettle combine potatoes, 6 carrots, 2 leeks, ham bone, and chicken broth. Cook until vegetables are tender. Discard ham bone. Stir in half and half. Transfer to food processor or blender in small batches. Purée until smooth. Cut remaining carrot and leek into thin julienne strips. Steam 2 or 3 minutes until tender-crisp. Refrigerate vegetables; reserve for garnish. Chill soup overnight. Before serving taste for seasoning. Serve soup in individual bowls. Garnish with julienned carrot and leek.

AVOCADO SOUP

Serves 6 to 8

An appetizing perk-up for the dog days of August.

2   cups peeled, sliced avocados
2   cups chicken consommé
½   teaspoon onion juice or minced onion to taste
1   cup half and half
1   cup sour cream
    juice of 1 lemon or to taste
    salt to taste
    pepper to taste
    paprika
    chopped parsley
    chopped scallion tops

In food processor or blender combine avocados, consommé, and onion juice. Process just until puréed. Transfer to large bowl. Add half and half, sour cream, lemon juice, salt, and pepper. Mix until smooth. Refrigerate. Garnish with paprika, parsley, and scallion tops.

NOUVELLE BORSCHT

Serves 4 to 5

32 ounces canned julienned beets
1 quart water
½ cup vinegar
3 eggs, well beaten
1 teaspoon dried dill weed
sugar to taste
salt to taste
sour cream
dill sprigs

In large kettle combine beets and water. Bring to boil; add vinegar. Remove from heat and cool. Add eggs, dill weed, sugar, and salt. Chill. Serve cold with dash of sour cream and dill sprig.

SCANDINAVIAN FRUIT SOUP

Serves 12

2 cups dried assorted fruit
6 cups cold water
2 cups cold peach nectar
2 cinnamon sticks
4 ¼-inch thick lemon slices
3 tablespoons lemon juice
4 tablespoons quick tapioca
1½ cups sugar
3 tablespoons golden raisins
2 tablespoons currants
1 large tart apple, peeled, cored, sliced
1½-2 cups blueberries
sour cream or whipping cream

In large enamel or stainless steel kettle soak dried fruit in water and nectar 45 minutes.

Add cinnamon stick, lemon slices, lemon juice, tapioca and sugar. Mix well. Bring to boil, reduce heat, cover and simmer 10 minutes, stirring occasionally.

Blend in raisins, currants, and apple slices. Simmer 5 minutes. Stir in blueberries, remove from heat and cool to room temperature. Remove cinnamon stick, cover and chill. Serve with a dollop of sour cream.

If desired, serve as a dessert, with cream, stiffly whipped.

May be prepared and refrigerated 2 to 3 days before serving.

STRAWBERRY ORANGE SOUP

Serves 6 to 8   *An extraordinary flavor, a visual treat.*

1   pint strawberries, hulled
     juice of 1 orange
1½   tablespoons Grand Marnier
3   tablespoons honey
1   teaspoon confectioners sugar
1   cup plain yogurt or sour cream
5½   ounces peach nectar
⅓   cup half and half
1   teaspoon grated orange rind
1   orange, peeled, thinly sliced
     mint leaves

In food processor or blender combine two-thirds of the strawberries and orange juice. Blend until smooth. Add Grand Marnier, honey, sugar, yogurt, nectar, half and half, and rind. Mix. Transfer to large bowl. Chill. Slice remaining one-third of the berries. Add to soup. Garnish with orange slices and mint.

SIX LILY SOUP

Serves 6 to 8   ½   cup unsalted butter
                       5   large onions, chopped
                       3   leeks, white portion, chopped
                       6   shallots, minced
                       3   cloves garlic, minced
                       4   cups chicken broth
                       3   cups beef broth
                       2   cups whipping cream
                           salt to taste
                           ground red pepper to taste
                     2-3   tablespoons cornstarch in 3 to 4 tablespoons cold water
                       ½   bunch chives, chopped
                       3   green onions, chopped

In large kettle melt butter over low heat. Add onions, leeks, shallots, and garlic. Simmer 20 minutes. Add chicken and beef broths. Increase heat and bring to boil. Reduce heat and simmer uncovered until reduced by 1 to 2 cups, about 45 minutes. Transfer mixture to food processor or blender in small amounts and purée until smooth. Return purée to kettle. Stir in cream. Heat through but do not boil. Season with salt and red pepper. Add cornstarch and stir until thickened. Garnish each serving with chives and green onions.

BASIC BEEF STOCK

Yield: 4 quarts

5   pounds meaty soup bones and beef neck bones
2   small unpeeled onions, quartered
4   teaspoons salt
4   quarts water plus ½ cup, divided
4   ribs celery with leaves, in chunks
2   carrots, sliced
4   cups tomatoes
2   teaspoons Worcestershire sauce
4   fresh parsley sprigs or 1 teaspoon dried parsley
3   bay leaves, crumbled
¼   teaspoon thyme
¼   teaspoon marjoram
¼   teaspoon celery seed

Place bones in large deep-sided roasting pan. Add onions and sprinkle with salt. Bake in preheated 450° oven 30 to 45 minutes or until browned. In large kettle combine remaining ingredients except ½ cup water. Add bones and onions to kettle. Scrape bottom of roasting pan with ½ cup water. Add drippings to soup. Bring soup to boil, removing foam from surface. Cover kettle; simmer 4 hours or until meat is easily removed from bones.

Remove meat and refrigerate. Replace bones in kettle and simmer at least 2 hours. Longer cooking will enhance flavor. Remove from heat; cool. Remove bones. Strain vegetables and purée. Add purée to soup. Adjust seasonings to taste. Refrigerate 24 hours before using. Skim congealed fat from soup's surface before reheating.

Soup may be frozen. An excellent base for other soups or chili.

FISH CHOWDER

Serves 12 to 14

10	cups water
7	ribs celery, chopped
4	carrots, chopped
2	onions, chopped
½	pound mushrooms, chopped
1½	cups parsnips, chopped
1½	cups chopped fresh parsley, divided
1½	cups chopped fresh dill, divided
½	cup barley
½	pound scallops
½	pound flounder, in 2-inch cubes
½	pound red snapper, in 2-inch cubes
1	pound peeled, deveined shrimp
1½	tablespoons Dijon mustard
8	ounces frozen corn niblets
	salt to taste
	pepper to taste
	dill sprigs

In large kettle bring water to boil. Add celery, carrots, onions, mushrooms, parsnips, 1 cup each parsley, dill, and barley. Reduce heat and simmer 1 hour and 15 minutes. Add scallops, flounder, red snapper, mustard, and remaining ½ cup each parsley and dill. Simmer 15 minutes. Add corn and shrimp during the last 5 minutes. Add salt and pepper. Garnish each serving with dill sprig.

SEAFOOD CHOWDER

Serves 10 to 12

3	cups seafood of your choice (shrimp pieces, crab, or fresh scallops—individually or combined)
10¾	ounces canned cream of shrimp soup
10¾	ounces canned cream of potato soup
10¾	ounces canned cream of mushroom soup
10¾	ounces canned tomato bisque soup
5	ounces sherry
1	quart half and half or milk
1	small onion, minced
	fresh dill or parsley

Precook seafood until barely tender or slightly underdone. Seafood will continue to cook in soup. In large kettle combine all remaining ingredients except dill or parsley. Heat slowly until hot but do not allow to boil. Garnish with fresh dill or parsley. Recipe doubles well.

WINTER SOUP

Yield: 2½ to 3 quarts

5   **pounds marrowbones of veal, beef, or oxtails with some meat**
3   **large carrots**
2   **ribs celery**
¼   **cup minced celery leaves**
1   **cup loosely packed chopped parsley**
1   **cup diced white turnips**
3   **small or 2 medium yellow onions**
3   **cloves**

Bouquet garni:
1   **clove garlic**
1   **tablespoon Herbes de Provence**
1   **teaspoon crushed marjoram**
5   **whole black peppercorns**
3   **whole allspice**
     triple-thick cheesecloth, 5 inches square

1   **cup sliced carrots**
½   **cup chopped onions**
½   **cup green beans**
½   **cup shredded cabbage**
2   **teaspoons coarse salt**
2   **envelopes dehydrated beef broth**
1   **pound lean beef stew meat, cubed**
     Parmesan cheese, grated

In 10 to 12 quart stockpot place marrowbones. Roast uncovered in preheated 375° oven 15 minutes. Turn bones and roast 15 minutes longer. Transfer stockpot to stove top. Add whole carrots, celery, celery leaves, parsley, turnips, and whole onions. Cover with cold water.

Tie garlic, Herbes de Provence, marjoram, peppercorns, and allspice into cheesecloth with string to make bouquet garni. Leave long tail. Submerge bouquet garni in stockpot, leave tail outside. Bring to boil; skim foam from surface until it disappears. Reduce heat. Simmer at least 4 to 6 hours with cover slightly ajar.

Remove stockpot from heat. Remove bouquet garni, and cool soup stock. Skim all fat.

Remove bones, marrow from bones, and vegetables. Remove meat from bones and discard bones. In food processor purée meat, marrow, and vegetables. Strain soup. Return purée and strained stock to stockpot. Reheat. Add sliced carrots, chopped onions, green beans, cabbage, salt, and broth. In a skillet sprayed with vegetable oil, brown stew meat quickly over high heat. Add to stock. Simmer until meat and vegetables are tender, about 30 minutes. Serve with Parmesan cheese.

HOT AND SOUR SOUP

Serves 6

If you are blessed with Oriental accessories, use them with this delicate soup.

4   dried black mushrooms
¼   cup dried wood ear (tree fungus, cloud ear)*
3   tablespoons soy sauce, divided
4   tablespoons cornstarch, divided
¼   pound or ½ cup lean pork, partially frozen, julienned
2   tablespoons vegetable oil
6   cups chicken broth
½   teaspoon ground red pepper or to taste
3   tablespoons vinegar or to taste
¼   cup water
½   pound tofu, cubed
2   eggs, beaten
2   teaspoons sesame oil, optional
2   scallions in ½-inch lengths

Place mushrooms and wood ear in separate bowls. Cover with boiling water and soak 4 hours or overnight. Remove and discard mushroom stems and woody sections of wood ear. Cut into julienne strips.

Combine 1 tablespoon soy sauce with 1 tablespoon cornstarch. Add pork strips. Heat oil in wok or 10-inch skillet. Stir fry pork in wok 5 minutes or until cooked. In 3-quart saucepan bring chicken broth to boil. Add pork, mushrooms, wood ear, remaining 2 tablespoons soy sauce, red pepper, and vinegar. Dissolve remaining 3 tablespoons cornstarch in ¼ cup water. Stir cornstarch mixture into soup. Add tofu and bring to boil. Remove from heat. Add eggs in slow, steady stream. Stir rapidly for 30 seconds. Add sesame oil and mix well. Garnish individual soup bowls with scallions.

*Available in Oriental food shops and some supermarkets.

THREE HOUR VEGETABLE SOUP

Serves 8 to 10

2	quarts water
16	ounces canned tomatoes with juice
1½	pounds lean beef, cubed
10¾	ounces canned tomato soup
2	tablespoons soy sauce
1½	cups coarsely diced celery
1½	cups coarsely diced onion
1	cup sliced carrots
2	tablespoons medium pearl barley
1	tablespoon sugar
½	cup sherry
	salt to taste
	pepper to taste

In large kettle combine water, tomatoes with juice, beef, tomato soup, and soy sauce; cover. Bring to boil. Reduce heat and simmer for 1 hour. Add celery and onion. Simmer a second hour. Add carrots, barley, sugar, sherry, salt, and pepper. Simmer a third hour. Remove from heat. Cool. Refrigerate overnight. Skim fat and reheat.

May be prepared in advance and stored for 1 week in refrigerator.

BROCCOLI BISQUE

Serves 6 to 8

1	cup minced onion
½	cup thinly sliced celery
½	cup thinly sliced leek
2	cloves garlic, minced
2	tablespoons butter
1½	pounds broccoli, trimmed
3	cups chicken stock
2	cups whipping cream
	pinch dry mustard
	pinch cayenne pepper
	salt to taste
	pepper to taste

In large covered kettle sauté onion, celery, leek, and garlic in butter until tender. Remove flowerets from broccoli. Slice stalks. Add slices and chicken stock to kettle. Simmer 15 minutes. Add broccoli flowerets. Simmer 15 minutes; remove from heat. Purée in food processor or blender. Return to kettle, stir in cream, and add seasonings. Simmer 10 minutes. Serve hot or cold.

ALMOND ZUCCHINI SOUP

Serves 6 to 8

This is a popular Nantucket recipe.

1   **Spanish onion, minced**
3   **tablespoons unsalted butter**
3   **medium zucchini, thinly sliced**
½   **cup slivered blanched almonds**
4   **cups chicken broth**
½   **cup ground blanched almonds**
1   **cup whipping cream**
1½   **tablespoons Amaretto**
1   **tablespoon brown sugar**
¼   **teaspoon cinnamon**
¼   **teaspoon nutmeg**
     zucchini slices
     slivered almonds

In large kettle sauté onion in butter over medium heat until soft, 4 to 5 minutes. Add 3 zucchini and ½ cup slivered almonds. Cook, stirring constantly, until zucchini is barely tender. Add chicken broth; simmer uncovered 25 minutes or until mixture is reduced by one-third. Add ground almonds and simmer 10 minutes, stirring. Add remaining ingredients except zucchini slices and almonds. Cook over low heat until warmed through. Serve soup in heated bowls. Garnish each serving with 1 or 2 paper-thin zucchini slices and several slivered almonds.

MUSHROOM SOUP

Serves 4 to 6

1   **pound mushrooms, finely chopped**
4   **tablespoons butter**
2   **tablespoons flour**
2   **cups strong chicken broth**
     salt to taste
     pepper to taste
1   **cup whipping cream**

Sauté mushrooms in butter 5 minutes over low heat. Stirring constantly, add flour. Mix well. Slowly add chicken broth, salt, and pepper. Transfer to double boiler to keep warm. Just before serving, add cream and heat thoroughly.

CREAM OF SORREL SOUP

Serves 6

½   cup chopped onion
4   tablespoons butter
4   tablespoons flour
4½   cups chicken broth
    salt to taste
    pepper to taste
½   pound sorrel leaves, stems removed
2   egg yolks
½-1   cup whipping cream
    nutmeg to taste
2   tablespoons chopped chives

In large kettle sauté onion in butter until transparent. Add flour and cook 2 minutes, stirring constantly. Add broth and simmer 5 minutes, stirring. Blend in salt, pepper, and sorrel. Remove from heat and cool slightly. In separate bowl beat egg yolks with a small amount of broth mixture. Add to kettle. Blend mixture in food processor or blender. Strain. Add cream and nutmeg to taste. May be served hot or cold. Garnish each serving with chives.

PAUL BERTOLLI'S SPINACH SOUP

Serves 10 to 12

From a renowned San Francisco chef.

3   tablespoons unsalted butter
1   cup water
1   large onion, finely chopped
1   carrot, peeled, sliced
1   celery rib, sliced
6   cups chicken broth
6   large bunches fresh spinach, stems removed
    salt to taste
    pepper to taste
    Parmesan cheese, grated
    croutons

In large kettle melt butter. Add water, onion, carrot, and celery. Cook until very soft. Add chicken broth and bring to boil. Add spinach. Cook 2 minutes uncovered until spinach wilts. Transfer to food processor in small batches. Purée until very smooth. Transfer to large bowl. Add salt and pepper. Serve immediately garnished with grated cheese and croutons if desired. Color changes if soup is allowed to stand.

CREAMY CARROT BISQUE

Serves 6

3 tablespoons butter
4 cups peeled, sliced carrots
2 tablespoons chopped onions
½ teaspoon sugar
½ teaspoon marjoram
¼ teaspoon thyme
2 tablespoons flour
2 cups milk
2 teaspoons fresh dill, or 1 teaspoon dried dill, divided
4 teaspoons dehydrated chicken soup base
2 cups half and half
1 cup whipping cream
  salt to taste
  white pepper to taste
1 carrot, peeled, grated

In medium saucepan melt butter. Add sliced carrots, onions, sugar, marjoram, and thyme. Cover and cook gently until fork pierces carrot easily. Uncover; sprinkle with flour. Cook slowly, stirring until flour is slightly browned. Over medium heat add milk slowly. Reduce heat and add 1 teaspoon dill. Simmer 25 to 30 minutes, stirring often. Transfer to blender or food processor and purée. Add soup base. With machine running add half and half. Blend well. Add whipping cream, salt, and pepper if needed. Blend well. Serve hot with grated carrot and remaining 1 teaspoon dill sprinkled on top.

If a lighter soup is desired, substitute milk for the whipping cream. Soup may be made ahead, refrigerated, and reheated. Do not boil.

SWISS POTATO SOUP

Serves 6

2 tablespoons butter
¼ cup chopped onion
2 cups seasoned mashed potatoes (instant seasoned mashed potatoes or leftover)
2 cups milk
2 cups grated Swiss cheese
½ teaspoon salt
dash pepper
crisp cooked bacon, crumbled
chives

In large kettle melt butter. Add onion and sauté until transparent. Add potatoes and milk. Blend well. (May be prepared to this point and refrigerated up to 2 days before serving.) Stir in cheese, salt, and pepper. Heat soup very slowly and stir until cheese melts (do not boil). Garnish with bacon and/or chives.

CHEESE SOUP

Serves 8

1 cup finely chopped scallions
⅓ cup peeled, finely chopped carrots
⅓ cup finely chopped celery
2 cups water
1 medium white onion, chopped
¼ pound butter
1 cup flour
4 cups milk
4 cups chicken broth
15 ounces Cheese Whiz
¼ teaspoon cayenne pepper
salt to taste
pepper to taste
1 tablespoon Dijon mustard

Simmer scallions, carrots, and celery in 2 cups water 5 minutes. Set aside onion mixture with cooking liquid. Sauté onion in butter. Add flour and blend well. In medium saucepan heat milk and chicken broth to boiling. Stir into onion mixture. Add cheese, cayenne, salt, and pepper. Stir in mustard, vegetable mixture, and reserved liquid. Bring to boil and serve.

EGYPTIAN CHICKPEA SOUP (Shorba Al Homus)

Serves 6 to 8

12 ounces chickpeas (garbanzos)
4 cups water
2 tablespoons vegetable oil
1 tablespoon butter
1 clove garlic, minced
½ cup finely diced mild or red onions
½ cup finely diced celery
⅓ cup peeled, finely diced carrots
¼ cup flour
½ teaspoon cumin
42 ounces chicken broth
1 cup diced tomatoes
1 bay leaf
salt to taste
freshly ground pepper to taste
½ cup uncooked rice
1½ tablespoons chopped parsley
lemon wedges
Parmesan cheese, freshly grated

Soak chickpeas overnight in 3 cups water. Drain, reserving liquid. Add enough water to make 4 cups. In large kettle heat oil and butter. Add garlic, onions, celery, and carrots. Cook, stirring, until onions are soft. Stir in flour and cumin; blend well. Add reserved water, stirring rapidly. Add chickpeas, broth, tomatoes, bay leaf, salt, and pepper. Stir until mixture comes to a boil. Cover and simmer 2 hours.

Add rice and simmer 20 minutes. Ladle 1 cup of chickpeas, rice, and vegetables into food processor or blender. Add small amount of liquid. Blend well. Return to kettle. Add parsley and stir to blend. Remove bay leaf. Serve in individual bowls with lemon wedges. Pass grated cheese.

HEARTY EGGPLANT SOUP

Serves 8

2 tablespoons olive oil
2 tablespoons butter
1 medium onion, chopped
1 pound ground beef
28 ounces canned Italian-style tomatoes (in pieces), liquid included
1 medium eggplant, peeled, diced
1-2 cloves garlic, minced or ⅛-¼ teaspoon garlic powder
½ cup peeled, chopped carrots
½ cup chopped celery
28 ounces beef broth
1 teaspoon salt
1 teaspoon sugar
½ teaspoon nutmeg
½ cup uncooked macaroni
2 tablespoons chopped parsley
 Parmesan cheese, grated

In large kettle heat oil and butter. Add onion. Cook, stirring, until soft. Add ground beef. Cook until brown. Drain fat. Add tomatoes, eggplant, garlic, carrots, celery, broth, salt, sugar, and nutmeg. Bring to boil; cover. Reduce heat and simmer 1 to 1½ hours. Add macaroni and parsley. Cover. Simmer until macaroni is tender, 10 to 15 minutes. Serve hot and pass Parmesan cheese.

Make this soup ahead. Its flavor improves with standing.

ITALIAN SAUSAGE SOUP

Serves 6 to 8

1½ pounds Italian sausage (hot or mild), in ½-inch slices
2   large onions, chopped
2   cloves garlic, minced
28 ounces canned Italian-style tomatoes with liquid
42 ounces canned beef broth, preferably unsalted
1½ cups dry red wine
½   teaspoon basil leaves, crumbled
2   cups uncooked bow or shell macaroni
2   medium zucchini, ¼-inch slices
1   medium green pepper, seeded, chopped
3   tablespoons chopped parsley
5   ounces Parmesan cheese, grated

In large kettle sauté sausage until lightly browned. Drain and discard fat. Add onions and garlic. Sauté until onions are limp. Stir in tomatoes, breaking them into small pieces. Add broth, wine, and basil. Simmer 30 minutes. Remove from heat. Cool, transfer to large bowl, and refrigerate. Skim fat from surface; discard. Return soup to kettle. Stir in macaroni, zucchini, green pepper, and parsley. Simmer covered 15 minutes or until macaroni and vegetables are tender-crisp. Serve with cheese.

See photo page 221.

BLACK BEAN SOUP

Serves 8 to 12

1   pound dried black beans
1½   pounds smoked ham hocks
2   quarts water
2   cups beef or chicken broth
1½   tablespoons olive oil
1½   cups seeded, finely chopped green pepper
1½   cups finely chopped onion
1   tablespoon minced garlic
1   teaspoon cumin
1   cup peeled, seeded, diced tomatoes
¼   cup red wine vinegar
     salt to taste
2   tablespoons finely chopped fresh coriander, optional
     dry sherry, optional

In large kettle combine beans, ham hocks, and water. Cover and bring to boil. Reduce heat and simmer until beans are tender, about 2 hours. Remove ham hocks and set aside. Drain beans, reserving cooking liquid; set aside. Measure cooking liquid (there should be about 4 cups) and add broth to make 6 cups liquid. In food processor or blender purée beans. Add small amount of cooking liquid and blend. Transfer beans to large bowl and combine with remaining liquid.

Heat oil in heavy kettle. Add pepper, onion, garlic, and cumin. Cook, stirring, until onion is wilted. Add tomatoes and vinegar. Simmer 15 minutes. Remove meat from ham hocks and chop. Discard skin and bones. Combine meat with puréed bean and vegetable mixtures. Taste and correct seasoning. Add coriander, if desired. Serve soup in bowls; add sherry to taste.

LENTIL SOUP

Serves 12

  2   cups dried lentils
  3   quarts water (part chicken broth may be substituted)
  1   ham bone with meat
  3   medium onions, chopped
1¼ cups thinly sliced celery with leaves
 ¾ cup peeled, sliced carrots
 ¼ cup chopped parsley
     salt to taste
     pepper to taste
     croutons or sliced frankfurters

In large kettle soak lentils in cold water to cover a minimum of 3 hours. Drain well. Return to kettle with 3 quarts water and ham bone. Simmer 3 hours. Add vegetables. Simmer 1 hour. Process three-fourths of the soup through food mill (one-fourth of the soup remains in kettle). Return to kettle. Season with salt and pepper. If desired, ham may be removed from bone, cut in bite size pieces, and served in soup. Reheat soup and serve with croutons or sliced frankfurters.

Variation:
For *Split Pea Soup* substitute split peas for lentils. Soaking is not necessary.

SOUTHERN PEANUT SOUP

Serves 8

 ½ cup finely chopped onion
 ½ cup finely chopped celery
  6   tablespoons butter
  6   tablespoons whole wheat flour
  2   cups 2% milk
 ½ cup peanut butter
  2   cups chicken broth
 ½ teaspoon Spike seasoning
     finely chopped peanuts to garnish

In large kettle sauté onion and celery in butter, stirring constantly until soft. One tablespoonful at a time, sprinkle flour over mixture. Add milk gradually, stirring constantly. When thickened gradually blend in peanut butter, Spike, and chicken broth. Cook over low heat until thickened. (Do not overcook.) Remove from heat; cool. Reheat before serving. Add more milk if thinner consistency is desired. Garnish with chopped peanuts.

For richer soup, half and half or whipping cream may be substituted for milk.

SALADS

Ravinia Notes

The Great Depression took its toll in the early '30's. Ravinia was forced to close its gates for four cheerless years. The Festival reopened in 1936. Rudolph Ganz was among the prominent guest conductors that first summer. It is NOTEWORTHY that Ganz was to become the teacher and mentor of Edward Gordon, Executive Director and Chief Operating Officer of Ravinia today.

Musical giant George Gershwin played at the revitalized Festival during that inaugural summer. He lived but one more brief year.

COMPOSED PEAR AND AVOCADO SALAD

Serves 6

1 medium bunch red-edged leaf lettuce
3 heads Belgian endive
3 pears, peeled, cored, (Comice preferably)
3 avocados, peeled

Fresh Pear Dressing:
2 small shallots
1 pear, peeled, cored, cut into 8 pieces
2 tablespoons red wine vinegar
¼ teaspoon salt or to taste
  freshly ground pepper to taste
4 tablespoons olive oil

Arrange lettuce decoratively on 6 salad plates. Place endive leaves in a circle with tips pointing toward plate edges. Just before serving cut each pear into quarters, then each quarter into 3 long wedges. Slice avocado in same way. Alternate pear and avocado slices on plate, making circle of fruit.

In food processor mince shallots. Add pear pieces and process until lumps disappear. Add vinegar, salt, and pepper. Slowly drizzle oil through feed tube. Process until smooth. Correct seasonings.

To serve, drizzle dressing over salad.

BLUE CHEESE STUFFED PEARS

Yield: 12

6 ripe pears, peeled, halved
  lemon juice
4 ounces blue cheese, crumbled
6 ounces cream cheese
2 tablespoons plus 1 teaspoon port wine
5 tablespoons margarine
½ cup chopped pecans or walnuts
  white or red seedless grapes
  leaf lettuce

Brush cut sides of pears with lemon juice to prevent discoloration. In food processor or blender combine cheeses, wine, and margarine. Mix well.

Core pears, enlarging cavities to hold 1 heaping tablespoon of cheese mixture. Fill cavities with mixture, mounding slightly. Sprinkle nuts over cheese. Decorate with halved grapes or small grape clusters. Serve individually on leaf lettuce or on platter as buffet accompaniment.

SEAFOOD PASTA SALAD

12 to 14 Servings   *May be prepared well in advance.*

Pasta:
1   pound fettucine, broken into 2-inch pieces
⅓   cup olive oil
¼   cup white wine vinegar
1   tablespoon sherry wine vinegar
     salt to taste
     freshly ground pepper to taste

Cook pasta "al dente" (slightly underdone). Drain, rinse in cold water, and drain again. Place in large bowl. Mix with oil and vinegars. Season to taste; mix again. Cover and refrigerate. This will keep 1 to 2 days in the refrigerator.

Vegetables:
16   thin asparagus spears (preferably fresh), trimmed,
          cut into 1½-inch lengths
2½   cups broccoli flowerets, in bite-size pieces
2½   cups tiny peas, fresh or frozen
6   scallions
1   pint cherry tomatoes
1   pound spinach leaves, stems removed

Separately boil or steam asparagus and broccoli until tender-crisp. Rinse in cold water. Drain. Steam fresh peas briefly or use defrosted uncooked frozen peas. Store each vegetable separately in plastic bags. Mince scallions; combine with tomatoes. Rinse and dry spinach. Store separately in refrigerator. May prepare everything but spinach 1 to 2 days in advance.

Seafood:
2   pounds bay scallops or halved sea scallops
2   pounds large shrimp, cooked, shelled, deveined
          or lobster and crabmeat equivalent
⅓   cup olive oil
3   tablespoons white wine vinegar
3   tablespoons sherry wine vinegar
1   clove garlic, minced
2   scallions, minced
     salt to taste
     freshly ground pepper to taste

continued

Poach scallops in simmering water until opaque (about 2 minutes). Drain.
Cut shrimp in half lengthwise. Combine scallops and shrimp (or lobster and
crabmeat) in bowl. Add oil, vinegars, and garlic; mix well. (Minced
scallions, salt, and pepper will be used during salad assembly.) This can be
done the morning of serving day.

HERB CREAM

⅓   cup white wine vinegar
2   tablespoons Dijon mustard
½   cup packed fresh basil leaves or 4 tablespoons
      dried, crushed basil
2   cloves garlic
⅓   cup vegetable oil
1   cup sour cream
½   cup whipping cream
3   tablespoons minced parsley
    salt to taste
    freshly ground pepper to taste

In food processor or blender combine vinegar, mustard, basil, and garlic.
Add oil slowly and process until smooth. Add sour cream, whipping cream, and
parsley. Process until smooth. Season to taste.

To assemble:

Arrange spinach leaves as border on large platter. Toss pasta with vegetables
and tomato-scallion mixture. Place in center of platter and make a well in
center of pasta. Drain seafood; toss with minced scallions, salt, and pepper.
Mound in center of pasta. Serve with herb cream.

Prepare at least 1 day ahead to blend flavors. Although this is time-consuming,
it is very simple to assemble on day of serving.

See photo on back cover.

MARINATED GOAT CHEESE SALAD

Serves 8

Marinated goat cheese:
- ½ cup virgin olive oil
- 2 cloves garlic, slivered
- 1 teaspoon fresh thyme
- 1 teaspoon rosemary
- ½ teaspoon fresh oregano
- ¼ teaspoon fresh savory
- 1 teaspoon chopped parsley
- 11 ounces Montrachet goat cheese, cut into 8 equal slices, ½-inch thick

Salad:
- 20 red lettuce leaves
- 1 head Boston lettuce
- 4 Belgian endives
- 1 bunch young rocket leaves, or other lettuce
- 4 sun-dried tomatoes, slivered or thinly sliced
- croutons

Dressing:
- 1 large shallot, minced
- 1 teaspoon Dijon mustard
- 2 tablespoons balsamic vinegar
- 1 tablespoon lemon juice
- 6 tablespoons virgin olive oil
- salt to taste
- pepper to taste

Combine oil, garlic, thyme, rosemary, oregano, savory, and parsley. Mix well. Marinate cheese in mixture 4 days at room temperature, turning occasionally.

Mix shallot with mustard, vinegar, and lemon juice. Slowly whisk in olive oil until it is incorporated. Season to taste.

Mix varieties of lettuce in large bowl. Toss with enough dressing to coat thoroughly. Arrange greens on 8 salad plates. Lay strips of tomato over greens and 1 slice cheese in center. Sprinkle with croutons.

SHRIMP AND VEGETABLE SALAD

Serves 4

1   large avocado and/or ½ cup pea pods
1   pound cooked, shelled, deveined shrimp, sliced lengthwise
8   ounces canned artichoke hearts, drained, quartered
    romaine lettuce, cut into ½-inch slices

Dressing:
1   egg yolk
1   cup oil, including 2 tablespoons olive oil
¼   cup wine vinegar
2   tablespoons Dijon mustard
1½   tablespoons minced parsley
1½   tablespoons minced chives
1   tablespoon minced shallots
    salt to taste
    pepper to taste

Peel avocado and cut into bite-size pieces. Simmer pea pods 2 minutes. Rinse in cold water.

In food processor or blender combine all dressing ingredients. Process until blended.

Marinate shrimp, artichoke hearts, avocado, and pea pods in dressing. Refrigerate 3 hours, turning occasionally. Blend in lettuce in desired quantity just before serving.

PASTA SALAD WITH PESTO DRESSING

Serves 4 to 6

Basil Pesto Dressing:
2   cups fresh basil leaves, coarsely chopped
2   tablespoons chopped, toasted pine nuts
¼   cup olive oil
2   cloves garlic, crushed
1   teaspoon salt
½   cup plus 3 tablespoons freshly grated Parmesan cheese, divided

3   cups freshly cooked, drained shell macaroni
    escarole or other lettuce
    pitted black olives

Combine basil, nuts, oil, garlic, and salt. Mix well. Stir in ½ cup cheese.
Pour enough of mixture over pasta to coat thoroughly. Toss well. Cool but do not chill. Serve in individual portions on plates lined with escarole or lettuce. Garnish with olives and sprinkle with remaining cheese.

PASTA SALAD WITH SPINACH PESTO

Serves 6 to 8

1   red pepper, in ½-inch pieces
8   ounces rotelli pasta (corkscrew)
10 ounces frozen tiny peas, thawed
7   ounces canned light tuna packed in water, drained

Pesto sauce:
10 ounces frozen spinach, thawed, squeezed dry
1   cup chopped parsley
⅔   cup freshly grated Parmesan cheese
½   cup walnut pieces
4   flat anchovies
2   cloves garlic, crushed
1   tablespoon dried basil
1   teaspoon salt
¼   teaspoon ground fennel
1   cup olive oil

Blanch red pepper in boiling water 30 seconds. Drain and rinse under cold water.

In food processor or blender process all pesto sauce ingredients except oil until smooth. With motor running, add oil gradually. This makes 2 cups. Salad requires 1 cup; remainder may be frozen.

Cook pasta in boiling salted water 7 minutes. Drain and rinse under cold water. In large bowl combine pasta with 1 cup pesto sauce, red pepper, peas, and tuna. Serve at room temperature.

ANTIPASTO PASTA SALAD

Serves 6 to 8   *A colorful salad for a portable feast.*

3½   ounces plain tortellini
3½   ounces spinach tortellini
4   ounces macaroni twists
2   cups broccoli flowerets
14   ounces canned artichoke hearts, drained, quartered
2   ounces sliced pimientos, drained
1   cup pitted ripe olives
6   slices Genoa salami, julienned
6   slices prosciutto, julienned
½   cup minced parsley
½   cup thinly sliced scallions, 1 inch of green
      included

Dressing:
¾   cup safflower oil (may use part olive oil)
¼   cup white wine vinegar
½   teaspoon garlic powder
1   teaspoon salt
1   teaspoon sugar
½   teaspoon freshly ground black pepper
2   tablespoons minced fresh basil or 1 teaspoon dried basil

Combine all dressing ingredients. Blend well.

Cook tortellini according to package directions. Drain and quickly rinse with cold water. Drain well. Transfer to large bowl. Follow same procedure with macaroni twists. Toss pastas with half of prepared dressing. This can be done up to 24 hours in advance and refrigerated.

Steam broccoli 3 to 5 minutes until tender-crisp. Combine with artichokes, pimientos, olives, salami, and prosciutto. Toss with remaining dressing.

Several hours before serving toss pasta mixture with vegetable mixture, parsley, and scallions. Transfer to glass bowl and serve at room temperature.

May also be served as an appetizer.

ORIENTAL NOODLE SALAD

Serves 8

Marinade:

1 teaspoon peanut butter
½ cup white rice vinegar
¼ cup soy sauce
1 teaspoon sesame oil
1 tablespoon plus 1 teaspoon sugar
2 teaspoons dry mustard
1 teaspoon ground ginger
¼ teaspoon salt
   freshly ground black pepper

Noodles and vegetables:

6 quarts water
2 tablespoons salt
12 ounces Oriental dried noodles
16 fresh pea pods, sliced in half lengthwise
1 large red pepper
1 large jicama, peeled, julienned
4 large scallions with green tops, sliced
4 large carrots, peeled, julienned
¼ cup sesame seeds

In food processor or blender combine all marinade ingredients. Process until mixed.

In large kettle combine 6 quarts water with 2 tablespoons salt. Bring to boil. Cook noodles 7 minutes or until soft. Drain immediately, rinse under cold water, and drain again. Transfer to large bowl and toss with marinade. Add pea pods, red pepper, jicama, scallions, carrots, and sesame seeds. Mix well. Cover and refrigerate.

SHELLS AND GRAPES

Serves 8

8 ounces uncooked shell macaroni
4 cups red seedless grapes
½ cup chopped scallions
3 ounces Roquefort or blue cheese, crumbled
   salt to taste
   pepper to taste
1 medium clove garlic, finely minced
1 cup mayonnaise
3 tablespoons fresh lemon juice
½ cup toasted walnut halves, optional

Cook macaroni "al dente" (slightly underdone). Drain. While hot, combine with grapes, scallions, cheese, salt, pepper, and garlic.

Combine mayonnaise and lemon juice. Mix well. Stir into macaroni until evenly mixed. Refrigerate, covered, for several hours or overnight.

Before serving, toss gently. Add walnuts if desired.

CHUTNEY CHICKEN SALAD

Serves 8

4 cups cooked white meat of chicken, in bite-size
   pieces
2 cups diagonally sliced celery
4 scallions with tops, sliced
5 ounces canned sliced water chestnuts, drained
   lettuce
8 slices bacon cooked, crumbled
½ cup slivered almonds, toasted
2 avocados, sliced in wedges

Dressing:
1 cup mayonnaise
¼ cup chopped mango chutney
¼ cup fresh lime juice
2 teaspoons grated lime peel
1 teaspoon curry powder
½ teaspoon salt

In large bowl combine chicken, celery, scallions, and water chestnuts. In jar with tight-fitting lid combine all dressing ingredients. Shake to blend thoroughly. Pour dressing over salad. Toss to coat well.

Line bowl or individual plates with lettuce. Mound salad on lettuce. Sprinkle with bacon and almonds. Surround with avocado slices.

WONG'S CHINESE CHICKEN SALAD

Serves 8

This ultimate Chinese chicken salad recipe comes directly from Hong Kong.

 4   whole chicken breasts, halved
 2   quarts cooking oil, preferably peanut oil
3¾ ounces cellophane noodles
11 ounces (8 or 9 squares) frozen won ton wrappers,
      cut into ⅛ inch strips
 1   cup nuts (dry roasted peanuts, almonds, or cashews)
 1   head iceberg lettuce, shredded
 1   cup scallions, cut diagonally into 1½ inch strips
 ½ cup chopped parsley

Marinade:
 6   tablespoons dry mustard
 3   tablespoons Oriental sesame oil
1½ cups soy sauce

Poach or steam chicken breasts 20 minutes or until barely tender. Do not overcook. Discard skin and bones; shred chicken with fingers into 2-inch pieces.

Heat oil to 350°. Test oil temperature by dropping in a cellophane noodle. It should become opaque and "explode" instantly. Drop noodles, in small amounts, into oil. Upon "explosion" remove immediately with slotted spoon to drain on paper towels. Using same oil, cook won ton strips in small amounts until lightly browned. Remove with slotted spoon to drain on paper towels. Drop nuts in same oil; cook until lightly browned. Remove with slotted spoon to drain on paper towels.

To prepare marinade place mustard in small bowl. Gradually add sesame oil while stirring to eliminate lumps. Add soy sauce. Mix well. Marinate chicken in one cup marinade for 20 minutes *only*.

Arrange shredded lettuce on large flat platter. Layer won ton strips over lettuce followed by cellophane noodles. Layer marinated chicken over noodles. Sprinkle with scallions, nuts, and desired amount of remaining marinade. Garnish with chopped parsley and serve immediately.

Noodles may be prepared several days in advance and stored in airtight container.

See photo page 228.

MANDARIN CHICKEN SALAD

Serves 4 to 5

8 to 10	leaves romaine lettuce, shredded in long pieces, chilled
3	ounces thin crisp Chinese rice noodles
6	teaspoons sesame oil
2	chicken breasts, cooked, cooled, julienned
4 to 5	scallions with tops, thinly sliced
½	cup chopped dry roasted peanuts
2	oranges, sectioned or sliced

Dressing:

6	tablespoons water
4	tablespoons soy sauce
3	tablespoons cream sherry
4	teaspoons red wine vinegar
2	teaspoons sugar
1½	large cloves garlic, minced
2	tablespoons peeled, chopped fresh ginger root
4	tablespoons creamy peanut butter

In jar with tight-fitting lid combine all dressing ingredients except peanut butter. Mix in peanut butter with spoon. Shake dressing vigorously until well blended.

Place chilled, shredded lettuce in shallow 9- or 10-inch glass bowl. Sprinkle 2 to 3 tablespoons dressing over lettuce. Spread noodles over lettuce. Spoon sesame oil onto noodles followed by 2 to 3 tablespoons dressing. Arrange chicken strips over noodles. Pour remaining dressing over chicken. Sprinkle scallions and nuts over top. Garnish with oranges. Serve immediately.

JAMES LEVINE'S CLASSIC CHICKEN SALAD

Serves 8

Our widely acclaimed Maestro's special salad.

4   large chicken breasts
2   carrots
2   celery ribs plus 1 cup chopped celery, divided
1   medium onion, quartered
1   cup clear French or Italian dressing
4   hard-boiled eggs
2   tablespoons capers or to taste
1   cup mayonnaise
1   tablespoon whipping cream
    salt to taste
    pepper to taste

In medium saucepan poach chicken breasts with carrots, 2 celery ribs, and onion 35 to 40 minutes. Cool. Discard skin and remove meat from bones. Cut chicken into large bite-size pieces. Marinate overnight in French or Italian dressing, basting occasionally.

Before serving, drain marinade thoroughly. Chop eggs and add to chicken with chopped celery and capers. Thin mayonnaise with cream. Add to salad gradually, using amount to achieve desired moistness of salad.

KATHY'S TACO SALAD

Serves 8

2½   pounds ground beef
2   tablespoons butter
6-8   ounces mild taco sauce
16   ounces Kraft Catalina dressing
1   head iceberg lettuce, shredded
1   Spanish onion, chopped
1   pint cherry tomatoes, halved
6   ounces sharp Cheddar cheese, grated
5   ounces taco chips, crumbled

Brown beef in butter. Drain well. Mix with taco sauce and dressing. Cool.

In large salad bowl arrange lettuce. Layer remaining ingredients except chips in order given. Add beef mixture. Top with taco chips. Toss before serving.

May be assembled hours ahead.

WARM CHICKEN SALAD

Serves 6 to 8

2   **whole fryers, cooked, at room temperature**
1   **bunch broccoli, in flowerets**
2   **medium zucchini, julienned**
½   **cup golden raisins**
6   **ounces canned bamboo shoots, drained**
     chopped parsley

Dressing:
2   **egg yolks**
4   **tablespoons sherry vinegar**
3   **tablespoons Dijon mustard**
1   **tablespoon Sauce Diable**
1   **teaspoon curry powder, or to taste**
2   **teaspoons salt**
½   **teaspoon freshly ground pepper**
2   **cups vegetable oil**

Remove meat from chicken, discarding skin and bones. Cut into large bite-size strips. Steam broccoli and zucchini until just tender-crisp. Plunge into cold water. Drain. Combine chicken, vegetables, raisins, and bamboo shoots, reserving a few vegetables for garnish.

In food processor or blender mix all dressing ingredients except oil until blended. Pour oil in a steady stream into blender. Process until blended.

When ready to serve pour sufficient dressing on salad ingredients to coat. If salad or dressing has been refrigerated, warm before serving. Garnish salad with reserved vegetables and chopped parsley.

CURRIED TUNA SALAD

Serves 4

13 ounces canned tuna in oil, drained
¼ cup golden raisins
2 tablespoons currants
1½ teaspoons crystallized ginger, in small pieces
¼ cup chopped celery
½ apple, in small pieces
3 tablespoons almonds, toasted

Dressing:
⅓ cup mayonnaise
1 tablespoon sour cream
1 tablespoon Miracle Whip
¼ teaspoon curry powder
⅛ teaspoon ground ginger
  salt to taste
  pepper to taste

In medium bowl combine tuna, raisins, currants, ginger, and celery.

In separate bowl combine all dressing ingredients. Mix well and pour over tuna mixture. Blend thoroughly. Add apple and almonds. Combine well. Refrigerate until served.

TUNA AND CANNELLINI BEAN SALAD

Serves 4 to 6

20 ounces canned cannellini beans, drained (white kidney beans)
½ cup finely chopped onions
1 small clove garlic, minced
2 tablespoons dried parsley
1 teaspoon dried oregano
1 tablespoon red wine vinegar
  juice of ½ lime
6 tablespoons olive oil
  salt to taste
  white pepper to taste
14 ounces canned water packed tuna, drained
  lettuce
  tomato wedges

In large bowl combine all ingredients except tuna, lettuce, and tomato. Mix well. Flake tuna into mixture and toss gently. Serve on bed of lettuce. Garnish with tomatoes. Prepare at least 24 hours ahead to allow flavors to mellow.

SALAD NIÇOISE

Serves 8 to 10　　　*A classic version of a classic salad.*

2　pounds green beans, ends trimmed, in 1½-inch lengths
2　green peppers, ribs removed, cut in thin rounds
2　cups thinly sliced celery
1　pint cherry tomatoes
5　medium red potatoes, cooked, peeled, sliced
21　ounces canned tuna, drained
2　ounces flat anchovies, drained, optional
10　black Greek olives
10　small pimiento-stuffed olives
1　large red onion, thinly sliced
2　tablespoons fresh basil, chopped, or 1 tablespoon
　　dried basil
⅓　cup finely chopped parsley
¼　cup finely chopped scallions
6　hard-boiled eggs, quartered

Dressing:
2　teaspoons Dijon mustard
2　tablespoons wine vinegar
1½　teaspoons salt
2　cloves garlic, minced
6　tablespoons vegetable oil
6　tablespoons olive oil
1　teaspoon fresh thyme or ½ teaspoon dried thyme
　　freshly ground pepper to taste

In large jar with tight-fitting lid combine all dressing ingredients. Shake until well blended. Set aside.

Steam beans until tender-crisp. Drain. Refresh under cold water. Drain.

Place beans, green pepper, celery, tomatoes, and potatoes in large salad bowl, arranging in symmetrical pattern. Flake tuna over vegetables. Arrange anchovies on top. Scatter olives and red onions over all. Sprinkle with basil, parsley, and scallions. Garnish with quartered eggs. Toss with dressing after garnished bowl has been presented.

ROYAL ROAST BEEF SALAD

Serves 8

2   **pounds rare roast beef, julienned (about 3 cups)**
8   **ounces canned beets, drained, julienned**
4   **large shallots, minced**
20   **ounces frozen peas**
     salt to taste
     pepper to taste
¼   **cup minced parsley**

In large bowl combine roast beef, beets, and shallots. Add sufficient basic vinaigrette to coat. Toss; cover and refrigerate 1 hour. Cook peas in boiling salted water 2 minutes. Drain. Rinse with cold water and drain again. Add three-fourths of the peas to beef mixture; season to taste with salt and pepper. Refrigerate covered at least 2 hours, or overnight. Transfer to serving bowl. Serve cold; garnish with parsley and remaining peas.

BASIC VINAIGRETTE DRESSING

Yield: ¾ cup

¼   **cup fresh lemon juice**
1   **teaspoon red wine vinegar**
¾   **teaspoon Dijon mustard**
1   **small clove garlic, minced**
¼   **teaspoon salt**
     freshly ground pepper
½   **cup vegetable oil**

In small bowl combine lemon juice, vinegar, mustard, garlic, salt, and pepper. Whisk in oil in slow, steady stream.

WILD RICE AND CHICKEN SALAD

Serves 4 to 6

1   **cup cooked wild rice**
1   **cup cooked chicken, cut into ½-inch pieces**
2   **tomatoes, peeled, juiced, seeded, cut into ½-inch pieces**
1   **bunch scallions, thinly sliced**
½   **cup chopped parsley**
     mayonnaise
     salt to taste
     pepper to taste

Combine all ingredients, using enough mayonnaise to bind salad. Toss lightly. Chill. Clear Dressing (page 104) may be substituted for mayonnaise.

WILD RICE SALAD

Serves 6

A creative salad with outstanding flavor.

1   cup uncooked wild rice
2¾ cups chicken stock
2¾ cups water
1   cup pecan pieces
1   cup currants
    rind of 1 orange, grated
10 ounces frozen tiny peas, thawed
¼   cup vegetable oil
⅓   cup fresh orange juice
1   teaspoon salt
    freshly ground pepper to taste

Rinse rice in strainer under cold water. Combine with chicken stock and water in saucepan. Bring to boil. Reduce heat and simmer uncovered 35 to 45 minutes. Rice should not be too soft. Drain.

Combine rice with remaining ingredients. Mix well. Let stand 2 hours. Serve at room temperature.

BROWN RICE SALAD

Serves 8

2   cups uncooked brown rice
4   cups water
12 scallions, thinly sliced
4   medium celery ribs, chopped or julienned
2   medium green peppers, chopped or julienned
4   ounces sliced ripe olives
½   pint cherry tomatoes, halved
1   tablespoon drained capers
    salt to taste
    pepper to taste
½   cup chopped parsley
½   cup sliced radishes
¼   cup olive oil
¼   cup white wine vinegar

In covered saucepan cook rice in water until liquid is absorbed and rice is fluffy, approximately 25 minutes. Remove from heat. Cool. Add remaining ingredients and toss.

Shrimp, crab meat, or flaked tuna may be added for variety.

CURRIED RICE AND FRUIT SALAD

Serves 8

A totable salad to accompany picnic chicken.

3   cups cooked, warm rice
2   teaspoons lemon juice
1   large Granny Smith apple, unpeeled, in bite-size pieces
1   cup red seedless grapes
⅔   cup golden raisins
2   cups thinly sliced celery
½   cup thinly sliced scallions with tops
¼   cup mayonnaise
1   teaspoon coarse grained mustard
1   teaspoon honey
    salt to taste

Marinade:
⅓   cup vegetable oil
1½   teaspoons white wine vinegar
1½   teaspoons coarse grained mustard
1½   teaspoons curry powder
    salt to taste
    pepper to taste

Place all marinade ingredients in jar with tight-fitting lid. Shake until well combined.

Sprinkle apple pieces with lemon juice to prevent discoloration. Combine rice, apple, grapes, raisins, celery, and scallions. Pour marinade over mixture. Stir. Chill, stirring occasionally.

In small bowl combine mayonnaise, mustard, honey, and salt. Add to chilled rice mixture, tossing to coat.

May substitute tart red apples for the green, and green seedless grapes for the red.

LENTIL AND WALNUT SALAD

Serves 10 to 12

- 2½ cups dried lentils, rinsed
- 1½ quarts chicken broth
- 1 bay leaf
- 2 teaspoons dried thyme
- ⅓ cup white wine vinegar
- 3 cloves garlic, minced
- ½ cup vegetable oil
  salt to taste
  pepper to taste
- 1 cup thinly sliced scallions
- 1 cup coarsely chopped walnuts
  finely chopped parsley

In large kettle combine lentils, chicken broth, bay leaf, and thyme. Simmer 25 minutes or until lentils are tender but hold their shape. Do not overcook. Drain.

In food processor or blender combine vinegar, garlic, oil, salt, and pepper. Mix well.

In large bowl toss warm lentils with dressing. Refrigerate overnight. Add scallions and walnuts. Mix well. Sprinkle top with parsley.

LAYERED LUNCHEON SALAD

Serves 12

- 1 cup mayonnaise
- 1 cup sour cream
- 1 large bunch leaf lettuce, in bite-size pieces
- 1 large green pepper, chopped
- 1½ cups diced celery
- 1 medium onion, chopped
- 10 ounces frozen tiny peas, thawed
- 3 whole chicken breasts, cooked, in bite-size pieces
- 2 tomatoes, chopped medium fine
- 1 cucumber, peeled, chopped medium fine
- 1 tablespoon sugar
- 1½ teaspoons curry powder
- ½ cup mango chutney, puréed
- 8 ounces Cheddar cheese, grated
- 8 slices bacon, cooked crisp, crumbled

Combine mayonnaise and sour cream. Set aside. Using 9-by 4-inch glass bowl, layer remaining ingredients in order given, topping with mayonnaise mixture. Refrigerate, covered, 8 hours or overnight.

ALSATIAN POTATO SALAD

Serves 8 to 10

2½ pounds russet potatoes
3 scallions, thinly sliced
6 slices bacon, crisply cooked
2-3 tablespoons bacon fat, strained
½ cup cider vinegar
3-4 tablespoons sugar
1 teaspoon salt
½ teaspoon freshly ground pepper
½ teaspoon caraway seed
½ teaspoon dill seed
⅛ teaspoon garlic powder
1 cup diagonally sliced celery
1 small green or red pepper, diced
½ cup chopped parsley
  lettuce leaves
  cherry tomatoes

Boil potatoes 20 to 25 minutes until cooked through but firm. Sauté scallions in bacon fat until transparent. Add vinegar, sugar, and seasonings. Bring to boil over medium heat. Remove from heat.

Peel potatoes and slice into ⅛-inch slices. Toss in bowl with bacon, celery, diced pepper, and parsley. Pour hot sauce over mixture.

Serve warm or at room temperature. Surround with lettuce leaves and cherry tomatoes.

COUNTERPOINT SALAD

Serves 18

3 large avocados
½ cup lemon juice
24 ounces alfalfa sprouts
6 large tomatoes, sliced ⅓-inch thick
1½ pounds bacon, cooked crisp, broken into bits

Dressing:
1 cup mayonnaise
½ cup yogurt, buttermilk, or milk
¼ cup minced chives
¼ cup chopped parsley
1½ tablespoons Worcestershire sauce
½ teaspoon freshly ground black pepper
¼ teaspoon Tabasco

Peel avocados; slice each into 8 wedges. Sprinkle avocados with lemon juice.

In large clear salad bowl layer a third each sprouts, tomatoes, avocados, and bacon. Repeat procedure twice. There should be 3 complete layers. Cover and refrigerate.

Combine all dressing ingredients. Mix well. Pour over salad and serve.

SPECIAL POTATO SALAD

Serves 8 to 12

4	pounds new potatoes
½	cup white wine vinegar
½	cup chicken stock
1	medium onion, chopped
1½	teaspoons sugar
	salt to taste
	freshly ground pepper to taste
10	tablespoons chopped parsley
6	tablespoons chopped dill
5	fresh sage leaves, chopped
1	branch lemon balm, snipped*
1	small cucumber, peeled, cubed
½	cup pickled baby onions
2	tablespoons chopped dill pickle
1	cup sour cream or crème fraîche (see page 423), divided
2	hard-boiled eggs, quartered
	dill sprigs

One day before serving, cook potatoes until just done. Peel and slice. In saucepan combine vinegar, stock, onion, sugar, salt, and pepper. Bring to boil. Pour, while hot, over potatoes. Potatoes should absorb liquid. Let stand overnight.

Mix chopped dill, parsley, sage, and lemon balm with potatoes. Stir in cucumber, onions, and pickle. Add sour cream or crème fraîche, reserving some for garnish.

To serve, garnish with eggs, dill sprigs, and remaining cream.

*Lemon balm is available in the herb section of specialty food stores.

RUSTIC RAVINIA SALAD

Serves 4 to 6

1 pound small new potatoes, unpeeled
4 tablespoons dry white wine
3 tablespoons white wine vinegar
3 tablespoons minced shallots
2 tablespoons Dijon mustard
¾ teaspoon salt
¼ teaspoon freshly ground pepper
½ cup plus 1 tablespoon olive oil
⅓ cup chopped parsley
¾ pound ham, julienned
½ pound Swiss cheese, julienned
  lettuce
2 beefsteak tomatoes, sliced
1 small red onion, thinly sliced

Boil potatoes in lightly salted water until just tender. Drain and cut into thinly sliced rounds, leaving skins intact where possible.

In jar with tight-fitting lid, combine wine, vinegar, shallots, mustard, salt, and pepper. Cover and shake well. Add oil and parsley; shake again. Pour half the dressing over warm potatoes and toss lightly. Cover. Cool to room temperature. Add ham, cheese, and remaining dressing. Blend well.

Line serving platter with lettuce. Mound salad on top and surround with tomato slices. Garnish with onion rings.

TOSSED SALAD WITH A DIFFERENCE

Serves 8

1 clove garlic, minced
½ teaspoon salt
¼ teaspoon dry mustard
3 teaspoons Worcestershire sauce, divided
3 tablespoons red wine vinegar
6 tablespoons chopped parsley
4 tablespoons chopped scallions
1 cup mayonnaise
½ cup sour cream
5 ounces canned chow mein noodles
3 tablespoons butter, melted
¾ teaspoon garlic salt
¾ teaspoon curry powder
  combination of salad greens sufficient for 8 people, in serving-size pieces
8 ounces canned water chestnuts, drained, sliced

In food processor or blender combine minced garlic, salt, mustard, 1 teaspoon Worcestershire sauce, vinegar, parsley, scallions, mayonnaise, and sour cream. Blend well.

In oven-proof dish combine noodles, butter, garlic salt, curry powder, and remaining 2 teaspoons Worcestershire sauce. Mix well. Heat in preheated 200° oven 15 minutes.

Place greens in large salad bowl. Just before serving add water chestnuts, then warm noodles. Add dressing. Toss well and serve immediately.

Dressing may be prepared 1 day ahead.

GREEK SALAD

Serves 4 to 6

1	clove garlic, halved
	salt
1	head Boston lettuce, shredded
3	heads Belgian endive, thinly sliced
4	celery ribs, sliced
8	radishes, sliced
1	bunch scallions, sliced
1	cucumber, thinly sliced
12	Greek olives (calamata)
½	cup virgin olive oil
	juice of 2 lemons
1	green pepper, sliced in thin rings
	salt to taste
	pepper to taste
½	pound feta cheese, cubed
1	teaspoon minced parsley
½	teaspoon oregano
3	tomatoes, cut in wedges

Rub large salad bowl with garlic and salt. Discard garlic. Combine lettuce, endive, celery, radishes, scallions, cucumber, and olives in salad bowl.

In small bowl combine oil and lemon juice. Shortly before serving pour over salad and toss well. Add pepper rings and feta cheese. Toss lightly. If desired, add salt and pepper.

Arrange salad with some pepper rings and cheese on top. Sprinkle with parsley and oregano. Garnish with wedges of tomato around outer edge of bowl.

DILLED LUNCHEON SALAD

Serves 4 to 6

¾ pound small zucchini, sliced
1 teaspoon salt
1 package dry ranch salad dressing mix, divided
1 cup water
6 ounces pitted small ripe olives
3 kosher dill pickles, chopped
1 tablespoon pickle juice
1 cup raw cauliflower, chopped
3 tablespoons lemon juice
1 tablespoon dried dill weed
1 cup sour cream
  lettuce
1 pint cherry tomatoes

In saucepan combine zucchini, salt, 1 tablespoon dressing mix, and water. Blend well and cover. Boil 1 minute. Drain and cool.

In large bowl combine zucchini mixture with remaining dressing mix, olives, pickles, pickle juice, cauliflower, lemon juice, dill weed, and sour cream. Toss and chill. Serve on lettuce. Garnish with cherry tomatoes.

MARINATED BROCCOLI

Serves 12 to 14

1 cup cider vinegar
1 tablespoon sugar
1 tablespoon dried dill weed
1 tablespoon Dippity Dill
1 teaspoon salt
1 teaspoon pepper
1 clove garlic, minced
1½ cups vegetable oil
3 bunches broccoli, in flowerets
1 pint cherry tomatoes
4½ ounces sliced ripe olives, drained

Combine vinegar, sugar, dill weed, Dippity Dill, salt, pepper, garlic, and oil. Mix well. Pour over broccoli, tomatoes, and olives. Refrigerate 24 hours, stirring several times.

Remove garlic. Drain in colander. Serve at room temperature.

ORIENTAL GREEN BEANS

Serves 10 to 12

2 pounds green beans, ends trimmed
1 3-inch piece of fresh ginger root, peeled
½ cup vegetable oil
3 tablespoons sherry vinegar
½ teaspoon sesame oil
½ teaspoon coarse salt
⅛ teaspoon sugar
⅛ teaspoon white pepper
4 tablespoons sesame seed, toasted

Cook beans in boiling water until tender-crisp, about 5 minutes. Rinse with cold water; drain. Refrigerate 1 hour.

Press ginger root in fine sieve, extracting juice into a bowl. Discard pulp. Combine juice with all ingredients except beans and sesame seed. Mix well. Add beans. Blend well. Refrigerate covered 4 hours. Transfer to serving bowl and sprinkle with sesame seed.

TOMATOES TOCCATA

Serves 8

Striking in appearance and easily portable. Elegant for a first course or buffet when tomatoes are at their peak.

8 firm ripe tomatoes, peeled
½ cup chopped parsley
1 clove garlic, minced
1 teaspoon salt
1 teaspoon sugar
¼ teaspoon pepper
¼ cup olive or vegetable oil
2 tablespoons tarragon or wine vinegar
2 teaspoons Dijon mustard

Cut stem ends from tomatoes. Cut vertical ½-inch slices partially through tomatoes and stuff 1 tablespoon parsley between slices. Place tomatoes in shallow dish.

Combine remaining ingredients. Mix well. Pour over tomatoes. Cover lightly and refrigerate. Let stand at room temperature 20 minutes before serving.

May be made 2 days ahead.

FIRE AND ICE TOMATOES

Serves 8 to 10

6 large tomatoes, sliced to medium thickness
1 large green pepper, sliced into thin rings
1 large red onion, sliced into thin rings
½ cup freshly chopped parsley

Marinade:
¾ cup cider vinegar
¼ cup water
4½ teaspoons sugar
1½ teaspoons celery salt
1½ teaspoons mustard seed
½ teaspoon salt
⅛ teaspoon black pepper
⅛ teaspoon cayenne

In saucepan combine all marinade ingredients. Boil 1 minute. Cool.

In large shallow serving dish alternate tomato slices with pepper and onion rings. Pour marinade over all. Garnish with parsley.

SWEET AND SOUR RED CABBAGE SALAD

Serves 12

1 small head red cabbage, shredded
1 teaspoon salt, optional
1 teaspoon whole cloves
½ cup white vinegar
½ cup water
1 tablespoon caraway seed
½ cup brown sugar
5 ounces currant jelly
   apple slices, optional
   curly endive, optional

In large kettle combine cabbage with water to cover, salt if desired, and cloves. Boil no more than 5 minutes. Drain, reserving cloves.

In saucepan combine vinegar, ½ cup water, cloves, caraway seed, sugar, and jelly. Bring to boil over medium heat. Cook until liquid begins to thicken. Pour over cabbage. Cool. Serve at room temperature in bowl surrounded by apple slices and curly endive.

PICKLED BEETS

Serves 8 to 10

2 bunches beets, cooked, cooled, thinly sliced
2 onions, thinly sliced
1 cup vinegar
1 cup sugar
½ cup water
¼ cup pickling spice

Layer beets and onions in bowl. In saucepan combine vinegar, sugar, water, and pickling spice. Bring to boil. Pour over vegetables. Cool, cover, and refrigerate. Serve cold.

CALORIFIC COLE SLAW

Serves 6 to 8

1   cup mayonnaise
1   teaspoon curry powder
1   teaspoon lemon juice
13 ounces canned pineapple tidbits, well drained
4   cups shredded cabbage
1   cup crushed peanut brittle

In large bowl combine mayonnaise, curry powder, and lemon juice. Mix well. Add pineapple and cabbage. Toss thoroughly with mayonnaise mixture. Chill. Before serving stir in peanut brittle.

WARM CARAWAY CABBAGE SLAW

Serves 4 to 6

2 tablespoons butter
3 cups shredded cabbage (½ small cabbage)
3 tablespoons cider vinegar
2 tablespoons water
1 tablespoon sugar
1 teaspoon caraway seed
½ teaspoon salt
1 large tart apple, unpeeled, cored, coarsely chopped

In large skillet melt butter. Add remaining ingredients except apple. Cook over medium heat 3 minutes, stirring, until cabbage is tender-crisp. Add apple; reduce heat to low. Cook, stirring, 1 minute. Serve warm.

CARROTS VINAIGRETTE

Yield: 1 quart

1 pound carrots, peeled, sliced diagonally
3½ cups water
1¾ teaspoons salt, divided
¾ cup vegetable oil
¼ cup vinegar
1 teaspoon sugar
1 teaspoon grated onion
¼ teaspoon paprika
¼ teaspoon dry mustard
6 pimiento-stuffed green olives, sliced
2 scallions, sliced
1 tablespoon sweet pickle relish
1 tablespoon minced parsley
1½ tablespoons drained capers
pimiento, optional
Boston lettuce

Gently boil carrots in water and 1 teaspoon salt 5 minutes. Drain and cool.

Combine oil, vinegar, sugar, ¾ teaspoon salt, onion, paprika, and mustard. Mix well. Stir in olives, scallions, pickle relish, parsley, and capers. Toss with carrots and chill.

Pimiento may be added for more color. Serve on lettuce leaves.

DIJON AND HONEY GLAZED CARROTS

Serves 4

Mustard lovers will enjoy this.

6 large carrots, peeled
½ cup Dijon mustard
¼ cup honey
juice of ½ lemon
½ teaspoon ground ginger
½ teaspoon salt
½ teaspoon freshly ground pepper
Boston lettuce leaves
¼ cup chopped parsley

Shred carrots into long strips with vegetable peeler, making about 6 cups. Combine all other ingredients except lettuce and parsley. Mix with carrot strips and chill.

To serve, place on lettuce leaf. Sprinkle with parsley.

CUCUMBERS DANOISE

Serves 4 to 6

6 medium or 3 large cucumbers, peeled, thinly sliced
   salt
½ cup white vinegar
⅓ cup sugar
1 teaspoon coarse salt
¼ teaspoon freshly ground pepper
2 teaspoons minced fresh or freeze-dried chives
   dill sprigs
   sweet paprika

Layer cucumbers in glass bowl, sprinkling each layer with a pinch of salt. Place a weighted plate on cucumbers. Chill at least 5 hours.

In jar with tight-fitting lid, combine vinegar, sugar, 1 teaspoon salt, pepper, and chives. Shake to mix well. Chill.

One hour before serving, drain cucumbers thoroughly, pressing with plate. Carefully lay cucumbers on towel. Fold in towel sides. Roll up tightly and place in plastic bag in refrigerator.

At serving time, toss cucumbers with dressing. Garnish with dill sprigs and paprika.

Serve with hot or cold fish.

SPINACH SALAD

Serves 8

A new spinach salad concept.

1 pound fresh spinach, stems removed, in bite-size pieces
1 pound creamed small curd cottage cheese
½ cup chopped pecans

Dressing:
½ cup sugar
3 tablespoons vinegar
½ cup sour cream or yogurt
2 teaspoons horseradish
½ teaspoon dry mustard
½ teaspoon salt

Combine spinach, cottage cheese, and pecans. Mix dressing ingredients. Toss with salad.

JAPANESE SALAD

Serves 8

4   **large cucumbers**
    salt
1   **medium carrot, peeled**
1   **small carrot, peeled**

Marinade:
½   **cup sugar**
½   **cup Japanese rice vinegar**
    pinch salt

Remove ends of cucumbers. With vegetable peeler remove lengthwise strips of outer skin every other strip to create striped effect. Slice each cucumber in half lengthwise and remove seeds. Slice horizontally ¼-inch thick. Sprinkle with salt and set aside 15 minutes. Drain well and press between paper towels.

Cut 4 equally spaced V-shaped grooves the length of each carrot (the points of each V should *not* meet). Then slice horizontally ¼-inch thick to achieve flower shape.

Combine marinade ingredients. Stir until sugar dissolves. Add cucumbers and carrots. Marinate 5 hours. Serve as relish or salad.

RAITA

Serves 6 to 8

A palate-cooling salad from India.

3   **medium cucumbers**
1   **tablespoon minced onion**
1   **tablespoon salt**
2   **tomatoes, in small cubes**
3   **cups plain yogurt**
½   **teaspoon pepper**
2   **tablespoons minced coriander leaves (cilantro or Chinese parsley)**
2   **teaspoons cumin seed**

Peel cucumbers. Slice lengthwise and remove seeds. Slice thinly. Combine with onion and salt. Mix well. Let stand 10 minutes. Drain well and press between paper towels. Drain tomatoes on paper towels. Combine cucumbers, tomatoes, yogurt, pepper, and coriander. Cover and chill at least 2 hours.

In dry skillet over medium heat cook cumin seed. Crush with spoon. Add to cucumber mixture or sprinkle over salad when serving. Serve in small bowls.

See photo page 225.

CURRIED SPINACH SALAD

Serves 6 to 8

10	ounces fresh spinach, stems removed, torn in pieces
1½	cups thinly sliced apples
½	cup golden raisins
½	cup peanuts
2	tablespoons sliced scallions

Dressing:

¼	cup white wine vinegar
¼	cup vegetable oil
2	tablespoons chopped mango chutney
2	teaspoons sugar
½	teaspoon salt
1½	teaspoons curry powder
1	teaspoon dry mustard

In jar with tight-fitting lid combine all dressing ingredients. Mix well. Cover and chill.

In large salad bowl combine spinach, apples, raisins, peanuts, and scallions. Shake dressing. Pour over salad and toss.

SNAPPY LIME CUCUMBER MOLD

Serves 6 to 8

3	ounces lime-flavored gelatin
¾	cup boiling water
½	cup cold water
¾	cup small curd cottage cheese
1	large unpeeled cucumber, seeded, grated, well drained
4	tablespoons horseradish
¾	teaspoon salt
2	teaspoons dill
1	medium onion, grated
½	cup whipping cream, lightly whipped

Dissolve gelatin in boiling water. Add cold water. Chill until mixture is partially set. Add remaining ingredients, blending in whipped cream last. Pour mixture into lightly oiled 4-cup mold. Refrigerate several hours or overnight. Unmold onto serving platter. Garnish as desired.

BROCCOLI MOLD

Serves 10 to 12

2 tablespoons unflavored gelatin, divided
2 cups water, divided
3 tablespoons chicken stock base, divided
3 cups broccoli flowerets, cooked tender-crisp
1 cup sour cream
1½ cups mayonnaise, divided
¼ cup chopped parsley
¼ cup chopped celery
2 teaspoons seasoned salt
½ teaspoon pepper
1 teaspoon lemon juice
1 ounce dry ranch dressing mix
1 cup milk
½ teaspoon dried dill weed

Dissolve 1 tablespoon gelatin in ½ cup cold water. Add 1 tablespoon chicken stock base to ½ cup boiling water. Add gelatin mixture to chicken stock mixture. Mix well. Pour into oiled 6-cup ring mold. Refrigerate until almost set.

Place 1 cup broccoli, flower side down, over gelatin mixture. Finely chop remaining broccoli. Add sour cream, mayonnaise, parsley, celery, seasonings, and lemon juice.

Dissolve remaining gelatin in ½ cup cold water. Add to ½ cup boiling water seasoned with 2 tablespoons chicken stock base. Combine thoroughly with broccoli mixture. Pour into mold. Refrigerate 4 hours or until set.

Combine dressing mix, 1 cup mayonnaise, milk and dill.

Invert mold onto serving platter. Garnish as desired. Serve with dressing.

COLD SPINACH MOLD

Serves 8

An unusual mold, outstanding for flavor and eye appeal.

2   hard-boiled eggs, sliced
1   tablespoon unflavored gelatin
10   ounces beef consommé, warmed
30   ounces frozen chopped spinach
¼   pound crumbled blue cheese
     salt to taste
     pepper to taste
2   tablespoons lemon juice
¼   teaspoon nutmeg
½   teaspoon Worcestershire sauce
½   pound cooked crumbled bacon

Horseradish Dressing:
½   cup mayonnaise
½   cup sour cream
1   tablespoon lemon juice
1½   tablespoons prepared horseradish
1   tablespoon sugar
¾   teaspoon salt
1   tablespoon snipped dill or 1½ teaspoons dried dill weed
1   tablespoon snipped chives or 1½ teaspoons
     freeze-dried chives
¼   teaspoon paprika

Grease an 8- by 8-inch pan or 6-cup ring mold. Line with egg slices. Dissolve gelatin in consommé. Pour a small amount over eggs. Refrigerate until firm.

Cook spinach and drain well. Combine remaining consommé with spinach, cheese, salt, pepper, lemon juice, nutmeg, and Worcestershire. Spread spinach mixture over eggs. Refrigerate overnight.

Combine mayonnaise, sour cream, and lemon juice. Mix until smooth. Stir in remaining dressing ingredients.

Invert mold onto serving platter. Sprinkle with bacon. Serve with horseradish dressing.

TOMATO ASPIC CON GUSTO

Serves 12

An unusually flavorful aspic.

6   cups tomato juice, California style
2   cups chopped onion
1   cup chopped celery
1   teaspoon basil
⅓   cup Worcestershire sauce
⅛   teaspoon red pepper flakes
3   tablespoons unflavored gelatin
¾   cup dry white wine
1   cup water chestnuts, drained, sliced
½   cup chopped green onion
5   tablespoons lemon juice
    fresh greens
    lemon slices
    ripe or green olives

In large saucepan over medium heat combine tomato juice, onion, celery, basil, Worcestershire sauce, and pepper flakes. Cook until vegetables are soft, about 5 minutes. Remove from heat.

Sprinkle gelatin over wine to soften, stirring. In food processor or blender purée tomato juice and cooked vegetables. Strainer may be used if very clear aspic is preferred. Combine tomato mixture with wine-gelatin mixture over very low heat. Stir until gelatin is dissolved.

Fill half an oiled 12-cup mold with aspic. Chill until jelled. Stir together water chestnuts, green onion, and lemon juice. Drain off half the lemon juice. Spread evenly over jelled aspic. Carefully spoon remaining aspic on top. Chill until very firm. Unmold and garnish with fresh greens, lemon slices, and ripe or green olives.

MOLDED GAZPACHO AND SHRIMP SALAD

Serves 6 to 8

2 tablespoons unflavored gelatin
14 ounces chicken broth, divided
15 ounces tomato sauce with tomato bits
½ cucumber, seeded, diced
½ green pepper, diced
⅓ cup finely sliced scallions
1 clove garlic, minced
2 teaspoons sugar
1 tablespoon lemon juice
½ teaspoon basil
2 dashes Tabasco, or to taste
10 ounces cooked, shelled, deveined large shrimp, halved

Dressing
⅔ cup sour half and half
⅓ cup mayonnaise
1 tablespoon Durkee Sauce
2 teaspoons lemon juice
1½ teaspoons horseradish
⅛ teaspoon white pepper

In small saucepan combine gelatin with 1 cup chicken broth. Cook over low heat, stirring to dissolve gelatin. Combine with remaining salad ingredients. Refrigerate until mixture is partially jelled. Spoon mixture into oiled 6-cup ring mold. Chill until jelled.

Combine all dressing ingredients. Mix well.

To serve, invert mold onto serving platter. Pour dressing into small bowl and place in center of mold.

DILLED SALMON MOLD

Serves 8 to 10

32 ounces canned salmon, drained, flaked
½ cup lemon juice
1 cup sour cream
1 cup grated Cheddar cheese
2 tablespoons grated onion
1 teaspoon dill
1 teaspoon salt
2 tablespoons unflavored gelatin
½ cup water
2 tablespoons vinegar
1 cup whipping cream, whipped
    cucumber, thinly sliced
    tomato, sliced
    green pepper, cut into strips
    pimiento, optional
    green olives, optional

In large bowl combine salmon and lemon juice. Add sour cream, cheese, onion, dill, and salt. Mix well.

In small saucepan combine gelatin, water, and vinegar. Heat slowly, stirring constantly, until gelatin is dissolved. Stir into salmon mixture. Gently fold in whipped cream. Pour into oiled 6-cup mold. Chill until firm.

Unmold onto serving platter. Garnish with cucumber, tomato, and green pepper.

A fish mold may be used. Garnish with cucumber for fins, pimiento for spine and mouth, and green olives for eyes.

BEET AND HORSERADISH RING

Serves 4 to 6

3 ounces lemon-flavored gelatin
1½ cups boiling water or beet juice
3 tablespoons vinegar
16 ounces canned beets, drained, chopped
4 tablespoons horseradish
   salt to taste

Dissolve gelatin in boiling water or beet juice. Stir in vinegar. Chill until partially set.

Add beets, horseradish, and salt. Mix well. Pour into oiled 3-cup ring mold. Chill. Unmold onto serving platter. Garnish as desired.

May be served with mayonnaise or sour cream mixed with small amount of horseradish.

CRANBERRY MOLD

Serves 10 to 12

Beautiful on a holiday table, garnished with fresh flowers and/or orange slices.

2 cups coarsely chopped fresh cranberries
2 cups sugar
6 ounces lemon-flavored gelatin
2 cups hot water
2 cups canned crushed pineapple, drained, reserving syrup
2 cups syrup from canned pineapple
2 cups chopped celery
1 cup broken walnuts

Combine cranberries and sugar. In large bowl dissolve gelatin in hot water. Add pineapple syrup to gelatin. Mix well; chill until partially set.

Add cranberry mixture, pineapple, celery, and walnuts. Pour into 2-quart melon mold and chill until firm.

Unmold onto serving platter. Garnish as desired.

MOLDED TUNA RING

Serves 8 to 10

2 tablespoons unflavored gelatin
½ cup cold water
20 ounces water packed tuna, drained, finely chopped
1 cup mayonnaise
1 cup ketchup
3 tablespoons lemon juice
½ teaspoon paprika
capers
cucumbers, thinly sliced

In saucepan, soften gelatin in cold water. Bring to boil. Remove from heat. Add remaining ingredients except capers and cucumbers. Mix well.

Pour into oiled 6-cup mold. Chill until firm. Unmold and garnish with capers and cucumbers.

CHILLED FISH AND VEGETABLE ASPIC

Serves 8

½ cup thinly sliced carrots
3 cups chicken stock
¾ cup cream sherry
2 tablespoons lemon juice
½ teaspoon salt
3 drops Tabasco
2 tablespoons unflavored gelatin
1½ cups cooked whitefish, flaked into small pieces
7 thin slices cucumber, halved.
½ cup frozen tiny peas, thawed
¼ cup finely chopped scallion tops

Cook carrots until just tender. Drain.

Combine chicken stock, sherry, lemon juice, salt, and Tabasco. Mix well. Pour 1 cup of mixture into small bowl. Stir in gelatin. Pour remaining mixture into saucepan and bring to boil. Remove from heat and add gelatin to hot mixture. Pour ¼-inch into bottom of well-oiled 6-cup ring mold. Refrigerate until set. Chill remaining mixture until it is consistency of unbeaten egg white.

Arrange cucumber slices in overlapping pattern on jelled aspic in mold. Return to refrigerator. Fold fish, peas, carrots, and scallions into remaining aspic when it begins to set. Spoon aspic over cucumbers. Refrigerate 4 hours or overnight. Unmold onto serving platter. Garnish as desired. May be served with a mildly flavored mayonnaise dressing.

CRANBERRY MOLD MANDARIN

Serves 12 to 14

6   ounces raspberry-flavored gelatin
2   cups boiling water
20 ounces frozen cranberry orange relish
22 ounces canned mandarin oranges with liquid

Dissolve gelatin in boiling water. Add frozen cranberry orange relish. Stir until thawed and well mixed. Fold in oranges with liquid. Pour into well-oiled 6-cup mold. Refrigerate until set. Unmold onto serving platter. Attractive garnished with sliced fresh fruit.

VINAIGRETTE SALAD DRESSING

Yield: 1 cup

2   tablespoons minced shallots
2   teaspoons Dijon mustard
¼   teaspoon salt
     freshly ground pepper
1   tablespoon lemon juice
3   tablespoons balsamic or red wine vinegar
½   cup virgin olive oil

In wooden bowl or food processor mix shallots, mustard, salt, pepper, lemon juice, and vinegar. Add oil in slow steady stream until well incorporated. Transfer to jar with tight lid and refrigerate.

Variation: Tangerine dressing:
Prepare dressing as for Vinaigrette, substituting 3 tablespoons tangerine juice and grated rind of 1 tangerine for vinegar, lemon juice, and mustard.

CLEAR DRESSING

Yield: 2¼ cups

¾ cup olive oil
¾ cup vegetable oil
⅔ cup garlic-flavored red wine vinegar
2 tablespoons honey
2 teaspoons seasoned salt
1 teaspoon basil
1 teaspoon dry mustard
1 teaspoon coarsely ground pepper

Combine all ingredients in jar with tight-fitting lid. Shake well. Store in refrigerator. Let stand at room temperature 30 minutes before using.

POPPY SEED DRESSING

Yield: 1½ cups

¾ cup sugar
⅓ cup white vinegar
1 teaspoon salt
1 teaspoon dry mustard
1 teaspoon grated onion or to taste
1 cup vegetable oil
1 tablespoon poppy seed

Combine sugar, vinegar, salt, and mustard. Mix well. Blend in onion. Add oil slowly while stirring. Beat until thick with electric mixer. Stir in poppy seed. Refrigerate covered. Bring to room temperature and stir before serving.

Excellent over fruit salad or grapefruit and avocado with lettuce.

May substitute celery seed for poppy seed.

Variation: Celery seed dressing
Prepare dressing as for Poppy seed, substituting 1 tablespoon celery seed for poppy seed.

SLIM-LINE CURRY DRESSING

Yield: 1½ cups

4   tablespoons white wine vinegar
2   tablespoons vermouth
4   teaspoons Dijon mustard
2   teaspoons soy sauce
1   teaspoon curry powder
1   teaspoon salt
½   teaspoon pepper
1   packet Equal, (Nutra Sweet low-cal sweetner) or 2 teaspoons sugar
⅔   cup vegetable oil

Place all ingredients in jar with tight-fitting lid. Shake until well mixed.

Delicious mixed with melon balls.

NORTH SHORE DRESSING

Yield: 2 cups

⅔   cup sugar
     pinch salt
1   small onion, chopped
½   cup cider vinegar
⅓   cup ketchup
1   tablespoon Worcestershire sauce
1   cup vegetable oil

In food processor or blender combine all ingredients. Process until smooth.

This dressing is particularly good with fresh spinach salad.

LORENZO DRESSING

Yield: 2 cups

1   cup chopped watercress
¾   cup vegetable oil
¼   cup vinegar
½   cup Bennett's chili sauce relish
½   cup Heinz's chili sauce
1   teaspoon salt

In jar with tight-fitting lid, combine all ingredients. Shake until well blended.

VENERABLE GREEN GODDESS DRESSING

Yield: 1½ cups

2/3 cup mayonnaise
1/3 cup sour cream
2 ounces canned anchovies, including oil
1/3 cup chopped parsley
3 scallions
1 clove garlic
3 tablespoons tarragon vinegar
1 tablespoon lemon juice
romaine lettuce

In food processor or blender combine all ingredients except romaine. Blend until smooth. Toss with romaine lettuce or lettuce of choice.

May be used as a dip for vegetables.

MANGO DRESSING

Yield: 1 cup

1 medium mango, peeled
2 shallots, finely diced
juice of 1 lime
1/2 cup virgin olive oil

In food processor purée mango. Add shallots and lime juice. Mix well. Add oil slowly to achieve desired consistency.

Use on fruit salad or crab-endive salad combined with fruit.

EGGS & CHEESE

Ravinia Notes

Jazz Great Benny Goodman played his first memorable concert at Ravinia in 1938. He returned with his original Quartet, Lionel Hampton, Gene Krupa, and Teddy Wilson, for a NOTE-WORTHY reunion in July, 1973. Upon the occasion of his eleventh concert in 1979, the park underwent a total power failure. Undaunted, and to the excitement of his vast audience, Goodman and the Sextet performed by candlelight. Ravinia installed a second generator within a short time.

Leonard Bernstein made his Ravinia conducting début in 1944, and a distinguished quartet of young conductors also established reputations at the Festival during the late '30's, early '40's and '50's: Fritz Reiner, Artur Rodzinski, Georg Solti, and Jean Martinon were all destined to become Music Directors of the Chicago Symphony Orchestra after their Ravinia débuts. The orchestra's present director, Sir Georg Solti, said, "I fell in love with the Chicago Symphony Orchestra at Ravinia in 1954, my second visit to America."

NESTED EGGS

Serves 6

An elegant brunch or luncheon presentation.

3   **English muffins, split**
    butter
6   **slices Canadian bacon, optional**
6   **eggs**
    pinch salt
    Hollandaise sauce

Toast English muffins; butter lightly. If using Canadian bacon, sauté slices
1 minute on both sides over moderate heat. Drain on paper towel:

Separate eggs, placing whites in large bowl and each unbroken yolk back in its
shell. Adding pinch of salt beat egg whites until stiff.

Place 1 slice bacon on top of each muffin half. Mound egg white over bacon.
(If no bacon is used, mound egg white directly on toasted muffin half.) In center
of white make an indentation with a spoon and gently place 1 yolk in well.
Place muffin halves on baking sheet. Bake in preheated 350° oven 15 minutes or
until yolks are set.

Using spatula, remove each muffin half to serving plate. Spoon warm
Hollandaise (see page 428) over yolks or pass in separate bowl. Serve
immediately.

BRUNCHEON EGGS

Serves 4

8   **ounces Gruyère cheese, grated**
4   **eggs**
2   **slices bacon, crisply cooked, crumbled**
1   **teaspoon chopped chives or scallion tops**
¼   **cup bread crumbs**

Place 1 ounce cheese into each of 4 buttered individual baking dishes. Break
1 egg into each dish. Cover with bacon, chives, and remaining cheese. Sprinkle
bread crumbs over top. (This can be done night before or early in day.)

Bake in preheated 300° oven 15 minutes or until mixture is set. Brown slightly
in broiler and serve immediately.

For a new taste combination, accompany with chutney.

Serves 6

A delightful hint of show business from your kitchen.

1	tablespoon unflavored gelatin
2	tablespoons port or Madeira
1½	cups undiluted consommé
1½	cups red madrilène
⅓	cup white vinegar
2	quarts water
6	eggs
10	ripe olives or 1 black truffle
½	pound fresh spinach leaves, washed, well drained, stems removed
12	slices smoked salmon (about ¾ pound)
2	ounces red caviar

Soak gelatin in wine. In large saucepan bring consommé and madrilène to boil. Add gelatin. Stir until dissolved. Cool. Refrigerate until mixture starts to thicken.

Combine vinegar with 2 quarts water. Bring to boil. Poach 3 eggs at a time in vinegar-water for 4 minutes. Using slotted spoon remove eggs to bowl of ice water.

Pour ¼-inch chilled aspic into 6 greased custard cups or muffin tins. Refrigerate 20 minutes or until set.

Cut ripe olives or truffle into thin oval slices to resemble flower petals. Arrange olive petals over aspic in cups, leaving room in center. Place dab of caviar in each center.

Drain chilled eggs. Dry with paper towel. Place egg over olives and caviar, yolk side down. Pour thick and syrup-like aspic around eggs. Chill 10 minutes. Fill cups with remaining aspic. Chill 30 minutes or until firm.

Arrange individual plates with bed of spinach leaves. Crisscross 2 slices salmon over leaves. Dot with remaining caviar. Dip cups in hot water 3 or 4 seconds. Unmold over salmon and serve.

EGG FU YUNG

Serves 6 to 8

Sauce:

2 cups strong clear broth, chicken or veal
2 tablespoons light soy sauce
¼ cup cold water
1½ tablespoons cornstarch

Pancakes:

5 eggs, lightly beaten
3 tablespoons vegetable oil
1 cup chopped, cooked shrimp, ham, pork or other desired meat
2 scallions, finely chopped or ½ cup finely chopped onion
½ cup sliced celery
2 tablespoons light soy sauce
¼-½ teaspoon ground ginger
1 clove garlic, crushed
2 cups fresh white bean sprouts, washed, dried

In saucepan combine broth and soy sauce. Bring to boil. Blend water and cornstarch. Add to broth. Reduce heat and simmer until sauce begins to thicken, stirring constantly. Remove sauce from heat.

In large bowl combine all pancake ingredients except sprouts. Mix well. Stir in sprouts until blended evenly.

In large skillet heat oil. Ladle ⅓-cup portions pancake batter into skillet. Brown on both sides. Remove with slotted spoon to paper towel. Drain. Repeat until all batter is cooked.

Arrange pancakes on hot platter. Reheat sauce and pour over pancakes. Serve immediately.

SUMMER FRITTATA

Serves 6

8   eggs
     salt to taste
     freshly ground pepper to taste
⅛   teaspoon Tabasco
1   cup diced bacon
4   tablespoons olive oil, divided
3   large scallions, chopped
1   clove garlic, crushed
1   green pepper, diced
3   tablespoons diced pimiento
2   small zucchini, finely cubed
3   medium new potatoes, cooked, peeled, cubed
2   teaspoons chopped parsley
2   tablespoons Parmesan cheese

In large bowl combine eggs, salt, pepper, and Tabasco. Beat until well combined.

In oven-proof pan sauté bacon until almost browned. Remove bacon to paper towel to drain.

Drain all but 1 tablespoon bacon fat from pan. Add 2 tablespoons oil, scallions, and garlic. Cook until scallions are soft and lightly browned. Add diced pepper, pimiento, and zucchini. Cover and cook over low heat 3 to 4 minutes or until vegetables are tender-crisp. Add potatoes and bacon. Cover and cook 1 to 2 minutes.

Add egg mixture and parsley. Stir. Increase heat and cook 1 to 2 minutes or until eggs are lightly set. Sprinkle with Parmesan cheese.

Transfer pan to preheated 350° oven. Bake 5 to 7 minutes or until eggs are completely set. Cut into 6 wedges for brunch or lunch.

May also be chilled, cut into small wedges or squares, and served as an appetizer.

SPANISH POTATO OMELET

Serves 4

½   **cup plus 1 tablespoon olive oil, divided**
2½   **cups diced potatoes**
1   **teaspoon salt, divided**
1   **cup finely chopped onion**
1   **clove garlic, minced**
4   **eggs**
      pepper to taste

In heavy 10-inch skillet heat ½ cup oil. Add potatoes. Sprinkle with ½ teaspoon salt. Cover and cook 10 minutes over moderate heat, stirring often to prevent potatoes from browning. Add onion and garlic. Continue cooking, stirring often, until potatoes are cooked.

Beat eggs lightly with ½ teaspoon salt and pepper. Remove potatoes and onion from skillet with slotted spoon. Drain in colander. Add potatoes and onion to eggs; mix well.

Remove any food particles from bottom of skillet. Two tablespoons olive oil should remain in skillet. Add more if necessary.

Heat oil in skillet. Pour in potato-egg mixture. Cook, shaking skillet occasionally, until egg is set and bottom of omelet is golden, about 3 minutes.

Turn omelet onto plate. Add 1 tablespoon oil to skillet. Slide omelet back into skillet, uncooked side down. Cook until set, about 1 minute. Omelet should be slightly soft inside.

Transfer to platter and serve hot or at room temperature.

Cut into wedges for light supper or small squares for appetizers.

QUICHE OLÉ

Serves 6

A Mexican version of quiche.

⅔ cup chorizo sausage, prepared at least 6 hours ahead (recipe follows)
3 eggs, beaten
1¾ cups hot milk
1 teaspoon salt
2 cups grated Monterey Jack cheese
¼ cup finely chopped, seeded green chilies
1 9-inch unbaked pie shell

Chorizo sausage:
½ pound lean pork, coarsely ground
1 tablespoon cider vinegar
1 clove garlic, minced
1 tablespoon chili powder
1 teaspoon salt
¼ teaspoon cumin

Combine all sausage ingredients. Refrigerate at least 6 hours to blend flavors.

Sauté sausage, stirring to break up pieces, until brown. Drain. Combine eggs, milk, salt, cheese, and chilies. Stir in sausage. Pour into pie shell. Place on lowest oven shelf.

Bake in preheated 400° oven 35 minutes or until set in center and browned on top. Let stand 10 minutes before cutting.

Serve with a green salad and red salsa for brunch or lunch.

SPINACH QUICHE

Serves 4

1 deep-dish pie crust
4 slices bacon
½ cup chopped onion
½ clove garlic, minced
4 large eggs, slightly beaten
1 cup whipping cream
½ cup milk
2 teaspoons Worcestershire sauce
½ teaspoon salt
½ teaspoon freshly ground pepper
¼ teaspoon nutmeg
5 ounces frozen chopped spinach, thawed, drained
1½ cups grated Swiss or Gruyère cheese

Line buttered quiche dish with pie crust. Pierce lightly with fork. Bake in preheated 375° oven 5 minutes. Remove from oven. Increase oven temperature to 450°.

In skillet cook bacon until crisp. Drain, cool, and crumble. Sauté onion and garlic in bacon drippings until transparent but not brown. Remove with slotted spoon and drain.

Combine eggs, cream, milk, Worcestershire sauce, salt, pepper, and nutmeg. Mix well. Blend in onion and garlic.

Layer bacon, spinach, and cheese alternately in crust. Pour egg mixture over. Bake at 450° 15 minutes. Reduce temperature to 375° and bake 30 minutes. Cool at least 20 minutes before serving.

May be half-baked and then frozen. Partially defrost before baking in preheated 375° oven 1 hour.

SWISS CHEESE SOUFFLÉ

Serves 3 to 4

3   tablespoons butter
3   tablespoons flour
½   cup half and half
¼   cup milk
¼   cup dry vermouth
¾   cup grated Swiss cheese (imported preferred)
¾   cup grated imported Gruyère cheese
4   eggs, separated
½   teaspoon salt
⅛   teaspoon white pepper
    dash cayenne, optional
½   teaspoon cream of tartar

In large saucepan melt butter. Blend in flour. Add half and half, milk, vermouth, and cheeses. Cook over low heat until cheeses are melted. Cool slightly. Add egg yolks, salt, and white and cayenne peppers. Beat mixture a few seconds.

Whip egg whites until foamy. Add cream of tartar and beat until stiff. Fold egg whites into cheese mixture gradually. Pour into 1½-quart soufflé dish that has been buttered on bottom *only*. Place in pan of hot water and bake in preheated 300° oven 1 hour to 1 hour and 15 minutes. Serve immediately.

LUSCIOUS CHEESE FLAN

Serves 6 to 8

A particularly "Noteworthy" dish.

Crust:
¾ cup bread crumbs
4   tablespoons butter, melted

Filling:
2   tablespoons butter
2   ounces blue cheese
16   ounces cream cheese
3   eggs, beaten
1⅓ cups sour cream, divided
1   teaspoon salt
     freshly ground pepper, to taste
1   teaspoon dried dill weed
¼   teaspoon Herbes de Provence

Mix crumbs and butter. Press onto bottom and sides of pie pan or quiche dish. Refrigerate.

Thoroughly blend butter and cheeses. Add eggs, ⅔ cup sour cream, salt, pepper, dill weed, and Herbes de Provence. Mix well. Pour into prepared crust.

Bake in preheated 375° oven 25 minutes or until custard has set. Remove from oven.

Spread remaining sour cream gently and smoothly over top of flan. Return to oven. Bake 10 minutes; remove from oven. Cool on rack briefly. Serve warm. May be reheated in preheated 300° oven 10 to 15 minutes.

One tablespoon finely chopped parsley and 2 teaspoons finely chopped chives may be substituted for the dill weed and herbs.

PUFF PASTRY CHEESE TART

Serves 10 to 12

This unusual recipe provides ample opportunity for the creative cook. The additional suggested fillings and seasonings serve to stimulate new food combination ideas.

2   sheets frozen puff pastry

Basic filling:
1   tablespoon butter, softened
2   cups grated sharp Cheddar cheese
2   cups grated Swiss cheese
1   cup grated white brick cheese
2   eggs, beaten
2   tablespoons whipping cream
    salt to taste
    pepper to taste
2   egg yolks, beaten

Additional optional fillings:
Fresh asparagus, trimmed, partially cooked, cut in 2-inch lengths; mushrooms, zucchini, red peppers, partially cooked; sliced shrimp, partially cooked, cleaned, deveined, seasoned with garlic; chicken cooked, cut in bite-size pieces, seasoned with curry and/or chutney; leaf spinach, washed, cut in large pieces, seasoned with shallots; sausage, grilled, cut in bite-size pieces; bacon crisply cooked, crumbled; fresh tomatoes, sliced, seasoned with basil.

Defrost puff pastry according to package directions. In large bowl combine butter, cheeses, whole eggs, cream, salt, and pepper. Mix well. Refrigerate until ready to use.

Place 1 sheet thawed pastry on 10- by 15-inch jelly roll pan or pizza pan, depending on shape desired. Shape dough to conform to pan. Place basic filling on top of pastry, using palm of hand to manipulate cheese mixture to cover pastry. At this point, if desired, add any combination of optional fillings over cheese layer.

Place second sheet of pastry over fillings, matching edges with bottom sheet. Seal completely with fork dipped in egg yolks.

Using heavy foil, shape funnel 1-inch in diameter. Butter funnel. Place funnel in center of tart, creating a steam hole opening. Funnel should remain until tart has been baked and cooled. Brush pastry top with beaten egg yolk.

Using razor blade, draw decorative lines from center point to edges of pastry, taking care not to pierce pastry. Bake in preheated 325° oven 30 to 40 minutes or until golden brown and puffed.

Cut in squares or wedges for appetizers, luncheon, or light supper.

MEXICAN EGG PUFF

Serves 10

10 eggs
½ cup flour
1 teaspoon baking powder
½ teaspoon salt
1 pint small curd cottage cheese
1 pound Monterey Jack cheese, grated
¼ pound butter
4 ounces diced, seeded green chilies (hot or mild)
¼ cup chopped red pimiento

Beat eggs until light. Add remaining ingredients. Mix well. Pour into buttered 9- by 13-inch baking dish. Bake in preheated 350° oven 35 minutes or until brown and puffed. Serve immediately.

For spicier version, add ⅛ teaspoon each: oregano, garlic powder, cumin, and black pepper.

SCOTCH EGGS

Serves 6

6 eggs
½ pound sausage meat
3 ounces ham, ground
¾ cup bread crumbs, divided
2 tablespoons hot milk
1 teaspoon finely minced onion
1 egg, separated
  salt to taste
  pepper to taste
  sage to taste
  shortening or oil for deep frying

Gently boil 6 eggs 12 minutes until hard-boiled. Peel.

Mix sausage meat and ham. Soak ¼ cup bread crumbs in milk. Combine with sausage mixture. Add onion, beaten egg yolk, salt, pepper, and sage. Mix well.

Divide mixture into 6 portions. Wrap each portion around a hard-boiled egg, covering it completely. Brush each with egg white, slightly beaten. Then coat with remaining bread crumbs.

Fry eggs in deep hot fat until golden. Drain on paper towel. Cut each egg in half and serve either hot, with broiled tomatoes, or cold, at a picnic.

Also a good addition to a cocktail buffet table.

HIDDEN EGGS

Serves 6

High drama at brunch.

6   large, uniform-size potatoes
oil
coarse salt
6   medium eggs
6   ounces mushrooms, sliced
4   tablespoons butter, divided
2   teaspoons flour
¼   cup chicken stock
salt to taste
pepper to taste
4   ounces ham, sliced, shredded
2-3   tablespoons hot milk
½   cup chives, optional
½   cup grated Cheddar cheese

Sauce Mornay:
2   tablespoons butter
3   tablespoons flour
1¼   cups milk
½   cup grated Cheddar cheese

Scrub potatoes. Brush lightly with oil. Sprinkle with coarse salt. Using fork pierce each potato in several places. Bake in preheated 350° oven 1 hour or until tender.

Boil eggs 5 to 6 minutes. Drain. Soak in cold water 7 to 8 minutes. Yolks should not be allowed to harden completely. Peel eggs.

Sauté mushrooms in 2 tablespoons butter. Stir in flour, stock, salt, and pepper. Bring to a boil, stirring constantly. Add ham. Remove from heat. Cool.

Cut off tops of potatoes lengthwise. Scoop out pulp carefully, leaving ½-inch wall. Purée pulp with remaining butter, hot milk, and chives if desired. Set aside.

To prepare Sauce Mornay: In medium saucepan melt butter. Stir in flour to make a smooth paste. Cook over low heat 2 minutes. Add milk. Stir constantly until thickened. Add cheese. Stir until melted and sauce is smooth.

Place spoonful of mushroom mixture in bottom of each potato and top with egg. Coat with Sauce Mornay. Using pastry bag, pipe puréed potato into rosettes over top. Sprinkle with grated cheese. Reheat in preheated 350° oven 8 to 10 minutes or until cheese melts.

Chicken or turkey may be substituted for ham. If desired, meat or poultry may be omitted.

APPLE PANCAKE RED STAR INN

*Yield: 4 to 5
large pancakes*

Filling:
3-4 pounds Granny Smith apples or other tart variety, peeled, sliced
¼ pound butter, melted
¾ cup sugar
    nutmeg to taste
    cinnamon to taste

Batter:
1½ cups milk
1½ cups flour
9 eggs
2 teaspoons sugar
    pinch salt
    sugar mixed with cinnamon to taste
¼ pound butter
    lemon juice to taste
    sugar, optional

Sauté apples in butter. Add sugar. Cook 6 minutes or until tender. Do not overcook. Season to taste with nutmeg and cinnamon. Keep fruit warm.

Combine milk, flour, eggs, sugar, and salt. Mix well. Melt enough butter to coat bottoms and sides of two 10-inch oven-proof skillets. For each pancake pour 1 cup batter in each skillet.

Bake in preheated 500° oven 10 to 15 minutes or until pancake is brown on bottom and sides. Sides should separate slightly from pan. Reduce heat to 400°. Sprinkle pancakes liberally with sugar-cinnamon mixture. Dot generously with butter. Bake 5 minutes. Top should brown only slightly because it will become inside of pancake. Remove skillets from oven.

Fill half of pancake with warm apples and fold other half over. With large spatula transfer to heated platter. Sprinkle with lemon juice and a little sugar if desired. Serve immediately.

Repeat procedure with remaining batter and filling.

Batter and filling may be frozen. Bring batter to room temperature and heat apples before using.

Apple Topping:
Heated filling may be spooned over coffee ice cream and served as dessert.

LOX AND CREAM CHEESE CRÊPES

Yield: 20

This is a nice variation on the standard lox and bagel brunch.

Crêpe batter:
4 eggs
1 cup milk
½ cup presifted flour
½ teaspoon salt
3 tablespoons butter, melted, slightly cooled

Filling:
8 ounces cream cheese
⅛ pound lox (3 or 4 slices), cut into small pieces
3 tablespoons sour cream
2 teaspoons dried dill weed
1 clove garlic, minced
1 slice lox, in thin strips
   fresh dill sprigs

In food processor or blender combine all batter ingredients except melted butter. Process 15 seconds. Scrape sides and blend briefly again. Add melted butter immediately and blend 10 seconds. Cover and refrigerate at least 1 hour. Batter may be made 1 day ahead and stored in refrigerator but may need thinning with 1 or 2 tablespoons of milk. Pour a small amount of batter into hot 7½-inch teflon-coated crêpe pan; cook crêpe on 1 side only. Place wax paper between crêpes as each is made.

For filling, place cream cheese, ⅛ pound lox, sour cream, and dill weed in food processor or blender. Process until mixture is blended and spreadable, about 15 seconds. Spread 1 tablespoon of filling over entire uncooked side of each crêpe and roll up. Garnish each crêpe with a thin strip of lox and dill sprig. Serve slightly warm or at room temperature. Allow 3 or 4 crêpes per person.

Crêpes may also be cut into bite-size pieces and served as an appetizer.

WHOLE GRAIN CRÊPES

Serves 3 to 4

1   egg
½   cup milk
⅓   cup whole wheat or rye flour
1   teaspoon vegetable oil
     pinch salt

In food processor or blender combine all ingredients. Mix until smooth.

Heat and grease crêpe pan. Pour one-sixth of batter into pan. Cook until bubbles form on top. Lift edges with spatula, turn, and cook on other side. Remove crêpe to plate. Repeat procedure with remaining batter. Fill crêpes with chicken, seafood, vegetables of choice, or serve plain.

Crêpes may be stacked and refrigerated in plastic bag for 2 days or frozen for 1 month. If frozen, thaw and heat in 350° oven 5 minutes.

TEA EGGS LAW (Cha-Yeh-Tan)

Serves 8 to 12

Traditionally served as part of a Chinese cold plate, these unusual eggs make an attractive garnish.

12   small or medium eggs
 2   tablespoons loose black tea
 1   whole star anise
 1   cinnamon stick
 2   tablespoons dark soy sauce
 2   tablespoons light soy sauce
1½   teaspoons sugar

Rinse eggs to remove any blemishes. In a saucepan combine eggs with water to cover. Slowly heat to boiling. Simmer 15 minutes. Cool and drain.

Tap each egg lightly with spoon until shell is covered with many fine cracks. Return cracked eggs to saucepan. Cover with water and add remaining ingredients. Bring to boil. Reduce heat and simmer gently 1½ to 2 hours. Drain and cool. Refrigerate if not serving immediately.

Before serving remove shells and slice lengthwise into 6 wedges.

Cracks in shells allow sauce to flavor eggs and produce pretty design.

FISH & SEAFOOD

Ravinia Notes

It was in the old Carousel that hot food was first made available to Ravinia patrons. In 1943 a cafeteria-style dinner was served with emphasis on spaghetti, chili, and hot dogs. The present-day restaurant complex, built thirty-five years later, caters to all tastes, and has wide appeal for marinated beef tenderloin fanciers as well as peanut butter and jelly devotées.

SCALLOPS IN FILO

Serves 8

½   pound plus 2 teaspoons unsalted butter, divided
¾   pound sliced mushrooms
½   cup dry white wine
8   ounces cream cheese, at room temperature
2   teaspoons flour
     salt to taste
     white pepper to taste
2   eggs, lightly beaten
2   pounds bay scallops, patted dry
16   sheets (¾ pound) filo dough

In large skillet sauté mushrooms in 4 tablespoons butter 4 to 5 minutes. With slotted spoon remove mushrooms.

Add wine to skillet. Increase heat and cook until liquid is reduced by half. Reduce heat. Add cream cheese and stir until melted. Simmer briefly.

Combine flour with 2 teaspoons butter. Blend into wine mixture until smooth. Season with salt and pepper. Cool. Blend in eggs. Mix well. Fold in mushrooms and scallops.

Melt remaining butter. Brush butter over 1 sheet filo. Cover with second sheet. Cut filo in half lengthwise. Spoon one-sixteenth of scallop mixture in strip along short end of filo, leaving 2-inch margin at each end of scallop strip. Roll up short end tightly until two-thirds rolled, making sure scallops are well sealed. Fold in sides of filo. Brush remaining one-third dough with butter. Complete rolling. Place seam side down on buttered baking sheet. Brush lightly with butter. Repeat procedure with remaining filo and scallop mixture.

Bake in preheated 400° oven 20 minutes or until golden brown. Serve immediately.

May be assembled on baking sheet up to 1 day in advance and refrigerated.

Serves 10 to 12

4   ounces spinach
1   teaspoon dried tarragon
½   teaspoon dried chervil
2¼ cups whipping cream, divided
½   teaspoon powdered saffron
1   pound scallops, minced
1   teaspoon coarse salt
1   egg
⅛   teaspoon Tabasco
    pinch nutmeg
    pinch white pepper
¾   pound fresh crab meat, in small pieces

Rinse spinach well. Drain partially. Transfer to saucepan. Bring to simmer and cook until nearly all liquid evaporates, stirring. Place in food processor or blender. Add tarragon and chervil. Purée. Pour into small bowl. Refrigerate.

In small saucepan combine ½ cup whipping cream and saffron. Bring to simmer, stirring to blend well, about 2 minutes. Pour into small bowl. Cool. Cover and refrigerate.

In food processor or blender combine scallops, egg, salt, Tabasco, nutmeg and white pepper. With motor running, slowly add 1 cup whipping cream in thin stream. Process additional 30 seconds. Remove processor or blender bowl from base, cover with plastic wrap. Refrigerate 30 minutes.

Return processor or blender bowl to base. With motor running, add ½ cup whipping cream. Adjust seasonings. Transfer half scallop mixture to small bowl. Cover and refrigerate.

With motor running, add ¼ cup whipping cream in thin stream to remaining scallop mixture in work bowl. Spoon half mixture into well-buttered 6-cup terrine. Smooth top. Transfer remaining scallop mixture to small bowl, cover and refrigerate.

Transfer half of previously refrigerated scallop mixture to food processor or blender. With motor running, add chilled saffron mixture. Process until smooth.

Distribute half of crab over scallop mixture in terrine. Cover with saffron-scallop mixture. Smooth top.

In food processor or blender combine chilled spinach and remaining refrigerated scallop mixture. Process until well blended.

continued

Distribute remaining crab over saffron-scallop mixture in terrine. Layer spinach mixture over crab. Smooth top.

Rap terrine sharply several times on hard, flat surface to expel air bubbles. Cover top loosely with buttered foil or terrine cover. Place terrine in large roasting pan. Fill pan with warm water to submerge two-thirds of terrine.

Bake in preheated 350° oven 1 hour 15 minutes or until tester comes out clean. Remove terrine from water. Cool on rack. Remove from pan onto plastic wrap. Wrap securely and refrigerate 1 to 2 days. Flavors blend more with longer refrigeration. Slice to serve.

CRAB STANLEY

Serves 4

1 cup mayonnaise
½ cup chili sauce
2 teaspoons horseradish
¼ cup sweet pickle relish
2 tablespoons chopped scallions
2 tablespoons lemon juice
  salt to taste
¼ teaspoon pepper
1 pound frozen crab meat, thawed, or 14 ounces canned
  Alaska king crab
1 head iceberg lettuce
2 tomatoes, cut in wedges
4 lemon wedges
2 hard-boiled eggs, quartered
4 ripe olives

Combine mayonnaise, chili sauce, horseradish, pickle relish, scallions, lemon juice, salt, and pepper. Mix well. Chill.

Drain crab. Reserve 4 pieces leg meat for garnish. Slice or shred remaining crab.

On 4 individual serving plates place lettuce cup. Shred remaining lettuce and divide among servings. Top with crab meat. Pour 2 tablespoons dressing over each. Garnish with reserved leg meat, tomato wedges, lemon wedges, quartered eggs, and olives. Serve remaining dressing on the side.

SCALLOPS AND MUSHROOMS

Serves 3 to 4

1   **pound bay scallops with natural broth**
½   **cup white wine**
1   **tablespoon fresh lemon juice**
½   **pound mushrooms, sliced**
3   **scallions with tops, sliced**
2   **tablespoons butter**
1   **tablespoon flour**
1   **tablespoon minced parsley**
2   **teaspoons grated Parmesan cheese**
    salt to taste
    white pepper to taste
    seasoned bread crumbs, optional
    butter, optional

In large skillet simmer scallops over low heat in broth, wine, and lemon juice. Cook 2 to 3 minutes, just until scallops become opaque. Do not overcook. Drain, reserving cooking liquid.

Sauté mushrooms and scallions in 2 tablespoons butter over medium heat 3 to 5 minutes. Remove from pan. Stir flour into pan. Stir in reserved cooking liquid, parsley, cheese, and seasonings. Cook, stirring continuously, until sauce is smooth and thickened. Add scallops and mushrooms. Cook 1 minute until reheated. Serve immediately.

If desired, spoon mixture into individual baking shells. Sprinkle with seasoned bread crumbs. Dot with butter. Brown slightly under broiler. Serve immediately.

SEAFOOD PASTA

Serves 6 to 8

1   quart half and half or 1 pint each half and half and
      whipping cream
3   tablespoons tomato paste
2   tablespoons unsalted butter
1   teaspoon dry mustard
      large pinch nutmeg, preferably freshly grated
      salt to taste
      white pepper to taste
1   pound linguini, fettuccine, plain or filled tortellini,
      or filled tortellacci
5   whole allspice
1½   pounds bay scallops
1   pound small shrimp, shelled, deveined
      dry white wine or vermouth
      freshly grated Parmesan cheese

In medium saucepan over very low heat simmer cream until thickened to consistency of medium white sauce. Stir in tomato paste, butter, mustard, nutmeg, salt, and pepper. Set aside over warm water.

Cook pasta in boiling salted water until "al dente" (slightly underdone). Drain, rinse in cold water, drain again. Put in large bowl. Add cream sauce. Toss.

In deep skillet combine allspice, scallops, and shrimp with enough wine or vermouth to barely cover seafood. Simmer until shrimp turn pink. Do not overcook. Remove seafood with slotted spoon. Add to pasta-cream sauce mixture. Toss. If desired, sprinkle with cheese. Serve immediately.

For added color tiny peas, bits of dried red pepper, and/or chopped parsley may be added before final tossing.

SHRIMP AND VEGETABLE COGNAC

Serves 4

5 tablespoons butter, divided
1½-2 pounds uncooked shrimp, shelled, deveined
　　salt to taste
　　freshly ground pepper to taste
3 tablespoons finely chopped shallots
2 cups thinly sliced mushrooms
1 cup finely chopped celery
1 cup thin julienne strips of sweet red pepper
1 cup fresh snow peas
3 tablespoons cognac
½ cup whipping cream

In 10- to 12-inch skillet melt 2 tablespoons butter. Add shrimp, salt, and pepper to taste. Cook over high heat 2 minutes, stirring constantly, or until shrimp turn pink. With slotted spoon remove shrimp to bowl.

Add 1 tablespoon butter and shallots to skillet. Cook 1 minute, stirring. Add mushrooms, celery, pepper, and snow peas. Cook 2 minutes. Sprinkle with cognac. Add cream and bring to boil. Add shrimp with any liquid that has accumulated. Mix well and heat thoroughly. Stir in remaining 2 tablespoons butter. Serve immediately.

CAJUN BARBECUED SHRIMP

Serves 2

1 pound jumbo raw shrimp, shelled, with tails left on
¼ pound butter or margarine
1 tablespoon lemon juice
1 tablespoon Worcestershire sauce
1 tablespoon coarsely ground pepper
½ teaspoon salt
　　Tabasco to taste

Put shrimp in single layer in 9-inch by 13-inch baking dish. Dot with butter. Combine remaining ingredients and pour over shrimp. Bake in preheated 350° oven 20 minutes, stirring occasionally.

Remove shrimp to tureen or individual bowls. Pour pan juices over shrimp. Serve immediately, accompanied by French bread for dipping.

Cajun "purists" may prefer to bake shrimp with shells on and shell while eating.

SHRIMP STROGANOFF

Serves 2 to 3

¼ pound unsalted butter
2 scallions, sliced
1 clove garlic, minced
¾ pound mushrooms, sliced
2 tablespoons flour
3 tablespoons milk
⅓ cup chicken broth
2 egg yolks, beaten
salt to taste
freshly ground pepper to taste
paprika to taste
2 teaspoons fresh dill, chopped, or 1 teaspoon dried dill weed
½ teaspoon Dijon mustard
4 tablespoons sauterne
1 pound cooked, shelled, deveined shrimp
½ cup sour cream

In skillet combine butter, scallions, garlic, and mushrooms. Cook 5 minutes or until browned.

Using a slotted spoon remove mushrooms. Reduce heat. Add flour and stir well. Add milk slowly, stirring constantly. When mixture thickens add chicken broth gradually. Pour a small amount of sauce over yolks. Stir well. Pour yolk mixture back into sauce. Add salt, pepper, paprika, dill, mustard, and sauterne. Mix well. Add mushrooms and shrimp. Heat, stirring.

Just before serving add sour cream. Heat 5 minutes. Do not boil. Serve immediately over rice.

SHRIMP SCAMPI

Serves 4

2 pounds uncooked jumbo shrimp, cleaned, shelled, tails left on
¼ pound butter, melted
½ cup olive oil
2 tablespoons lemon juice
¼ cup finely chopped shallots
1 tablespoon finely chopped garlic
1 teaspoon salt
pinch pepper
3 tablespoons chopped parsley
sprigs of parsley

Combine butter, oil, juice, shallots, garlic, salt, pepper, and chopped parsley. Mix well. Pour over shrimp. Turn to coat well.

Arrange shrimp in single layer in broiler-proof dish. Pour sauce over shrimp. Cover and refrigerate until 10 minutes before serving. Remove cover. Broil 3 to 4 minutes. Turn. Broil additional 3-4 minutes. Serve over rice. Garnish with parsley sprigs.

SWEET AND SOUR SHRIMP

Serves 4 to 6

1 cup sliced celery
1 cup green pepper strips
½ cup sliced onions
¼ cup vegetable oil
1½ cups tomato juice, divided
2 tablespoons cornstarch
¼ cup brown sugar
½ teaspoon salt
1 tablespoon grated lemon peel
¼ cup lemon juice
2 pounds cooked, cleaned, deveined shrimp

Sauté celery, green pepper, and onions in oil, browning slightly. Over medium heat add 1¼ cups tomato juice. Combine cornstarch with remaining ¼ cup tomato juice. Add to vegetable mixture, stirring until thickened. Blend in sugar, salt, lemon peel, and lemon juice. Cook 5 minutes, stirring occasionally. Add shrimp. Heat thoroughly. Serve with rice.

TROUT LOUIS

Serves 6

6   9-12 ounce fresh rainbow trout heads and fins removed, boned for stuffing
4   tablespoons unsalted butter, melted
    salt
    white pepper
    dried dill weed
    garlic salt
    cracker meal
6   thin slices lemon

Dijon mustard sauce:
6   tablespoons Dijon mustard
    rind of 1 lemon, grated
    juice of 1 lemon
3   cloves garlic, crushed
1   medium onion, grated
4   tablespoons flour
¼   pound unsalted butter, melted

Crab mousse stuffing:
12 ounces canned crab meat, drained
1   small onion, grated
1   teaspoon freshly ground white pepper
2   eggs, beaten
½   cup cracker meal
½   teaspoon Tabasco

Combine all mustard sauce ingredients except butter. Mix well.

Combine all stuffing ingredients. Blend until mixed. Do not overmix.

Line large shallow baking dish with foil. Oil liberally with vegetable oil. Brush inside of trout with 4 tablespoons butter. Sprinkle inside lightly with salt, pepper, and dill weed. Divide crab mousse stuffing into 6 portions. Stuff each fish with 1 portion.

Add ¼ pound melted butter to mustard sauce. Mix well. Spread sauce heavily on 1 side of fish. Sprinkle fish lightly with dill weed and garlic salt. Coat well with cracker meal. Transfer trout to baking pan, sauced side down. Repeat procedure for other side.

Bake trout in preheated 425° oven 35 minutes. Transfer to heated serving dish. Garnish each trout with lemon slice. Serve immediately.

FILLET OF FLOUNDER WITH MUSTARD

Serves 4

8   **small flounder fillets, skinned, boned**
    salt to taste
    pepper to taste
1   **tablespoon vegetable or corn oil**
2   **tablespoons mayonnaise**
1   **tablespoon Dijon or Düsseldorf mustard**
2   **teaspoons chopped parsley**
4   **lemon or lime wedges**

Season fillets with salt and pepper. Brush with oil. Arrange fillets in single layer in baking dish.

In bowl combine mayonnaise, mustard, and parsley. Blend well. Brush evenly over fish. Place baking dish 3 to 4 inches under preheated broiler for 1 minute or until fish is golden brown. Serve immediately with lemon wedges.

ORANGE ROUGHY MORNAY

Serves 3 to 4

1½   **pounds orange roughy or fish of choice**
3   **tablespoons butter, divided**
2   **tablespoons flour**
1   **cup milk**
    salt to taste
    pepper to taste
2   **ounces Gruyère cheese, grated**
    pinch nutmeg
1   **tablespoon bread crumbs**
1   **tablespoon grated Parmesan cheese**

Cut fish into serving pieces. Arrange in buttered oven-proof dish.

In saucepan melt 2 tablespoons butter. Remove from heat. Stir in flour then milk. Season with salt and pepper. Return to heat. Bring to boil, stirring constantly. Reduce heat. Add Gruyère and nutmeg. Cook until cheese is melted. Do not boil.

Spoon sauce over fish. Sprinkle with crumbs mixed with Parmesan cheese. Drizzle 1 tablespoon melted butter over all. Bake in preheated 350° oven 20 to 25 minutes. Serve immediately.

MARINATED GROUPER

Serves 6

¾ cup vegetable oil
6 tablespoons olive oil
6 teaspoons Dijon mustard
   juice of 1½ lemons
1 teaspoon fresh rosemary or ¾ teaspoon dried rosemary
3 cloves garlic, slivered
   salt to taste
   freshly ground pepper to taste
3 pounds grouper, in serving pieces (salmon, halibut, or
      haddock may be substituted)

Combine oils, mustard, lemon juice, rosemary, garlic, salt, and pepper. Mix well. Marinate fish in mixture 2 hours or longer. Drain marinade and reserve.

Arrange fish in pan. Broil 5 to 6 minutes, basting with marinade. Turn and broil 5 to 6 additional minutes, basting again. Serve immediately.

RED SNAPPER INDIENNE

Serves 4

1½ tablespoons curry powder
¼   teaspoon cumin
2   tablespoons vegetable oil, divided
1   tablespoon sesame oil
    juice of ½ lemon
1   clove garlic, minced
2   tablespoons chopped coriander
2   pounds red snapper
½   green pepper, julienned
¼   onion, julienned
4   mushrooms, julienned
½   small tomato, julienned
¼   cup grated coconut, optional
⅓   cup chopped peanuts, optional

Preheat broiler. Combine curry powder, cumin, 1 tablespoon vegetable oil, sesame oil, lemon juice, garlic, and coriander. Mix well into thin paste.

Place fish in broiling pan and spread paste over top. Broil until fish flakes, about 10 minutes.

While fish is cooking sauté pepper, onion, mushrooms, and tomato in remaining 1 tablespoon vegetable oil. Cook 5 minutes. Remove from heat. Spoon over fish which has been placed on warm platter. Sprinkle with coconut and peanuts if desired. Serve with Raita (See page 94). See photo page 225.

COLD GLAZED PIKE

Serves 6 to 8

1   **4-pound pike, dressed with head and tail**
    (trout, whitefish, or salmon may be substituted)
1   **lemon, sliced**
1   **small onion, sliced**
    salt to taste
    pepper to taste
½   **cup white wine or dry vermouth**
1   **tablespoon unflavored gelatin**
2   **tablespoons cold water**
½   **cup boiling water**
1   **cucumber, thinly sliced**
2   **pimiento-stuffed olives, optional**
    parsley

Stuff fish with lemon and onion slices. Salt and pepper lightly. Place fish in shallow oven-proof baking dish. Pour wine over fish. Cover with foil. Bake in preheated 350° oven 20 to 25 minutes or until fish is firm and flakes easily with fork. Cool.

Remove skin only from top side of fish. Remove lemon and onion. Drain pan juices and reserve. Soften gelatin in cold water. Add to boiling water to dissolve. Combine with pan juices.

Place fish on serving platter. Arrange cucumber slices to simulate scales. Two olives may be used to simulate eyes. Spoon layer of gelatin and pan juice mixture over cucumber. Chill 15 minutes. Spoon another layer of mixture over cucumber. Chill 15 minutes. Repeat until cucumber slices are firmly glazed in place. Refrigerate.

To serve, decorate with parsley and hollowed-out lemons filled with tartar sauce.

BROWN SUGAR BAKED SALMON

Serves 6

6   salmon steaks, 1-inch thick, or 2-pound salmon fillet in 1 piece

Marinade:
½   cup brown sugar
4   tablespoons melted butter
3   tablespoons soy sauce
2   tablespoons fresh lemon juice
2   tablespoons dry white wine or water

In small bowl combine all marinade ingredients. Place salmon steaks or fillet on foil-covered baking pan that holds fish snugly in one layer. Pour marinade over fish. Cover and marinate in refrigerator from 30 minutes to 6 hours.

Uncover pan. Place on middle rack of preheated 400° oven. Bake 15 to 20 minutes or until fish is done, basting every 5 minutes. Do not turn fish. Serve immediately.

SALMON STRAVINSKY

Serves 4

1   quart dry white wine
6-8   medium shallots, chopped
½   cup whipping cream
1   pound butter, divided
    salt to taste
    cayenne to taste
    juice of ¼ lemon
4   ounces salmon caviar
⅓   pound spinach
2   pounds fresh salmon, in fillets

In medium saucepan combine wine and shallots. Bring to boil, reduce heat, and simmer until liquid evaporates. Add whipping cream. Simmer until cream is reduced by half. Cool to room temperature.

Add ⅓ pound butter in small pieces to cream-shallot mixture, stirring constantly with wire whisk. Season to taste with salt and cayenne. Stir in lemon juice. Purée 1 tablespoon caviar. Add to sauce. Set aside; keep warm.

Blanch spinach in boiling water. Drain well. In medium skillet, sauté spinach in ⅓ pound butter. Keep warm.

Sauté salmon fillets in remaining ⅓ pound butter. Do not overcook.

Arrange bed of spinach in center of each serving plate. Top with salmon fillet. Sprinkle with remaining 3 ounces caviar. Spoon sauce around salmon.

POACHED SALMON STEAKS WITH CUCUMBER-CAPER SAUCE

Serves 8

2   whole cloves
1   medium onion
2   quarts water
8   ounces clam juice
1   cup white wine
6   peppercorns
4   sprigs parsley
4   sprigs thyme
1¼   tablespoons salt
½   bay leaf
8   salmon steaks

Cucumber-caper sauce:
1   egg yolk
⅔   cup vegetable oil, divided
1   tablespoon lemon juice
2   teaspoons Dijon mustard
1   teaspoon minced parsley
1   teaspoon chopped chives
1   teaspoon chopped fresh dill or 2 teaspoons dried dill weed
    freshly ground white pepper to taste
1   large cucumber, peeled, seeded, grated
1   tablespoon drained capers
½   cup whipping cream, whipped

Insert cloves in onion. In large kettle combine onion, water, clam juice, wine, peppercorns, parsley, thyme, salt, and bay leaf. Bring to boil and cook on high heat 10 minutes. Reduce heat, add salmon, and simmer 10 minutes per inch thickness of salmon. Remove from kettle, chill, and serve with cucumber-caper sauce.

In food processor or blender combine egg yolk, 2 tablespoons oil, lemon juice, mustard, parsley, chives, dill, salt, and pepper. Process 10 seconds. With motor running add remaining 8 to 9 tablespoons oil in thin steady stream. Pour into bowl. Stir in cucumbers and capers. Fold in whipped cream. Refrigerate 2 hours.

May be served hot with hollandaise sauce (page 428).

VODKA SOLE WITH CAVIAR SAUCE

Serves 6

	dry vermouth
	water
2	lemon slices
2	scallions
1	stalk celery
1	carrot, sliced
2	parsley sprigs
1	bay leaf
	pinch salt
12	small fillets of sole
	watercress

Sauce:

½	cup mayonnaise
½	cup sour cream
1	small clove garlic, crushed
2	teaspoons Dijon mustard
1½	teaspoons lemon juice
4	ounces red caviar
	vodka to taste

In saucepan combine equal parts of vermouth and water to measure 3 inches. Add lemon, scallions, celery, carrot, parsley, bay leaf, and salt. Bring to boil. Reduce heat and simmer 20 minutes. Remove from heat. Cool thoroughly.

Roll up fillets. Place seam side down in liquid. If necessary add equal amounts vermouth and water to cover fish. Simmer gently 10 minutes. Drain. Cover and chill fillets.

Combine all sauce ingredients. Mix well. Chill overnight.

To serve, arrange rolled fillets on bed of watercress. Spread with sauce.

BAKED STUFFED SOLE

Serves 4

9 fillets of sole, divided
16 mushroom caps, divided
6 tablespoons unsalted butter, divided
1 shallot, finely minced
½ teaspoon salt, divided
¼ teaspoon pepper, divided
12 uncooked shrimp in shells
water
½ onion, sliced
bouquet garni
½ cup dry white wine
salt
pepper
¼ cup whipping cream
2 egg yolks
chopped parsley

Finely chop 1 fillet of sole. Finely mince 8 mushroom caps. In 2 tablespoons butter sauté shallot and minced mushroom caps. Combine with chopped fish. Season with ¼ teaspoon salt and dash pepper. Stuff remaining fillets by rolling each around a tablespoonful of fish mixture. Fasten each with toothpick. Stand rolls upright and close together in buttered baking dish.

Gently boil shrimp in water to cover with onion, bouquet garni, ¼ teaspoon salt, and ⅛ teaspoon pepper. Drain, reserving liquid. Shell shrimp. Pour ½ cup each wine and shrimp stock over fillets in dish. Sprinkle lightly with salt and pepper. Cover dish with buttered paper or foil. Bake sole in preheated 325° oven 25 to 30 minutes, basting occasionally.

While fish is baking sauté 8 whole mushroom caps in 2 tablespoons butter. When fish is baked remove all liquid to small saucepan. Reduce liquid over high heat to ¾ cup. Remove from heat. Stir in 2 tablespoons butter. Beat cream and egg yolks together. Add to sauce. Reheat, stirring, until just thickened.

Arrange 4 shrimp down center of baking dish. Spoon sauce over all. Place 1 sautéed mushroom cap and 1 shrimp on each fish roll. Garnish with parsley.

LEMON SOLE PARMESAN

Serves 2 to 3

4   **fillets or 1 pound lemon sole**
3   **tablespoons mayonnaise**
2   **tablespoons chopped scallions**
½   **cup grated Parmesan cheese**
2   **tablespoons melted butter**
    dash lemon juice
    dash Tabasco
    watercress

Broil fish 6 to 8 minutes. While fish is cooking combine remaining ingredients except watercress. Mix well and spread over fish. Broil 2 minutes or until cheese bubbles and browns slightly. Watch closely to prevent topping from burning. Serve immediately, garnished with watercress.

Other types of fish may be substituted for lemon sole.

GRILLED SWORDFISH WITH GINGER BUTTER

Serves 4

2   **tablespoons shallots**
¼   **cup lemon juice**
¼   **cup dry white wine**
2   **tablespoons finely chopped fresh ginger root**
½   **pound unsalted butter**
    salt to taste
    freshly ground pepper to taste
⅛   **teaspoon cayenne pepper, optional**
2½ **pounds swordfish, in 2 steaks, 1 inch thick**
2   **tablespoons corn oil**
    chopped basil
    chopped parsley

In small saucepan combine shallots, juice, wine, and ginger root. Cook until liquid is reduced to ¼ cup. Over low heat add butter 1 tablespoon at a time, stirring constantly. Do not boil. Season with salt, pepper, and cayenne.

Sprinkle both sides of swordfish with salt and pepper. Brush both sides with oil. Broil fish on outdoor grill or preheated broiler 7 minutes. Turn carefully. Broil 3 minutes. Transfer to serving plates and cover with sauce. Garnish with basil and parsley.

SWORDFISH WITH PESTO

Serves as many as desired

6   ounces fresh swordfish, ½ inch thick per person
    salt to taste
    white pepper to taste
    olive oil

Pesto sauce:
1   pint tightly packed basil
¾   cup pine nuts, toasted
1   large clove garlic
1   cup virgin olive oil
½   cup freshly grated Parmesan cheese

    salad greens or spinach
    red or yellow peppers, in strips

Trim skin from fish. Season with salt and pepper. Sauté in olive oil until springy to touch. Do not allow fish to brown. Cool to room temperature until served.

In food processor combine basil, nuts, and garlic. Process until smooth. With motor running add 1 cup olive oil in stream. Blend cheese into mixture.

Place fish on bed of greens or spinach. Top each piece with dollop of pesto sauce. Decorate plate or platter with pepper strips.

Remaining pesto sauce may be frozen.

LAKE SUPERIOR WHITEFISH

Serves 4 to 6

The pride of the Great Lakes.

3   tablespoons olive oil
2   fresh whitefish, filleted
    juice of ½ lemon
¼   cup dry vermouth
    salt to taste
    pepper to taste
⅓   cup chopped parsley
    lemon wedges
    parsley

Spread olive oil in bottom of large flat baking dish. Place fish in dish and coat with oil. Sprinkle lemon juice, vermouth, salt, pepper, and chopped parsley over fish. Bake in preheated 400° oven 8 minutes or less, without turning, until fish flakes. Serve immediately with lemon wedges and parsley.

BLACKENED FISH

Serves 4

It doesn't have to be redfish to be "blackened".

2 teaspoons minced fresh ginger root
1 clove garlic, minced
2 tablespoons fermented black beans, rinsed well
1 tablespoon soy sauce
¼ cup vegetable oil
1 tablespoon sesame oil
juice of ½ lemon
2 tablespoons rice vinegar
1 tablespoon hot chili bean paste or 1 tablespoon hoisin sauce
2 pounds fish fillets (sea bass, halibut, or monkfish)
1 tablespoon chopped parsley
1 lemon, quartered

Combine ginger root, garlic, black beans, and soy sauce. Mash together, mixing well. Stir in oils, lemon juice, vinegar, and bean paste. Marinate fish in mixture, covered, in refrigerator several hours or overnight.

Place fish in barbecue basket. Grill 10 minutes on each side or until fish flakes. Do not overcook. Sprinkle with parsley. Serve immediately with lemon.

DOOR COUNTY FISH BOIL

Serves 6

6 quarts water
½ cup salt
1 bay leaf
6 peppercorns
1 whole allspice
2 tablespoons white vinegar
1 slice fresh ginger root
12 new potatoes, scrubbed, unpeeled
12-18 boiling onions, peeled
3 pounds fresh fish, cut into 1½-inch steaks
1½ lemons, quartered
½ pound butter, melted

In large pot combine water, salt, bay leaf, peppercorns, allspice, vinegar, and ginger root. Bring to boil. Add potatoes and onions. Cook 15 minutes. Add fish. Cook 8 to 10 minutes after water has returned to boil. Drain. Serve immediately with lemon wedges and melted butter.

CRAB AND SHRIMP CREOLE

Serves 6 to 8

6 tablespoons butter, divided
3 medium onions, chopped
48 ounces canned plum tomatoes, coarsely chopped
2 quarts chicken broth
6 beef bouillon cubes
1½ pounds okra, thinly sliced
1 clove garlic, minced, optional
5 tablespoons flour
2 drops Tabasco
salt to taste
pepper to taste
sherry to taste
chopped parsley
1 pound crab meat
1 pound cooked, shelled shrimp

In large kettle melt 3 tablespoons butter. Add onions and cook until opaque. Add tomatoes, chicken broth, bouillon cubes, okra, and garlic, if desired. Lower heat and simmer 2 hours.

In medium skillet melt remaining 3 tablespoons butter. Add flour and cook over low heat, stirring constantly, until smooth. Slowly add 1 cup tomato-broth mixture to butter-flour mixture. Cook over low heat, stirring, until thickened. Gradually add flour mixture to tomato-broth mixture. Stir in Tabasco, salt, pepper, and sherry. Stir in crab meat and shrimp. Heat through. Garnish with chopped parsley.

SEAFOOD GUMBO

Serves 6 to 8

1	pound okra, in 1-inch slices
5	tablespoons vegetable oil, divided
2	ribs celery, chopped
1	large onion, chopped
1	garlic clove, minced
½	green pepper, chopped
3	ounces tomato paste
28	ounces canned tomatoes, drained, in small pieces
2	quarts soup stock*
2	tablespoons flour
1	slice uncooked ham, cut in 1-inch squares
1	bay leaf
½	teaspoon thyme
	cayenne to taste
	salt to taste
	pepper to taste
½	pound crab meat
1	pound uncooked medium shrimp, shelled, deveined

In medium skillet sauté okra in 2 tablespoons oil until soft. Set aside. In large heavy kettle sauté celery, onion, garlic, and green pepper in 2 tablespoons oil until soft. Add tomato paste and cook, stirring, 5 minutes. Add tomatoes and simmer 5 minutes. Gradually stir in stock. Blend well.

In small skillet brown flour in remaining 1 tablespoon oil. When flour turns dark brown, add small amount stock-tomato mixture. Stir until smooth. Add to stock-tomato mixture in large kettle. Add ham, okra, bay leaf, thyme, cayenne, salt, and pepper. Bring to boil. Reduce heat, cover, and simmer 3 hours.

If serving same day, add crab meat and shrimp 15 minutes before end of cooking time. If serving next day or freezing, add seafood at end of cooking time, stir, remove from heat, cool to room temperature, and refrigerate or freeze. To reheat, bring to room temperature, heat through over medium-low heat. Do not boil.

Serve in bowls over rice. Flavors blend best when prepared a day ahead.

*Prepare stock by cooking shrimp heads and shells in 2 quarts water, or use canned fish, chicken, or beef stock.

GOLDEN GATE CIOPPINO

Serves 6

¼ cup olive oil
3 medium onions, sliced
2 cloves garlic, minced
1 tablespoon grated lemon peel
¼ teaspoon thyme
¼ teaspoon basil
28 ounces canned stewed tomatoes with liquid
3 tablespoons lemon juice
2 tablespoons sugar
½ teaspoon pepper
½ teaspoon paprika
¾ pound fresh fish fillets (grouper, monkfish, halibut, snapper, or French turbot)
8 ounces king crab legs in shell, cracked slightly
1½ pounds seafood (scallops, uncooked lobster tail cut into large pieces, and/or large uncooked shrimp, shelled, deveined)
12 littleneck clams, scrubbed
lemon wedges

In large kettle heat oil. Add onions and garlic. Cook 10 minutes. Add lemon peel, thyme, basil, tomatoes, lemon juice, sugar, pepper, and paprika. Cook 20 minutes or until mixture is slightly thickened.

Cut fish fillets into 2-inch pieces. Remove bones. Add fish, crab, other seafood, and clams to cioppino sauce. Simmer gently 10 to 15 minutes or until cooked. Serve in bowls with lemon wedges.

MEATS

Ravinia Notes

In May of 1949 the charming little Pavilion with its breeze-swept Japanese lanterns burned to the ground. Construction began immediately on a new stage and shell, and the Festival opened six weeks later, on schedule. That season, however, the temporary roof was a thirty-three ton canvas cover, used during World War II to shelter bomber planes.

It was in this NOTEWORTHY setting that the "Million Dollar Trio", Gregor Piatigorsky, Jascha Heifetz, and Arthur Rubinstein, played four performances. Wags said that Rubinstein got first billing, Heifetz got the most money, and Piatigorsky got to play solo.

FLAMED STEAK

Serves 2

2   **steaks, sirloin or fillet**
     freshly ground pepper
2   **tablespoons butter**
¼   **cup brandy, warmed**
1   **tablespoon finely chopped shallots**
1   **tablespoon chopped chives**
½   **teaspoon Worcestershire sauce**
¼   **teaspoon dry mustard**
     salt to taste
¼-½   **cup dry red wine**

Pound pepper into both sides of steaks. In skillet brown meat in butter on both sides. Pour brandy over meat and ignite. When flame dies remove meat with slotted spoon and keep warm.

To pan juices add remaining ingredients. More butter may be added. Simmer 2 to 3 minutes. Pour sauce over steaks and serve.

GRILLED MARINATED FLANK STEAK

Serves 4 to 6

1½   **cups beer**
4   **scallions, minced**
⅓   **cup vegetable oil**
3   **tablespoons soy sauce**
2   **tablespoons light brown sugar**
2   **cloves garlic, minced**
1   **teaspoon salt**
1   **teaspoon red pepper flakes**
     pinch ground ginger
1½-1¾   **pounds flank steak**

In large glass bowl combine all ingredients except steak. Mix well. Add steak, coating it well with marinade. Cover bowl. Refrigerate steak in marinade overnight or up to 3 days, turning occasionally. Drain steak.

Grill steak on barbecue or broil 2 inches from heat about 5 minutes on each side. Cool. Cut across grain into thin slices.

Grilled steak may be stored up to 2 days in refrigerator.

PEPPER STEAK PIQUANT

Serves 10 to 12

2   **sirloin steaks, 1 to 1¼ inches thick**
2   **tablespoons butter**
2   **large Spanish onions, cut into ½-inch rings**
2   **pounds medium mushrooms, caps only**
3   **large green peppers, cut into ½-inch rings**

Sauce:

2   **large cloves garlic, minced**
6   **tablespoons butter**
3   **tablespoons brown sugar**
1⅓   **cups ketchup**
⅓   **cup soy sauce**
⅓   **cup A-1 sauce**
2   **tablespoons lemon juice**
¼   **teaspoon black pepper**
4   **dashes Tabasco**

    chopped parsley

Broil steaks to rare. Cool. In 2 tablespoons butter sauté onions, mushroom caps, and green peppers until tender-crisp. Using sharp knife, remove all fat, bone, and sinews from steaks. Slice into ⅓-inch strips, collecting juices from meat.

In large skillet, sauté garlic in butter a few seconds. Blend in brown sugar. Add remaining sauce ingredients and meat juices. Blend thoroughly. Simmer over low heat 5 minutes. Add meat strips and vegetables. Heat through. Sprinkle with chopped parsley.

Serve with crisp Chinese noodles or crusty French bread.

STUFFED ROLLED FLANK STEAK WITH SPICY SAUCE

Serves 4 to 6

1½ pounds flank steak
1 tablespoon lemon juice
1 tablespoon olive oil
½ teaspoon dried or 2 tablespoons fresh coriander
¼ teaspoon coarse salt
¼ teaspoon coarsley ground pepper
¼ cup chopped parsley
10 ounces frozen leaf spinach, cooked, well drained
2 medium carrots, shredded
1 small onion, finely chopped
2 quarts beef broth or stock

Spicy sauce:
2 medium tomatoes, peeled, seeded, finely chopped
1 medium onion, finely chopped
½ green pepper, seeded, finely chopped
2 green chilies, roasted, peeled, seeded, finely chopped, or to taste
1 clove garlic, minced
¼ cup olive oil
2 tablespoons red wine vinegar
salt to taste
freshly ground pepper to taste

Using meat mallet, pound steak to ¼-inch thickness. Combine lemon juice, oil, coriander, salt, pepper, and parsley. Spread mixture over steak, leaving 1-inch border. Cover with spinach. Combine carrots and onion. Spread over spinach. Press flat. Roll up steak, jelly roll fashion. Tie with string at 2-inch intervals.

Place steak in Dutch oven. Pour beef stock over meat. Heat to boil. Skim. Simmer covered 1½ to 2 hours or until fork tender, turning several times. Remove steak from broth. Cool.

Combine all sauce ingredients. Mix well. Serve steak warm or cold, thinly sliced, with spicy sauce.

JEWEL OF A POOR MAN'S STEAK

Serves 4 to 6   *A pot roast masquerading as a steak.*

8 ounces Italian dressing
¼-½ cup red wine vinegar
2 ounces honey
1 ounce bourbon
1 tablespoon Worcestershire sauce
3 strips orange peel
3-4 pounds blade-cut pot roast

Combine all ingredients except meat. Mix well. Pierce top and bottom of pot roast with fork and place in large bowl. Pour marinade over meat. Cover and refrigerate overnight.

One hour before barbecuing drain marinade. To barbecue, sear each side of meat 1 minute over hot coals. Grill to taste. Carve ⅜-inch thick on slanted diagonal.

GRAM'S BEEF AND SAUERKRAUT

Serves 4 to 5   *This "Gram" was a beloved North Shore hostess.*

1 large onion, sliced
2-3 tablespoons butter, divided
3-4 pound pot roast, fat trimmed
¾-1 cup boiling water
1 pound sauerkraut, drained
1 apple, peeled, grated
1 large uncooked potato, peeled, grated
½ teaspoon salt
pepper to taste
1 teaspoon caraway seeds

In Dutch oven sauté onion in 1 to 2 tablespoons butter until golden. With slotted spoon remove onion from pan. Add remaining butter to pan. Add roast and sear until browned on all sides. Add water and onion. Cover tightly. Bake in preheated 375° oven 1 hour.

Spread sauerkraut over meat. Sprinkle with apple and potato. Season with salt and pepper. Sprinkle with caraway seeds. Cover and bake 3 hours or until tender.

OVEN BARBECUED POT ROAST

Serves 6 to 8   *A traditional method using updated ingredients.*

5	ounces soy sauce
¼	cup brown sugar
¼	cup bourbon
1	tablespoon lemon juice
1	teaspoon Worcestershire sauce
1½	cups water
3½-5½	pounds pot roast

In large bowl combine all ingredients except meat. Mix well. Add meat. Cover and marinate pot roast in mixture in refrigerator overnight. Drain marinade and reserve. Place roast in heavy Dutch oven. Bake, covered, in preheated 300° oven 3½ to 4 hours or until tender. After 1 hour, baste every 30 minutes.

WINTER POT ROAST AND NOODLES

Serves 8

4	pounds chuck pot roast
2	tablespoons steak sauce
2	tablespoons butter
2	medium onions, sliced
2	cups tomato sauce
1	cup ketchup
1	teaspoon salt
1	teaspoon sugar
¼	teaspoon pepper
1½	tablespoons horseradish
16	ounces uncooked noodles, fine or medium
1	teaspoon caraway seeds
	chopped parsley

Coat meat on all sides with steak sauce. In large skillet brown roast in butter over medium heat. Transfer to large shallow oven-proof pan or casserole. Place onions on top of meat. Combine tomato sauce, ketchup, salt, sugar, pepper, and horseradish in skillet. Bring to boil, stirring. Pour sauce over meat and onions. Cover pan tightly.

Bake in preheated 350° oven 2 hours or until fork tender. Cool and refrigerate overnight. Skim fat from gravy and meat. Remove bone and gristle. Slice for serving and reheat in half of gravy. Cook noodles. Drain and mix with 3 cups remaining gravy. Stir in caraway seeds. Sprinkle with parsley.

CAJUN EYE OF ROUND

Serves 8 to 10

3½-4 pound eye of round roast, well trimmed
1 tablespoon lemon juice
1 teaspoon salt
freshly ground pepper
¼ teaspoon ground allspice
1 large Spanish or Bermuda onion, thinly sliced
1 bell pepper, green or red, thinly sliced
1 tablespoon vegetable oil
1 tablespoon margarine
1 pound canned tomatoes, crushed, drained, liquid reserved

Sauce:
4-8 ounces beef bouillon
reserved liquid from tomatoes
½ cup Burgundy wine
½ cup cold coffee
½-¾ teaspoon Tabasco or to taste

Add enough beef bouillon to liquid from tomatoes to make 1½ cups. In saucepan combine mixture with remaining sauce ingredients. Bring to boil over medium heat. Reduce heat and simmer 5 minutes or until thickened.

Rub roast with lemon juice. Sprinkle with salt, pepper, and allspice. Place meat in roasting pan. In skillet over medium heat sauté onion and pepper separately in combined oil and margarine. Spoon vegetables and tomatoes over roast. Pour a third of the sauce over all.

Bake meat in preheated 500° oven 10 minutes. Reduce heat to 300° and roast 40 minutes for rare and 50 minutes for medium rare. Turn off oven. Open oven door and leave roast in oven 10 minutes. Drain pan juices and add to remaining sauce. May be served hot or cold with sauce.

BRISKET OF BEEF

Serves 10 to 12

5	pound trimmed first cut brisket of beef
21½	ounces canned undiluted consommé
½	cup ketchup
2	teaspoons A-1 sauce
2	teaspoons Escoffier sauce
¼	teaspoon Worcestershire sauce
	cornstarch or flour, optional

Wrap brisket in large sheet heavy foil, sealing well. Place in shallow roasting pan. Bake in preheated 325° oven 3 hours.

While meat is cooking bring consommé to boil. Reduce heat and simmer until soup is reduced by half. Add ketchup, A-1 sauce, Escoffier sauce, and Worcestershire sauce. Mix and heat thoroughly.

Remove roast from oven. Open foil. Drain off liquid. Spoon soup mixture over roast. Rewrap roast and return to oven for 1 hour.

If thicker gravy is desired, remove roast and thicken liquid with small amount of cornstarch or flour. If browner roast is desired, broil several minutes.

Roast is more flavorful if prepared 1 day ahead.

MARINATED BEEF TENDERLOIN

Serves 8

1	cup soy sauce
¾	cup peanut oil
½	cup olive oil
1¼	cups sherry
7	cloves garlic, minced
1½	teaspoons Tabasco
½	teaspoon salt
½	teaspoon freshly ground pepper
7	pound fillet of beef, well trimmed
	parsley sprigs
	cherry tomatoes

Combine all ingredients except beef, parsley, and tomatoes. Marinate beef in mixture 8 hours, turning several times. Remove beef from marinade. Dry. Place on rack in roasting pan. Bake in preheated 475° oven 25 minutes for very rare, 30 minutes for rare. Baste every 5 minutes with marinade. Remove to platter. Cool. Do not refrigerate. Before serving slice and arrange in overlapping decorative pattern on platter. Garnish with parsley sprigs and cherry tomatoes.

May be grilled outdoors and served on buns.

Serves 6 to 8

3-4	pound trimmed beef fillet
	salt to taste
	pepper to taste
4	tablespoons butter, divided
1	carrot, finely chopped
1	leek, white part only, finely chopped
1	rib celery, finely chopped
1	tablespoon vegetable oil
1	clove garlic, minced
¾	pound bacon, cut into 1-inch pieces
¼	pound mushrooms, sliced
1½	cups sour cream
1	tablespoon grated onion
2	teaspoons horseradish
1	tablespoon finely chopped parsley
1	teaspoon thyme
1	teaspoon chervil

Season beef with salt and pepper. Dot with 2 tablespoons butter. Melt remaining 2 tablespoons butter in small roasting pan. Add carrot, leek, and celery. Sauté over low heat 8 minutes. Place beef in pan. Bake in preheated 500° oven 25 minutes. Cool in pan juices 1 hour.

In medium skillet heat oil and garlic. Cook 1 minute. Add bacon. Sauté until barely crisp. Drain on paper towels. Drain all but 3 tablespoons drippings. Add mushrooms. Cook over moderate heat 3 to 5 minutes. Remove, drain, and set aside.

Place cooled meat on cutting board, pouring pan juices into bowl. Add remaining ingredients to pan juices, blending well. Add bacon and mushrooms. Taste for seasoning. Cut wedge 1 inch wide and 1 inch deep along top length of beef. Remove long triangular wedge. Spoon stuffing evenly into cavity, filling with about 3 tablespoons of stuffing. Replace wedge. Chill. To serve, cut beef into ¾-inch slices. Accompany with remaining chilled stuffing.

BEEF TENDERLOIN DUET

Serves 10 to 12

4-5	pound beef tenderloin
	salt to taste
	pepper to taste
1	tablespoon flour
4	slices bacon, divided
1	clove garlic, slivered
½	pound mushrooms, sliced
2	medium onions, sliced
6	tablespoons butter, melted
¼	pound ground round steak
2	tablespoons chili sauce
¼	teaspoon marjoram
¼	teaspoon thyme
¼	teaspoon hickory salt
4	drops Tabasco
⅛	teaspoon Worcestershire sauce
2	beef bouillon cubes

Sprinkle beef with salt and pepper. Rub with flour. Place 2 slices bacon over meat and broil 7 minutes. Turn, cover with remaining bacon, and broil 7 minutes. Remove to shallow oven-proof pan.

Sauté garlic, mushrooms, and onions in butter until soft but not brown. Add ground round. Cook, stirring, until brown. Drain. Add chili sauce, seasonings, Tabasco, Worcestershire sauce, and bouillon cubes. Simmer 20 minutes.

Pour sauce over tenderloin in pan. Let stand at room temperature until ready to roast.

Bake in preheated 400° oven 25 minutes. Spoon sauce over slices of meat when serving.

STIR FRIED BEEF WITH BROCCOLI
(Chieh Lan Ch'al Niv)

Serves 3

½   pound boneless beef, flank or tenderloin
3   teaspoons cornstarch, divided
1½   tablespoons soy sauce
1   tablespoon water
1   teaspoon sugar
½   teaspoon salt
2   tablespoons dry sherry
1   tablespoon oyster sauce
5   cups broccoli, in 2- by ½-inch pieces
3   tablespoons vegetable oil
2   thin slices ginger root

Slice beef into 2- by 1- by ¼-inch pieces. Combine with 2 teaspoons cornstarch, soy sauce, and water. Mix well. Combine sugar, salt, remaining 1 teaspoon cornstarch, sherry, and oyster sauce. Mix well.

Drop broccoli into boiling water and cook uncovered 1 minute. Drain and rinse under cold water.

Heat wok or electric skillet until very hot. Add oil, ginger, and beef pieces. Stir quickly to cook beef. Blend in broccoli. Cook 2 to 3 minutes. Add oyster sauce mixture. Stir until sauce thickens and clear glaze develops. Remove ginger root. Serve immediately.

Serve with rice. Accompany with bean sprout salad.

BEEF TERIYAKI

Serves 4 to 6

From a fine Hawaiian chef.

1½   cups soy sauce
1   cup sugar
½   cup sake or dry vermouth
2   cloves garlic, finely chopped
2   slices fresh ginger root, finely chopped
1   tablespoon sesame seed
2   tablespoons scallion tops, chopped
2   flank steaks

continued

In saucepan bring to boil soy sauce, sugar, sake or vermouth, garlic, and ginger root. Let cool. Add sesame seed and scallions. Marinate flank steak in sauce for 2 hours. Barbecue on grill to desired doneness, basting occasionally. Slice thinly on the diagonal and serve over rice. Pass warmed marinade.

Variation:
For *Chicken Teriyaki* substitute chicken pieces or boneless chicken breasts for flank steaks.

BEEF STROGANOFF

Serves 6

1½ **pounds fillet of beef, in 1½- by 2- by ½-inch strips**
    juice of 1 lemon
1   **cup sliced mushrooms**
¼   **pound butter, divided**
¼   **cup thinly sliced onion**
1   **teaspoon dehydrated beef bouillon**
1   **teaspoon water**
½   **cup flour**
1   **cup sour cream**
1   **cup pitted small ripe olives**

Sprinkle beef strips with lemon juice. Refrigerate overnight. Drain on paper towels.

Sauté mushrooms in butter until lightly browned. Remove from pan. Sauté onion in butter until lightly browned. Remove from pan.

Dissolve bouillon in water. Dredge beef strips in flour, shaking off excess. Sauté beef in butter until almost done. Sprinkle with bouillon. Add mushrooms and onion. Cook 3 to 5 minutes. Add sour cream and olives. Mix well. Heat briefly and serve immediately.

Prepare ahead to let flavors blend and develop.

A 4-pound sirloin steak trimmed of all fat and bone may be substituted for fillet.

ALL AMERICAN MEAT LOAF

Serves 6 to 8

The much-maligned meat loaf, elevated to new heights.

Meat loaf:
1   pound lean ground beef
½   pound lean ground pork
½   pound ground veal
1   teaspoon salt, optional
½   teaspoon freshly ground pepper
¼   teaspoon ground allspice
⅛   teaspoon ground coriander
⅛   teaspoon ground cardamom
1-2   tablespoons Worcestershire sauce
1½   cups quick rolled oats
½   cup chili sauce
½   cup sour cream or cottage cheese, puréed
1   heaping tablespoon dried chopped onions
2   eggs, beaten
½   cup chopped parsley

    parsley

Sauce:
1   cup ketchup
1   cup barbecue sauce
1   cup port
½   cup cold coffee
1   teaspoon Liquid Smoke, optional

In saucepan combine all sauce ingredients. Simmer uncovered until reduced by a third.

Combine meats. Mix well. In large bowl blend meat with remaining ingredients. Form into loaf 8- by 4- by 3-inches. Place loaf in greased 9- by 13-inch glass baking dish. Cover with heavy foil. Chill 1 hour. Remove from refrigerator. Let come to room temperature.

Bake covered in preheated 350° oven 1 hour. Drain all juices and fat. Use paper towel to absorb any remaining juice on meat loaf. Spoon half of sauce over loaf. Bake uncovered 30 to 40 minutes or until glazed dark red-brown. Turn off oven. With door ajar leave meat loaf in oven 10 minutes. Remove to warm platter. Garnish with parsley. Serve with remaining sauce.

STUFFED MEAT LOAVES

Yield: 2 large meat loaves

Meat loaf:

5	pounds ground round steak or meat loaf mixture
2	eggs
¼	cup milk
2-3	medium onions, chopped
8	thin slices whole wheat or whole grain bread, crumbled
1	teaspoon salt or to taste
2	tablespoons Worcestershire sauce
1	tablespoon sage
1	tablespoon dry mustard
¾	teaspoon garlic powder
⅔-1	cup ketchup

Stuffing:

1	pound mushrooms, finely chopped
1	tablespoon butter or margarine
8	ounces cream cheese or low-calorie cream cheese
8-10	drops Tabasco

In large bowl combine all meat loaf ingredients. Mix well by hand.

Sauté mushrooms in butter. Drain well. Mix with cheese and Tabasco. Divide meat loaf mixture into fourths. Shape each quarter into equal oblongs making depression in center of each. Divide stuffing in half and spread over 2 quarters. Top with remaining quarters. Seal carefully around all sides to prevent stuffing from escaping during baking. Place loaves on large baking pan with shallow sides.

Bake in preheated 350° oven 1 hour. Meat loaf may be frozen, baked or unbaked.

Stuffing also is good under skin of boned chicken breasts and is proper amount for 8 halves.

KOREAN BARBECUED SHORT RIBS

Serves 3

1 cup soy sauce
5 cloves garlic, minced
2 tablespoons chopped scallions
1 teaspoon finely chopped ginger root
¼ cup sugar
2 tablespoons sesame oil
1½ teaspoons sesame seed
¼ teaspoon black pepper
3 pounds beef short ribs

In large bowl combine all ingredients except ribs. Mix well. Score ribs and marinate in mixture 2 to 3 hours at room temperature. Remove ribs from marinade. Broil or cook over charcoal grill 30 to 45 minutes, basting occasionally with marinade. May reheat in foil in oven.

Serve with kim chee, a spicy Korean cabbage available in Oriental food markets.

CHILI

Serves 4

1 large onion, thinly sliced
1 clove garlic, minced
1 green pepper, chopped
1 pound ground beef
3 tablespoons olive oil
16 ounces canned chopped tomatoes
8 ounces tomato paste
1 bay leaf
2 tablespoons chili powder
1 teaspoon sugar
1 teaspoon cumin seed
1 teaspoon salt
½ tablespoon basil
¼ teaspoon crushed red pepper
 dash cayenne pepper
10 ounces canned kidney beans, drained

In large kettle brown onion, garlic, green pepper, and beef in oil. Add all remaining ingredients except kidney beans. Simmer covered 1 hour. Uncover and simmer additional 1 hour, stirring occasionally. Add kidney beans. Heat and serve.

STUFFED ONIONS CASABLANCA

Serves 6

The flavor of exotic Morocco sets this recipe apart.

6 Spanish onions, about ⅔ pound each, peeled
1 tablespoon vegetable oil
½ pound lean ground beef
½ pound lean ground pork
16 ounces canned plum tomatoes, drained, coarsely chopped
4 ounces canned mild green chili peppers, drained, coarsely chopped
⅓ cup golden raisins
2 tablespoons tomato paste
3 cloves garlic, minced
1 tablespoon cider vinegar
¼ teaspoon cinnamon
⅛ teaspoon ground cloves
 salt to taste
 pepper to taste
1 cup pimiento-stuffed green olives, coarsely chopped
2 teaspoons grated Parmesan cheese
13 ounces canned beef consommé
2 teaspoons chopped parsley

Carefully cut thin slice from root end of each onion to provide flat base, preserving leak-proof shell. Cut 1-inch slice off each top. Scoop out centers leaving ¼-inch shell. Chop removed centers to measure 1 cup. Steam onion shells 5 minutes. Invert on rack to drain.

In large skillet cook chopped onion in oil until soft. Add beef and pork, stirring to break up meat. Cook until brown. Drain excess fat. Add tomatoes, peppers, raisins, tomato paste, garlic, vinegar, cinnamon, cloves, salt, and pepper. Cook mixture, stirring, about 10 minutes. Mixture should be moist but not runny. Stir in olives. Remove from heat.

Mound stuffing inside onion shells, shaping with spoon. Sprinkle top of each with Parmesan cheese. Place in casserole. Pour consommé in bottom. Bake in preheated 350° oven 35 to 40 minutes. Garnish with parsley. Serve on brown rice or spinach bed.

May be prepared 1 day ahead, refrigerated, and baked before serving.

EMPAÑADAS DE HORNO

Yield: 12

Filling:

2 cups chopped onions
2 tablespoons butter
1 pound ground beef
2½ teaspoons cumin
   salt to taste
   pepper to taste
   chili powder to taste
   raisins, optional
2 hard-boiled eggs, sliced
1 egg white, beaten

Dough:

4 cups flour
1 cup vegetable shortening
1 cup hot milk, not boiled
1 egg
2 teaspoons salt

In large skillet sauté onions in butter until transparent. In separate skillet sauté meat. Stir meat into onions. Add cumin, salt, pepper, and chili powder. Refrigerate filling several hours or overnight.

Combine all dough ingredients. Mix well. Let stand 20 minutes at room temperature. Roll dough into log shape. Divide into 12 equal parts. With rolling pin flatten each piece into round at least ¼ inch thick.

Spoon 1½ tablespoons filling on each round of dough. Sprinkle with several raisins if desired. Top with slice of hard-boiled egg. Fold round of dough over to form half moon, carefully sealing edges. Brush tops of empañadas with beaten egg white. Bake in preheated 350° oven 20 to 25 minutes or until golden brown.

Unbaked empañadas freeze well. May be baked frozen with increased baking time.

GRILLED VEAL CHOPS

Serves 4

¾   cup dry white wine
2   tablespoons olive oil
½   teaspoon rosemary
½   teaspoon marjoram
½   teaspoon oregano
½   teaspoon cracked pepper
4   teaspoons minced onion
½   teaspoon minced garlic
   salt to taste
4   large rib veal chops, 1 inch thick
   parsley

In 9- by 13-inch dish combine all ingredients except veal chops and parsley. Mix well. Add chops, turning to coat all surfaces. Marinate at least 3 hours, turning chops halfway through marinating time.

Arrange chops on charcoal grill. Brush with marinade. Cover and grill 10 to 15 minutes. Turn. Brush with marinade. Cover and grill 5 to 10 minutes. Uncover. Baste and grill until done as desired. Garnish with parsley before serving.

VEAL CHOPS AND MUSHROOMS

Serves 4

3   tablespoons butter or margarine
4   lean loin veal chops
   salt to taste
   pepper to taste
2   medium onions, chopped
1   pound mushroom caps
1   tablespoon flour
1   tablespoon tomato paste
¾   cup beef or chicken broth
⅔   cup dry white wine
1   teaspoon Herbes de Provence or fines herbes
1   small bay leaf
1   tablespoon minced parsley

In large heavy skillet melt butter or margarine. Season veal chops with salt and pepper. Brown quickly in skillet over high heat. Transfer chops to shallow casserole.

In same skillet over medium heat, sauté onions. Add remaining ingredients except parsley. Cover skillet and cook 5 minutes. Pour mixture over chops. Cover casserole. Bake in preheated 325° oven 1 hour. Sprinkle with parsley before serving.

VEAL CHOPS ST. MICHEL

Serves 4

4   rib or loin veal chops
4   tablespoons unsalted butter
4   tablespoons Dijon mustard
4   tablespoons whipping cream, divided
½   pound grated Swiss cheese
2   tablespoons applejack brandy
    salt to taste
    freshly ground pepper to taste

Sautéed apples:
4   apples, cored, thinly sliced
¼   pound unsalted butter
    pinch cinnamon
    pinch sugar

Sauté chops in butter until brown. Transfer to buttered oven-proof dish.

Combine mustard, 2 tablespoons cream, and cheese. Mix well. Spread over chops. Deglaze skillet with brandy and simmer until reduced. Stir in remaining 2 tablespoons cream and seasonings. Pour sauce over each chop and around edge of baking dish. Bake in preheated 350° oven 30 minutes.

Sauté apples in butter. Add cinnamon and sugar. Cook until apples are glazed but still retain their shape.

Serve chops immediately with sautéed apples.

VEAL PATTIES

Serves 3 to 4

2   thin slices white bread
1   pound veal shoulder, ground 3 times
1   tablespoon grated onion
1½   teaspoons salt
⅛   teaspoon freshly ground pepper
1   egg
1   cup whipping cream
3   tablespoons butter, divided
     lemon juice to taste
2   tablespoons drained capers
1   tablespoon chopped parsley

continued

Soak bread in water. Squeeze out excess water. Combine bread, veal, onion, salt, pepper, and egg. Mix well. Chill 1 hour. Add cream gradually, beating with spoon until light and fluffy. Chill additional hour.

With wet hands form mixture into patties. Over high heat in 1 tablespoon butter sauté patties quickly on both sides. Reduce heat and simmer 20 minutes, turning once.

Brown remaining 2 tablespoons butter. Combine with lemon juice, capers, and parsley. Pour over patties. Serve immediately.

VEAL SMITH

Serves 3

6   **veal scallops, flattened to ¼-inch thickness**
½   **cup flour**
5   **tablespoons butter, divided**
3   **tablespoons corn oil, divided**
1   **cup brandy or dry sherry**
1   **cup crème fraîche, (see page 423)**
1   **cup sliced mushrooms**
     salt to taste
     freshly ground pepper to taste
1½ **cups peeled, cored, sliced Granny Smith or other tart apples**

Dry veal on paper towel. Place flour in plastic bag. Add scallops 1 at a time. Shake to coat veal lightly. In 10-inch skillet heat 3 tablespoons butter and 1½ tablespoons oil over moderately high heat. When butter foam subsides, sauté 3 slices of veal 2 minutes on each side or until lightly browned. Remove scallops to oven-proof dish. Repeat with remaining scallops, adding 1½ tablespoons oil. Transfer dish to preheated 250° oven.

Pour off all fat from skillet. Add brandy while skillet is heated. Scrape bottom of skillet, incorporating scraps into brandy. Add crème fraîche and mushrooms. Simmer until sauce is reduced and thickened, about 5 to 8 minutes. Add salt and pepper to taste.

While sauce is thickening sauté apples in remaining 2 tablespoons butter in another skillet. Remove veal from oven. Spoon sauce over scallops and top with sautéed apples. Serve immediately.

OSSO BUCCO MILANESE

4	tablespoons butter
1½	cups chopped onions
½	cup finely chopped carrots
½	cup finely chopped celery
1	clove garlic, minced
6-7	pounds veal shanks, 2½-inches long, tied
1½	teaspoons salt
½	teaspoon pepper
¼	cup flour
½	cup olive oil, divided
1	cup dry white wine
¾	cup beef or chicken stock
½	teaspoon dried basil
½	teaspoon dried thyme
3	cups canned tomatoes, drained, coarsely chopped
6	parsley sprigs
2	bay leaves

Gremolata:

3	tablespoons finely chopped parsley
1	tablespoon grated lemon rind
1	small clove garlic, finely chopped

In heavy shallow casserole or Dutch oven with tight-fitting cover, melt butter. Add onions, carrots, celery, and garlic. Cook over medium heat 10 to 12 minutes, stirring occasionally. Remove from heat.

Sprinkle veal with salt and pepper. Dust with flour. Heat 6 tablespoons olive oil in heavy 10- or 12-inch skillet. Add veal pieces, a few at a time, to brown over moderate heat. Add more oil if needed. Place browned pieces over vegetables in casserole.

Drain all but small amount of fat from skillet. Add wine. Boil briskly over high heat until reduced to ½ cup. Stir in stock, spices, tomatoes, parsley, and bay leaves. Bring mixture to boil. Pour over veal. Veal should be half submerged in liquid. Add more stock if needed. Cover. Place in lower third of preheated 350° oven. Bake 60 to 75 minutes, basting occasionally. If necessary, adjust oven heat to keep casserole simmering gently. Test veal for tenderness with sharp knife.

When tender, strain liquid from casserole. Cool liquid. Skim fat. Return defatted liquid to casserole. Stand shanks on end. Reheat, covered. May place casserole under broiler briefly to brown shank ends.

Combine all gremolata ingredients. May be served from casserole or heated platter. Sprinkle with gremolata. Serve with plain buttered pasta or rice.

VEAL SHANKS WITH LEMON AND ORANGE

Serves 4

3   pounds veal shanks, in 2-inch pieces
5   oranges, divided
2   lemons
2   tablespoons fresh basil or 1 teaspoon dried basil
1   bay leaf
4   whole cloves
1   tablespoon fresh thyme or 1½ teaspoons dried thyme
1½   pounds onions, chopped
     salt to taste
     pepper to taste
     flour
3   tablespoons vegetable oil
4   cups chicken stock
2   teaspoons brown sugar
1   teaspoon water
1   tablespoon white wine vinegar

Place veal in large glass or enamel pan. Remove rinds of 2 oranges. Reserve. Juice all citrus and pour over veal. Add basil, bay leaf, cloves, thyme, onions, salt, and pepper. Cover. Refrigerate 24 hours.

Remove meat and dust lightly with flour. In skillet over high heat sear meat in oil in 3 to 4 batches. Lightly brown 2 to 3 minutes per side to seal. In heavy kettle bring marinade to simmer. Add meat and cover. Bake in preheated 325° oven 1 hour 45 minutes. Add chicken stock, ¼ cup at a time, if mixture gets too dry.

In small saucepan combine sugar with 1 teaspoon water. Carmelize over high heat. Remove from heat; add vinegar. Add some juice from stew pot to keep mixture liquid. When meat is roasted, purée marinade in food processor or blender. Add vinegar mixture to purée. Grate reserved orange rinds and add to sauce. If sauce is too liquid, reduce over low heat. Spoon sauce over meat and serve.

May be prepared in advance and reheated in slow oven.

VEAL WITH EGGPLANT

Serves 6 to 8

1   cup flour
1   cup zwieback crumbs
½   teaspoon mace
½   teaspoon white pepper
¼   teaspoon salt
6-8 slices eggplant, ⅜-inch thick, unpeeled
6-8 slices veal scallops, ⅓ to ¼ pound each
3   tablespoons vegetable oil, divided
3   tablespoons butter, divided
1   cup grated mozzarella cheese
2   cups tomato sauce
1   clove garlic, minced
½   teaspoon oregano
½   teaspoon basil
½   teaspoon rosemary
⅛   teaspoon cinnamon
½   cup grated Parmesan cheese
½   cup minced parsley

Cover 2 cookie sheets with wax paper. Combine flour, crumbs, mace, pepper, and salt. Dip eggplant in mixture. Shake off excess. Place slices on prepared cookie sheets. Cover with wax paper. Refrigerate at least 1 hour. Repeat procedure using veal scallops.

In large skillet, sauté eggplant in 1½ tablespoons oil and 1½ tablespoons butter until very lightly browned. Drain on paper towels. Sauté veal, adding remaining oil and butter as needed, until golden. Drain on paper towels.

Arrange eggplant in single layer in 9- by 13-inch baking dish. Cover with veal slices. Sprinkle with mozzarella.

Combine tomato sauce, garlic, oregano, basil, rosemary, and cinnamon. Pour over veal. Sprinkle with Parmesan cheese. Cover lightly with foil. Bake in preheated 350° oven 30 minutes. Remove foil. Bake 15 minutes. Sprinkle liberally with parsley before serving.

VITELLO TONNATO

Serves 8

1 cup minced onion
½ cup minced celery
½ cup minced carrots
3 tablespoons butter
4 pounds boneless veal loin, tied
3 tablespoons vegetable oil
6 parsley sprigs
2 thyme sprigs or ⅛ teaspoon dried thyme
1 bay leaf
5 cups chicken stock, divided
1 cup dry white wine

Sauce:
6 ounces tuna in oil
6 anchovy fillets, drained, rinsed
1 cup braising liquid, divided
½ cup whipping cream
1 tablespoon lemon juice or to taste
¼ teaspoon pepper
2 cups mayonnaise

lemon slices
capers
Italian parsley
ripe pitted olives

In large kettle sauté onion, celery, and carrots in butter. Cover and cook until tender. In heavy skillet brown veal in oil. Add to vegetables with parsley, thyme, bay leaf, and 1 cup chicken stock. Simmer, basting veal, until stock is reduced. Add second cup stock. Simmer and reduce, basting veal until glaze forms. Add remaining 3 cups stock and wine. Cover tightly with foil and lid. Simmer 1½ hours or until tender. Remove from heat. Strain stock and cool. Skim fat. Remove meat from kettle. Return 2 cups strained stock to kettle. Reduce to 1 cup, cool and reserve.

In food processor or blender combine tuna, anchovies, ½ cup reserved braising liquid, whipping cream, 1 tablespoon lemon juice, and pepper. Blend well. Transfer to bowl and stir in mayonnaise. Add more of reserved braising liquid until mixture has creamy consistency. Adjust seasoning and add more lemon juice if desired.

Pour layer of sauce on serving platter. Arrange thinly sliced meat on sauce. Pour remaining sauce over top. Garnish with lemon slices, capers, Italian parsley, and olives.

Pork loin or turkey breast may be substituted for veal loin.

Remaining braising liquid is excellent soup base.

LAMB CHOPS WITH GOAT CHEESE

Serves 4

8   small lamb chops
    olive oil
    dry white wine
    whole peppercorns
    thyme to taste
2   bay leaves
5   whole allspice
8   ½-inch slices goat cheese
2   cloves garlic, minced

Marinate chops overnight in equal amounts of oil and wine, (enough to cover chops), peppercorns, thyme, bay leaves, and allspice. Marinate cheese slices overnight in olive oil, thyme, and garlic.

Broil chops, basting with marinade. Five minutes before done, place 1 slice cheese on each chop. Cheese should almost melt and lightly brown. Serve immediately.

See photo page 230.

ROAST RACK OF LAMB

Serves 3

1½-1¾   pound rack of lamb
1   tablespoon Dijon mustard
2-3   teaspoons finely chopped mint or 1 teaspoon dried mint
        freshly ground pepper to taste
        salt to taste
⅛-¼   teaspoon garlic powder
1   tablespoon bread crumbs

Coat meat portion of rack with mustard. Sprinkle with mint, pepper, salt, and garlic powder. Pat bread crumbs into mustard.

Bake lamb in preheated 500° oven 10 minutes. Reduce heat to 300° and bake 25 to 35 minutes. Lamb should be pink. Serve with mint sauce. (See page 426).

LEG OF LAMB NEW ZEALAND STYLE

Serves 8

6-7 pound leg of lamb
1-2 cloves garlic, slivered
½ teaspoon salt
½ teaspoon pepper
½ teaspoon ground ginger
16 small white potatoes
2-3 yams, in serving size pieces
1 butternut squash, in serving size pieces
3-4 parsnips, in 1-inch slices
⅓ cup white wine

Gravy:
¼ cup lamb drippings
¼ cup flour
2 cups chicken stock
3-4 anchovies, drained
2 tablespoons chopped parsley
1 teaspoon grated lemon rind

Make series of small cuts across top of roast. Insert slivers of garlic. Rub meat with salt, pepper, and ginger. Bake meat in preheated 350° oven 20 to 23 minutes per pound. Drain small amount of drippings from roast into baking dish large enough to accommodate vegetables. Roast vegetables in preheated 350° oven 1 hour.

Wrap meat in foil and return to 200° oven for 20 minutes, basting occasionally with white wine.

To make gravy drain fat from roasting pan. Stir in flour. Brown. Add chicken stock, anchovies, parsley, and rind. Stir over low heat until thickened. Place lamb on serving platter surrounded by vegetables. Pass gravy.

MINTED ROAST LEG OF LAMB

Serves 8 to 10

5-6   **pound leg of lamb, well trimmed of fat, at room temperature**
2   **tablespoons dried mint, divided**
1   **teaspoon dried rosemary**
2   **cloves garlic, slivered**
2   **tablespoons olive oil**
4   **tablespoons melted butter**
½   **cup dry vermouth**
¼   **cup mint jelly**
    cornstarch combined with water, optional
    watercress sprigs
    salt to taste
    pepper to taste

Currant mint sauce: (optional)
¾   **cup chili sauce**
1   **cup red currant jelly**
½   **cup butter**
3   **tablespoons bottled mint sauce**

Rub lamb completely with 1 tablespoon mint and rosemary. Make small slits in meat and insert garlic slivers. Rub meat with oil. Let stand at room temperature 2 to 3 hours. Bake on rack in open roasting pan in preheated 450° oven 15 minutes. Reduce heat to 350°. Bake 1½ to 1¾ hours (check with meat thermometer, 140° for medium). During roasting, brush occasionally with combination of melted butter and remaining 1 tablespoon mint.

Transfer meat to platter. Skim fat from drippings and add vermouth and jelly to pan juices. If desired, thicken liquid with cornstarch and water mixture, cooking until desired consistency.

For additional sauce increase vermouth and jelly and combine with cornstarch and water mixture to desired consistency. Add salt and pepper to taste.

Slice meat thinly. Garnish with watercress sprigs. Pass sauce.

May substitute water for some of the vermouth. For added color, use a drop of commercial gravy seasoning sauce.

For alternate or additional sauce, combine all currant mint sauce ingredients. Heat. Serve warm with lamb.

LEBANESE LEG OF LAMB

Serves 6 to 8

7   pound leg of lamb
3   cloves garlic, 1 slivered, 2 minced
¼   pound plus 2 tablespoons butter, divided
1   onion, chopped
½   cup uncooked rice
1   cup beef broth, divided
¼   cup pine nuts
3   tablespoons raisins
⅛   teaspoon ground allspice
⅛   teaspoon cinnamon
⅛   teaspoon nutmeg
     salt to taste
     pepper to taste

Have butcher bone lamb and scoop or cut out ½ pound from 1 end. Have removed meat ground twice. Insert garlic slivers deep into lamb cavity.

In large saucepan melt 4 tablespoons butter. Add onion and brown. Stir in rice and minced garlic. Add ground lamb, and cook, stirring, until meat is no longer red. Add ½ cup broth and remaining ingredients. Simmer until liquid is absorbed.

Stuff lamb with mixture and sew up cavity. Place lamb in roasting pan greased with remaining butter. Bake in preheated 425° oven 30 minutes. Reduce heat to 375° and bake 1¼ hours, basting frequently with remaining ½ cup broth.

LAMB SHANKS

Serves 4 to 6

4-6   lamb shanks
2   tablespoons butter or margarine
½   cup chicken or beef broth
3   tablespoons wine vinegar
1   medium onion, chopped
1   teaspoon salt
¼   teaspoon pepper

In large skillet brown shanks in butter or margarine. Transfer meat to baking dish and arrange in single layer.

Combine broth, vinegar, and onion. Mix well and pour over shanks. Season with salt and pepper. Cover pan. Bake in preheated 350° oven 2 to 2½ hours or until meat is tender.

LAMB SHISH KEBAB

Serves 6 to 8

Marinade:
4 tablespoons vinegar
2 tablespoons red wine, optional
2 teaspoons salt
½ teaspoon dried marjoram or 2 teaspoons fresh marjoram
¼ teaspoon dried basil or 1 teaspoon fresh basil
¼ teaspoon freshly ground black pepper
4 slivers garlic
3 thin slices lemon
½ cup vegetable oil

Shish kebab:
3 pounds lamb, cut into 2-inch cubes
20 small white stewing onions
3 green peppers, cut into 2-inch squares
1 box cherry tomatoes
20 large mushrooms

Combine all marinade ingredients. Mix well. Marinate meat, covered, 12 hours in refrigerator, either in bowl or plastic bag. Turn occasionally.

In boiling water cook onions 5 minutes. Rinse in cold water. Drain and set aside. One hour before cooking, skewer meat and vegetables alternately. (Tomatoes may be placed on separate skewer as they broil quickly.) Brush with marinade. Grill kebabs on barbecue about 15 minutes, turning once and brushing frequently with marinade.

May also be broiled about 10 minutes on each side.

LAMB RAGOUT WITH DILL AND CREAM

Serves 4

1½ pound leg of lamb, boned, in ¾-inch cubes
2 tablespoons olive oil
½ cup dry white wine
½ cup beef stock
½ cup whipping cream
   salt to taste
   pepper to taste
   juice of 1 lemon
4 tablespoons dill, divided
1 tablespoon cornstarch

continued

In heavy skillet brown meat in oil. Add wine, stock, and cream. Simmer 10 minutes. Add salt and pepper. Simmer 25 minutes. Stir in lemon juice and 2 tablespoons dill. Mix cornstarch with small amount of water and blend into ragout. Simmer 5 minutes. Serve sprinkled with remaining dill.

Sherry and chicken broth may be substituted for wine and beef stock. Parsley may be substituted for dill.

LAMB AND COUSCOUS

Serves 4

2	pound boned leg of lamb, in small cubes
2	tablespoons olive oil
3	tablespoons butter, divided
2	medium onions, chopped
4	carrots, sliced
3	celery ribs, sliced
3	large or 4 medium tomatoes, peeled, in chunks
½	pound green beans, in 2-inch lengths
1	small zucchini, cubed
8½	ounces canned garbanzo beans or chick peas, drained
	salt to taste
	pepper to taste
⅛	teaspoon each: celery salt, ground cloves, ground ginger, ground saffron, turmeric, mace, cumin, ground allspice, curry
5-6	drops Tabasco
1	beef bouillon cube
2	tablespoons hot water
2	cups salted water
2	cups couscous

In large kettle brown meat in oil and 1 tablespoon butter. Add onions and brown. Add carrots, celery, tomatoes, green beans, zucchini, and garbanzo beans. Blend in salt, pepper, celery salt, cloves, ginger, saffron, turmeric, mace, cumin, allspice, curry, and Tabasco. Dissolve bouillon cube in 2 tablespoons hot water. Add to meat and vegetables. Over low heat cook covered 40 minutes or until meat is cooked and vegetables are tender-crisp.

In large bowl pour 2 cups boiling salted water over couscous. Let stand 5 minutes. Fluff up with fork. Brown remaining 2 tablespoons butter and pour over couscous. Stir and fluff again. Add salt to taste.

To serve, pass lamb and couscous separately.

MOUSSAKA

Serves 12

Meat sauce:
1 cup finely chopped onion
1 clove garlic, minced
1½ pounds ground lamb or beef
2 tablespoons butter
1 teaspoon dried basil
½ teaspoon dried oregano
½ teaspoon cinnamon
1 teaspoon salt
16 ounces tomato sauce

Eggplant layers:
2 1¼-pound eggplants
salt to taste
½ cup melted butter or margarine

Cream sauce:
2 tablespoons butter
2 tablespoons flour
½ teaspoon salt
dash pepper
2 cups milk
2 eggs

½ cup grated Parmesan cheese
½ cup grated Cheddar cheese
2 tablespoons dry bread crumbs

In 3½-quart Dutch oven sauté onion, garlic, and meat in 2 tablespoons butter, stirring until brown. Add basil, oregano, cinnamon, salt, and tomato sauce. Bring to boil, stirring constantly. Simmer uncovered 30 minutes.

Halve unpeeled eggplants lengthwise. Slice halves crosswise ½-inch thick. Sprinkle lightly with salt. Brush lightly with melted butter. In broiler pan broil eggplant 4 inches from heat, 4 minutes per side, or until golden.

In saucepan melt 2 tablespoons butter. Stir in flour, salt, and pepper. Add milk and cook until thickened, stirring constantly. Remove from heat. In small bowl beat eggs well. Still beating, slowly add hot mixture. Mix well.

In bottom of shallow 9- by 13-inch baking dish layer half of eggplant. Sprinkle with 2 tablespoons each of grated cheeses. Stir bread crumbs into meat sauce and spoon evenly over eggplant. Layer remaining eggplant. Pour cream sauce over all, followed by remaining cheeses. Bake in preheated 350° oven 40 minutes or until top is set and golden brown. If desired, brown under broiler 1 minute. Cool slightly before serving. Cut into 12 squares.

May be baked 1 day ahead, refrigerated, and reheated before serving.

CASSOULET

1	pound dried Great Northern beans
3	large onions, sliced
14	thick bacon slices, in 1-inch pieces
28	ounces canned tomatoes, chopped, juice reserved
	freshly ground pepper to taste
4	cloves garlic, minced
½	teaspoon dried thyme
5	parsley sprigs, chopped
1	large bay leaf
3	cups chicken stock
1	pound kielbasa (Polish sausage), in ½-inch slices
1	pound lamb, cubed
1	pound pork, cubed
	olive oil
1	duck, partially cooked, in serving pieces, optional

Soak beans overnight in water to cover. Sauté onions and bacon until bacon begins to brown. Drain fat. Add tomatoes, including juice. Stir in pepper, garlic, thyme, parsley, bay leaf, and stock. Simmer 15 minutes.

Brown kielbasa, lamb, and pork in olive oil. Cook beans until almost done. In large casserole layer enough beans to cover bottom. Top with meats. Add remaining beans, then onion mixture. Add duck if using. Stir gently to combine. Bring to boil over low heat. Remove from heat.

Cover and bake in preheated 325° oven 1 to 1½ hours. If using on same day, skim fat from top 2 or 3 times during baking. If preparing a day ahead, cool, refrigerate, and remove fat from top before reheating.

Kielbasa is essential to this recipe; other meats may be adjusted to meet personal preference, keeping total weight constant. Leftover pork or lamb may be used.

Cassoulet may be prepared 2 days in advance. May be frozen.

PORK CHOPS AND APPLES

Serves 4

4 center cut loin pork chops, 1½-inches thick, well trimmed
    freshly ground pepper to taste
1 tablespoon safflower oil
2 Golden Delicious apples, peeled, cored, quartered
¼ cup chopped onion
1 tablespoon brown sugar
2 tablespoons red wine vinegar
1 tomato, peeled, cubed
½ cup chicken broth

Sprinkle both sides of chops with pepper. In large skillet heat oil. Cook chops 2 to 3 minutes or until browned on each side. Reduce heat. Continue cooking chops 15 minutes, turning occasionally. Arrange apples around meat. Cover and cook 5 minutes. Remove chops and apples to serving platter. Drain fat.

Cook onion in skillet until slightly limp. Stir in sugar and vinegar. Add tomato and broth. Cook mixture 2 minutes, stirring constantly. Pour hot sauce over chops and apples. Serve immediately.

ROAST LOIN OF PORK WITH APPLE HORSERADISH SAUCE

Serves 8

5 pound loin of pork
1 tablespoon Dijon mustard
½ teaspoon salt
¼ teaspoon pepper
¼ teaspoon thyme
½ cup plus 2 tablespoons tawny port, divided
¼ cup plus 1 tablespoon soy sauce, divided
3 cloves garlic, minced
2 teaspoons ground ginger
10 ounces currant jelly
2 tablespoons lemon juice

Apple horseradish sauce:
4 tart apples, peeled, cored, quartered
½ cup water
2 tablespoons lemon juice
1 3-inch vanilla bean, split
1 cinnamon stick
½ cup sugar
3 tablespoons horseradish

Rub meat with mustard, salt, pepper, and thyme. Place in plastic bag. Combine ½ cup port, ¼ cup soy sauce, garlic, and ginger. Pour in bag and seal. Refrigerate overnight, turning bag occasionally.

Reserving marinade, transfer meat to roasting pan. Cover and bake in preheated 325° oven 1 hour. Uncover and bake additional 1½ to 2 hours, basting frequently with marinade. Combine jelly, remaining 2 tablespoons port, and remaining 1 tablespoon soy sauce. Boil 5 minutes, stirring constantly. Pour jelly mixture over roasted meat. Let stand at room temperature 1 hour, basting with jelly several times.

Combine all sauce ingredients except horseradish. Cook until apples are tender, about 20 minutes. Remove vanilla bean and cinnamon stick. Purée in food processor or blender. Add horseradish. Chill.

Remove pork to serving platter. Strain jelly. Pour over meat to serve. Pass apple horseradish sauce.

BRAISED PORK WITH BOURBON

Serves 8

4	pound pork loin, center cut, tied, trimmed
½-¾	cup Dijon mustard
¾-1	cup brown sugar
2	tablespoons peanut oil
⅔	cup plus 1 tablespoon bourbon, divided
2	cups beef stock
	salt to taste
	freshly ground pepper to taste
	bouquet garni of thyme, parsley, bay leaves, marjoram
1	teaspoon arrowroot

Brush pork liberally with mustard. Roll pork in brown sugar. In heavy casserole or Dutch oven heat oil. Brown meat on all sides, taking care that sugar does not burn. Sugar will carmelize. Coat meat with residue from casserole. Pour ⅓ cup bourbon over meat and flame it, shaking pan vigorously so alcohol will burn evenly when flame subsides. Add stock. Place sheet of parchment over meat and cover casserole. Bake in preheated 375° oven 45 minutes. Turn meat. Season with salt and pepper; add bouquet garni. Reduce heat to 350°. Bake 45 to 50 minutes. Remove pork from casserole.

Strain liquid and skim carefully to remove all fat. Return liquid to casserole. Over medium heat bring to boil. Add ⅓ cup bourbon and stir to deglaze. Cook until stock is reduced to ¾ cup. Skim top. Sauce should be syrupy. Dissolve arrowroot in remaining 1 tablespoon bourbon. Add to sauce; let bubble gently to thicken. Remove strings from roast and serve with sauce.

ROAST PORK CALYPSO

Serves 8 to 10

5-6	pound loin of pork
1	teaspoon salt
½	teaspoon pepper
1	teaspoon ground ginger
½	teaspoon ground cloves
2	cloves garlic, minced
2	bay leaves, crumbled
1	cup dark rum, divided
2½	cups chicken stock, divided
½	cup brown sugar
⅓	cup lime juice
2	teaspoons arrowroot

Have butcher saw through shinbone of pork loin. Score fatty side in diamond pattern. Combine salt, pepper, spices, and garlic. Rub into scored surface thoroughly. Sprinkle bay leaves on top. Place roast on rack in pan with ½ cup rum and ½ cup stock.

Bake in preheated 325° oven 30 minutes to the pound. Halfway through cooking, baste roast with sauce made of brown sugar, lime juice, and remaining ½ cup rum. Baste several times, adding more stock if necessary.

When done, remove roast to warm place. Remove bay leaves. To make gravy, skim excess fat. Increase liquid to 2 cups by adding remaining basting liquid and stock. Bring to boil. Mix arrowroot with small amount of water and stir into pan. Continue stirring until gravy has thickened. Adjust seasoning. Serve with roast.

PORK TENDERLOIN

Serves 4

3	tablespoons butter
2	¾- to 1-pound whole pork tenderloins, fat removed
	salt to taste
	pepper to taste
½	cup apple jelly
½	cup Calvados
¼	cup Dijon mustard
1	tablespoon cornstarch, optional
3	tablespoons cream or water, optional

continued

In large skillet melt butter. Sauté pork until lightly browned on all sides, about 5 to 6 minutes. Place in 6-inch by 10-inch baking pan; season with salt and pepper.

In small saucepan combine jelly, Calvados, and mustard. Cook over medium heat until smooth, stirring constantly. Pour over pork. Bake in preheated 325° oven 60 to 70 minutes, basting every 15 minutes. Cut into 1½-inch slices. Arrange on warm serving platter, and spoon sauce over meat or serve separately.

For thicker sauce, combine cornstarch with cream or water. Stir until smooth. Remove meat from baking dish. Stir cornstarch mixture into sauce and simmer until thickened.

Variation:
Substitute currant jelly and vermouth for apple jelly and Calvados. Apple juice may be substituted for Calvados.

PORK TENDERLOIN WITH MUSTARD SAUCE

Serves 5 to 6

¼ **cup soy sauce**
¼ **cup bourbon**
2 **tablespoons brown sugar**
3 **1-pound pork tenderloins**

Sauce:
⅓ **cup sour cream**
⅓ **cup mayonnaise**
1 **tablespoon finely chopped scallions**
1 **tablespoon dry mustard**
 salt to taste
1½ **tablespoons vinegar**

Combine soy sauce, bourbon, and sugar. Mix well. Marinate pork in mixture 2 to 3 hours, turning occasionally. Remove meat from marinade. Bake in preheated 325° oven 1 hour, basting occasionally.

Combine all sauce ingredients. Mix well. Carve pork into thin diagonal slices and serve with sauce.

See photo page 231.

PORK POCKETS

Serves 4 to 6

This is an excellent entrée for family, teenagers, or casual entertaining.

- ½ cup water
- ¼ cup vinegar
- 2 tablespoons sugar
- 1 tablespoon prepared or Dijon mustard
- 1½ teaspoons salt
- ½ teaspoon pepper
- dash cayenne pepper
- 1 thick slice lemon
- 1 onion, sliced
- ⅛ pound butter or margarine
- 2 cups thinly sliced cooked pork
- ½ cup ketchup
- 2 tablespoons Worcestershire sauce
- 3 whole large pita breads

In large saucepan or skillet combine water, vinegar, sugar, mustard, spices, lemon, onion, and butter. Bring to boil. Add sliced pork. Reduce heat and simmer uncovered 20 minutes. Add ketchup and Worcestershire sauce. Bring to boil. Warm pita breads in preheated 350° oven. Split each, creating "pocket," and fill with pork and sauce. Serve immediately.

A good use for leftover pork roast.

BARBECUED BACK RIBS

Serves 4 to 6

- 4 pounds baby back ribs, in 3- to 4-rib serving pieces
- salt
- pepper
- paprika

Sauce:
- ¾ cup ketchup
- ¼ cup brown sugar or honey
- 2 tablespoons cider vinegar
- 1 teaspoon salt
- 1 teaspoon chili powder

continued

Season ribs with salt, pepper, and paprika. Place ribs bone side down in shallow roasting pan. Cover tightly with foil. Bake in preheated 350° oven 1 hour. May be done early in day or day ahead and refrigerated.

Combine sauce ingredients. Mix well. Place cooked ribs bone side down on grill over medium heat. Cook 20 minutes or until heated through. Brush occasionally with sauce. Do not turn ribs.

May be broiled in oven. Sauce is also good for barbecued chicken.

LOUISIANA HAM AND RED BEANS

Serves 16

2 pounds dried kidney beans
2-3 cloves garlic, minced
2 cups chopped onion
½ cup thinly sliced scallion tops
½ cup chopped green pepper, optional
1⅓ tablespoons finely minced parsley
1 pound baked ham, in 1-inch cubes
1 pound salt pork in large chunks, boiled 5 minutes, rinsed
    salt to taste
½ teaspoon freshly ground black pepper
⅛ teaspoon cayenne pepper
⅛ teaspoon crushed red pepper
2 bay leaves, quartered
½ teaspoon dried thyme
⅛ teaspoon dried basil

Soak beans overnight in water to cover. Drain. In 8- to 10-quart kettle combine beans with remaining ingredients. Add just enough cold water to cover. Bring to boil. Lower heat and cover. Simmer gently 2½ to 3 hours or until beans are tender and thick gravy has formed. Stir frequently to prevent scorching. If mixture becomes too dry during cooking, add 1 cup water. When beans are cooked remove from heat. Serve over boiled rice.

May be prepared 1 day in advance and reheated.

ROAST VENISON

4	strips salt pork
3-4	pound loin of venison
	salt to taste
	pepper to taste
2	whole cloves
2	small onions
½	cup unsalted butter, melted
1	teaspoon rosemary
1	cup orange juice
½	cup currant jelly
1	tablespoon grated lemon peel
	parsley
1	tablespoon flour

Place strips of salt pork on venison. Sprinkle generously with salt and pepper. Place in roasting pan. Insert 1 clove in each onion. Add onions, butter, rosemary, and orange juice to pan. Cover and bake in preheated 300° oven, basting with pan liquid, 3 to 4 hours.

Ten minutes before removing roast from oven, melt jelly and stir in lemon peel. Brush roast with mixture. Bake 10 minutes longer. Transfer roast to serving platter. Garnish with parsley.

Prepare gravy by thickening pan juices with flour. Pass gravy with roast.

POULTRY

Ravinia Notes

In July of 1961 famed German composer-conductor Paul Hindemith spent a week at the Festival conducting his own compositions. At first sight of Ravinia Mrs. Hindemith exclaimed, "Everywhere I look I see Renoirs."

Two years later, in 1963, Seiji Ozawa made an impromptu début, filling in for the ailing scheduled conductor. Within several months "Seiji San" was appointed Musical Director, a post that he held for five years. The Seiji Years were exciting ones, due in large measure to Ozawa's burgeoning talent and personal magnetism. One long-time Ravinia watcher has said that it was not uncommon to see Ozawa jump into his white Mustang convertible after the concert, en route to a downtown dawn patrol jazz session. His graceful, slight figure was frequently observed on the golf courses of the North Shore. He is remembered with enduring affection by orchestra and audiences alike, and is a warmly received guest conductor today.

CHICKEN FLORENTINE WITH ROQUEFORT CRÈME

Serves 6

2   **bags spinach, stems removed**
6   **chicken breasts, split, boned**
4   **tablespoons butter**
2   **cups crème fraîche (page 423)**
¼   **pound Roquefort, crumbled**
1-1½   **tablespoons cornstarch, optional**

Cook spinach in simmering water until softened, about 2 to 3 minutes. Drain. Sauté chicken breasts in butter, 7 minutes on each side. Skin should be well browned.

In saucepan combine crème fraîche and Roquefort. Heat very slowly until Roquefort is melted, stirring frequently. If thicker sauce is desired combine 3 tablespoons sauce with cornstarch. Add to crème fraîche mixture and cook very slowly until thickened.

To serve, spoon sauce on individual warmed serving plates. Cover with bed of spinach. Place chicken breast over spinach, and add a little sauce over chicken.

LEMON-LIME CHICKEN

Serves 6

½   **cup chopped parsley**
½   **cup chopped dill**
½   **cup chopped mint**
2   **cloves garlic, minced**
6   **chicken breasts, boned, skinned**
  salt to taste
  freshly ground pepper to taste
3   **lemons, sliced**
3   **limes, sliced**
4   **tablespoons margarine**
  fresh mint leaves

Combine parsley, dill, mint, and garlic. Mix well. Arrange chicken in single layer in baking dish. Season with salt and pepper. Sprinkle with parsley mixture. Arrange lemon and lime slices over top. Dot with margarine. Cover with heavy duty foil. Bake in preheated 350°oven 35 minutes.

Garnish with fresh mint leaves and serve immediately.

See photo page 230.

CHICKEN WITH NECTARINES

Serves 6 to 8

6   chicken breasts, split, boned
1   teaspoon seasoned salt or to taste
4   tablespoons butter
1   small onion, chopped
11 ounces peach nectar
¾   teaspoon dry mustard
1   teaspoon ground ginger
½   teaspoon curry powder
½   teaspoon Worcestershire sauce
½   cup fresh orange juice
3   tablespoons honey
15 ounces strained peaches (baby food)
3   tablespoons lemon juice
3   tablespoons applesauce
1   clove garlic, minced
9   small nectarines, quartered, pitted

Season chicken with seasoned salt. In large skillet sauté chicken lightly in butter. Remove chicken to large shallow baking pan. In same skillet sauté onion until soft. Add remaining ingredients except nectarines. Mix well. Scatter nectarine pieces over chicken. Pour sauce over all. Bake in preheated 350° oven 55 minutes, basting frequently.

Serve with brown or wild rice.

CHICKEN DUBONNET

Serves 4

⅓   cup flour
1   tablespoon salt
4   chicken breasts, split, boned, skinned
¼   pound plus 2 tablespoons butter, divided
½   cup white Dubonnet or dry sherry
2   tablespoons soy sauce
¼   teaspoon confectioners sugar
    chopped parsley

Combine flour and salt. Mix well. Dredge chicken in mixture, coating well. In skillet brown chicken in ¼ pound butter. Remove chicken and discard fat.

Melt 2 tablespoons butter in skillet. Add remaining ingredients except parsley. Bring to boil, stirring to mix. Place chicken in baking dish. Pour sauce over chicken. Bake covered in preheated 350° oven 50 to 60 minutes or until tender, basting occasionally. Arrange chicken on serving platter. Sprinkle with parsley.

CHICKEN AND ORANGES

Serves 6   *Submitted by Dale Clevenger, principal horn of the Chicago Symphony Orchestra.*

1	clove garlic, crushed
3	tablespoons butter, softened
6	chicken breasts
1½	cups orange juice
½	cup chutney
½	cup raisins
1	tablespoon curry powder
½	teaspoon cinnamon
	pinch nutmeg
11	ounces canned mandarin oranges with juice
	salt to taste
	pepper to taste
1	banana, sliced

Combine garlic and butter. Rub chicken breasts with mixture. Place in baking dish skin side up. Bake in preheated 475° oven 15 minutes.

While chicken is baking combine orange juice, chutney, raisins, curry, cinnamon, nutmeg, and juice from mandarin oranges. Pour over baked chicken. Season with salt and pepper. Reduce heat to 325°. Bake chicken 1 hour, basting frequently. Before serving add oranges and bananas. Return to oven until fruit is heated thoroughly. Serve immediately.

CHICKEN PICCATA

Serves 4

2	chicken breasts, split, boned, skinned
⅓	cup flour
	seasoned salt to taste
¼	cup corn oil
½	cup chopped onion
1	lemon, thinly sliced
1	cup chicken broth
2	tablespoons chopped parsley

Pound chicken to ¼-inch thickness. Dredge in flour and season to taste. In large skillet heat oil. Sauté chicken 5 minutes on each side or until golden brown. Remove. Add onion. Sauté 1 minute. Scrape bottom of pan. Return chicken to pan. Top with lemon slices and add broth. Cover and simmer 5 minutes or until chicken is tender. Serve sprinkled with parsley.

ANCIENT CHINESE CHICKEN

Serves 12

8   **whole chicken legs**
4   **chicken breasts, split**
½   **cup vegetable oil**
2   **teaspoons Herbes de Provence**
2   **teaspoons coarse salt**
½   **teaspoon freshly ground pepper**
2   **tablespoons lemon juice**

Sauce:

1⅓   **cups ketchup**
⅔   **cup red currant jelly**
4   **tablespoons Worcestershire sauce**
2   **tablespoons Chinese rice vinegar**
1   **tablespoon light soy sauce**
½   **teaspoon Tabasco**
1   **teaspoon minced crystallized ginger**
⅛   **teaspoon Chinese Five Star Powder**
1   **clove garlic, minced**
¼   **cup plum jam, sieved**

Rub chicken with oil. Sprinkle Herbes de Provence, salt, pepper, and lemon juice evenly over chicken. Arrange chicken in broiler pan and cover. Bake in preheated 350° oven 1 hour. Remove from oven and uncover. Drain half of juices.

While chicken is baking combine all sauce ingredients in heavy saucepan. Heat to slow simmer and cook 10 minutes, stirring occasionally. Transfer chicken to moderately hot barbecue. Baste frequently with sauce, turning chicken often. Grill until brown and tender.

Alternate method: Leave chicken in broiler pan. Spoon sauce generously over chicken. Increase oven temperature to 375°. Bake chicken uncovered 30 to 40 minutes. Serve with remaining sauce.

Serves 4 to 6

3 chicken breasts, boned, skinned, cubed
   salt to taste
1 tablespoon sugar or to taste
½ cup white wine
1 tablespoon soy sauce
1 teaspoon cornstarch
1-2 egg whites, lightly beaten
1 clove garlic, minced
1 tablespoon ground ginger
   vegetable oil
2 tablespoons water
8 ounces canned bamboo shoots, drained
2 tablespoons Chinese wine or Chablis
8 ounces walnuts, in large pieces
3 scallions, chopped
   cooked rice, optional

Sauce:
1 teaspoon cornstarch
1 teaspoon light soy sauce
1½ cups water
1 tablespoon sesame oil
1 teaspoon sugar

Sprinkle salt, sugar, wine, and soy sauce over chicken. Mix well. Stir in cornstarch and egg whites.

In large skillet or wok brown chicken mixture with garlic and ginger in small amount of oil. Add 2 tablespoons water. Simmer until chicken is tender. Stir in bamboo shoots and wine.

Combine all sauce ingredients. Mix well and add to chicken. Stir over low heat until thickened. In separate pan brown walnuts in small amount of oil. Add to chicken. Transfer to serving dish and top with scallions. Serve immediately with rice if desired.

CHICKEN WITH ARTICHOKES

Serves 4

4   chicken breasts, split, boned, cut into bite-size pieces if desired
     butter
17   ounces canned artichoke hearts, drained
2   cups sliced mushrooms
½   cup chopped shallots
1   clove garlic, minced
     salt to taste
     pepper to taste
1   cup dry white wine
1   tablespoon flour

In skillet brown chicken in butter. Remove chicken from pan using slotted spoon. Sauté artichokes, adding butter as needed. Remove artichokes from pan. Sauté combined mushrooms, shallots, and garlic. Return chicken and artichokes to pan. Season with salt and pepper. Add wine. Simmer until chicken is tender. With slotted spoon remove chicken and vegetables from pan to warm serving platter. Thicken juices with flour and pour over chicken. Serve immediately.

STUFFED CHICKEN BREASTS SALTIMBOCCA

Serves 6 to 8

4   chicken breasts, split, boned, and pounded
8   slices prosciutto or baked ham
4   slices mozzarella
2   tomatoes, chopped, drained
1   teaspoon sage
½   cup dried bread crumbs
3   tablespoons Parmesan
3   tablespoons chopped parsley
4   tablespoons butter, melted
     parsley sprigs

Place chicken breasts skin side down. Top each with slice of ham followed by a half slice mozzarella. Sprinkle each with tomato and sage. Roll up each breast. Combine bread crumbs, cheese, and parsley. Dip each breast in butter. Dip in bread crumb mixture. Arrange seam side down in single layer in oven-proof baking dish. Bake in preheated 350° oven 40 to 45 minutes.

Garnish with parsley sprigs. Serve immediately.

CHICKEN FILLETS WITH PLUM SAUCE

Serves 8 to 12

8   chicken breasts, split, boned
    salt to taste
    pepper to taste
4   eggs, beaten
2   cups ground walnuts
⅔   cup dry bread crumbs
¼   pound butter
1   tablespoon vegetable oil

Plum sauce:
1½   cups canned plums with juice
6   ounces plum preserves
2   tablespoons butter
6   ounces chicken broth
¼   cup sherry
1½   teaspoons lemon juice
1-2 teaspoons cornstarch, optional
1   tablespoon cold water, optional

Season chicken with salt and pepper. Dip in eggs, then coat with combined nuts and bread crumbs. Sauté in combined butter and oil until tender. Set aside on heated platter.

In saucepan combine all sauce ingredients except cornstarch. Simmer 30 minutes, stirring occasionally. Combine cornstarch with cold water. Add to sauce and simmer until thickened. Spoon over chicken or pass separately.

May be prepared earlier in the day and reheated at 400°.

Serves 6

3   1-pound chicken breasts, split
½   cup dry sherry
3   chicken bouillon cubes
2½   cups hot water
6   tablespoons prepared mustard
¾   teaspoon garlic salt
¾   teaspoon fines herbes
6   4-by 6-inch slices Monterey Jack cheese
6   4-by 6-inch slices cooked ham
1   10-ounce package frozen patty shells or frozen
        puff pastry sheets, thawed
1   egg white, beaten
      poppy or sesame seed, optional

In large pan combine chicken, sherry, and bouillon dissolved in hot water. Bring to boil. Reduce heat and cover. Simmer 20 minutes or until tender. Cool in broth 30 minutes. Remove chicken from broth; skin and bone. Refrigerate until thoroughly cooled.

Combine mustard, garlic salt, and fines herbes. Mix well. Spread 1 tablespoon of mixture over each chicken piece, coating thoroughly. Wrap 1 slice cheese followed by 1 slice ham around each piece. On lightly floured board, roll each pastry shell into 8-inch circle. Place 1 chicken piece seam side down, in center of each pastry circle. Bring up sides of pastry to overlap in center. Moisten and pinch to seal.

Place bundles, seam side down, at least 2 inches apart on large ungreased baking sheet. Brush with egg white and sprinkle with poppy or sesame seeds if desired. Chill 30 minutes. Bake in preheated 425° oven 30 minutes or until brown and crisp. Cool 20 minutes on rack. May be served warm or cold.

CHICKEN STRUDEL

Serves 6 to 8   *A show-off entrée that may be prepared in advance*

2   whole chicken breasts, boned, cooked, skinned, finely chopped
½   cup finely chopped scallions
¼   cup chopped parsley
¼   teaspoon tarragon
4   eggs, beaten
    salt to taste
    pepper to taste
8   leaves filo pastry
    melted butter
    bread crumbs

Combine chicken, scallions, parsley, tarragon, eggs, salt, and pepper. Mix well. On large damp towel place 1 filo leaf. Brush with butter and sprinkle lightly with bread crumbs. Top with another filo leaf. Repeat procedure until a stack of 4 leaves is prepared.

Spread half the chicken mixture down center of filo in a strip, leaving 1 inch at each end. Fold in edges and, using the towel, roll up leaves. Place on buttered baking sheet, seam side down. Brush with melted butter. Repeat procedure with remaining ingredients to make second strudel. Bake in a preheated 375° oven until golden brown, about 20 minutes. Serve warm or at room temperature sliced into serving pieces.

May substitute the following filling:

Variation: Spinach-feta Strudel
20   ounces frozen chopped spinach, thawed, squeezed dry
1   cup scallions
½   pound feta cheese, crumbled
4   eggs, beaten
1   tablespoon dried dill weed
¼   cup chopped parsley
     salt to taste
     pepper to taste

Combine all ingredients. Mix well. Follow instructions for chicken filling.

SPINACH STUFFED CHICKEN BREASTS

Serves 6 to 8

10 ounces frozen chopped spinach, thawed, drained
4 ounces canned water chestnuts, drained, finely chopped
8 ounces cream cheese or low-calorie cream cheese
¾ cup sour cream or sour half and half
1⅝ ounces dry vegetable soup mix
4 boneless chicken breasts, split

Combine all ingredients except chicken. Mix well. Divide mixture into eighths. At neck end of each piece of chicken carefully lift skin. With long handled spoon fill space between skin and meat with one-eighth spinach mixture, taking care not to break membrane connecting skin to meat. Tuck ends of chicken under and place in oven-proof baking dish. Repeat process with remaining chicken. Bake covered in preheated 350° oven 30 minutes. Uncover and bake additional 30 minutes.

May be served hot or cold. Cold chicken breasts are attractive sliced and arranged on platter.

See photo page 227.

INDONESIAN GRILLED CHICKEN AND COCONUT RICE

Serves 4 to 6

Chicken:
2 red chilies, seeded
2 medium onions, chopped
3 tablespoons finely chopped ginger root
2 tablespoons fresh lemon juice
1½ teaspoons salt
2 tablespoons light soy sauce
2 tablespoons dark soy sauce
2 tablespoons sesame oil
2 tablespoons sugar
4-6 chicken breasts, split
½ cup canned coconut milk

Coconut Rice:
1½ cups long grain white rice
½ teaspoon salt
2 cups water
1 cup coconut milk

continued

In food processor or blender combine chilies, onions, ginger root, lemon juice, salt, and soy sauces. Process until smooth. Add oil and sugar. Blend well. Marinate chicken in mixture 2 hours at room temperature or overnight in refrigerator. Grill chicken 20-30 minutes, basting often with marinade.

In saucepan combine remaining marinade with coconut milk. Simmer until smooth and thick, stirring constantly. Serve sauce with chicken and rice.

Prepare rice according to package directions, substituting equal amount of coconut milk for one-third the required amount of water.

Wear rubber gloves to handle chilies.

BREAST OF CHICKEN TONNATO

Serves 6 to 8

4 **whole chicken breasts, boned, skinned**
salt to taste
pepper to taste
olive oil
1 **cup dry white wine**

Sauce:
7 **ounces canned tuna, drained**
5 **flat anchovy fillets, drained**
½ **cup olive oil**
3 **tablespoons lemon juice**
3 **tablespoons capers**
1-2 **cups mayonnaise**
ripe olives
capers
lemon slices
parsley

Season chicken with salt and pepper. Sauté in oil over low heat. Add wine and cook 10 minutes. Remove chicken from pan. Cool and cut into thin slices. Reserve pan juices.

In food processor or blender combine tuna, anchovies, oil, lemon juice, capers, and reserved pan juices as needed. Process until smooth and creamy. Remove to bowl and blend in mayonnaise.

Spread half of sauce over bottom of shallow dish. Layer chicken slices over sauce. Cover with remaining sauce. Cover and refrigerate. Serve at room temperature. Garnish with olives, capers, lemon slices, and parsley.

CHICKEN WITH GINGER (Kai Phat Khing)

Serves 4

An authentic Thai dish.

2   ounces dried sliced mushrooms
2   tablespoons corn or peanut oil
2   small onions, thinly sliced
4   cloves garlic, finely minced
2   large chicken breasts, boned, skinned, cut into bite-size pieces
1   tablespoon plus 1 teaspoon finely grated ginger root
      or 2 teaspoons ground ginger
2   tablespoons soy sauce
2   tablespoons fish sauce
2   tablespoons red wine vinegar
2   tablespoons sugar
1   cup chopped scallions with tops
½   teaspoon dried coriander

In small bowl combine mushrooms with hot water to cover. Let stand 20 minutes. Drain.

In large skillet heat oil. Add onion rings and garlic. Cook, stirring until onion rings start to brown. Add chicken and mushrooms. Sauté, stirring until opaque. Stir in ginger. In small bowl combine soy sauce, fish sauce, vinegar, and sugar. Mix well. Add to skillet. Cover and cook no more than 3 minutes. Remove from heat, stir in scallions and coriander. Serve immediately.

Dried mushrooms may be found in Oriental food sections of supermarkets.

INCREDIBLE CHICKEN

Serves 2 to 3

This unlikely combination of ingredients is delicious.

1   chicken, quartered
        garlic salt
¼-⅓   cup brown sugar

Arrange chicken skin side up in lightly oiled baking pan. Season fairly heavily with garlic salt. Sprinkle generously with brown sugar. Bake in preheated 375° oven 1 hour. Cover with foil after 30 to 45 minutes if chicken appears too dry. May be served hot or cold.

JUST GOOD CHICKEN

Serves 6 to 8

2   **broiler-fryers, in serving pieces**
     Dijon mustard
     salt to taste
     paprika
     fresh or dried thyme, basil, or rosemary

Brush chicken with mustard. Season with salt and paprika. Sprinkle with herb of choice. Arrange, skin side up, in shallow roasting pan. Bake in preheated 350° oven 1 hour, basting occasionally.

Variation:
When using boneless, skinless chicken breasts, drizzle with oil or melted butter after sprinkling with herbs. Bake 50 minutes, basting frequently.

STIR FRY CHICKEN WITH BROCCOLI AND CASHEWS

Serves 4 to 6

¼   **cup soy sauce**
1½   **tablespoons dry sherry**
¾   **teaspoon ground ginger**
1½   **pounds boneless chicken breast in 1-inch pieces**
1   **pound broccoli, peeled**
7   **tablespoons vegetable oil, divided**
½   **cup sliced scallions**
1   **large clove garlic, crushed**
1½   **cups cashews**

In small bowl combine soy sauce, sherry, ginger, and chicken. Let stand 10 minutes. Trim flowerets from broccoli and reserve. Cut tough ends from stalks and discard. Slice stalks diagonally into ¼-inch pieces. Steam flowerets and stalk slices 3 to 4 minutes until tender-crisp. Drain and rinse under cold water.

Heat 4 tablespoons oil in wok or large skillet. Add scallions, garlic, and nuts. Cook 3 minutes, stirring constantly. Transfer mixture to bowl. Heat remaining oil in wok. Add chicken mixture and broccoli. Stir fry 6 minutes or until chicken is opaque. Stir in nut mixture. Serve immediately.

CHICKEN VINAIGRETTE

Serves 6

4 chicken breasts, boned, quartered
1 teaspoon salt
1 teaspoon thyme
¼ teaspoon marjoram
5 tablespoons butter, divided
3 tablespoons vegetable oil
1 clove garlic, minced
3 scallions, chopped
⅔ cup dry white wine
⅔ cup red wine vinegar
1 cup chicken broth
2 tablespoons tomato paste
  salt to taste
  pepper to taste
4 tablespoons chives

Combine chicken in bowl with salt, thyme, and marjoram. Mix well.

In large skillet combine 2 tablespoons butter and oil. Heat and add garlic. Add chicken and brown both sides. Remove chicken. Add scallions to skillet. Stir in wine and deglaze. Add vinegar and chicken broth. Mix well. Boil 3 minutes. Blend in tomato paste. Return chicken to skillet. Simmer covered 30 minutes. With slotted spoon remove chicken to oven-proof serving platter. Keep warm in preheated 325° oven.

One tablespoon at a time, add 3 tablespoons firm butter to skillet, beating well with fork after each addition. Season with salt and pepper to taste.

Spoon sauce on warmed plates and arrange chicken over sauce. Sprinkle with chives.

BALSAMIC GRILLED CHICKEN

Serves 8 to 10

1 cup vegetable oil
½ cup balsamic vinegar
3 tablespoons sugar
3 tablespoons ketchup
1 tablespoon Worcestershire sauce
2 medium scallions, tops included, minced
1 teaspoon salt
½ teaspoon cracked pepper
1 teaspoon dry mustard
1 medium clove garlic, minced
  Tabasco to taste
5 pounds chicken, in serving size pieces

Combine all ingredients except chicken. Dip chicken in marinade to coat. Arrange chicken in two 9-inch square pans. Pour remaining marinade over chicken. Cover and refrigerate at least 6 hours, preferably overnight.

Bring chicken to room temperature. Bake in preheated 325° oven 30 to 40 minutes. Remove chicken from marinade. Grill on barbecue 4 to 5 minutes on each side or until tender and browned, basting with marinade.

Serve with Special Potato Salad, page 85 and Fire and Ice Tomatoes, page 90.

GLAZED CHICKEN

Serves 6

4 tablespoons butter
½ cup honey
¼ cup prepared mustard
1 teaspoon salt
1 teaspoon curry powder
2 tablespoons soy sauce
6 chicken breasts, split, boned

In shallow baking dish melt butter. Stir in remaining ingredients except chicken. Roll chicken in mixture, coating both sides. Arrange chicken in dish skin side up. Bake in preheated 375° oven 1 hour, basting occasionally.

Serve immediately accompanied by rice noodles.

BARBECUED APRICOT CHICKEN

Serves 4

Glaze:

5½ ounces canned apricot nectar
2 tablespoons brown sugar
1 tablespoon grated orange peel
1 tablespoon ketchup
2 teaspoons cornstarch
1 teaspoon prepared horseradish
½ teaspoon salt

3 pound broiler-fryer, quartered
   salt, optional
16 ounces canned peeled whole apricots, drained
   leaves

In small saucepan combine apricot nectar, sugar, orange peel, ketchup, cornstarch, horseradish, and salt. Mix well. Boil 1 minute. Reduce heat and simmer 5 minutes.

To barbecue:

Rub chicken lightly with salt. Grill over medium heat until golden on both sides. To avoid charring stand pieces upright, leaning 1 against the other. Rearrange pieces occasionally and cook until tender, about 25 minutes. During last 5 to 10 minutes brush frequently with glaze. Arrange chicken on warm platter. Garnish with heated apricots and leaves.

To broil:

Place lightly salted chicken skin side down on broiling pan brushed with oil. In preheated broiler, broil 7 to 9 inches from heat 20 minutes or until golden. Brush generously with glaze. Broil 2 to 3 minutes. Turn chicken and broil 10 minutes. Brush with glaze and broil 10 minutes or until fork tender. Garnish with heated apricots and leaves.

SESAME CHICKEN

Serves 4

3-4	pound chicken, quartered
1	onion, peeled, quartered
¼	cup vegetable oil
¼	cup soy sauce
2	cloves garlic, peeled
3	tablespoons sesame seed
2	tablespoons brown sugar
1	teaspoon chili powder
¼	teaspoon ground ginger
	chopped green onion or chives

Rinse chicken in cold water. Pat dry. Arrange in 8- by 12-inch nonmetal baking dish. Combine remaining ingredients except green onion in food processor or blender. Blend until smooth. Pour over chicken. Cover and refrigerate at least 8 hours, turning chicken several times. Remove from refrigerator 30 minutes before cooking.

Bake chicken in marinade in preheated 350° oven 1 hour, turning and basting with marinade every 20 minutes. Transfer chicken to serving platter. Garnish with chopped green onion or chives. Skim fat from pan marinade.

Serve marinade separately as sauce.

JAMAICAN CHICKEN

Serves 2 to 4

This chicken derives its unique flavor from the use of a pungent West Indian sauce.

1	chicken broiler, quartered
1	lemon, cut into 8 pieces
½	cup teriyaki sauce
5	ounces Pickapeppa Sauce
	watercress sprigs

Trim excess fat from chicken. Line broiler pan with heavy foil. Place chicken on foil. Squeeze juice from lemon pieces over it. Arrange lemon pieces, rind side down, around chicken. Pour teriyaki sauce over all, followed by Pickapeppa Sauce. Bake in preheated 400° oven 1 hour or until chicken is crisp and brown, basting after 30 minutes. If chicken is not brown, broil 1 to 2 minutes.

To serve place 2 carmelized lemon pieces, rind side up, on each chicken quarter. Garnish with sprigs of watercress.

PLUM CHICKEN

Serves 6 to 8

An irresistible flavor combination.

2   chickens, quartered
1   teaspoon seasoned salt
1   medium onion, chopped
2   tablespoons butter
4   tablespoons lemon juice
12 ounces plum preserves
4   teaspoons soy sauce
1   teaspoon dry mustard
1   teaspoon ground ginger
    dash Worcestershire sauce
6   ounces tomato paste
1   clove garlic, minced
3   tablespoons brown sugar
6-7 fresh plums, pitted, quartered

Season chickens with seasoned salt. Brown in preheated broiler 10 minutes. In medium saucepan sauté onion in butter until soft. Add remaining ingredients except plums. Simmer 15 minutes.

Arrange chicken in single layer in baking dish. Cover with sauce. Scatter plum quarters around dish. Bake in preheated 350° oven 45 minutes or until tender, basting frequently.

YOGURT BAKED CHICKEN

Serves 2 to 3

1   chicken, quartered
    salt to taste
    pepper to taste
6   tablespoons butter or margarine, divided
2   tablespoons flour
1   tablespoon paprika
2   cups plain yogurt
¼   pound mushrooms, sliced
2   tablespoons fresh lemon juice
2   tablespoons chopped dill or 1 tablespoon dried dill
        weed or 2 tablespoons chopped parsley

continued

Season chicken with salt and pepper. Sauté chicken in 4 tablespoons butter until golden brown. Remove to buttered shallow baking dish. Pour half the pan juices over chicken. Sprinkle flour and paprika into remaining pan juices and cook 1 minute, stirring constantly. Stir in yogurt. Mix well. Spoon mixture over chicken.

Sauté mushrooms in remaining 2 tablespoons butter 1 minute. Stir in lemon juice. Spoon mushroom mixture over chicken. Sprinkle with dill or parsley. Cover and bake in preheated 325° oven 1 hour or until chicken is tender.

CHICKEN WITH TARRAGON SAUCE

Serves 2 to 4

1   **whole broiler-fryer chicken, quartered, or chicken pieces of choice**
     salt to taste
     pepper to taste
½   **teaspoon fines herbes**
     flour
2   **tablespoons butter**
2   **tablespoons vegetable oil**
1   **cup finely chopped leeks**
½   **cup finely chopped carrots**
1½   **cups dry white wine**
2   **teaspoons dehydrated chicken bouillon**
½   **teaspoon tarragon**
½   **cup crème fraîche (see page 423) or ¼ cup sour cream and ¼ cup whipping cream**

Season chicken with salt, pepper, and fines herbes. Dredge in flour to coat.

In heavy skillet sauté chicken in butter and oil until browned on both sides. Remove chicken from skillet. Sauté leeks and carrots in drippings until tender. Stir in wine and scrape any particles from bottom of pan. Add bouillon and tarragon. Return chicken to skillet. Cover and simmer 30 minutes. Turn chicken. Simmer uncovered 15 minutes. Remove chicken to heated platter.

Stir crème fraîche or sour cream and whipping cream into skillet. Simmer gently several minutes to reduce sauce. Season to taste. Pour over chicken and serve immediately.

MEXICAN CHICKEN WITH OLIVES

Serves 4

3½ pound fryer, cut into serving size pieces
    salt to taste
    freshly ground pepper
2   tablespoons olive oil
1   cup finely chopped onion
2   cloves garlic, finely minced
¼   cup dry sherry, divided
1   scant teaspoon chili powder
1   teaspoon cumin
1   teaspoon ground oregano
2   tablespoons flour
2½ cups chopped fresh tomatoes or 17 ounces canned
       Italian peeled plum tomatoes, drained
20 pitted green olives

Season chicken with salt and pepper. In heavy skillet heat olive oil. Add chicken pieces skin side down and cook until golden brown. Turn and brown other side. Remove with slotted spoon and transfer to Dutch oven.

Add onion to skillet and cook until wilted, stirring constantly. Add garlic and half of sherry. Cook until most of liquid has evaporated. Stir in chili powder, cumin, oregano, and flour. Blend well. Add tomatoes and salt and pepper to taste. Cook until thickened, stirring. Spoon sauce over chicken. Cover Dutch oven. Cook over moderate heat 30 minutes or until chicken is tender. Add olives and remaining sherry. Bring to boil. Remove from heat and serve with rice.

ORIENTAL ROAST CHICKEN

Serves 4

3   pound whole fryer
2   tablespoons soy sauce
2   tablespoons dry vermouth
1   teaspoon salt or to taste
1   teaspoon ginger root, finely chopped

Tuck wings under chicken. Place in sealable plastic bag. In bowl combine remaining ingredients. Mix well. Pour mixture over chicken and seal bag. Refrigerate 4 hours, turning bag several times. Remove chicken from bag. Place on rack in shallow baking pan filled with small amount of water. Reserve marinade. Bake chicken in preheated 450° oven 1 hour 20 minutes, basting occasionally with marinade.

May be served hot or cold.

SKEWERED CHICKEN WITH MAPLE MARINADE

Serves 3 to 4

3   chicken breasts, split, boned

Marinade:
½   cup maple syrup
    juice of 1 orange
⅛   cup soy sauce
3   tablespoons Worcestershire sauce
1   tablespoon freshly grated ginger root
    dash Sherry Peppers Sauce or Tabasco

Cut each split chicken breast into 3 pieces, leaving skin on. Combine marinade ingredients. Mix well. Marinate chicken in mixture at least 2 hours. Thread 4 pieces chicken on small skewers. Grill on barbecue 7 to 8 minutes on each side.

May also be cooked in preheated 450° broiler 10 minutes on each side. Baste frequently.

Serve with Wild Rice Salad, page 81.

Marinade may also be used with beef tenderloin.

CHICKEN COUNTRY CAPTAIN

Serves 10

10 whole chicken breasts, boned, skinned, quartered
    seasoned salt to taste
    garlic salt to taste
1   cup flour
    vegetable oil
3   large onions, diced
4   large green peppers, diced
36 ounces Brooks ketchup
2   cups water
    curry powder to taste
    currants
    slivered almonds

Season chicken with seasoned and garlic salts. Dredge in flour. In deep skillet heat oil. Sauté chicken pieces 6 to 8 at a time until lightly browned. Drain well. Arrange in single layer in large baking dish. Combine remaining ingredients. Pour over chicken. Bake uncovered in preheated 350° oven 1 hour, stirring occasionally and adding more water if mixture gets dry.

Serve over rice.

CHICKEN WELLINGTON WITH CHAMPAGNE SAUCE

Serves 6

6   **small chicken breasts, boned, skinned (may substitute 3 large breasts, split)**
3   **tablespoons butter**
       salt to taste
       white pepper to taste
1   **package frozen puff pastry**
6   **thin slices ham**
6   **thin slices cheese (Gruyère, Swiss, or Fontina)**
6   **sweet gherkin pickles**
1   **egg, lightly beaten**

Champagne sauce:
1   **pound mushrooms, sliced**
2   **tablespoons butter, if needed**
3   **tablespoons flour**
4-5   **cups whole milk or half and half, warmed**
⅛   **teaspoon salt**
⅛   **teaspoon white pepper**
⅛   **teaspoon thyme**
1   **cup champagne, room temperature**
       minced parsley

Sauté breasts in 3 tablespoons butter until golden brown on both sides. Season with salt and pepper. Remove with slotted spoon. Save pan and remaining butter. Open breast and place 1 slice ham on ½ breast. Top with 1 slice cheese, cut to fit, and 1 gherkin. Fold other half breast over top. Roll dough to 6 squares twice size of each breast. Place 1 breast diagonally in center of each square. Fold 1 corner of dough square to center. Brush top of corner with egg. Fold in each corner, brushing tops. Roll remaining dough thinly. With cookie cutter; e.g. hen, chicken, leaf, cut form. Brush top of dough "envelope" and stick cutout to top. Place chicken packages in large, shallow baking pan. Brush tops with egg. Bake in preheated 350° oven 45-60 minutes or until golden brown.

While chicken bakes sauté mushrooms 5 minutes in reserved pan with butter. Remove with slotted spoon. Add enough butter to measure 4 tablespoons. Blend in flour. Stir over high heat 2 minutes, making sure roux does not brown. Add salt, pepper, and thyme. Reduce heat and add milk slowly until thoroughly blended. Do not boil. Stir in wine. Add mushrooms. Simmer 15 minutes or until sauce is reduced by one-third. Taste and correct seasonings. Pour into sauce boat. Sprinkle with parsley. Serve immediately with chicken.

STUFFED CHICKEN LEGS

Serves 6

6 chicken legs with thighs attached
½ pound mushrooms, coarsely chopped
1 medium onion, coarsely chopped
½ large green pepper, coarsely chopped
1 tablespoon butter
1½ teaspoons Worcestershire sauce
½ teaspoon sage
   salt to taste
   pepper to taste
2 cups cooked wild rice

Basting sauce:
½ cup melted butter
   juice of 1 lime
1½ teaspoons paprika

Wash and dry chicken. Sauté mushrooms, onion, and green pepper in butter. Add Worcestershire sauce, sage, salt, and pepper. Stir in wild rice. Separate skin from meat of chicken leg and thigh and stuff tightly with rice mixture. Secure with toothpick. Arrange legs in shallow baking pan.

Combine basting sauce ingredients and pour over chicken. Basting frequently bake in preheated 350° oven 1 hour or until chicken is tender and skin is glazed, golden brown, and crisp. Remove toothpicks and serve.

May be prepared early in the day and baked prior to serving.

CHICKEN LIVERS WITH APPLES

Serves 2 to 3

1 pound chicken livers
   flour
4 tablespoons butter, divided
2 Granny Smith apples, peeled, cored, sliced
2 tablespoons chopped scallion

Dredge livers lightly in flour. In skillet heat 2 tablespoons butter until bubbly. Add livers. Sauté 3 minutes. Remove with slotted spoon to heated platter.

In separate skillet heat 2 tablespoons butter. Sauté apple slices 1 to 2 minutes.

Combine apples with livers. Top with scallions. Serve immediately.

PAELLA

Serves 6 to 8

- 6 tablespoons olive oil
- 3 pounds chicken breasts, boned, in serving size pieces
- ¼ pound chorizo or hot Italian sausage, in 1-inch pieces
- ½ pound medium shrimp, shelled, deveined
- 8 jumbo shrimp, in shells
- 2 green peppers, coarsley chopped
- 1 onion, chopped
- 2 cloves garlic, minced
- 2 tomatoes, skinned, quartered
- 6½ ounces pimiento, chopped
- 3 teaspoons paprika
- ¼ teaspoon saffron
- 2 cups uncooked short grain rice
- 5 tablespoons chopped parsley
- 1 bay leaf, crumbled
- 3½ cups chicken broth
- 1 teaspoon lemon juice
- ½ cup dry white wine
- salt to taste
- pepper to taste
- 1 cup tiny peas
- lemon wedges
- chopped parsley

In 10- to 14-inch paella pan or large heavy oven-proof skillet heat oil. Sauté sausage over medium heat 5 minutes. Add chicken. Cook additional 5 minutes, stirring, until chicken is golden. Remove chicken and sausage to warm bowl. Add all shrimp to pan. Sauté 3 minutes or until shrimp is barely pink. Remove to warm bowl.

Add peppers, onion, and garlic to pan. Sauté 2 to 3 minutes. Stir in tomatoes and pimiento. Cook 10 minutes over low heat. Add paprika, saffron, and rice. Stir to coat rice well with oil. Add parsley and bay leaf.

Bring chicken broth to boil. Add to rice mixture. Stir. Add lemon juice, wine, salt, and pepper. Stir in peas. Bring to boil over medium heat. Cook uncovered 6 to 8 minutes, stirring occasionally.

Add chicken, sausage, and shrimp. Bake uncovered in preheated 325° oven 15 minutes. More broth may be added if mixture seems too dry. Remove from oven and cover lightly. Let stand for 10 minutes before serving.

Garnish with lemon wedges and parsley.

JAMBALAYA

Serves 8 to 10   *A timeless Southern specialty.*

3	pounds chicken, in serving size pieces
	salt to taste
	pepper to taste
3-4	tablespoons bacon drippings or butter, divided
2	onions, chopped
1	green pepper, diced
1	clove garlic, minced
2	tablespoons flour
1	pound smoked sausage, sliced
3	cups peeled, seeded, chopped tomatoes
½	teaspoon thyme
½	teaspoon pepper
½	teaspoon Tabasco
1	cup water
1	cup tomato juice
¾	cup uncooked rice
½	pound shelled, deveined jumbo shrimp
2	small lobster tails, shelled and quartered, or
	12 ounces shrimp, shelled and deveined
½	cup thinly sliced scallions
¼	cup parsley

Season chicken with salt and pepper. Sauté in 2 tablespoons bacon drippings or butter. Remove chicken from pan.

In same skillet sauté onions, green pepper, and garlic. Remove from skillet. Add remaining drippings or butter and flour. Stirring often, simmer until light brown.

Stir in sausage, chicken, onions, pepper, garlic, and 2 cups tomatoes. Stirring constantly, cook 10 minutes. Add thyme, ½ teaspoon pepper, Tabasco, water, tomato juice, and rice. Mix well. Bring to boil. Reduce heat and cover. Simmer 30 minutes. Stir in shrimp, lobster, scallions, remaining 1 cup tomatoes, and parsley. Cook 5 minutes.

Serve in large bowls.

BRUNSWICK STEW

Serves 8 to 10

1	pound ground beef
1	pound pork sausage, crumbled
1	large onion, chopped
32	ounces canned whole kernel corn with liquid
32	ounces canned creamed corn with liquid
32	ounces canned tomatoes, mashed
3	chicken legs, cooked, skinned, in bite-size pieces
3	chicken thighs, cooked, skinned, in bite-size pieces
2	chicken breasts, cooked, skinned, in bite-size pieces
10	drops Tabasco
1	cup ketchup
	Worcestershire sauce to taste
	thyme to taste
	oregano to taste
	salt to taste
	pepper to taste
	chicken consommé or tomato juice, as needed
10	ounces frozen okra or frozen green beans

In large kettle sauté beef and pork sausage until well browned. Drain all fat. Remove meat. Sauté onion until transparent. Return meat to kettle. Add corn, tomatoes, chicken, Tabasco, ketchup, and seasonings to taste. If more liquid is needed, add consommé or tomato juice. Simmer 20 minutes. Mixture may be frozen at this point. Add okra or beans and simmer until vegetable is cooked. Serve stew in mugs.

PICKLED CORNISH GAME HENS

Serves 3

4 onions, thinly sliced
2 medium carrots, thinly sliced horizontally
3 Cornish game hens, in serving pieces
2 cloves garlic, minced
2 pimientos, thinly sliced
3 tablespoons chopped parsley
1 rib celery, chopped
2 bay leaves
½ cup tarragon vinegar
½ cup white wine
1 cup olive oil
½ teaspoon pepper
⅛ teaspoon dried ground chili peppers
2 teaspoons salt
   watercress
1 small lemon, thinly sliced

In large casserole arrange half of onions and carrots. Cover with game hens. Sprinkle with remaining onions and carrots, garlic, pimientos, parsley, celery, and bay leaves.

Combine vinegar, wine, oil, pepper, chili peppers, and salt. Pour over ingredients in casserole. Cover. Cook over low heat 45 minutes or until hens are tender.

Remove hens to shallow serving dish. Bring sauce to boil and cook until reduced by half. Remove bay leaves. Pour vegetable sauce over hens. Refrigerate.

Serve hens slightly chilled or at room temperature. Place on bed of watercress. Garnish with lemon slices.

May be used as a first course. May be prepared 1 day before serving.

STUFFED CORNISH HEN WITH BLUEBERRY SAUCE

Serves 3

3   Rock Cornish Hens, 1-1½ pounds each
⅛   teaspoon seasoned salt
⅛   teaspoon garlic powder
⅛   teaspoon oregano
2   cups cooked converted long grain rice and wild rice
2-3   tablespoons peanut oil
⅛   teaspoon garlic salt
⅛   teaspoon freshly ground pepper
    juice of 1 orange

Blueberry sauce:
2   cups blueberries, fresh or frozen
½   cup sugar
¼   cup water
1   tablespoon lemon juice
1   tablespoon cornstarch
¼   cup port wine
1   teaspoon grated lemon rind

Rinse insides of hens with cold water. Pat dry. Mix seasoned salt, garlic powder, and oregano. Rub mixture into cavities of hens. Fill cavities with rice and skewer openings. Brush skins of hens with peanut oil. Sprinkle with garlic salt and pepper. Place birds in roasting pan. Bake uncovered in preheated 350° oven 1 hour. Baste frequently with orange juice and pan juices.

Remove pan from oven. Spread Blueberry sauce (directions below) over hens. Return pan to oven. Raise temperature to 375°. Bake 15 minutes without basting. Remove skewers and serve hens immediately with sauce.

While hens bake combine blueberries, sugar, water, and lemon juice in a saucepan. Bring to boil. Lower heat and simmer 3 to 5 minutes, stirring constantly. Mix cornstarch with port wine. Add to blueberry mixture. Stir in lemon rind. Add more lemon juice if desired. Simmer until mixture thickens.

ROAST DUCKLING WITH ORANGE SAUCE

Serves 6 to 8

½   teaspoon ground ginger
3   cloves garlic, crushed
4   tablespoons soy sauce
2   5-7 pound ducks, quartered

Orange Sauce:
4   oranges, peeled, sectioned
4   tablespoons Madeira wine
4   tablespoons sugar
4   tablespoons red wine vinegar
1   cup beef or chicken stock
2   teaspoons cornstarch
2   tablespoons cold water

Combine ginger, garlic, and soy sauce. Mix well. Rub duck generously with mixture. Let stand at room temperature 1 to 2 hours. Place on rack in baking pan. Roast in preheated 300° oven 3 hours or until crisp.

Peel orange sections, reserving juice. Combine orange sections with wine. Let stand at room temperature. In heavy large saucepan combine sugar and vinegar. Cook uncovered over high heat until carmelized, about 2 to 3 minutes. Stir in stock immediately.

Skim off fat from duck pan juices. Add pan juices and drained juice from orange sections to carmelized stock. Combine 2 teaspoons cornstarch with 2 tablespoons cold water. Add to saucepan. Cook over medium heat until thickened and bubbly, stirring constantly. Stir in orange sections. Spoon over duck sections and serve.

Sour Cherry Sauce (See page 427) may be substituted for Orange Sauce.

See photo page 231.

SLOW DUCK

Serves 2 to 3

4½-5	pound duck
3	large fresh peaches, poached, peeled, sliced
1½	cups peach nectar or apple juice
½	cup dry white wine
5	tablespoons honey
	salt to taste

Sauce:

1	tablespoon cornstarch
1	tablespoon cold apple juice or peach nectar
	reserved peach purée
2	large peaches, sliced

Truss duck. Pierce with skewer in 4 or 5 places. Place on rack in casserole with cover. In food processor or blender combine peaches, nectar or juice, and wine. Purée. To 1 cup purée add honey and salt. Reserve remaining purée. Pour purée-honey mixture over duck. Cover and bake in preheated 200° oven 8 hours, basting once or twice. Remove cover and drain juices. Increase heat to 375° and bake 15 minutes or until browned.

In small saucepan dissolve cornstarch in juice or nectar. Stir in reserved purée. Heat until thickened, stirring frequently. Add peach slices.

Serve duck on rice accompanied by sauce.

Two pounds canned sliced peaches may be substituted for fresh peaches, using drained juices for purée.

CURRIED TURKEY WITH WATER CHESTNUTS

Serves 4 to 5   *A colorful, low-calorie dish*

¼   cup vegetable oil, divided
1   bunch green onions, sliced diagonally ½ inch thick
3   ribs celery, sliced diagonally ½ inch thick
½   green pepper, sliced
½   red pepper, sliced or ¼ cup sliced pimiento
½   cup sliced mushrooms
1½ cups thinly sliced water chestnuts
1½ cups diced, cooked turkey
2   tablespoons flour
1   teaspoon paprika
¾-1½ teaspoons curry powder or to taste
¼   teaspoon thyme
1   cup chicken broth
¾   cup drained pineapple tidbits

In large skillet or wok heat 3 tablespoons oil. Sauté onions, celery, and peppers until lightly browned. In a small skillet sauté mushrooms in 1 tablespoon oil. Add to first mixture. Stir in water chestnuts and turkey. Stir in flour, paprika, curry, and thyme. Add broth and pineapple. Stir. Cover and steam briefly. Serve on cooked rice or chow mein noodles.

Chicken or duck may be substituted for turkey.

TURKEY PARMESAN

Serves 3 to 4

6   3-ounce turkey breast slices, skinned
¼   cup flour
1   cup fine bread crumbs
1   cup grated fresh Parmesan
    rind of 2 lemons, grated
½   teaspoon garlic powder
1   tablespoon salt
¼   teaspoon pepper
2   eggs, beaten well
4   tablespoons butter
1   large lemon, quartered
    parsley

Pound turkey slices until thin. Place flour in shallow bowl. In another shallow bowl combine crumbs, cheese, rind, garlic powder, salt and pepper. Mix well. Place eggs in third shallow bowl. Dredge turkey slices in flour. Shake off excess. Dip in egg. Coat with crumb-cheese mixture. In skillet sauté turkey slices in butter 2 minutes or until golden brown. Do not overcook. Serve immediately with lemon quarters. Garnish with parsley.

For **Veal Parmesan,** substitute veal scallops for turkey.

Italian Sausage Soup

Left to right: Cheese Piroshky, Confetti Cocktail Mold, Garden Pizza, and Marinated Shrimp with Orange

Layered Vegetable Terrine

Left to right: Raita and Red Snapper Indienne

225

226

Clockwise from upper left: Herbed Challah Bread, White Sangria,
Spinach Stuffed Chicken Breasts, Country Terrine, and Melon in Rum-Lime Sauce

Wong's Chicken Salad

Clockwise from upper left: Green Pepper Jelly, Tomato Marmalade, Five Herb Vinegar, Quick Sweet Zucchini Pickles, Cantaloupe Pickles, and Red Pepper Jelly

Clockwise from upper left: Lamb Chops with Goat Cheese, Pork Tenderloin with Mustard Sauce, Roast Duckling with Orange Sauce, and Lemon Lime Chicken and Sweet Potato Curls

231

Clockwise from upper left: Lime Cheesecake and Chocolate Leaves, Chocolate Torte with Raspberry Glaze, Plum Kuchen, and Sour Cream Apple Pie

Front row left to right: Coffee Break Treats, Festive Fruitcake Cookies, Lemon Drop Cookies, Raspberry Almond Wreaths, Mint Brownies, Little Lebkuchen, and Almond Butter Cookies; rear row left to right: Peanut Brittle, White Chocolate Macadamia Bark and Bourbon Balls

VEGETABLES

Ravinia Notes

In 1968 Edward Gordon was appointed
Executive Director of Ravinia. A highly
respected concert pianist who had
successfully turned to management, Mr.
Gordon was most influential in shaping
the Festival's future. Today he remains
the vital and dynamic force behind
Ravinia.

FRESH CARROT PUFF

Serves 6 to 8

2 pounds carrots, peeled, cooked, puréed
2 teaspoons lemon juice
2 tablespoons minced scallions
¼ pound butter, softened
¼ cup sugar
1½ tablespoons flour
½ teaspoon salt
¼ teaspoon cinnamon
1 cup milk
3 eggs
1 egg white, stiffly beaten

Combine all ingredients except egg white. Mix well. Fold in egg white. Pour into well-greased, 2-quart soufflé dish. Bake in preheated 350° oven 50 to 60 minutes or until center is firm to touch. Serve immediately.

CHEDDAR CARROT RING

Serves 8

2 cups mashed, cooked carrots (2 pounds)
1 cup cracker crumbs
1 cup milk
¾ cup grated sharp Cheddar cheese
½ cup melted butter
¼ cup grated onion
1 teaspoon salt
¼ teaspoon pepper
3 eggs

In large bowl combine all ingredients except eggs. Mix well. Beat eggs well and fold into carrot mixture. Pour into greased 6-cup ring mold. Bake in preheated 350° oven 45 to 50 minutes. Unmold onto serving platter while hot.

Center of ring may be filled with cooked tiny peas, mushrooms, or vegetable of choice, or ring may be garnished with parsley.

GINGER CANDIED CARROTS

Serves 6 to 8

12 medium carrots, peeled, julienned
4 tablespoons butter, melted
¼ cup brown sugar
1½ teaspoons ground ginger
½ teaspoon caraway seed

In saucepan combine carrots with water to cover. Cook until tender-crisp.

Melt butter in small saucepan. Add sugar, ginger, and caraway seed. Mix well. Drain carrots, return to pan and add butter mixture. Cook over low heat 5 minutes, stirring occasionally.

PEAS EXTRAORDINAIRE

Serves 6

1 pound frozen tiny peas, thawed
½ cup crumbled cooked bacon
8 ounces canned water chestnuts, drained, chopped
¼ cup chopped onion
11 ounces canned cream of celery soup
½-1 cup seasoned poultry stuffing
2 tablespoons melted butter
¼ cup sherry

Spread peas over bottom of greased 1-quart casserole. Combine bacon, water chestnuts, onion, and soup. Spoon mixture over peas. Sprinkle stuffing over mixture. Drizzle butter over stuffing. Pour sherry over top. Bake in preheated 350° oven 30 minutes.

To double recipe, repeat pea and soup layers. Add stuffing, butter, and sherry to top only.

MUSHROOMS PAYSANNE

Serves 4 to 6

6   slices bacon
2   pounds mushrooms, sliced
1   teaspoon lemon juice
1   small onion, finely chopped
1   clove garlic, minced
2   tablespoons fine bread crumbs
½   teaspoon salt
    freshly ground pepper to taste
1   tablespoon finely chopped parsley

In large skillet over low heat cook bacon until crisp. Drain on paper towel. Crumble. Drain fat from skillet, leaving small amount.

In same skillet sauté mushrooms 3 minutes. Stir in lemon juice. Add onion, garlic, and bread crumbs. Sauté over high heat 3 minutes, stirring constantly. Add bacon, salt, pepper, and parsley. Mix well. Serve immediately.

MUSHROOM CASSEROLE

Serves 8

1   pound mushrooms, coarsely chopped
2   tablespoons butter
8   slices white bread, crusts removed, cut into
      1-inch squares, divided
½   cup chopped onion
½   cup chopped celery
½   cup chopped green pepper
½   cup mayonnaise
¾   teaspoon salt
¼   teaspoon pepper
2   eggs
1½   cups milk
10¾   ounces canned cream of mushroom soup
1   cup grated sharp Cheddar cheese

Sauté mushrooms in butter. Place squares from 3 slices of bread on bottom of 8-inch square baking pan. Combine mushrooms, onion, celery, green pepper, mayonnaise, salt, and pepper. Mix well. Pour mixture over bread cubes. Layer squares from 3 slices of bread over mixture.

Combine eggs and milk. Beat well. Spoon over bread layer. Cover with soup. Add remaining bread squares. Bake in preheated 300° oven 1 hour. Sprinkle top with cheese. Bake 10 minutes. Serve immediately.

MUSHROOM TART

Serves 6

1   pound mushrooms with stems, chopped (reserve 8 caps for garnish)
1   medium onion, chopped
1   clove garlic, minced
3   tablespoons butter
3   tablespoons flour
½   cup milk
2   tablespoons plus 1 teaspoon medium dry sherry
2   teaspoons Worcestershire sauce
1½   teaspoons salt or to taste
½   teaspoon pepper
⅛   teaspoon nutmeg
½   cup chopped parsley
3   eggs, well beaten
    chopped parsley

In large skillet sauté mushrooms, onion, and garlic in butter over medium heat until mushrooms lose their juices, about 4 to 5 minutes. Blend in flour. Stir in milk. Cook 4 to 5 minutes, stirring. Remove from heat. Blend in remaining ingredients except chopped parsley.

Turn into greased, shallow 8-inch pie pan. Bake in preheated 350° oven 40 to 45 minutes or until edges are browned and tart is puffy.

During baking sauté whole mushrooms caps. Garnish tart. Replace in oven 2 to 3 minutes to reheat. Sprinkle with chopped parsley. Serve immediately.

BROCCOLI CASSEROLE

Serves 8 to 10

20   ounces frozen chopped broccoli
½   pound carrots, peeled, julienned 1½-inches long by ⅛- to ¼-inch square
1   head broccoli, cut into very small flowerets
8   ounces Velveeta cheese, thinly sliced (do not substitute)
¼   pound butter, melted
1   cup Ritz cracker crumbs
⅓   cup sliced or slivered almonds

continued

Cook frozen broccoli until just softened. Do not overcook. Drain thoroughly. Cook carrots and broccoli flowerets until tender-crisp. Drain. Spread chopped broccoli in bottom of lightly greased 9- by 13-inch baking dish. Cover with cheese.

Combine butter and cracker crumbs. Mixture will be lumpy. Drop by spoonful over cheese and spread evenly. Cover with mixture of carrots and broccoli flowerets, arranging attractive pattern around outer edge. Pat gently into cracker mixture so vegetables are one-third submerged. Sprinkle with almonds. Bake in preheated 350° oven 20 minutes or until hot.

May be assembled early on day of serving, refrigerated, and brought to room temperature before baking.

ONE PRETTY ONION

Serves 1

1   8-ounce well-shaped Spanish onion
2   broccoli flowerets, steamed tender-crisp
3-4 baby carrots, peeled, steamed tender-crisp
1   teaspoon melted butter
     salt to taste
     pepper to taste
     green or red pepper strips, optional

Peel onion. Cut thin slice from bottom so onion rests evenly on plate. Cut a third from other end. Place onion in small saucepan. Add 1½ inches water. Cover and bring to boil. Reduce heat and simmer 10 minutes. Remove onion and drain on paper towel until cool.

Carefully remove inside layers of onion, leaving shell of 3 to 4 thicknesses. Arrange broccoli inside shell to 1 side. Stand carrots on other side. Pour melted butter over top and season to taste. If desired, tuck red or green pepper strips into onions to form "handles".

May be made ahead and reheated in preheated 350° oven 10 minutes.

SCOTCH ONIONS

Serves 8

3 large well-shaped white onions, peeled, sliced ½-inch thick
6 tablespoons butter
13 ounces beef consommé
    salt to taste
    pepper to taste
½ teaspoon sugar
½ cup Scotch whiskey
    chopped parsley

In large skillet sauté onions in butter, turning once carefully. Pour consommé over onions. Cover tightly. Lower heat and steam 15 minutes. Remove onions to warmed shallow serving dish. Sprinkle with salt and pepper if desired.

Add sugar and whiskey to skillet. Stir to deglaze. Pour over onions. Sprinkle with parsley.

May be prepared in advance and reheated.

HEAVENLY ONIONS

Serves 6

2 large Bermuda onions, sliced, separated into rings
2 tablespoons butter
½ pound Swiss cheese, grated
¼ teaspoon pepper
10¾ ounces canned cream of chicken soup, undiluted
½ cup milk
1 teaspoon soy sauce
8 slices French bread, buttered
    chopped parsley

In heavy saucepan over low heat simmer onions in butter until tender, stirring frequently. Pour into 1½-quart baking dish. Top with cheese and pepper.

Heat soup, milk, and soy sauce, blending well. Pour soup mixture into baking dish. Stir lightly with knife to allow sauce to mix thoroughly. Top with overlapped bread slices arranged in circle. Bake in preheated 350° oven 30 minutes. Sprinkle with chopped parsley. Serve immediately.

LEEK AND CHÈVRES TART

Serves 6 to 8

Unlike other members of its onion family, the leek boasts a delicate flavor.

1 sheet frozen puff pastry
4 large leeks
⅓ cup plus 1 tablespoon butter or margarine, divided
⅓ cup sour cream
¼ teaspoon salt
¼ teaspoon pepper
¼ teaspoon curry powder
6 ounces Chèvres cheese, crumbled

Thaw pastry 20 minutes. Line cookie sheet with brown paper. Cut two ½-inch strips from both long and short sides of pastry, totalling 4 strips. Moisten edges of pastry with water. Place cut strips over edges of remaining uncut sheet to form border around top. Using back of wooden spoon or spatula flatten inside pastry area to measure 8- by 8-inches. Trim edges of pastry case. Place on cookie sheet. Pierce bottom in 8 to 10 places. Bake in preheated 375° oven 25 to 30 minutes or until golden. Remove to rack. Cool pastry completely and cover. Reduce oven temperature to 350°.

Trim leeks, removing root ends and green stems. Wash thoroughly. Cut diagonally into ¼-inch slices to make 4 cups. Sauté 3 cups leeks in ⅓ cup butter 5 minutes. Stir in sour cream, salt, pepper, and curry powder. Mix well. Spread mixture over bottom of tart shell. Top with Chèvres.

Sauté remaining 1 cup leeks in remaining 1 tablespoon butter 3 minutes, stirring. Sprinkle over top of tart. Bake in preheated 350° oven 10 to 15 minutes or until hot.

ASPARAGUS WITH PINE NUTS

Serves 4

1 pound asparagus, ends trimmed
3 quarts boiling salted water
3 tablespoons unsalted butter
½-1 teaspoon minced garlic
¼ cup chopped prosciutto
1 teaspoon chopped fresh basil or ½ teaspoon dried basil
3 tablespoons toasted pine nuts*
freshly ground pepper to taste
¼ cup grated Parmesan cheese, divided

Cook asparagus in boiling water 6 to 8 minutes or until tender-crisp. Drain. Rinse immediately under cold water. Drain. Transfer to broiler-proof dish.

In small saucepan melt butter. Add garlic and sauté 1 to 2 minutes. Add prosciutto. Sauté 2 minutes.

Combine basil, pine nuts, pepper, and ⅛ cup cheese. Add prosciutto mixture. Combine well. Spread over asparagus spears. Sprinkle with remaining ⅛ cup cheese. Broil 2 minutes or until cheese is almost melted.

Serve as first course or luncheon dish. Topping may be used for other green vegetables.

*To toast nuts: spread on foil-covered cookie sheet. Bake in preheated 350° oven 3 to 5 minutes, watching carefully.

CRUSTLESS SPINACH PIE

Serves 12

1 pound ricotta cheese
1 cup grated mozzarella cheese
3 eggs, slightly beaten
10 ounces frozen chopped spinach, thawed, drained
2 tablespoons vegetable oil
1 teaspoon salt
½ teaspoon dill
½ teaspoon garlic powder
⅓ cup chopped salami, pepperoni, or ham, optional
¼ cup combined sliced, sautéed mushrooms and zucchini, optional

Combine cheeses with eggs. Mix well. Blend in spinach. Add remaining ingredients. Pour into buttered 10-inch springform pan. Drizzle top with small amount of oil for golden brown color. Bake in preheated 350° oven 40 minutes. Serve warm or at room temperature.

SPINACH SOUFFLÉ

Serves 8 to 10

20 ounces frozen chopped spinach, thawed, drained
2 pounds small curd creamed cottage cheese
¼ pound sharp Cheddar cheese, grated
¼ pound Swiss cheese, grated
6 eggs, beaten
6-8 tablespoons flour
¼ pound butter, melted
salt to taste
pepper to taste
¼ cup chopped scallions, sautéed, optional

Combine all ingredients. Mix well. Pour into greased 9- by 13-inch baking dish. Bake in preheated 350° oven 1 hour or until browned.

ITALIAN SPINACH

Serves 4 to 6

20 ounces spinach, stems trimmed
1 medium onion, chopped
8 ounces mushrooms, sliced
2 tablespoons butter
4 slices smoked bacon, cooked, crumbled or
    7 slices prosciutto, in thin strips
½ cup mayonnaise
¼ cup sour cream
¾ cup plus 3 tablespoons grated Parmesan cheese, divided
1 medium tomato, diced
¼ cup dry bread crumbs, optional
2 tablespoons butter, melted, optional

Cook spinach 1 to 2 minutes or until just wilted. Drain and chop.

Sauté onion and mushrooms in 2 tablespoons butter until onion is soft. Combine with bacon. Combine mayonnaise, sour cream, and ¾ cup Parmesan cheese.

Spread chopped spinach over bottom of lightly buttered 6-cup baking dish. Cover with onion-mushroom mixture. Spread with mayonnaise mixture. Cover with tomato. Sprinkle with remaining 3 tablespoons Parmesan cheese.

If desired, combine crumbs and 2 tablespoons melted butter. Sprinkle over cheese. Bake in preheated 325° oven 25 minutes.

For darker appearance, combine spinach, onion-mushroom mixture, and mayonnaise mixture. Place in baking dish. Sprinkle with tomato and 3 tablespoons Parmesan.

SPINACH STUFFED TOMATOES

Serves 6

20 ounces frozen chopped spinach, thawed
½ cup pine nuts
¾ cup safflower oil, divided
2 medium onions, chopped
2 cloves garlic, minced
  salt to taste
  pepper to taste
⅛ teaspoon nutmeg
6 medium tomatoes
1½ teaspoons sugar
1½ teaspoons basil

Squeeze moisture from spinach. Sauté pine nuts in ¼ cup oil until golden, watching carefully to avoid burning. Stir in onions and garlic. Sauté 1 to 2 minutes. Add ¼ cup oil, spinach, salt, pepper, and nutmeg. Remove from heat.

Cut thin slice from each tomato top. Hollow out tomatoes and drain well. Sprinkle inside of each with salt, pepper, sugar, and basil. Fill with spinach mixture. Arrange tomatoes in buttered baking dish large enough to hold tomatoes without crowding. Sprinkle with remaining ¼ cup oil. Bake in preheated 350° oven 15 minutes. Serve warm or chilled.

SAUSAGE STUFFED TOMATOES

Serves 8

8 small tomatoes
½ teaspoon salt
  freshly ground pepper to taste
¼ cup finely chopped onion
1 clove garlic, mashed
2½ tablespoons butter, divided
¾ teaspoon olive oil
¾ pound Italian sausage
2 teaspoons red wine vinegar
½ teaspoon sugar
½ teaspoon beef bouillon powder
¾ cup cooked rice
⅛ cup pine nuts
⅛ cup chopped parsley
1½ tablespoons freshly grated Romano cheese
1 tablespoon fresh basil or ½ teaspoon dried basil
1 egg, slightly beaten
⅛ cup fresh bread crumbs

Slice tops from tomatoes and discard. Remove pulp and juice. Reserve. Sprinkle insides of tomatoes with salt and pepper. Invert and drain on paper towel.

In large skillet over medium heat sauté onion and garlic in ½ tablespoon butter and oil. Add sausage, breaking up lumps. Stir in reserved tomato pulp and juice, vinegar, sugar, and bouillon powder. Cook until liquid evaporates. Remove from heat. Add rice, pine nuts, parsley, cheese, basil, and egg. Mix well. Fill tomatoes with mixture. Top with bread crumbs and remaining 2 tablespoons butter in small pieces. Place in greased baking dish large enough to hold tomatoes without crowding. Bake in preheated 350° oven 30 minutes. Serve immediately.

SQUASH IN CREAM

Serves 4

2   pounds summer squash, peeled, sliced
2   tablespoons lemon juice
    salt
2   tablespoons butter
1   cup whipping cream
2   tablespoons drained capers, optional
1   tablespoon minced dill
    pepper to taste
    dash Tabasco

Toss squash with lemon juice. Sprinkle with salt and drain on paper towel 30 minutes.

Heat butter in skillet and add squash. Cook, stirring, 5 minutes or until just tender. Remove with slotted spoon to warm serving dish. Add cream to skillet. Cook over medium heat, stirring constantly, 10 to 12 minutes or until sauce is reduced to ½ cup. Stir in remaining ingredients. Pour sauce over squash. Serve immediately.

SQUASH SOUFFLÉ

Serves 8 to 10

Superb soufflé!

5	tablespoons unsalted butter
½	cup sugar
½	cup flour
2	cups whole milk
4	large eggs, separated
10	ounces frozen squash, thawed, mashed
1	teaspoon salt
1	teaspoon freshly ground nutmeg
1	teaspoon cream of tartar

In large saucepan melt butter over medium low heat. Stir in sugar. Cook 2 minutes, stirring constantly. Add flour, a little at a time, blending well after each addition. Mixture will appear dry.

In separate saucepan heat milk. Do not boil or let skin form. Add a third of milk to butter-flour mixture. Blend well. Add another third. Blend well. Add remaining milk and stir until mixture is smooth. Cook over medium heat until mixture bubbles. Remove from heat immediately.

In large bowl beat egg yolks. Add small amount of cooked mixture to yolks. Mix well. Continue to add small amounts of mixture, blending well after each addition, until cooked mixture is completely combined. Stir in squash, salt, and nutmeg. Cool 1 hour.

Beat egg whites until frothy. Add cream of tartar and beat until stiff peaks form. Gently fold whites into squash mixture, taking care not to blend completely. Do not overmix. Pour into 2½-quart soufflé dish sprayed liberally with vegetable oil. Submerge soufflé dish in large shallow baking pan filled with 2 inches hot water. Place pan in center of preheated 350° oven. Bake 1¾ to 2 hours. Serve immediately.

Soufflé custard may be prepared night before and refrigerated. Bring to room temperature before adding beaten egg whites.

TOM'S STUFFED ASPARAGUS SQUASH

Serves 6

6   asparagus squash, 3 inches in diameter
4   slices bacon*
1   tablespoon chopped parsley
½   teaspoon minced thyme
¼   teaspoon minced rosemary
7   tablespoons bread crumbs, divided
6   tablespoons butter, divided
3   tablespoons shallots, finely chopped
1   pound mushrooms, finely chopped
1   tablespoon flour
⅓   cup whipping cream
½   teaspoon salt
     freshly ground pepper to taste

Steam squash until just tender. Cool. Cut thin slice from bottom of each squash so squash rests evenly on plate. Cut wide circle from tops, leaving ½-inch sides and bottom, hollowing center to hold stuffing. Discard seeds from scooped-out portion. Chop scooped-out portion.

In skillet cook bacon. Reserving fat, remove bacon to drain. Sauté chopped squash in bacon fat 5 minutes. Remove from heat. Add parsley, thyme, rosemary, and 3 tablespoons bread crumbs. Mix well. Transfer to bowl.

Melt 4 tablespoons butter in skillet. Add shallots and sauté 4 minutes, stirring constantly. Add mushrooms and cook 10 minutes or until most of moisture has evaporated. Add flour and mix well. Add cream and cook 1 to 2 minutes. Season with salt and pepper.

Combine mushrooms and squash mixtures. Mix well. Stuff squash with mixture.

In small saucepan melt remaining 2 tablespoons butter. Add remaining 4 tablespoons bread crumbs. Cook, stirring constantly until brown. Sprinkle over squash. Place squash on baking sheet and bake in preheated 350° oven 15 minutes.

*For more authentic Italian flavor, substitute 4 ounces pancetta.

SQUASH MEDLEY

Serves 8 to 12

¼ pound butter, melted
¼ cup chopped onion
1 butternut squash, peeled, cubed
1 buttercup squash, peeled, cubed
2-3 zucchini, unpeeled, sliced
2 tomatoes, quartered
2 teaspoons sugar
1 teaspoon salt
½ teaspoon pepper
⅛ teaspoon oregano
4-5 tablespoons grated Parmesan cheese

Combine all ingredients except cheese in greased 8-cup casserole. Mix well. Sprinkle with cheese. Cover and bake in preheated 350° oven 1 hour.

SPAGHETTI SQUASH PRIMAVERA

Serves 8

3½ pounds spaghetti squash
2 cups broccoli flowerets
½ pound carrots, peeled, cut into 1-inch lengths
1 zucchini, sliced
½ cup minced scallions
½ pound mushrooms, sliced, optional
3 tablespoons olive oil
3 cups tomato sauce

Tomato sauce:
4-5 tomatoes, peeled, seeded, coarsely chopped
⅓ cup olive oil
1 cup minced basil
1 cup minced parsley
3 tablespoons grated Parmesan cheese
3 cloves garlic, minced
salt to taste
pepper to taste

continued

Combine all tomato sauce ingredients at least one hour before using. Mix well. Do not cook.

Bake squash in preheated 350° oven 1¼ hours. Cool. Slice in half. Using fork scrape long strands into bowl.

Steam broccoli, carrots, and zucchini until tender-crisp. Rinse under cold water. Drain.

In large skillet sauté scallions and mushrooms in oil. Stir in all vegetables. Add tomato sauce. If serving warm, heat over medium heat. May be served at room temperature.

For an effective presentation, serve in the squash shell.

SWEET AND SOUR WAX BEANS

Serves 4 to 6

¾   **pound yellow wax beans, ends and strings removed**
1   **tablespoon butter**
1   **tablespoon vegetable oil**
2   **tablespoons flour**
½-¾   **cup cooking liquid from beans**
1   **tablespoon white vinegar**
2   **teaspoons sugar**
½   **teaspoon salt or to taste**
¼   **teaspoon white pepper or to taste**
½   **teaspoon dried dill weed, optional**
4   **ounces canned water chestnuts, drained, sliced**

French cut beans, if desired. Gently boil in water to cover until tender-crisp. Drain, reserving liquid. Rinse beans with cold water. Drain.

Melt butter and oil in saucepan. Stir in flour to make a smooth paste. Gradually add ½ to ¾ cup reserved cooking liquid, stirring constantly over medium heat until sauce thickens. Stir in remaining ingredients except water chestnuts. Add beans and water chestnuts. Toss to heat and coat with sauce. Serve immediately.

GREEN BEANS WITH BACON

Serves 8

1 medium onion, chopped
5 slices bacon, cooked, crumbled, fat reserved
2 pounds green beans
1 teaspoon red pepper flakes
 salt to taste
1 cup boiling water
3 tablespoons melted butter
3 teaspoons white vinegar
1 large tomato, diced

In large saucepan sauté onion in reserved bacon fat until soft. Add green beans, pepper flakes, and salt. Sauté over high heat for 2 minutes. Reduce heat to low. Add 1 cup boiling water and cover. Cook 15 minutes, shaking pan occasionally. Add butter, vinegar, and tomato. Heat thoroughly. Sprinkle with crumbled bacon. Serve immediately.

CUCUMBERS IN SWEET-SOUR SAUCE

Serves 8

4 large cucumbers, peeled, halved lengthwise, seeded, and
 cut into ⅓-inch pieces
2 tablespoons flour
2 tablespoons butter, melted
1 cup beef broth
2 tablespoons white wine vinegar
2 tablespoons sugar
2 tablespoons chopped dill
4 ounces drained capers

Cook cucumbers in salted boiling water several minutes. Do not overcook. Drain well.

In saucepan over medium heat stir flour into melted butter. Slowly add broth, stirring until sauce thickens. Add remaining ingredients. Mix well. Combine with cucumbers and serve warm.

BRUSSELS SPROUTS IN BUTTER SAUCE

Serves 4

¼ pound butter
4 tablespoons chopped chives
1 tablespoon prepared mustard
1 tablespoon Worcestershire sauce
⅛ teaspoon garlic salt
⅛ teaspoon pepper
   dash celery salt
1 pint fresh Brussels sprouts or 10 ounces frozen Brussels sprouts

In saucepan melt butter. Stir in chives, mustard, Worcestershire sauce, garlic salt, pepper, and celery salt. Simmer 30 minutes.

Cook sprouts in boiling salted water until tender. Drain. Return to pan. Pour butter sauce over sprouts. Place over low heat, turning sprouts to coat. Remove from heat and serve immediately.

CABBAGE TART

Serves 6 to 8

The humble cabbage in a gourmet guise.

6 cups shredded cabbage
¼ pound butter
5 eggs, beaten
2 cups whipping cream
1 teaspoon nutmeg
¼ teaspoon garlic powder
   salt to taste
   pepper to taste
1 9-inch unbaked pie shell, optional

In heavy skillet cook cabbage in butter over medium heat, stirring until golden. Combine eggs, cream, and seasonings. Place cabbage in pie shell or lightly greased shallow baking dish. Pour egg mixture over cabbage. Bake in preheated 350° oven 45 minutes or until custard is set and lightly browned. If omitting pie shell, place baking dish in pan of hot water for baking.

DILLED CABBAGE

Serves 4

½ large head cabbage, thinly sliced
½ teaspoon chopped dill or to taste
4-6 tablespoons Italian dressing
6-8 tablespoons water
cherry tomatoes, halved

In skillet combine cabbage with dill. Let stand 5 to 10 minutes. Add dressing and water. Stir fry over medium high heat until cabbage is tender-crisp. Add additional water if desired. Garnish with halved tomatoes. Serve warm.

May substitute ⅔ pound Brussels sprouts, quartered, for cabbage.

RED CABBAGE

Serves 6 to 8

5 cups shredded red cabbage
2 large tart apples, peeled, cored, thinly sliced
3 tablespoons bacon drippings
2 tablespoons walnut oil
6 tablespoons brown sugar
1 cup water
½ cup cider vinegar
½ teaspoon salt
freshly ground pepper to taste
1 tablespoon caraway seed
1 teaspoon cornstarch, optional
1 tablespoon water, optional

In large, heavy skillet combine all ingredients except cornstarch and water. Bring to boil. Cover, reduce heat, and simmer 20 minutes until cabbage is tender-crisp. If thicker consistency is desired, combine cornstarch and water, stir into cabbage, and simmer additional 1 minute.

ROMAINE SOUFFLÉ

Serves 6

3   scallions, chopped
4   tablespoons butter, melted
3   tablespoons flour
1   cup half and half
4   eggs, separated
1   cup grated Cheddar cheese
1   medium bunch romaine lettuce, finely chopped
1   teaspoon salt
½   teaspoon Worcestershire sauce
2   dashes Tabasco
2-3   tablespoons grated Parmesan cheese, or as needed

In large saucepan sauté scallions in butter. Stir in flour. Cook 2 to 3 minutes. Gradually add half and half and cook until thickened, stirring constantly. Beat egg yolks and blend into mixture. Stir in Cheddar cheese. Cook until smooth. Add lettuce, salt, Worcestershire sauce, and Tabasco. Mix well and remove from heat.

Butter 1½-quart soufflé dish. Sprinkle with Parmesan cheese. Cut 4-inch strip of foil. Attach to soufflé dish to create 3-inch collar above top of dish.

Beat egg whites until stiff but not dry. Fold into lettuce mixture. Pour into soufflé dish. Bake in preheated 375° oven 50 to 60 minutes or until brown and puffed. Serve immediately.

EGGPLANT SOUFFLÉ

Serves 4

1   medium large eggplant
1   teaspoon salt
2   tablespoons butter
1   small clove garlic, finely minced
2   tablespoons flour
1   cup milk, warmed
3   egg yolks, lightly beaten
2-3   ounces Parmesan cheese, grated
½   teaspoon freshly ground pepper
4   egg whites

Bake eggplant in preheated 350° oven 40 to 50 minutes or until thoroughly cooked. When cool slice in half. Drain well. Remove all pulp and mash well. Stir in salt.

In large saucepan melt butter and add garlic. Stir in flour. Cook slowly 2 to 3 minutes. Stirring constantly, add milk and cook until mixture thickens. Remove from heat. Blend in egg yolks, cheese, pepper, and eggplant.

Beat egg whites until stiff but not dry. Add a third of egg whites to eggplant mixture. Fold in gently. Add another third and finally remaining third, folding gently with each addition. Pour mixture into 6-cup soufflé dish. Bake in preheated 350° oven 45 to 50 minutes. Serve immediately.

EGGPLANT CHEESE PIE

Serves 6 to 8

1   pound eggplant, peeled, in ¼-inch slices
3   eggs, lightly beaten
6   ounces cream cheese with chives
1½   cups ricotta cheese
¾   cup grated Parmesan cheese
½   cup fresh bread crumbs
½   teaspoon salt
¼   teaspoon white pepper
5   scallions, thinly sliced
¼   cup chopped parsley

continued

Arrange eggplant slices in greased, large, shallow pan. Cover tightly with foil. Bake in preheated 400° oven 20 minutes or until soft. Remove from oven and reduce heat to 350°.

In large bowl combine eggplant with remaining ingredients except parsley. In food processor or blender blend in 2 batches with several quick on and off pulses. Mixture should be combined but not puréed. Transfer mixture to greased 8-inch round quiche or pie pan. Bake 45 minutes or until brown and crusty. Sprinkle with parsley and serve immediately.

ARTICHOKE CHEESE TART

Serves 8 to 10

½ **pound plus 2 tablespoons unsalted butter, divided**
8 **ounces cream cheese**
2 **cups flour**
17 **ounces canned whole artichoke hearts, drained, mashed**
½ **cup ricotta cheese**
3 **eggs, beaten**
2 **slices white bread**
½ **cup milk**
1 **shallot, minced**
1 **large onion, chopped**
½ **pound mushrooms, chopped**
½ **teaspoon parsley**
1 **teaspoon oregano**
¼ **teaspoon salt**
¼ **teaspoon pepper**

Cream ½ pound butter with cream cheese. Blend in flour. Roll into ball. Wrap in wax paper and chill 1 hour.

Combine artichokes, ricotta cheese, and eggs. Mix well. Soak bread in milk and add to mixture. Sauté shallot, onion, and mushrooms in remaining 2 tablespoons butter. Blend in parsley and seasonings. Combine with artichoke mixture.

Divide chilled dough in half and roll into 2 rounds. Place 1 round in 9- or 10-inch pie pan. Pour in artichoke mixture. Cover with other round. Cover edge with cuff of foil. Bake in preheated 450° oven 25 minutes. Remove foil. Bake 10 minutes. Cool 10 minutes before slicing. Serve immediately.

BAKED ZUCCHINI

Serves 6

Fear not the seasonal burgeoning of the zucchini. Here is the first of five flavorful preparations.

4   cups grated zucchini
1   cup Bisquick
⅔   cup chopped onion
½   cup grated Parmesan cheese
2   tablespoons chopped parsley
½   teaspoon salt
½   teaspoon oregano
1   large clove garlic, minced
4   eggs, beaten
½   cup vegetable oil

In large bowl combine all ingredients. Mix well. Pour into greased 8-inch square or 9-inch quiche baking pan. Bake in preheated 350° oven 45 to 50 minutes.

ZUCCHINI-RICE CASSEROLE

Serves 10

¾   cup uncooked rice
1   cup cold water
1   cup dry white wine
8   slices bacon, thickly sliced
2   cups thinly sliced zucchini
½   cup finely chopped onion
⅛   teaspoon minced garlic
6   eggs
1   cup sour cream
1   teaspoon salt
1¼ cups grated Cheddar cheese, divided

In saucepan combine rice, water, and wine. Cook until rice is "al dente" (slightly undercooked).

In large skillet cook bacon until crisp. Drain, reserving 2 tablespoons bacon fat in skillet. Crumble bacon. Add zucchini, onion, and garlic to fat in skillet. Cook 5 minutes, stirring occasionally.

In large bowl beat eggs. Add sour cream, salt, cooked rice, 1 cup cheese, vegetable mixture, and bacon. Mix well. Pour into 8- by 10-inch baking dish. Sprinkle with remaining ¼ cup cheese. Bake in preheated 350° oven 55 minutes or until set.

HASHED BROWN ZUCCHINI PATTIES

Serves 4

4   cups grated zucchini
½   teaspoon salt
2   eggs, beaten
6   tablespoons grated Parmesan cheese
1   clove garlic, finely minced
     salt to taste
     pepper to taste
3-4   tablespoons butter, divided
     tomato wedges

Mix zucchini with salt. Let stand 15 minutes. Squeeze with hands to press out moisture. Stir beaten eggs into zucchini. Add cheese, garlic, salt, and pepper. Combine well.

Melt 2 tablespoons butter in 10- to 12-inch skillet over medium heat. When butter is hot, spoon zucchini mixture into skillet in mounds of about 2 tablespoons each. Flatten slightly. Patties should not touch. Sauté uncovered until golden brown, turning once, about 4 minutes on each side. Transfer patties to warm platter. Repeat procedure until entire zucchini mixture is used. Add remaining butter as needed. Garnish with tomato wedges. Serve immediately.

ZUCCHINI PUDDING

Serves 8

4   eggs, beaten
1½   pounds zucchini, coarsely grated
1   onion, chopped
1   cup corn muffin mix
     salt to taste
     freshly ground pepper to taste
1   cup grated Cheddar cheese

Mix eggs with zucchini and onion. Add corn muffin mix, salt, and pepper. Mix well. Pour into greased 8-inch square glass baking dish. Sprinkle with cheese. Bake in preheated 350° oven 30 minutes. If edges are brown, cover them with strips of foil. Bake additional 15 minutes or until entire top is golden brown.

ZUCCHINI LENORE

Serves 4

3 medium zucchini, shredded
1 teaspoon salt
1 medium onion, chopped
3 tablespoons margarine
3 tablespoons wine vinegar
½ cup water
   dill to taste
   sugar to taste
½ cup sour cream
2 tablespoons flour

Place zucchini in sieve. Sprinkle with salt. Let stand 30 minutes. Squeeze dry.

Sauté onion and zucchini in margarine until tender-crisp, about 5 minutes. Stir in vinegar, water, dill, and sugar.

Before serving blend sour cream and flour into zucchini mixture over low heat until just warm. Do not allow sour cream to curdle. Serve immediately.

CAULIFLOWER NORMANDE

Serves 6

1 large cauliflower
1 tablespoon butter
1 tablespoon flour
⅔ cup apple cider
⅔ cup whipping cream
¼ teaspoon salt
¼ teaspoon pumpkin pie spice
1 tablespoon chopped chutney
1 Granny Smith apple, peeled, cored, diced

Gently boil cauliflower in water 10 minutes or until just tender. Drain. Place in serving dish. Keep warm.

In heavy kettle melt butter. Blend in flour and cook 2 minutes, stirring constantly. Blend in cider and cream. Stirring constantly, cook mixture until boiling and thickened. Add remaining ingredients. Mix well and heat thoroughly. Pour sauce over cauliflower and serve immediately.

BAKED LIMA BEANS

Serves 12

4 cups small dried lima beans
¾ pound bacon, cooked, diced
1-2 tablespoons bacon fat
1¼ cups boiling water, divided
6 tablespoons molasses
4 tablespoons brown sugar
1 tablespoon dry mustard
1 tablespoon salt
1 teaspoon freshly ground pepper
¼ teaspoon ground ginger
1-2 ounces sliced pimientos

Soak beans overnight in cold water to cover. Drain. In saucepan cover beans again with cold water. Over medium heat bring to boil. Reduce heat. Simmer, stirring occasionally until tender, about 40 to 50 minutes. Drain and transfer beans to 3-quart casserole. Blend in bacon and bacon fat.

In small bowl stir ¼ cup boiling water into molasses. Add sugar, mustard, salt, pepper, ginger, and pimiento. Pour mixture over beans. Add remaining 1 cup boiling water. Stir well. Cover and bake in preheated 250° oven 3 to 4 hours, adding more hot water if beans seem dry. Stir occasionally. Increase oven temperature to 300° and uncover beans. Bake until tender and brown on top, about 30 minutes.

PEPPERS ROQUEFORT

Serves 8

4 green bell peppers
1 cup bread crumbs
  dash salt
1 cup crumbled Roquefort or blue cheese
⅔ cup mayonnaise
⅔ cup milk
  dash paprika

Cut peppers in half lengthwise. Remove seeds. Place peppers in saucepan. Cover with water and simmer 5 minutes. Remove and drain.

Combine remaining ingredients except paprika. Mix well. Fill pepper halves with mixture and place in large shallow baking pan. Add 1 inch water to pan. Bake in preheated 350° oven 25 minutes. Sprinkle with paprika. Serve hot or cold.

WALNUT AND CHEESE STUFFED PEPPERS

Serves 6

6   medium to large green bell peppers
4   small onions, chopped
1   cup chopped celery
2   cloves garlic, minced
2   tablespoons margarine
2   cups brown rice cooked in consommé
2   cups coarsely chopped walnuts
1   cup packed grated sharp Cheddar cheese
3   eggs, lightly beaten
2   teaspoons caraway seed
½   teaspoon thyme
½   teaspoon marjoram
1   teaspoon salt
½   teaspoon pepper
1   cup dry white wine
    dash paprika

Remove tops, ribs, and seeds from peppers. Sauté onions, celery, and garlic in margarine until tender-crisp. Combine sautéed vegetables with rice and remaining ingredients except wine and paprika.

Spoon mixture into pepper shells and place upright in oven-proof casserole just large enough to hold peppers without touching. Sprinkle with paprika. Pour wine into bottom of casserole. Bake in preheated 350° oven 25 to 30 minutes, or until bubbly and golden. Transfer to heated serving dish.

Serve hot with broiled steak or chicken or with salad as a meatless entrée.

MÉLANGE OF VEGETABLES

Serves 12

¼   cup vegetable or olive oil
4   large onions, peeled, thickly sliced
4   green peppers, seeded, cut into chunks
1   large eggplant, peeled, cut into 1-inch cubes
4   cloves garlic, minced
4   zucchini, thickly sliced
6   large tomatoes, cut into chunks
½   cup chopped parsley
2   teaspoons salt or to taste
2   teaspoons oregano or to taste
½   cup packaged herb stuffing mix, optional

In large skillet heat oil. Sauté onions and peppers only until transparent. Stir in eggplant and garlic. Cook 5 minutes. Stir in zucchini, cooking 5 minutes. Add tomatoes.

Simmer covered 15 to 20 minutes, stirring to prevent sticking. Add more oil if necessary. Stir in parsley, salt, and oregano. If desired, at end of cooking time stir in stuffing mix to absorb excess liquid in skillet.

Serve hot or cold. Should be made at least 24 hours ahead to mingle flavors.

CALICO BAKED BEANS

Serves 12

1	pound ground beef
1	large onion, chopped
2	tablespoons butter or margarine
1	pound bacon, cooked, drained, in 1-inch pieces
½	cup sugar
½	cup brown sugar
¼	cup ketchup
¼	cup barbecue sauce
2	tablespoons prepared mustard
2	tablespoons molasses
¾	teaspoon chili powder
1	teaspoon salt
½	teaspoon pepper
16	ounces canned kidney beans, drained
16	ounces canned lima beans, drained
28	ounces canned pork and beans

In large skillet brown beef and onion in butter. Drain well. Place in large casserole with bacon.

In medium bowl combine sugar, brown sugar, ketchup, barbecue sauce, mustard, molasses, chili powder, salt, and pepper. Mix well. Add kidney beans, lima beans, and pork and beans to casserole. Pour sugar mixture on top. Blend well.

Cover casserole and bake in preheated 350° oven 45 minutes. Uncover casserole and bake additional 15 minutes. This casserole can be held, covered, in low oven for 1 hour.

CHUNKY CAPONATA

Serves 12

1 large eggplant, unpeeled, in bite-size pieces
6 medium zucchini, unpeeled, in bite-size pieces
½ pound mushrooms, thickly sliced
1½ cups chopped onions
1 cup sliced celery
1 clove garlic, crushed
¾ cup olive oil
½ cup red wine vinegar
¼ cup drained capers
2 teaspoons salt
¼ teaspoon pepper
⅛ teaspoon cayenne
3 large tomatoes, in chunks
4½ ounces pimiento-stuffed olives, drained

In large kettle cook eggplant, zucchini, mushrooms, onions, celery, and garlic in hot oil 10 minutes, stirring occasionally. Stir in vinegar, capers, and seasonings. Reduce heat, cover, and simmer vegetables 5 to 10 minutes or until fork tender. Stir in tomatoes and olives. Heat to boiling. Pack in hot sterilized jars or transfer to large bowl. Cool. Cover and refrigerate until well chilled.

Serve cold as appetizer or side dish with meat.

RATATOUILLE COBEY

Serves 10 to 12

An excellent version from the well-known Chicago caterer.

2 cups thinly sliced onions
2 cups red pepper in large chunks
4 cloves garlic, finely chopped
¾ cup olive oil, or as needed
4 cups zucchini in large chunks
4 cups eggplant in chunky strips
2 teaspoons thyme
2 teaspoons salt or to taste
   freshly ground pepper to taste
1 cup tomato purée

continued

In large kettle sauté onions, red pepper, and garlic in oil until partially softened. Transfer mixture to large casserole. Sauté zucchini slightly. Add to casserole. Using generous amount of oil, sauté eggplant until soft. Add to casserole. Season with thyme, salt, and pepper. Stir in tomato purée. Mix well. Bake in preheated 400° oven 30 minutes.

GHIVETCH

Serves 8

A colorful and crisp vegetable casserole.

2	medium carrots, peeled, thinly sliced
2	medium potatoes, diced
2	medium tomatoes, cored, quartered
1	cup green beans, sliced into ½-inch diagonals
1	large rib celery, sliced into ¼-inch diagonals
1	yellow squash, thinly sliced
1	zucchini, thinly sliced
1	Bermuda onion, thinly sliced
1	small cauliflower, cut into flowerets
½	cup red pepper strips
½	cup green pepper strips
1	cup beef or chicken bouillon
½	cup olive oil
3	cloves garlic, minced
2	teaspoons salt
1	bay leaf
½	teaspoon savory
¼	teaspoon tarragon

Combine all vegetables. Mix well. Pour into 3-quart ungreased casserole.

In saucepan combine bouillon, oil, garlic, salt, and spices. Bring to boil. Pour mixture over vegetables. Cover casserole with tight-fitting lid or foil. Bake in preheated 350° oven 60 to 75 minutes. Stir occasionally. Vegetables should remain crisp. Do not overcook.

May substitute any colorful seasonal vegetables.

TORTA TARASCA (Mexican Casserole)

Serves 8

1 medium onion, finely chopped
2 green bell peppers, thinly sliced
½-¾ cup vegetable oil, divided
3 cups tomato sauce
1 cup water
salt to taste
pepper to taste
1 pound frozen corn niblets
16 corn tortillas
½ pound mozzarella cheese, grated
½ pound Cheddar cheese, grated
½ pound Monterey Jack cheese, grated
1 pint sour cream

In saucepan over medium heat sauté onion and peppers until soft in 3 tablespoons oil. Add tomato sauce and water. Cover and simmer 1 hour. Add more water if sauce thickens too much. Season with salt and pepper. Stir in corn. Remove from heat and cool.

In skillet over medium heat pour oil to ½-inch depth. When oil is very hot fry tortillas singly a few seconds on each side to soften them. Drain tortillas on paper towel.

Combine 3 cheeses. Spoon 3 tablespoons cooled tomato sauce into 3- to 4-quart casserole. Top with layer of 4 tortillas. Follow with another layer of sauce, then layer of cheese mixture. Repeat until all ingredients are used, finishing with layer of cheeses. Bake in preheated 350° oven 45 minutes, uncover, and bake additional 15 minutes or until cheese has browned. Serve with sour cream on the side.

May be assembled in advance. Cover and refrigerate. Bring to room temperature before baking.

NEAPOLITAN VEGETABLE CHEESECAKE

Serves 8

Far from being a dessert, this "cheesecake" is an excellent accompaniment to broiled meat or chicken. The name is derived from the texture, which resembles the dessert.

3	cups packed coarsely grated zucchini
1	teaspoon salt, divided
1	onion, chopped
1	tablespoon butter
3	cloves garlic, finely minced
1	cup coarsely grated carrots
3	tablespoons flour
½	teaspoon basil
½	teaspoon oregano
¼	cup packed chopped parsley
1½	tablespoons lemon juice
4	eggs
3	cups ricotta cheese
½	pound mozzarella cheese, grated
¾	cup grated Parmesan cheese, divided
	salt to taste
	freshly ground pepper to taste
⅓	cup fine bread crumbs
5-6	plum tomatoes, thinly sliced
	rolled anchovies, optional

Sprinkle grated zucchini with ½ teaspoon salt. Place in sieve and let drain 15 minutes. Squeeze out all moisture.

In large skillet combine onion, butter, and remaining ½ teaspoon salt. Sauté 3 to 4 minutes. Add zucchini, garlic, carrots, flour, basil, and oregano. Stir over medium heat 5 to 6 minutes. Remove from heat. Add parsley and lemon juice.

In large bowl combine eggs, ricotta, mozzarella, and ⅔ cup Parmesan cheese. Beat well. Add vegetable mixture and blend thoroughly. Stir in salt and pepper.

Butter 10-inch springform pan and sprinkle a few bread crumbs on bottom. Pour mixture into pan. Bake uncovered in preheated 375° oven 30 minutes. Remove from oven. Decorate with tomato slices dredged in remaining bread crumbs and optional anchovies. Sprinkle with remaining Parmesan cheese.

Reduce oven temperature to 350° and bake additional 30 minutes. Turn oven off, open door, and leave "cake" inside 15 minutes. Remove from oven. Cool on rack 10 minutes before serving.

LAYERED VEGETABLE TERRINE

Serves 8

Spinach layer:
20   ounces cooked spinach (thawed if frozen)
½   small onion, minced
3   tablespoons half and half
1   egg
1   teaspoon salt
⅓   teaspoon garlic powder
¼   teaspoon pepper

Cauliflower layer:
1   medium cauliflower, cut up, cooked
1   egg
1-2   tablespoons half and half
1   tablespoon minced parsley
1   teaspoon salt
½   teaspoon lemon and pepper seasoning

Carrot layer:
1   pound carrots, cooked
1   egg
1-2   tablespoons half and half
1   teaspoon dried dill weed
¾   teaspoon salt
½   teaspoon ground ginger
    sugar to taste

    carrot flowers

Press moisture out of spinach. In food processor or blender combine spinach layer ingredients, adding as much half and half as necessary to make smooth purée. Mixture should be moist but not runny. Pack evenly and firmly into bottom of greased 9- by 5-inch loaf pan.

For cauliflower layer, follow directions for spinach layer, adding half and half as necessary. Purée and layer evenly in pan over spinach.

For carrot layer, proceed as before, puréeing all ingredients. Layer evenly in pan over cauliflower. Cover top with buttered wax paper and place in larger pan. Add water to reach 1 to 2 inches up side of loaf pan.

Bake in preheated 300° oven 1 to 1½ hours. Test for doneness by lifting wax paper and shaking loaf pan; terrine is baked when firm. Remove from oven and let stand 15 minutes. Remove paper and run knife around edges. Invert onto serving plate. Garnish with carrot flowers.

Slice and serve hot or cold. If served hot, accompany with hot melted butter flavored with lemon juice. If served cold, accompany with homemade Quick Mayonnaise (page 422).

See photo page 224.

PASTA, RICE, & POTATOES

Ravinia Notes

Ravinia had evolved, through the years, into a major festival of the arts. Important future goals were the building of a new stage and back stage area, and the installation of a new sound system for the lawn audience. To implement these goals the Festival's first capital campaign "To Rebuild Ravinia" was established. Opera stars Sherrill Milnes and Martina Arroyo flew in for a benefit performance that earned a quarter of a million dollars.

The opening night concert of 1970 was performed on the new stage that had been especially designed by the New York City Ballet's George Ballanchine to achieve resilience for dancers. The event was aired on national television.

VEGETARIAN LASAGNA

Serves 12

2½ tablespoons olive oil, divided
10 uncooked lasagna noodles
1 onion, minced
1 clove garlic, minced
1 pound mushrooms, sliced
1 pound carrots, peeled, shredded
¾ cup pitted ripe olives, sliced
15 ounces tomato sauce
6 ounces tomato paste
1½ teaspoons oregano
½ teaspoon salt
⅛ teaspoon freshly ground pepper
2 cups creamed cottage cheese, well drained, divided
2 pounds spinach, cooked, well drained, divided
1 pound 12 ounces Monterey Jack cheese, grated, divided
3 tablespoons grated Parmesan cheese

In 2-gallon kettle bring 6 quarts salted water to rapid boil. Add 1 tablespoon olive oil and lasagna noodles, 2 or 3 at a time. Cook 8 to 10 minutes. Drain. Return to kettle with warm water to cover to prevent sticking.

In 10-inch skillet heat 1 tablespoon oil. Stir in onion and garlic. Sauté over moderate heat 2 minutes, stirring continuously. Add mushrooms. Stirring occasionally, sauté until moisture evaporates, about 12 to 15 minutes. Add carrots. Cook 3 to 5 minutes. Stir in olives, tomato sauce, tomato paste, oregano, salt, and pepper. Combine well. Remove from heat.

Grease 9- by 13-inch baking pan with remaining ½ tablespoon oil. Line bottom of pan with 5 drained lasagna noodles. Spread over noodles half the cottage cheese, half the spinach, and a third of the Monterey Jack cheese in that order. Cover with half the tomato mixture. Repeat procedure. Top with remaining Monterey Jack cheese. Sprinkle with Parmesan cheese. Bake in preheated 375° oven 45 minutes.

MARY'S LASAGNA

Serves 20

Discover the pleasures of homemade pasta. Unequaled for texture, flavor, and personal satisfaction.

½   cup dried mushrooms
2-3   tablespoons vegetable oil
2   medium onions, chopped
2   cloves garlic, minced
1   small green pepper, chopped
1⅓   ribs celery with leaves, chopped
1   teaspoon chopped parsley
3   pounds ground chuck
¾   pound ground pork
¾   pound ground veal
12   ounces tomato paste
6   ounces chili sauce
18   ounces water
½   cup white wine
      salt to taste
      pepper to taste
4   tablespoons butter

Cream sauce:
¼   pound butter
1   cup flour
1   quart whole milk
1½   teaspoons salt
      freshly ground pepper to taste

Pasta dough:
6   eggs, divided
5¼   cups flour, divided
½   teaspoon salt, divided
1   tablespoon vegetable oil, divided
6   tablespoons water, divided

8   ounces Parmesan cheese, grated

continued

Soak mushrooms in hot water to cover 20 to 30 minutes. Drain, reserving water. Chop mushrooms. Set aside.

In large Dutch oven heat oil. Add onions, garlic, green pepper, celery, and parsley. Sauté until brown. Add meat. Stirring frequently and breaking meat into small pieces, cook until meat is brown, about 20 minutes. Add tomato paste, chili sauce, water, wine, mushrooms, and reserved water from mushrooms. Season with salt and pepper to taste. Simmer 1½ hours. Remove from heat and stir in butter.

In large saucepan melt ¼ pound butter. Stir in 1 cup flour until smooth. Stirring constantly, add milk slowly until mixture is thickened and smooth. Add salt and pepper. Remove from heat.

Combine a third of all pasta dough ingredients in food processor. Blend well with quick on and off pulses. Run motor steadily until dough forms a ball and is well kneaded, about 1 minute. Repeat procedure for each third of dough ingredients. Combine 3 balls of dough. Put in bowl, cover, and place in warm area 30 minutes.

Using hand pasta machine roll out dough, resetting machine 5 or 6 times to make dough as thin as possible. Hang or lay on counter to dry. When ready to assemble lasagna, cook in boiling salted water until just tender, about 2 minutes.

Butter three 9- by 13-inch baking pans. Cover bottom of each pan with meat sauce. Cover sauce with cooked drained pasta placed lengthwise in single layer, overlapping slightly. Spread meat sauce over pasta. Cover meat sauce with cream sauce. Sprinkle with Parmesan cheese. Repeat procedure for 3 layers, topping with generous layer of Parmesan cheese. Bake in preheated 350° oven 30 to 40 minutes or until bubbly and lightly browned.

May be frozen after assembling.

ELEGANT LASAGNA

Serves 8 to 10

½ **pound uncooked lasagna noodles**

Meat sauce:
1 **pound ground beef**
½ **cup chopped onion**
3 **cloves garlic, minced**
1 **tablespoon olive oil**
3 **pounds tomatoes, peeled, seeded, chopped**
2 **tablespoons chopped parsley**
1½ **teaspoons seasoned salt**
1 **teaspoon basil**
½ **teaspoon oregano**
¼ **teaspoon pepper**

Béchamel sauce:
¼ **pound butter**
4 **tablespoons flour**
1 **cup milk**
1 **cup chicken broth**
1 **chicken bouillon cube, optional**
⅛ **teaspoon salt**

Ricotta filling:
1 **egg, beaten**
½ **pound ricotta cheese**
¼ **cup grated Parmesan cheese**
½ **teaspoon salt**
⅛ **teaspoon nutmeg**

1½ **cups grated Parmesan cheese**
4 **ounces sliced mozzarella cheese**
4 **ounces grated Monterey Jack cheese**
3 **tablespoons butter**

Cook lasagna noodles in boiling, salted water until "al dente" (slightly underdone). Drain. Transfer to bowl of cold water until ready to assemble. Sauté beef, onion, and garlic in olive oil until meat is browned. Add remaining meat sauce ingredients. Simmer until sauce is quite thick, about 30 minutes. Skim fat from surface.

In saucepan melt butter. Add flour, and cook 1 minute, stirring with whisk. Continuing to stir, slowly add liquids and bring to boil. Taste and add bouillon cube if desired. Stir in salt. Remove from heat.

Combine all ricotta filling ingredients. Mix well.

In lightly greased 9- by 13-inch baking pan, layer ingredients in following order:

continued

small amount meat sauce, half the drained noodles, half the remaining meat sauce, ½ cup béchamel sauce, ½ cup Parmesan cheese, 2 ounces mozzarella cheese, 2 ounces Monterey Jack cheese, half the ricotta filling, remaining drained noodles, remaining meat sauce, ½ cup béchamel sauce, ½ cup Parmesan cheese, remaining mozzarella cheese, Monterey Jack cheese, ricotta filling, béchamel sauce, and Parmesan cheese. Dot with butter.

Bake uncovered in preheated 400° oven 30 to 40 minutes until bubbling.

FETTUCCINE DE JONGHE

Serves 6

2	scallions, minced
3	cloves garlic, minced
½	pound unsalted butter, divided
1¼	cups white bread crumbs
½	cup dry Marsala or sauterne wine
¼	cup Italian parsley, chopped
¼	cup grated Parmesan cheese
½	teaspoon salt
⅛	teaspoon freshly ground pepper
8	ounces uncooked spinach fettuccine
½	cup half and half
1½	pounds cooked, shelled, deveined, medium shrimp
12	small pitted ripe olives
	parsley sprigs

In large skillet, sauté scallions and garlic in ¼ pound plus 4 tablespoons butter 2 minutes. Add bread crumbs, wine, chopped parsley, cheese, salt, and pepper. Sauté 3 minutes, stirring constantly. Remove from heat.

Cook fettuccine until "al dente" (slightly underdone). Drain and toss with half and half and remaining 4 tablespoons butter. When well coated pour into baking dish. Top with half of garlic-crumb mixture. Cover with shrimp and olives. Sprinkle with remaining garlic-crumb mixture.

Bake in preheated 375° oven 30 minutes. Garnish with parsley sprigs before serving.

Scallops may be substituted for shrimp. White fettuccine may be substituted for green; if so, replace ripe olives with pimiento-stuffed green olives.

Garlic-crumb mixture and pasta mixture may be made 1 day ahead and refrigerated. Assemble before baking.

CRAB FETTUCCINE

Serves 2 as
main course
4 to 6 as
first course

½ pound uncooked fettuccine
3-4 cloves garlic, minced
¼ pound butter, divided
¾ cup whipping cream
½ cup grated Parmesan cheese
10 ounces crab meat
salt to taste
pepper to taste

Cook fettuccine in salted boiling water until soft. While pasta is cooking sauté garlic in 3 tablespoons butter. Add cream and heat. Stir in cheese.

In separate skillet sauté crab meat in remaining 5 tablespoons butter. Add to creamed mixture with salt and pepper. Heat through. Toss with hot, drained fettuccine. Serve immediately.

FETTUCCINE WITH TOMATO-ANCHOVY-CAPER SAUCE

Serves 10 to 14

6 scallions, chopped
2 cloves garlic, finely minced
2 tablespoons vegetable oil
10 plum tomatoes or 28 ounces canned, coarsely chopped tomatoes
2 ounces flat anchovies, drained, chopped
12 ounces tiny capers, drained
¼ cup chopped parsley
¼ cup chopped basil
2 pounds uncooked fettuccine
2 tablespoons butter, melted, kept warm
10 Sicilian olives
10 cherry tomatoes, sliced
basil leaves
freshly ground pepper
grated Parmesan cheese

continued

278

Sauté scallions and garlic in oil 3 minutes. Add tomatoes, anchovies, and capers. Sauté 10 minutes. Add chopped parsley and basil. Cook 3 minutes. Remove from heat. Keep hot or reheat before pouring over noodles.

In rapidly boiling salted water cook fettuccine noodles until "al dente" (slightly underdone). Toss with warm melted butter. Transfer noodles to large serving platter. Spoon sauce over. Decorate with olives, sliced tomatoes, and basil leaves. Season with pepper and serve with Parmesan cheese.

Tomato-anchovy-caper sauce may be stored in refrigerator 1 to 2 days.

SPRINGTIME PASTA

Serves 6

Eye-appealing, light, and flavorful.

1   cup water
1   cup dry white wine
1½ pounds bay scallops
1   medium onion, minced
1   large clove garlic, minced
¼   pound unsalted butter
2   cups pea pods
1   cup diagonally sliced peeled carrots
3   cups asparagus tips, in 1-inch pieces
2   cups halved mushrooms (approximately ½ pound)
1   cup whipping cream
½   cup chicken stock
2   tablespoons chopped fresh basil or 2 teaspoons dried
1   pound fettuccine or linguine, cooked, drained
1½ cups freshly grated Parmesan cheese

In large saucepan combine water and wine. Bring to boil. Remove from heat, add scallops, and let steep 30 minutes. Drain.

In large skillet or wok sauté onion and garlic in butter until onion is softened, about 2 minutes. Add pea pods, carrots, asparagus, and mushrooms. Stir fry 2 minutes. Stir in stock and basil. Simmer 3 minutes. Add scallops and cream. Simmer 1 minute.

Combine pasta with scallop mixture, tossing until well mixed. Pour into large serving bowl. Add cheese and toss again. Serve immediately.

FETTUCCINE PARMA

Serves 4 to 6

8 ounces uncooked fettuccine
5 tablespoons butter, divided
1-2 cups cubed baked ham
½ cup whipping cream
1 egg yolk
¼ pound Parmesan cheese
1 cup sliced pitted ripe olives
2 tablespoons chopped parsley

Cook noodles in boiling salted water and 1 tablespoon butter until soft. While noodles are cooking, melt remaining 4 tablespoons butter in saucepan. Add ham and warm through. Remove from heat.

Beat together whipping cream and egg yolk. Stir into ham mixture over low heat. Do not allow to boil. Stir cheese, olives, and parsley into hot, drained noodles. Toss lightly with cream-ham mixture. Serve immediately.

THE JUDGE'S ARTICHOKE FETTUCCINE

Serves 4

1 tablespoon olive oil
2 tablespoons butter
1 teaspoon flour
¾ cup chicken stock
2 cloves garlic, minced
1 tablespoon lemon juice
½ cup minced parsley
8 cooked artichoke hearts, quartered (may use canned)
2 tablespoons grated Parmesan cheese
¼ pound ham or prosciutto, slivered, optional
¼ pound mushrooms, sliced, sautéed, optional
½ pound fettuccine, cooked, drained
salt to taste
pepper to taste

In large skillet heat oil and butter. Stir in flour until smooth. Add stock, garlic, lemon juice, and parsley. Stir over medium heat 5 minutes. Add artichoke hearts, cheese, ham, mushrooms, and salt and pepper if desired. Cover. Cook over low heat 5 to 7 minutes. Toss with fettuccine. Additional grated Parmesan may be sprinkled on individual serving.

PASTA WITH FOUR CHEESES

Serves 6

¼ pound butter
¼ pound Bel Paese cheese, cubed
¼ pound Gorgonzola cheese, crumbled
¼ pound Fontina cheese, cubed
½ cup freshly grated Parmesan cheese
1 cup whipping cream
   freshly ground pepper
1 pound uncooked spinach fettuccine
   finely chopped parsley

In top of double boiler melt butter over low heat. Add Bel Paese, Gorgonzola, and Fontina, stirring until melted. Stir in Parmesan, cream, and pepper. Blend well. Hold on very low heat while cooking pasta until "al dente" (slightly underdone). Drain pasta. Toss with sauce. Garnish with parsley. Serve immediately.

ZUCCHINI PASTA

Serves 6 to 8

4 tablespoons butter
2 onions, sliced medium thick
4 zucchini, sliced medium thick
4 tomatoes, peeled, sliced medium thick
4 cloves garlic, minced
½ cup chopped parsley
1 teaspoon thyme
1 teaspoon marjoram
1 teaspoon basil
1 teaspoon oregano
1 teaspoon salt or to taste
½ teaspoon pepper or to taste
1 pound uncooked vermicelli, capellini, or spaghettini
   grated Parmesan cheese

In large skillet melt butter. Separate onions into rings. Sauté in butter over low heat. Cut zucchini slices in half. Add to skillet. Cut tomato slices in half. Add to skillet. Stir in garlic, parsley, herbs, salt, and pepper. Sauté mixture over medium heat until vegetables are tender-crisp, 5 to 6 minutes.

In large kettle of boiling salted water, cook pasta until "al dente" (slightly underdone). Drain. Transfer to serving platter. Spoon vegetable mixture over pasta. Serve with grated Parmesan cheese.

HARRY'S BAR VERMICELLI

Serves 6 to 8

½ cup minced onion
3 tablespoons chopped parsley
1 cup diced celery
⅓ cup mayonnaise
⅓ cup vegetable oil
8 ounces uncooked vermicelli
   salt to taste

In food processor combine onion, parsley, celery, mayonnaise, and oil. Process until well blended.

Cook vermicelli in boiling salted water until "al dente" (slightly underdone). Drain. Do not rinse. Immediately place in large bowl and toss with mayonnaise-oil mixture. Season with salt to taste. Serve immediately.

ANGEL HAIR PANCAKES

Serves 4 to 6

8 ounces uncooked angel hair noodles
2 eggs, lightly beaten
   salt to taste
   pepper to taste
   butter
   sour cream
   fresh dill
   chives, optional

Boil noodles in salted water 1 minute. Drain. Combine noodles, eggs, salt, and pepper. Mix well. Spoon small mounds of mixture on hot griddle or skillet coated with melted butter. Cook until brown on both sides. Serve immediately topped with sour cream and dill.

If stronger flavor is desired, add dill and/or chives to taste to noodle mixture.

Serve with meat, poultry, or fish.

CARAMEL PECAN NOODLE DELIGHT

Serves 10 to 12

1 pound uncooked medium egg noodles
1 cup sour cream
  salt to taste
4 eggs, beaten
1¼ cups brown sugar, divided
1 cup creamed cottage cheese
1 teaspoon cinnamon
1 tablespoon vanilla
¼ pound plus 4 tablespoons butter, melted
8 ounces pecan halves

Cook noodles in boiling salted water until tender. Rinse in cold water. Drain. Combine sour cream and salt. Mix eggs with ¼ cup brown sugar, cottage cheese, cinnamon, and vanilla. Stir in sour cream. Fold mixture into noodles.

Pour melted butter into lightly greased 10-cup casserole. Sprinkle remaining 1 cup brown sugar over butter. Press nuts into mixture in attractive pattern, flat side up. Spread noodle mixture evenly over all.

Bake in preheated 350° oven 45 to 50 minutes. Cool on rack 10 minutes. Loosen noodles by running knife around inside edge. Invert onto serving dish. Keep casserole in place over noodles 10 minutes. Remove casserole. Cut noodles in wedges. Serve immediately.

LEMON PASTA WITH CAVIAR

Serves 4

8 ounces uncooked angel hair noodles
¼ pound butter, melted
  juice of 3 lemons, strained
7 ounces large red lumpfish or golden caviar

Cook noodles in boiling salted water 1 minute. Drain well. Combine butter, juice, and caviar. Toss with hot noodles. Serve immediately.

If stronger flavor is desired, add ⅛ teaspoon each oregano, garlic powder, cumin, and pepper to butter mixture.

May also be served as a first course.

SPINACH AND GREEN NOODLE CASSEROLE

Serves 6 to 8

8   ounces uncooked green noodles
2   eggs, beaten
1   large onion, chopped
¼   pound butter
1   cup sour cream
20   ounces frozen chopped spinach, cooked, drained
    salt to taste
    pepper to taste

Cook noodles until "al dente" (slightly underdone). Rinse in cold water and drain well. Combine noodles and eggs. Sauté onion in butter until golden. Add onion with butter, sour cream, and spinach to noodles. Season with salt and pepper. Mix well. Pour into casserole and bake in preheated 350° oven 45 minutes.

SPICY PEANUT NOODLES

Serves 6

A Chinese-inspired picnic treat.

8   ounces very fine noodles, cooked, drained
3   tablespoons olive oil, divided
2   teaspoons creamy peanut butter
2   tablespoons soy sauce
1   tablespoon water
1   tablespoon sugar
¼   cup chopped scallions
½   tablespoon freshly grated ginger
    dash Tabasco
1   small cucumber, peeled, seeded, cut into slivers

Toss noodles with 1 tablespoon oil, coating well. Chill. In large bowl combine remaining ingredients except cucumbers and noodles. Mix well. Blend in noodles. Top with cucumber.

Serve chilled or at room temperature.

APRICOT NOODLES

Serves 16

4 eggs, beaten
¼ cup sugar
1 pint small curd creamed cottage cheese
1 pint sour cream
4 tablespoons butter or margarine, melted, optional
½ teaspoon vanilla
12 ounces apricot preserves
   dash salt
1 pound broad noodles, cooked, drained
   cornflake crumbs

In large bowl combine eggs, sugar, cottage cheese, sour cream, butter if desired, vanilla, preserves, and salt. Mix well. Blend in noodles. Pour into large buttered casserole. Sprinkle crumbs liberally over top. Bake in preheated 350° oven 1¼ hours.

RICE AND NOODLE CASSEROLE

Serves 12 to 14

½ pound butter or margarine
½ pound uncooked very fine noodles
2 cups uncooked instant rice
21½ ounces canned onion soup
21½ ounces canned chicken broth
1 teaspoon soy sauce
1 cup water
8 ounces canned sliced water chestnuts, drained

In large kettle melt butter or margarine. Add noodles. Cook until lightly browned, stirring frequently. Add remaining ingredients. Mix well. Pour mixture into 3-quart casserole. Bake in preheated 350° oven 45 minutes.

BROWN RICE WITH MUSSELS

Serves 4 to 6

1½   pounds cleaned, cooked, shucked mussels or
     3 pounds mussels in shells
1   cup mussel liquid
1   cup chicken broth
1   cup uncooked brown rice
2   tablespoons butter
2   tablespoons olive oil
¾   cup finely chopped onions
2   cloves garlic, minced
⅓   cup chopped parsley
½   cup dry white wine
1¼   teaspoons oregano
    pinch black pepper
    grated Parmesan cheese

If using mussels in shells, steam in large covered kettle in small amount of water 10 to 12 minutes until shells open. Discard any that do not open. Remove mussels from shells. Strain liquid, reserving 1 cup. If using precooked mussels, strain liquid, reserving 1 cup.

Combine mussel liquid with chicken broth. Bring to boil. Add rice. Cover tightly and reduce heat to simmer. Cook 45 minutes until liquid is absorbed and rice reaches desired degree of softness.

While rice is cooking, melt butter in large saucepan. Blend in oil. Add onion and sauté until transparent. Stir in garlic, parsley, wine, oregano, and pepper. Simmer a few minutes, stirring. Combine with cooked rice. Add mussels to rice-onion mixture just before serving and reheat briefly, stirring well. Sprinkle with Parmesan cheese.

Whole clams, fresh or canned, and bottled clam juice may be substituted for mussels and mussel liquid.

OYSTERED WILD RICE

Serves 8 to 10

4   tablespoons butter, divided
1   pound mushrooms, thinly sliced
1   tablespoon olive oil
4   large shallots, finely chopped
3   ribs celery, finely chopped
½   large green pepper, finely diced
½   teaspoon salt
3   cups cooked wild rice (1 cup uncooked)
7   ounces smoked oysters

In large skillet melt 2 tablespoons butter. Sauté mushrooms until liquid evaporates, 5 to 6 minutes. Set mushrooms aside.

Add remaining 2 tablespoons butter and olive oil to skillet. Sauté shallots, celery, and green pepper until tender-crisp. Sprinkle with salt. Combine vegetables with wild rice. Drain oysters on paper towel. Combine with rice mixture. Place in 2-quart casserole. Cover. Bake in preheated 325° oven 20 to 25 minutes.

May be prepared ahead and refrigerated. Bring to room temperature before baking.

Serve with poultry. May be used as stuffing for Cornish hens.

RISOTTO AND MUSHROOMS

Serves 4 to 6

1	cup uncooked rice
2	cups chicken broth
¼	pound pancetta
4-5	tablespoons unsalted butter
1	clove garlic, minced
3	shallots, chopped
1	pound large mushrooms, sliced
	salt to taste
	pepper to taste
¼	teaspoon fresh thyme leaves, chopped

In saucepan cook rice with 1 cup broth, adding more broth as needed as rice cooks and liquid is absorbed. Keep covered. Simmer 20 minutes. Turn off heat and steam a few minutes.

In small skillet, sauté pancetta, turning, until crisp and brown. Drain on paper towel. Reserve 1 or 2 tablespoons of drippings.

In large saucepan melt butter. Add garlic and shallots and cook 2 to 3 minutes. Do not brown. Add mushrooms and sauté until browned, about 10 minutes. Add salt and pepper to taste.

Combine pancetta and a fourth of the mushroom mixture in food processor or blender. Chop finely. Mix rice, pancetta mixture, and remaining mushroom mixture. Adjust seasoning. Add pancetta drippings and/or more butter if desired. Add parsley and thyme. Mix well and serve.

Lean bacon may be substituted for pancetta.

May be prepared early on day of serving and reheated in top of double boiler.

CHINESE FRIED RICE WITH SHRIMP

Serves 10

4 tablespoons vegetable oil, divided
2 eggs, beaten
4½ ounces tiny whole shrimp, shelled
½ cup frozen green peas, thawed
1 whole scallion, chopped
5 cups cooked white rice, cooled
½ teaspoon salt
4 tablespoons soy sauce

In large skillet heat 2 tablespoons oil. Scramble eggs and transfer to plate. In same skillet sauté shrimp, peas, and scallion 1 to 2 minutes or until shrimp turn pink. Remove to plate with eggs. Add remaining 2 tablespoons oil to pan. Blend in rice and cook over medium-low heat 5 minutes, stirring often. Add eggs and shrimp mixture to rice. Stir together over medium heat. Sprinkle with salt and soy sauce. Toss and serve.

Leftover ham, pork, or chicken may be substituted for shrimp.

OVEN CHIPPED POTATOES

Serves 4

A welcome change from time-worn French fries.

6 baking potatoes, unpeeled
4 tablespoons butter or margarine, melted, or enough to coat potatoes
½ cup grated Parmesan cheese, optional
salt to taste

Scrub potatoes. Cut into ¼- to ½-inch slices, discarding ends. Soak slices in ice water at least 45 minutes. Drain well on paper towels.

Dip slices in butter and arrange in single layer on cookie sheet. Sprinkle with cheese if desired. Bake in preheated 350° oven 25 to 35 minutes, turning once, until crisp and browned. Season with salt and serve immediately.

ACCORDION POTATOES

Serves 6

6 medium Idaho potatoes, peeled
⅔ cup melted butter
1½ tablespoons vegetable oil
1¼ teaspoons salt
⅛ teaspoon pepper
⅔ cup grated Cheddar cheese, optional

Thinly slice each potato three-fourths of the way through vertically, leaving bottom of potato whole. Roll potatoes in combined butter and oil. Place potatoes in shallow roasting pan. Pour remaining butter mixture over potatoes. Season with salt and pepper. Bake in preheated 375° oven 2 hours, basting frequently. If desired, sprinkle Cheddar cheese over tops of baked potatoes and bake an additional 5 minutes or until cheese melts.

BACON STUFFED POTATOES

Serves 6

6 8-ounce Idaho potatoes, skins pierced
9 slices bacon
1½ cups chopped onions
⅓ cup sour cream
2 large eggs, lightly beaten
  salt to taste
  pepper to taste

Bake potatoes in preheated 425° oven 1 hour. Fry bacon until very crisp. Reserve bacon fat. Drain bacon and crumble in bowl.

Sauté onions in reserved fat. Remove with slotted spoon and drain on paper towels. Add to bacon. Measure 3 tablespoons of remaining bacon fat. Add to bacon-onion mixture.

When potatoes are baked, cut thin slice from tops. Scoop out interiors, leaving ⅓-inch shell. Rice scooped-out potatoes. Add to bacon-onion mixture. Stir in sour cream, eggs, salt, and pepper. Beat until fluffy. Return mixture to shells, mounding slightly and smoothing with fork tines. When ready to serve reheat in 425° oven 15 to 20 minutes. Watching closely, broil 5 minutes to brown tops.

Serve immediately.

OLD COUNTRY POTATO HASH

Serves 7 to 8

The salami flavor predominates

3   large baking potatoes (1 ¼ pounds), peeled
1   cup fresh whole wheat bread crumbs, divided
3   tablespoons olive oil
½   cup plus 2 tablespoons grated Parmesan cheese, divided
6   ounces mozzarella cheese, in small cubes
2   eggs, lightly beaten
6   ounces salami, in small cubes
3   tablespoons chopped parsley, divided
1   clove garlic, minced
¼   teaspoon thyme
    freshly ground pepper to taste
2   tablespoons vegetable oil
2   tablespoons butter or margarine
    parsley

Cut potatoes in small cubes and soak in cold water. Drain and cook in boiling salted water until barely tender, about 5 minutes. Drain and cool in cold water. Drain again, dry with paper towels, and place in large bowl.

Sauté ½ cup bread crumbs in olive oil, stirring until brown. Combine crumbs, ½ cup Parmesan cheese, mozzarella cheese, eggs, salami, 2 tablespoons parsley, garlic, thyme, and pepper to taste. Mix with potatoes.

In 8-to 9-inch skillet with flameproof handle, heat vegetable oil, coating sides of pan. Press potato mixture firmly into skillet to form an even layer. Cook over medium heat until bottom is browned. Remove pan from heat. Sprinkle potato mixture with remaining ½ cup crumbs, 1 tablespoon parsley, and 2 tablespoons Parmesan cheese. Dot with butter. Place pan under broiler until top is browned. Run knife around edge of pan to loosen potatoes. Garnish with parsley.

Serve hot with eggs at lunch or brunch, or as an accompaniment to grilled meats.

May be prepared ahead. Brown under broiler, cool in pan, and refrigerate. To reheat, place in preheated 350° oven 10 to 15 minutes or until heated through.

SWEET POTATO RING MOLD

Serves 10 to 12   *This mold features a beautiful praline glaze.*

8 large sweet potatoes
¼ pound butter
½ cup light brown sugar
5.3 ounces evaporated milk
1 teaspoon nutmeg
1 egg, lightly beaten
¾ cup raisins
4 tablespoons butter or margarine
¾ cup dark brown sugar
1 cup pecan halves

Cook potatoes until soft, about 20 minutes. Peel and mash. Add butter, light brown sugar, evaporated milk, nutmeg, and egg. Mix well. Fold in raisins.

Grease 6½-cup ring mold generously with butter or margarine. Sprinkle dark brown sugar into mold bottom and halfway up sides, patting sugar into butter or margarine. Press pecan halves flat side up into bottom of mold. Fill with potato mixture. Bake in preheated 350° oven 45 minutes. Cool 5 minutes. Invert onto round serving plate. Serve immediately.

SWEET POTATO CURLS

Serves 4

vegetable shortening or oil
1 pound sweet potatoes, peeled
salt to taste

In deep fryer heat 1½ inches shortening or oil to 380°.

Cut potatoes in 3-inch long, ⅛- to ¼-inch square julienne strips. Fry potato sticks in small batches 45 seconds to 1 minute, or until bubbles in fat subside. Do not let potatoes brown. Remove potatoes and drain on paper towels. Sprinkle with salt. Potatoes will crisp as they cool.

Shortening must be maintained at 380° during frying.

May be made 2 hours ahead and reheated in preheated 300° oven 10 minutes.

See photo page 230.

YAM AND APPLE CASSEROLE

Serves 8

2　pounds yams or sweet potatoes
¼　pound butter, melted, divided
⅓　cup plus 2 tablespoons light brown sugar
¼　teaspoon salt
2　tablespoons dry sherry
½　cup dark corn syrup
1　teaspoon cinnamon
2　Granny Smith apples, peeled, cored, sliced

Cook yams until tender. Peel and cool.

In food processor or blender purée yams, 5 tablespoons butter, sugar, salt, sherry, corn syrup, and cinnamon. Spread half of purée in greased 9-inch baking dish. Layer half of sliced apples over purée. Repeat both layers. Brush top layer of apples with remaining 3 tablespoons butter. Bake in preheated 350° oven 30 minutes.

May be assembled, covered, and refrigerated. To bake, bring to room temperature. Bake in preheated 350° oven 30 minutes.

APRICOT SWEET POTATOES

Serves 6

1½　cups dried apricots
6　medium sweet potatoes, cooked, peeled, thickly sliced
1　cup light brown sugar
3　tablespoons melted butter
2　teaspoons orange juice
1　teaspoon grated orange peel

In medium saucepan combine apricots with water to cover. Simmer until apricots are tender. Cool. Drain apricots, reserving liquid.

In lightly greased 6-cup casserole put a third of the potatoes. Cover with a third of the apricots, then a third of the sugar. Continue procedure two more times.

Combine butter, juice, peel, and ¼ cup reserved apricot liquid. Mix well and pour over potatoes and apricots. Bake in preheated 375° oven 40 minutes. Baste and bake additional 5 minutes.

BREADS

Ravinia Notes

On the warm opening night of 1971,
James Levine, twenty-seven years old,
made his Ravinia début. Substituting at
a week's notice, he rehearsed and conducted the Mahler Second Symphony
without a score. Levine had known and
committed to memory the Mahler score
at the age of twelve.

Other factors contributing heat to that
summer were the appearances of Dionne
Warwick and Janis Joplin, the latter in
one of her last performances. The
NOTEWORTHY staging of the rock
opera, Jesus Christ Superstar, filled the
Pavilion, the lawn, the petunia beds,
and the maple trees to capacity. An un-
precedented, unscheduled second
performance was arranged to accommodate the overflow audience the following
Saturday morning.

ONION TWIST

Serves 10

1 package active dry yeast
¼ cup warm water (105° to 115°)
4 cups flour, divided
¼ cup sugar
1½ teaspoons salt
½ cup hot water
½ cup milk
⅛ pound butter, softened
1 egg

Filling:

⅛ pound butter
1 cup chopped onion
1 tablespoon grated Parmesan cheese
1 tablespoon sesame or poppy seed
1 teaspoon garlic salt
1 teaspoon paprika

In large bowl dissolve yeast in warm water. Add 2 cups flour. Mix well. Add sugar, salt, hot water, milk, butter, and egg. Beat 2 minutes at medium speed. Stir in remaining 2 cups flour. Cover with thin towel. Let stand in warm place until doubled, 45 to 60 minutes. Punch down dough.

Combine all filling ingredients. Mix well. Toss dough on floured surface until no longer sticky. Roll out to 18- by 12-inch rectangle. Spread filling on dough. Cut lengthwise in thirds. With hands roll each dough strip lengthwise, jelly-roll fashion, enclosing filling. Pinch shut and place seam side down. Braid strips. Tuck ends under. Transfer to greased cookie sheet. Bake in preheated 350° oven 35 to 40 minutes. Remove to rack. Cool.

See photo page 232.

HERBED CHALLAH BREAD

Yield: 2 large loaves

2   **packages active dry yeast**
2   **cups warm water (105° to 115°)**
½   **cup plus 1 teaspoon honey, divided**
3   **eggs, lightly beaten**
1¼   **cups vegetable oil**
1½   **cups whole wheat flour**
4   **teaspoons salt**
2-3   **tablespoons minced rosemary**
7-8   **cups unbleached flour**

Combine yeast, warm water, and 1 teaspoon honey. Let stand 5 to 10 minutes. Reserve small amount of beaten eggs for glaze.

Pour remaining eggs into large bowl. Add oil, mixing well. Blend in remaining ½ cup honey. Add egg-oil mixture to yeast mixture. Stir. Add whole wheat flour to yeast mixture ½ cup at a time. Using wooden spoon, blend in salt and rosemary thoroughly. Add unbleached flour, stirring until dough is slightly sticky in consistency. Knead on lightly floured board several minutes until dough is smooth and elastic.

Place dough in oiled bowl, turning so all sides of dough are greased. Cover bowl with clean, damp towel. Set in warm place to rise until doubled, 1 to 1½ hours.

When dough has risen, punch down. Divide in half. Divide each half into 3 equal pieces. Using palms of hands roll each piece into 18-inch rope. Each loaf will require 3 ropes. Join ends of 3 ropes and tuck under. Braid ropes, join ends, and tuck under. Place braided loaves on greased cookie sheets. Cover with damp towel. Set in warm place to rise about 40 minutes. Brush with reserved egg glaze. Bake in preheated 350° oven 1 hour or until golden brown.

See photo page 226.

PEASANT RYE BREAD

Yield: 1 large loaf

1½ cups rye flour
1½ cups unbleached flour
1 tablespoon margarine
2 tablespoons brown sugar
1 tablespoon molasses
2 teaspoons coarse salt
1 teaspoon caraway seed
1 package active dry yeast
¼ cup warm water (105° to 115°)
¾ cup ice water
¼ cup crumbled crisply cooked bacon
1 tablespoon yellow cornmeal
1 egg
⅛ teaspoon salt

In food processor fitted with steel knife combine flours, margarine, sugar, molasses, salt, and caraway seed. Process 5 to 10 seconds with quick on and off pulses.

Dissolve yeast in warm water. Let stand 5 minutes. Add to mixture in processor. Start motor and quickly pour ice water through tube. Process 1 minute. Remove dough from processor, shape into ball, and transfer to glass or china bowl. Cover with damp towel. Place in warm area until dough has doubled, about 1½ hours.

Punch down dough. On floured surface roll out to 9-by 10-inch rectangle. Sprinkle with bacon. Fold both outside edges inward to reach each other in center, halving size of rectangle. Roll again to 9- by 10-inch rectangle. Repeat folding from opposite ends of rectangle. Roll to form 10-inch oval loaf with tapered ends.

Place on greased baking sheet sprinkled with cornmeal. Let rise again until doubled in bulk. Brush with egg beaten with salt. Bake in preheated 400° oven 25 minutes. Cool on rack.

HONEY LEMON BREAD

Yield: 2 loaves

1¼ cups warm water (105° to 115°)
½ cup plus 1½ teaspoons honey, divided
2 tablespoons active dry yeast
1 cup hot water (120° to 130°)
4 tablespoons butter, divided
1 tablespoon salt
  peel of 1 lemon, finely grated
2 tablespoons sesame seed
4 cups whole wheat flour, divided
3 cups white bread flour , divided
  vegetable oil

In small bowl combine 1¼ cups warm water, 1½ teaspoons honey, and yeast. Let stand 5 minutes.

In large bowl combine 1 cup hot water and 3 tablespoons butter. When butter has melted, add remaining ½ cup honey. Stir until dissolved. Add salt, lemon peel, and sesame seed. Stir in yeast mixture. Add 2 cups whole wheat flour. Mix until flour is blended. Add remaining 2 cups whole wheat flour. Mix well. Add 2 cups white bread flour. Continue cutting through mixture until well mixed.

Turn dough onto floured wooden board. Knead in remaining 1 cup white bread flour, or as needed. Dough should be slightly sticky. Let dough rest.

Grease large bowl generously. Roll dough around bowl to coat. Cover with light towel. Let rise in warm place 1 hour, or until doubled. Punch down dough and divide in half. Roll again on board to remove all air bubbles. Shape into 2 loaves.

Place loaves, seam side down, in 2 generously buttered loaf pans. With knife make ¼-inch deep slit down length of each loaf. Cover again and let rise 20 to 30 minutes. Bake in preheated 400° oven 40 minutes. Remove to rack. Rub remaining butter over top of loaves. Remove from pans and cool.

EASIEST FOOD PROCESSOR WHITE BREAD

Yield: 1 loaf

1   package active dry yeast
2   teaspoons sugar
⅓   cup warm water (105° to 115°)
3   cups flour
3   tablespoons plus 1 teaspoon butter, divided
1   teaspoon salt
⅔   cup ice water

Dissolve yeast and sugar in warm water. In food processor fitted with steel knife combine flour, 3 tablespoons butter, and salt. Process 20 seconds. Add yeast mixture. With motor running pour ice water through tube in steady stream. Process until ball forms and spins. Process additional 50 to 60 seconds. Remove and, if desired, knead briefly by hand. Shape into ball.

Place dough in lightly floured 1-gallon plastic bag. Press out air and seal, allowing rising space. May use oiled bowl if desired. Cover with towel or buttered plastic wrap. Let rise until doubled, about 50 to 60 minutes.

Open bag; punch down dough in bag. Remove from bag and shape into loaf. Place in greased bread pan and cover lightly with plastic wrap. Let rise until loaf is 1½-inches above top of pan.

Bake in center of preheated 375° oven 35 minutes or until lightly browned and starting to pull away from sides of pan. Remove bread from pan. Place on rack. Spread lightly with 1 teaspoon softened butter. Cover top with wax paper or light towel. Cool before slicing.

HERBED FRENCH BREAD

Yield: 4 loaves

1   teaspoon garlic salt
1   teaspoon seasoned salt
1   teaspoon basil
1   teaspoon rosemary
½   teaspoon marjoram
¼   pound butter or margarine, softened
4   small loaves French bread

Mix salts and herbs with butter. Slice loaves ¾-inch thick diagonally. Spread butter mixture between slices and over top. Place loaves on cookie sheet. Bake in preheated 425° oven until slightly browned. Serve immediately.

PEANUT BUTTER CHIP-FIG BREAD

Yield: 1 loaf

¼ pound butter
⅔ cup sugar
1 egg
1 teaspoon vanilla
2 cups flour
1 teaspoon baking powder
1 teaspoon baking soda
1 teaspoon cinnamon
½ teaspoon nutmeg
1 cup chunky applesauce
¼ cup milk
1 cup peanut butter chips
1 cup chopped dried figs

Cream butter and sugar until light and fluffy. Add egg and vanilla. Beat well. Combine flour, baking powder, baking soda, cinnamon, and nutmeg. Add alternately with applesauce and milk to creamed mixture, beating well after each addition. Stir in peanut butter chips and figs. Pour into buttered 9- by 5-inch loaf pan.

Bake in preheated 350° oven 1 hour 15 minutes or until inserted tester comes out clean. Cool in pan 10 minutes. Remove. Cool completely. Wrap tightly and store overnight before serving.

BLUEBERRY BREAD

Yield: 1 large loaf or 2 small loaves

1 pint blueberries, rinsed, dried
3 cups flour, divided
4 teaspoons baking powder
½ teaspoon salt
2 eggs
½ cup sugar
½ cup brown sugar
1 cup milk
5⅓ tablespoons butter, melted

Toss blueberries with small amount of flour. Sift remaining flour, add baking powder and salt, and sift together. Combine eggs and sugars. Beat well and add milk and butter. Combine with flour mixture and stir only until blended. Fold in blueberries, taking care not to bruise them. Pour batter into greased 9½- by 5½-inch loaf pan or 2 8- by 4-inch pans. Bake in preheated 350° oven 1 hour or until inserted tester comes out clean. Cool in pan 5 minutes. Transfer to rack.

PUMPKIN BREAD

Yield: 1 loaf

1⅔ cups sifted flour
1½ cups sugar
1 teaspoon baking soda
¼ teaspoon baking powder
¾ teaspoon salt
½ teaspoon nutmeg
½ teaspoon cloves
½ teaspoon cinnamon
¼ teaspoon ground allspice
½ cup vegetable oil
½ cup orange juice
1¼ cups canned pumpkin
2 eggs, lightly beaten

Glaze:
¼ cup confectioners sugar
2 teaspoons warm water
½ teaspoon lemon juice

Sift together flour, sugar, baking soda, baking powder, salt, nutmeg, cloves, cinnamon, and allspice. In large bowl combine oil, juice, pumpkin, and eggs. Mix well. Add dry ingredients, blending thoroughly. Pour into greased 9- by 5-inch loaf pan. Bake in preheated 350° oven 60 to 65 minutes. Cool 15 minutes. Remove from pan and place on rack.

Combine glaze ingredients and spread on loaf. Cool 1 hour before slicing.

GARLIC-CHEESE FRENCH BREAD

Serves 6 to 10

1 large loaf French bread
½ pound Swiss cheese, grated
2-3 cloves garlic, crushed
¼ cup half and half
1-2 tablespoons minced parsley

Slice bread into 1½-inch slices, taking care not to cut all the way through. Combine remaining ingredients. Mix well. Spread between slices. Wrap loaf lightly in foil. Bake in preheated 400° oven 20 to 25 minutes. Serve warm.

RASPBERRY PICNIC BREAD

Yield: 1 loaf

10	ounces frozen raspberries, thawed, undrained
1	tablespoon raspberry jam
2	eggs
¾	cup vegetable oil
1½	cups flour
1	cup sugar
1	teaspoon cinnamon
½	teaspoon baking soda

In food processor or blender purée raspberries and jam. In small bowl combine eggs and oil using wire whisk. Sift flour, sugar, cinnamon, and baking soda into second bowl. Make well in center of dry ingredients. Pour in egg mixture and raspberry purée. Blend well. Pour batter into greased 9- by 5-inch loaf pan. Bake in preheated 350° oven 50 to 60 minutes, or until tester inserted in center comes out clean. Cool in pan 5 minutes. Remove to rack. Cool completely before slicing.

APRICOT NUT BREAD

Yield: 1 loaf

1	cup dried apricots
1	egg, beaten
1	cup sugar
2	tablespoons butter or margarine, melted, cooled
2	cups sifted flour
2	teaspoons baking powder
½	teaspoon baking soda
1	teaspoon salt
¾	cup orange juice
¾	cup chopped pecans

If apricots are very dry, soak in water 45 minutes and drain. Mix egg with sugar and melted butter or margarine. Sift together flour, baking powder, baking soda, and salt. Add alternately with orange juice to egg mixture. Cut apricots into ¼-inch pieces. Add with nuts to batter. Pour into greased 9- by 5-inch loaf pan. Bake in preheated 350° oven 45 minutes or until inserted tester comes out clean. Cool in pan 5 minutes. Remove to rack.

BANANA NUT BREAD

*Yield: 1 large loaf
or 2 small loaves*

¼   **pound plus 3 tablespoons unsalted butter**
1⅓   **cups sugar**
4   **eggs, beaten**
4   **cups sifted flour**
4   **teaspoons baking powder**
½   **teaspoon baking soda**
½   **teaspoon salt**
3   **cups mashed, very ripe bananas**
1   **cup chopped walnuts**

In large bowl cream butter and sugar. Add eggs and mix well. Sift together flour, baking powder, baking soda, and salt. Add alternately with bananas to egg mixture. Fold in nuts. Pour into 1 greased 9- by 5-inch loaf pan or 2 greased 7- by 4-inch loaf pans. Bake in preheated 350° oven 60 to 70 minutes. Cool in pan 5 minutes. Remove to rack.

ZESTY LEMON TEA BREAD

Yield: 2 loaves

½   **pound unsalted butter**
3   **cups sugar, divided**
4   **eggs**
3   **cups flour**
¼   **teaspoon salt**
2   **teaspoons baking powder**
2½   **tablespoons grated lemon rind**
½   **cup milk**
½   **cup half and half**
    juice of 3 large lemons

In large bowl cream butter and 2 cups sugar. Add eggs, 1 at a time, beating after each addition. Sift together flour, salt, and baking powder. Combine with rind. Add to butter mixture, alternating with combined milk and half and half. Mix well.

Pour into 2 lightly greased 9- by 5-inch or 8- by 4-inch bread pans. Bake in preheated 350° oven 50 minutes or until inserted tester comes out clean. While bread is baking, combine 1 cup sugar and lemon juice. Mix until sugar is dissolved. Pierce top of hot baked bread with fork in 10 to 20 places. Loosen sides from pan and spoon juice mixture over top and sides. Cool in pan 30 minutes. Remove from pan and cool on rack.

ITALIAN COFFEE BREAD

Serves 12 to 16

6 eggs
2 cups sugar
4½ cups plus 1 tablespoon flour, divided
2 tablespoons baking powder
1 cup orange juice or milk
1 cup vegetable oil
1 teaspoon grated tangerine, orange, or lemon rind
1 teaspoon anise extract
1 cup golden raisins
1 cup coarsely chopped walnuts
confectioners sugar

In large bowl beat eggs well. Slowly add sugar, mixing thoroughly. Add 2¼ cups flour and baking powder. Mix at low speed. Stir in orange juice and oil. Add 2¼ cups flour. Mix well. Stir in grated rind and anise extract. Coat raisins and nuts with remaining 1 tablespoon flour. Fold into mixture. Pour into lightly greased 10-inch tube pan. Bake in preheated 375° oven 1 hour. While still hot, sprinkle generously with confectioners sugar. Excellent toasted and buttered generously.

CRUNCHY CINNAMON APPLE CAKE

Serves 12

½ pound butter
1 cup sugar
1 cup brown sugar
2 eggs, beaten
1 cup buttermilk
2½ cups flour
1 teaspoon baking powder
1 teaspoon baking soda
1 teaspoon salt
1 teaspoon cinnamon
2 cups peeled, coarsely chopped apples

Topping:
½ cup sugar
½ cup brown sugar
2 tablespoons flour
1 tablespoon butter
1 teaspoon cinnamon
½ cup chopped nuts

In large bowl cream butter and sugars. Add eggs and buttermilk. Sift together flour, baking powder, baking soda, salt, and cinnamon. Add half of dry ingredients to butter mixture. Mix well. Add apples and remaining dry ingredients. Blend well. Pour into greased 9- by 13-inch pan.

Combine all topping ingredients. Mix well. Sprinkle over cake. Stir in slightly. Bake in preheated 350° oven 35 to 40 minutes. Cool in pan on rack.

PRUNE AND APRICOT COFFEE CAKE

Serves 12 to 15

An original recipe from a master baker.

¾   cup dried prunes, pitted
¾   cup dried apricots
      boiling water
2   cups plus 1 tablespoon sifted flour, divided
2   teaspoons baking powder
½   teaspoon salt
⅔   cup packed brown sugar
1   tablespoon cinnamon
¼   pound plus 4 tablespoons butter, softened
¾   cup sugar
2   eggs
¾   cup milk
1   teaspoon vanilla
6   tablespoons melted butter
⅓   cup chopped walnuts

Cover prunes and apricots with boiling water. Let stand 5 minutes. Drain and chop finely. In small bowl sift 2 cups flour with baking powder and salt. In another small bowl combine brown sugar with remaining tablespoon flour and cinnamon. Set aside.

Cream butter until fluffy. Add ¾ cup sugar, mixing well. Add eggs, 1 at a time, beating until light. At low speed add flour mixture to butter mixture alternately with milk and vanilla until just blended. Fold in chopped fruit.

Pour a third of batter into greased 9-inch tube pan. Spread evenly and sprinkle with a third of brown sugar mixture. Drizzle with a third of melted butter. Repeat for 2 additional layers. Top with chopped nuts.

Bake in preheated 350° oven 55 minutes or until inserted tester comes out clean. Cool on rack 10 minutes. Remove cake from pan and return to rack to cool thoroughly.

APRICOT MERINGUE COFFEE CAKE

Serves 10 to 12

1 ounce cake yeast
¼ cup scalded milk, cooled to lukewarm
1 cup plus 3 tablespoons sugar, divided
½ pound butter
2¼ cups flour
 pinch salt
3 eggs, separated
12½ ounces canned apricot filling
3 ounces coarsely chopped pecans
¼ cup raisins, optional
 confectioners sugar

Dissolve yeast in milk. Blend in 3 tablespoons sugar. In large bowl cut butter into flour combined with salt. Stir in yeast mixture. Add egg yolks, 1 at a time, beating well after each addition. Cover loosely and refrigerate overnight. Refrigerate egg whites.

On floured board roll dough thin. Beat egg whites until frothy. Add 1 cup sugar. Beat until stiff peaks form. Spread whites over dough. Layer apricot filling over whites. Sprinkle nuts over all. Sprinkle with raisins if desired.

With hands roll dough jelly-roll fashion to form long, narrow cylinder. Arrange in buttered springform tube pan. Bake in preheated 350° oven 30 minutes. When cool, remove pan sides. Sprinkle with confectioners sugar.

BLUEBERRY BRUNCH CAKE

Serves 8

4 tablespoons butter
¾ cup sugar
1 egg
2 cups flour
2 teaspoons baking powder
½ teaspoon salt
½ cup milk
2 cups blueberries, rinsed, dried

Topping:
½ cup sugar
⅓ cup flour
½ teaspoon cinnamon
4 tablespoons butter

Cream butter and sugar. Add egg. Mix well. Sift together flour, baking powder, and salt. Add to creamed mixture alternately with milk. Stir blueberries into mixture just until blended. Pour batter into greased 8- or 9-inch square pan.

Combine sugar, flour, and cinnamon. Cut butter into mixture. Sprinkle over batter in pan. Bake in preheated 350° oven 45 minutes. Cool in pan.

CAPE COD CRANBERRY COFFEE CAKE

Serves 16

Perfect for Thanksgiving or Christmas breakfast.

Cake:
1/4   pound unsalted butter
1   cup sugar
2   eggs
2   cups flour
1   teaspoon baking powder
1   teaspoon baking soda
1/2   teaspoon salt
1/2   pint sour cream
1   teaspoon almond extract
12   ounces canned whole cranberry sauce, divided
1/2   cup chopped pecans

Topping:
1   cup confectioners sugar
3   tablespoons warm water
1/2   teaspoon almond extract

In large bowl cream butter. Add sugar gradually. Beat in eggs 1 at a time. Sift flour, baking powder, baking soda, and salt together. Add to creamed mixture alternately with sour cream. Add almond extract.

Pour half of batter into greased and floured 9-inch tube pan. Spread half of cranberry sauce over batter. Pour in remaining batter. Top with remaining cranberry sauce. Sprinkle nuts over top. Bake in preheated 350° oven 55 to 60 minutes. Cool on rack 5 minutes. Remove from pan. Combine topping ingredients and drizzle over cake. Cool 1 hour before slicing.

BUNDT COFFEE CAKE

Serves 16

3   tablespoons unsalted butter, softened, or non-stick
       baking spray

½   cup plus 3 tablespoons sugar, divided

1   tablespoon plus ½ teaspoon cinnamon, divided

1-2   tablespoons ground pecans

1   package yellow cake mix

4   eggs

½   pint sour cream

½   cup vegetable oil

3   ounces instant vanilla pudding mix

1   teaspoon vanilla

½   teaspoon almond extract

¼   pound butter

1   tablespoon cocoa

1   cup finely chopped pecans

Spray 10-inch bundt cake pan with baking spray or coat pan with 3 tablespoons softened butter. Combine 3 tablespoons sugar with ½ teaspoon cinnamon and pour into prepared pan. Shake to coat bottom and sides. Sprinkle ground nuts evenly over bottom of pan.

Combine cake mix, eggs, sour cream, oil, pudding mix, vanilla, and almond extract in large bowl. Beat for 7 minutes.

In small saucepan melt butter. Add remaining ½ cup sugar, cocoa, remaining 1 tablespoon cinnamon, and finely chopped nuts. Mix well. Pour half of cake mixture into prepared pan. Add half of butter mixture and cut lightly through batter with knife using care not to reach bottom or sides of pan, to marbelize. Pour in remaining cake mixture. Add remaining butter mixture and marbelize carefully. Bake in preheated 350° oven 55 to 60 minutes. Cool before removing from pan.

DOUBLE BERRY SOUR CREAM COFFEE CAKE

Serves 8 to 10

¼	pound butter, softened
1½	cups sugar, divided
2	eggs
2	cups flour
⅛	teaspoon salt
1	teaspoon baking powder
1	teaspoon baking soda
½	pint sour cream
1	teaspoon vanilla
1	teaspoon cinnamon
2	cups blueberries
12	medium strawberries, quartered*

Cream butter and 1 cup sugar. Add eggs 1 at a time, beating after each addition. Sift together flour, salt, baking powder, and baking soda. Add to creamed mixture. Blend in sour cream and vanilla. Batter will be stiff.

Pour batter into greased 10-inch springform pan. Combine cinnamon with remaining ½ cup sugar. Sprinkle half of cinnamon-sugar mixture over batter. Insert knife and make zigzag movements through batter to marbelize. Smooth top.

Sprinkle blueberries evenly over batter. Arrange half of strawberries decoratively around outer edge, spoke-fashion. Sprinkle remaining strawberries over blueberries. Pat berries gently into batter so they are one-half submerged. Sprinkle with remaining cinnamon-sugar mixture. Bake in preheated 350° oven 50 to 60 minutes, or until lightly browned around edges and tester inserted in center comes out clean. Cool in pan on rack 30 minutes. Remove pan sides and cool completely.

Variation:
Combine 1 pint sour cream, 2 egg yolks, ½ cup sugar, and 1 teaspoon vanilla. Pour over berries. Bake and cool as above.

*If strawberries are used, cake should be consumed within 24 hours. Otherwise, substitute 1 cup blueberries for strawberries.

SWEET FRUITED SCONES

Yield: 1 dozen

2 cups flour
½ teaspoon baking soda
½ teaspoon cream of tartar
pinch salt
3 tablespoons unsalted butter
¼ cup dried currants, sultanas, or raisins
¼ cup sugar
5 ounces sour milk or buttermilk
3 tablespoons milk

Sift together flour, baking soda, cream of tartar, and salt. Combine with butter in food processor or with electric mixer. Blend to consistency of fine bread crumbs. Combine currants and sugar. Add to dough. Gradually stir in sour milk or buttermilk, mixing to light dough.

To bake American style, drop dough by tablespoonsful on ungreased, heated baking sheet. To bake English style, turn dough onto lightly floured surface and knead lightly until smooth. Roll to ½-inch thickness and cut with 2-inch plain or fluted pastry cutter. Reknead trimmings and repeat. Place on ungreased, heated baking sheet.

For both methods brush tops of scones with milk. Bake in top third of preheated 450° oven 10 minutes. Cool on wire rack.

Serve with clotted cream, crème fraîche (page 423), or sweet butter and homemade preserves.

ENGLISH SCONES

Yield:
approximately 10

2　**cups flour**
4　**teaspoons baking powder**
2　**teaspoons sugar**
½　**teaspoon salt**
4　**tablespoons butter (do not use margarine)**
2　**eggs, well beaten**
⅓　**cup half and half**

Sift together flour, baking powder, sugar, and salt. Cut in butter with pastry blender until mixture resembles cornmeal. Add eggs and half and half. Mix well.

Turn dough onto floured board. Knead several times and shape into ball. Press down to ½-inch thickness. Cut into 2½- to 3-inch rounds. Arrange on buttered baking sheet. Bake in preheated 425° oven 12 to 15 minutes or until golden brown. Serve warm.

May be cut in half before serving. Traditionally served with butter, jam, and clotted cream.

MILE HIGH POPOVERS

Yield: 6

The name says everything.

1　**cup flour**
¼　**teaspoon salt**
2　**eggs, lightly beaten**
1　**cup milk**
1　**teaspoon butter, melted**

Sift flour and salt together. Combine eggs with milk and butter. Blend into dry ingredients, stirring until smooth. Pour into 6 well-greased 6-ounce custard cups. Place on cookie sheet in *cold* oven. Set oven to 425° and bake 30 minutes. Lower temperature to 350° and bake 20 to 25 minutes or until puffed and browned. Insert sharp knife into each popover to let steam escape. Serve hot.

May be cooled, frozen, and reheated in preheated 350° oven 5 to 10 minutes.

JULIE'S PRETZELS

Yield: 32

A large, soft pretzel typical of the type served in ball parks and on New York City streetcorners.

2 **cups warm water (105° to 115°)**
2 **packages active dry yeast**
½ **cup sugar**
2 **teaspoons salt**
4 **tablespoons butter, softened**
1 **egg plus 1 yolk, divided**
6-7 **cups unsifted flour, divided**
2 **tablespoons water**
coarse salt

Pour warm water into large warmed bowl. Sprinkle yeast over water. Stir until yeast dissolves. Add sugar, salt, butter, 1 egg, and 3 cups flour. Beat until smooth. Add enough additional flour to make stiff dough. Cover bowl tightly with foil. Refrigerate 2 to 24 hours.

Turn dough onto lightly floured board. Divide into 32 equal pieces. Roll each piece into 20-inch long "pencil". Twist into pretzel shape. Place on lightly greased cookie sheets.

Combine egg yolk and water. Mix well. Brush over pretzels. Sprinkle liberally with coarse salt. Let rise in warm place until doubled, about 30 minutes. Bake in preheated 400° oven 15 minutes. Serve warm.

To freeze, cool completely on rack. Wrap for freezer. To serve, bring to room temperature. Unwrap. Warm in 350° oven 2 to 3 minutes.

PRETZEL BREAD

Yield: 10 small or 6 medium loaves

Follow pretzel directions through refrigeration. Divide dough into 10 equal parts. Roll each into 20- to 22-inch long "pencil". Form into pretzel shape. Place on lightly greased cookie sheet. Brush with combined egg yolk and water. Sprinkle with salt. Let rise in warm place until doubled, about 30 minutes. Bake in preheated 400° oven 15 to 20 minutes, or until nicely browned and hollow-sounding when tapped on bottom. Serve hot or freeze according to pretzel directions.

For larger loaves, divide dough into 6 equal parts. Follow rolling, forming, rising, and baking instructions above, baking 20 to 25 minutes or until hollow-sounding when tapped on bottom.

For variety, form dough into other shapes such as braids, circles, or twisted sticks.

PRETZEL MELBA TOAST

Yield: as desired

leftover pretzel bread
butter, softened

Slice pretzel bread thinly. Butter lightly on 1 side. Place on cookie sheet. Bake in preheated 250° oven 30 to 35 minutes, or until lightly browned and crisp. Cool on rack.

These keep well in sealed plastic bag.

HERBED BREAD STICKS

Yield: 20 sticks

¼   **pound butter**
2   **tablespoons finely minced chives**
½   **teaspoon sweet basil**
¼   **teaspoon summer savory**
1   **loaf soft white bread, thinly sliced**
    salt to taste

Combine butter and herbs. Mix well. Cover and refrigerate 24 hours before using.

Remove crust from bread. Using rolling pin, flatten slices. Spread each slice with butter-herb mixture and roll from corner. Secure with toothpick. Place on cookie sheets. Bake in preheated 350° oven 35 minutes or until lightly browned and crisp. Serve immediately.

Variation:
Slice 1 loaf French bread. Spread slices with herb butter. Reassemble, wrap in foil, and heat through.

PIZZA

Yield: one
14-inch pizza

Crust:

½ package active dry yeast
½ cup warm water (105° to 115°)
1 teaspoon sugar
1¾ cups flour, divided
½ teaspoon salt
½ tablespoon vegetable oil

Sauce:

½ pound pork sausage
16 ounces tomato sauce
¼ teaspoon salt or to taste
¼ teaspoon pepper or to taste
¼ teaspoon oregano or to taste
¼ teaspoon anise seed or to taste
¼ teaspoon garlic powder or to taste
¼ teaspoon fennel seed or to taste
dash red pepper

Topping:

vegetables as desired:
scallions, thinly sliced
green peppers, sliced
mushrooms, sliced
½ pound mozzarella cheese, grated

Dissolve yeast in warm water. Stir in sugar. Let stand 5 minutes. Add ¾ cup flour. Mix well. Stir in salt, oil, and remaining 1 cup flour. Knead until smooth. Place dough in buttered bowl, cover, set in warm place, and let rise approximately 45 minutes.

Brown sausage and drain well. Add remaining sauce ingredients. Simmer 30 minutes. Cool and refrigerate.

On floured board roll out dough. Fit dough into buttered pizza pan. Spread chilled sauce over dough. Sprinkle vegetables over sauce and cheese over vegetables. Bake in preheated 525° oven 5 minutes. Reduce heat to 475°. Bake 5 to 10 minutes or until cheese bubbles and crust browns. Serve immediately.

BALTIC BACON CRESCENTS

Yield: 24

A Latvian Easter breakfast tradition.

1   pound bacon, diced
1   cup chopped onion
½   teaspoon cracked pepper
1   pound frozen bread dough, thawed
1   egg, beaten, optional
    poppy seed, optional
    softened butter, optional

Sauté bacon and onion 2 to 3 minutes or until onion is soft but not browned. Drain well. Transfer to bowl. Add pepper and mix well.

Slice dough into 8 equal pieces, then each slice into thirds. Mold each piece into a 3-inch round. Mound 1 tablespoon bacon mixture along center. Fold in half. Pinch edges together. Form into crescent shape. Place on lightly greased baking sheets. Bake in preheated 350° oven 15 minutes or until lightly browned. Serve warm.

If desired, glaze with beaten egg and sprinkle with poppy seeds before baking. Or, glaze top lightly with softened butter after baking.

SPOON BREAD SOUFFLÉ

Serves 4

Not the customary Southern spoon bread but an elegant soufflé version.

1   pint milk
¾   cup white cornmeal
1   tablespoon butter
1   teaspoon salt
4   eggs, separated

In large saucepan warm milk over low heat. Add cornmeal, stirring until thickened. Remove from heat. Add butter and salt. Stir in beaten egg yolks. Beat egg whites until stiff peaks form. Fold into mixture. Pour into buttered 1½-quart baking dish. Bake in preheated 350° oven 40 minutes. Serve immediately with butter on the side.

Serve for breakfast, brunch, or supper.

SOUTHERN CORNMEAL CUSTARD BREAD

Serves 6 to 8

8½   ounces cornmeal muffin mix
½   teaspoon salt
½   teaspoon baking soda
1   egg, well beaten
1   cup milk, divided
½   cup sour cream
     maple syrup, optional

In bowl combine cornmeal mix, salt, and baking soda. Add egg, ½ cup milk, and sour cream. Stir just until dry ingredients are moistened. Pour into greased 9-inch pie pan. Pour remaining ½ cup milk over mixture. Do not stir. Bake in preheated 400° oven 20 minutes. Serve immediately.

Top with maple sryup if desired.

DELICATE CINNAMON ROLLS

Yield: 4 dozen

½   cup warm water (105° to 115°)
2   envelopes active dry yeast
1¾   cups plus 1 teaspoon sugar, divided
1½   cups milk
6   tablespoons butter
2   teaspoons salt
6   cups flour, divided
2   eggs, lightly beaten
¼   pound butter, melted
1½   teaspoons cinnamon

In small bowl combine warm water, yeast, and 1 teaspoon sugar. Set aside.

In small saucepan combine milk, butter, and salt. Bring to boil, stirring occasionally. Pour into large bowl. Add ¼ cup sugar and 4 cups flour, 1 cup at a time, mixing well after each addition. Add eggs. Knead with dough hook attachment of electric mixer on low speed 3 to 4 minutes or by hand 10 to 12 minutes. When dough is lukewarm add yeast mixture and remaining flour. Mix on medium speed with mixer or by hand until well combined, about 5 minutes.

Divide dough in half. Roll each half into ¼-inch thick rectangle. Brush with melted butter. Combine remaining 1½ cups sugar with cinnamon. Sprinkle over melted butter. Roll rectangles tightly, ending with seam side down. Slice into ½-inch rounds. Put in greased muffin tins. Cover with light towel. Set in warm place until doubled. Bake in preheated 400° oven 10 to 12 minutes or until golden brown. Remove to rack. Serve warm.

CINNAMON STICKS

Serves 15 to 20

1   loaf firm white bread, preferably home-made, unsliced
¼   pound unsalted butter, melted
½   cup brown sugar
¼   cup sugar
2   tablespoons confectioners sugar
1   teaspoon cinnamon

Remove bread crust. Slice loaf into sticks 1-inch square by 4-inches long. Dip sticks into butter. Roll in mixture of sugars and cinnamon. Place on cookie sheets or foil. Bake in preheated 350° oven 15 minutes. Serve warm.

Prepare as close to serving time as possible.

COFFEE-BREAK TREAT

Serves 8

3   ounces cream cheese
¼   pound plus 4 tablespoons unsalted butter, divided
1   cup flour
     melted butter, divided
1½   teaspoons cinnamon, divided
½   cup brown sugar
1   tablespoon maple syrup
½   cup chopped pecans
     raisins, optional
2   tablespoons sugar

Cream cheese and ¼ pound butter well. Stir in flour, mixing just until well blended. Flatten dough into 1-inch thick round disk. Wrap in wax paper. Refrigerate at least 2 hours.

Roll dough into 8- by 16- by ⅛-inch rectangle. Brush liberally with melted butter. Sprinkle with ½ teaspoon cinnamon.

In saucepan combine remaining 4 tablespoons butter, brown sugar, and maple syrup. Bring to boil, stirring constantly. Reduce heat. Add nuts and ½ teaspoon cinnamon and boil 3 minutes or until mixture thickens.

Spread filling on dough, leaving a 2-inch border. Add raisins if desired. Roll dough widthwise ending with seam side down. Brush with more melted butter. Sprinkle with mixture of ½ teaspoon cinnamon and 2 tablespoons sugar. Cut into 1½-inch slices. Place on greased cookie sheets seam side down. Bake in preheated 350° oven 18 to 20 minutes. Cool on rack.

See photo page 236.

STONE TOASTS

Yield: 36 to 40

Wonderful with patés, soups, and salads.

1   loaf very thin sliced **Pepperidge Farm** white bread, frozen
¾   pound unsalted butter, softened
     finely grated Parmesan cheese

Spread each bread slice with softened butter. Sprinkle heavily with grated Parmesan cheese. Slice diagonally to create 2 triangles. Place on cookie sheets. Bake in preheated 250° oven 1 hour or until dry. Cool on rack. Store in airtight container.

ORANGE STICKY BUNS

*Yield: 8 large
16 miniature*

A quick no-knead recipe

¼   cup plus 2 tablespoons sugar, divided
2   tablespoons orange juice
1   tablespoon corn syrup
2   teaspoons grated orange rind, divided
1   8-ounce can crescent roll dough
4   teaspoons butter, melted
⅛   teaspoon cinnamon

Grease 8 large or 16 miniature tins. Combine ¼ cup sugar, orange juice, corn syrup, and 1 teaspoon grated orange rind. Mix well. Spoon 1 tablespoon of mixture into each tin, or 1½ teaspoons if using miniatures.

Separate crescent dough into rectangles and seal perforations. Spread with melted butter. Combine remaining 2 tablespoons sugar, cinnamon, and remaining 1 teaspoon grated orange rind. Mix well. Sprinkle over dough. Starting at shorter side, roll dough. Slice into 8 to 16 slices, depending on tins used. Place in tins cut side down.

Bake in preheated 375° oven 18 to 23 minutes. Invert immediately. Serve warm.

BECKER'S SCHNECKEN

Yield: 24
large rolls

3   tablespoons warm water (105° to 115°)
5   tablespoons warm milk (105° to 115°), divided
1   rounded tablespoon active dry yeast
2   eggs, beaten
¼   cup sugar
3   cups flour
¼   pound plus 4 tablespoons butter, divided
¾   teaspoon salt
    pinch cardamom
¼   teaspoon grated lemon peel
1   cup light brown sugar or as needed
24 whole pecans
¾   cup finely chopped pecans
    cinnamon
    raisins, optional

In small bowl combine warm water and 2 tablespoons milk. Add yeast and let stand 5 minutes. Add eggs and sugar. Mix well.

In food processor fitted with steel knife combine flour, 4 tablespoons butter, salt, cardamom, and lemon peel. Process until mixed, about 10 seconds. With motor on, slowly drizzle yeast mixture through feed tube. Add enough additional milk so dough forms ball and cleans side of bowl. Process until ball circles bowl about 25 times. Dough should be sticky.

Transfer dough to lightly buttered bowl, rolling dough to coat completely with butter. Cover with plastic wrap and let rise until doubled, about 1 hour.

Butter muffin tins generously. Spoon 1 teaspoon brown sugar in each followed by 1 whole pecan placed upside down.

Punch down dough. Divide in half. On well-floured surface roll half dough into thin rectangle. Spread rectangle generously with 4 tablespoons softened butter. Sprinkle with half chopped pecans and ¼ cup brown sugar. Top with cinnamon and raisins if desired. Roll up jelly roll fashion. Cut into 1-inch slices. Place 1 slice in each muffin tin cut side down. Repeat procedure with remaining half of dough.

Let schnecken rise again in warm place until doubled, about 1 hour. Bake in preheated 350° oven about 20 minutes or until golden. Remove muffin tins to rack and cool 1 minute. Place wax paper across pan, tucking under ends to secure. Invert quickly and carefully onto rack. Slowly and carefully remove pan, leaving schnecken nut side up.

SPECIAL ORANGE MUFFINS

Yield: 15

¼ pound unsalted butter
1 cup sugar
2 eggs
1 teaspoon baking soda
1 cup buttermilk
2 cups flour
¼ teaspoon salt
½ cup dark raisins
½ cup golden raisins
¼ cup chopped pecans
    rind of 1 large orange, cut into very thin strips
    juice of 1 large orange
¼ cup superfine sugar

In large bowl combine butter and sugar. Beat until fluffy. Add eggs 1 at a time, beating after each addition. Combine baking soda and buttermilk. Combine flour and salt. Add buttermilk mixture to egg mixture in thirds, alternating with flour mixture. Stir together until just combined. Do not beat.

In food processor or blender combine raisins, nuts, and rind. Process just until finely chopped. Stir into batter lightly. Pour into greased muffin tins to within ½-inch of top. Bake in preheated 400° oven 15 minutes or until golden brown.

Cool in pan several minutes. Remove muffins to rack placed over wax paper. Brush tops with orange juice. Sprinkle with sugar.

MOLASSES BRAN MUFFINS

Yield: 1 dozen

1 cup flour
2 teaspoons baking powder
1 teaspoon baking soda
¾ cup buttermilk
½ cup molasses
1½ cups natural bran
1 egg
½ cup raisins
2 tablespoons melted butter

Combine all ingredients except butter. Mix well. Let stand 2 minutes. Stir in butter. Fill 12 greased muffin tins two-thirds full. Bake in preheated 400° oven 15 minutes. Remove from pan. Cool on rack.

STRAWBERRY MUFFINS

Yield: 15 large

¼   pound unsalted butter
1½ cups sugar, divided
2   eggs
2   cups flour
2   teaspoons baking powder
    salt to taste
½   cup half and half or whipping cream
1   teaspoon vanilla
18-20 medium to large strawberries, hulled, chopped

Cream butter and 1¼ cups sugar until light and fluffy. Add eggs 1 at a time. Blend well but do not overbeat. Sift together flour, baking powder, and salt. Add alternately with cream to butter mixture. Add vanilla. Fold in strawberries.

Fill greased muffin tins nearly full with batter. Sprinkle with remaining ¼ cup sugar. Bake in preheated 375° oven 30 minutes or until lightly browned. Cool on rack.

MACADAMIA NUT MUFFINS

Yield: 12

5⅓ tablespoons butter, melted, cooled slightly
1   egg, beaten
½   cup milk
1½ cups flour, sifted
½   cup sugar
2   teaspoons baking powder
½   teaspoon salt
½-¾ cup coarsely chopped macadamia nuts

Topping:
4   tablespoons butter
½   cup sugar

In a small bowl combine butter, egg, and milk. Mix well. In a medium bowl sift together flour, sugar, baking powder, and salt. Add nuts. Pour liquid mixture over dry ingredients. Stir only until dry ingredients are moistened. Batter will be lumpy. Spoon into 12 well-greased muffin tins, filling cups ⅔ full. Bake in preheated 400° oven 20 minutes.

While muffins bake combine butter and sugar. Spoon over muffins immediately after removing from oven. Cool muffins on rack.

BLUEBERRY MUFFINS RITZ-CARLTON

Yield: 18

3½ cups sifted flour
2 tablespoons baking powder
1¼ cups sugar, divided
pinch salt
5 eggs, lightly beaten
½ cup milk
4-5 cups fresh or frozen blueberries
5 ounces unsalted butter, melted, cooled

Heat oven to 425°. Sift together flour, baking powder, ¾ cup sugar, and salt. Blend in eggs, milk, and melted butter. Do not overmix. Stir in berries carefully.

Grease top surfaces of large muffin tins. Insert paper baking cups. Spoon batter to top of cups. Sprinkle generously with remaining ½ cup sugar. Reduce oven temperature to 400°. Place muffin tins on center rack of oven. Bake 35 minutes or until muffins are golden brown. Remove from tins and cool on rack.

APPLE BRAN MUFFINS

Yield: 2 dozen

1 cup 100% bran
1 cup boiling water
½ cup vegetable oil or shortening
1½ cups sugar
2 eggs, beaten
2½ cups flour
2½ teaspoons baking soda
2 cups buttermilk
2 cups All Bran
½ teaspoon salt
1 Granny Smith apple, peeled, cored, coarsely chopped

Mix 100% bran with boiling water. In large bowl combine oil, sugar, eggs, flour, baking soda, and buttermilk. Add bran mixture. Mix well. Fold in All Bran, salt, and apple.

Pour into 24 greased muffin tins. Bake in preheated 400° oven 15 minutes.

Variation:
For *Apple Oatmeal Muffins* substitute 2 cups uncooked rolled oats for 2 cups All Bran.

DESSERTS

Ravinia Notes

A highlight of the 1982 season was Shostakovich Times Three—the composer's music conducted by his son Maxim, with his namesake grandson Dmitri as piano soloist.

Ravinia "spent the day with J. S. Bach" at a three-part Bach marathon honoring the composer's 300th. birthday. The Festival presented Pinchas Zukerman, who not only conducted the Saint Paul Chamber Orchestra but also thrilled the audience with solo violin and viola performances.

In addition to honoring the seventeenth century composer, the 1985 anniversary season brought to the pavilion stage Kiri Tekanawa in her Ravinia debut.

FESTIVAL OF FRUIT TART

Serves 12 to 16

10 ounces packaged **refrigerated sugar cookie dough,**
     in ¼-inch slices

2 tablespoons unflavored gelatin

2 cups milk, divided

6 ounces cream cheese, in pieces (light may be used)

⅓ cup sugar

6 tablespoons apricot brandy or brandy, divided,
     or 6 tablespoons lemon or orange juice, divided

1 teaspoon vanilla

1 cup ice cubes

1 egg white, beaten

4-5 cups assorted sliced fresh fruit

½ cup apricot preserves

Arrange cookie dough slices to cover bottom of greased 15½- by 10½-inch jelly roll pan. Pat gently to seal slices together and to cover pan sides with dough. Bake in preheated 350° oven 12 minutes or until browned. Cool.

While crust is baking, sprinkle gelatin over ½ cup cold milk in food processor or blender. Let stand until gelatin is moistened. Add 1 cup very hot milk. Process at low speed 2 minutes. Add ½ cup cold milk, cream cheese, sugar, 3 tablespoons brandy or juice, and vanilla. Process at high speed, adding ice cubes 1 at a time. Continue until ice is melted. Let stand until mixture starts to thicken, about 10 minutes.

Paint crust with egg white. Spread gelatin mixture evenly over prepared crust. Arrange fruit on top (strawberries, peaches, bananas, oranges, grapes, cherries, blueberries, kiwi, or whatever fresh fruit is available). In small saucepan heat preserves with remaining brandy or juice. Carefully brush mixture over fruit. Chill tart until firm, at least 2 hours.

APPLE KUCHEN

Serves 8

A particularly delectable apple tart.

¼ pound butter
1 cup presifted flour
¼ teaspoon baking powder
1 tablespoon sugar
5 medium to large Granny Smith apples, peeled, cored, sliced
½ teaspoon cinnamon

Streusel topping:
¾ cup sugar
¼ cup flour
4 tablespoons butter

Combine butter, flour, baking powder, and sugar. Mix until dough forms a ball. Press dough onto bottom and sides of 8-inch tart pan with removable sides. Arrange apples on crust in overlapping circles, until crust is very full.

Combine topping ingredients. Mix well. Spoon generously over apples. Sprinkle with cinnamon. Bake in preheated 350° oven 1 hour or until juices bubble. Cool. Remove pan sides. Best served warm.

TARTE AUX POMMES STRASBOURG

Serves 6 to 8

1   10-inch unbaked pie shell
7-8   medium Granny Smith apples, peeled, cored, thinly sliced
1¼   cups sugar, divided
½   teaspoon cinnamon
4   egg yolks
½   cup whipping cream

Line bottom and sides of 10-inch fluted, removable rim tart pan with pie dough. Arrange apples attractively over dough, mounding slightly in center. Sprinkle with combined ¾ cup sugar and cinnamon. Bake in preheated 350° oven 30 minutes. If crust edges appear brown, cover with foil.

Combine yolks, remaining ½ cup sugar, and cream. Mix well. Pour over apples. Bake 10 to 15 minutes or until topping is golden brown. Serve warm or cold.

ALMOND TART

Serves 6 to 8

Crust:
1 cup flour
1 tablespoon sugar
¼ pound unsalted butter, chilled
1 tablespoon water
½ teaspoon vanilla
¼ teaspoon almond extract

Pastry filling:
½ cup packed, finely ground almonds
1 cup confectioners sugar
1 egg plus 1 egg white
2 tablespoons unsalted butter, melted
1 teaspoon grated lemon rind

Almond filling:
1¼ cups sliced blanched almonds
1 cup superfine sugar
1 cup whipping cream
2 teaspoons Grand Marnier
¼ teaspoon almond extract
    pinch salt

Combine flour, sugar, and butter. Mix until consistency of coarse meal. Add water, vanilla, and almond extract, stirring until liquid is absorbed. Press evenly into 9-inch flan or pie pan. Chill 45 to 60 minutes. Cover dough with wax paper. Layer raw rice or other pie weight over paper. Bake in preheated 400° oven 6 minutes. Remove rice and paper. Cool slightly.

In food processor or blender combine ground almonds, sugar, egg, and egg white. Blend until mixture forms a paste. Add butter and lemon rind. Spread over cooled crust. Bake at 400° 5 minutes. Remove. Reduce heat to 375°.

Combine blanched almonds, sugar, cream, Grand Marnier, almond extract, and salt. Let stand 20 minutes. Mix well and pour over pastry filling in crust. Bake at 375° 35 to 45 minutes. Cool and serve at room temperature.

PLUM KUCHEN

Serves 8

¼   **pound plus 4 tablespoons butter, divided**
1¼   **cups sifted flour, divided**
    pinch baking powder
¾   **cup plus 1 tablespoon sugar, divided**
1   **tablespoon whipping cream**
20-24   **blue Italian plums, pitted, quartered**
½   **teaspoon cinnamon**

Combine ¼ pound butter, 1 cup flour, baking powder, 1 tablespoon sugar, and cream. Mix well. Spread mixture on bottom and sides of 9-inch tart pan with removable sides.

Starting at edge of pan, place plum quarters evenly in overlapping circles, covering entire crust. Using 2 knives mix together remaining ¾ cup sugar, ¼ cup flour, 4 tablespoons butter, and cinnamon. Mixture should resemble small peas. Spinkle over plums. Bake in preheated 350° oven 1 hour 20 minutes.

To freeze kuchen, bake 1 hour only. Cool. Freeze. Remove directly from freezer to preheated 350° oven. Bake 30 minutes or until filling bubbles.

If desired, buy extra plums in season. Clean, pit, halve, and freeze. Prepare kuchen using frozen plums.

See photo page 235.

CHEESE FILLED PASTRY SLICES

Yield: 8 large slices
16 small slices

A mock cheese strudel.

16   **ounces cream cheese, softened**
¾   **cup sugar**
1   **teaspoon vanilla**
1   **teaspoon lemon juice**
1   **egg, separated**
2   **8-ounce packages crescent roll dough**
    confectioners sugar

continued

In medium bowl combine cream cheese, sugar, vanilla, juice, and egg yolk. Mix until smooth.

With rolling pin, flatten 1 package of rolls, closing up seams. Cover bottom of greased 9- by 13-inch baking dish with rolled pastry. Pour in cream cheese mixture. Roll out remaining dough on wax paper to 9 by 13 inches. Invert pastry over cheese mixture. Remove wax paper.

Beat egg white until frothy. Spread over top crust. Bake in preheated 350° oven 30 minutes or until golden brown. Cool. Sprinkle with confectioners sugar.

To serve, cut in slices or squares.

CHOCOLATE WHISKEY TORTE

Serves 12

¼   **cup raisins**
¼   **cup bourbon**
4   **ounces semi-sweet chocolate**
2   **ounces sweet chocolate**
3   **tablespoons water**
1   **ounce unsweetened chocolate**
¼   **pound butter**
3   **eggs, separated**
⅔   **cup sugar**
¼   **cup flour**
⅔   **cup ground almonds**
    pinch salt
    confectioners sugar, optional

Soak raisins in bourbon. In top of double boiler melt all chocolate with water. Add butter. Blend into chocolate and remove from heat.

Beat egg yolks with sugar until mixture is pale creamy yellow. Combine with chocolate. Mix flour with almonds. Stir into chocolate mixture. Blend in raisins and bourbon. Beat egg whites with salt until stiff but not dry. Fold whites into chocolate mixture.

Butter 9-inch cake pan, line with wax paper, then butter and flour. Shake off excess flour. Pour batter into pan. Bake in preheated 375° oven 20 minutes or until inserted toothpick comes out clean. Cool 10 minutes; unmold onto serving platter. Sprinkle with confectioners sugar if desired.

CHOCOLATE TORTE WITH RASPBERRY GLAZE

Serves 8 to 10

A spectacular dessert, rich in chocolate, gilded with raspberries.

Torte:
1¼ cups graham cracker crumbs
1   cup plus 1 tablespoon sugar, divided
4   tablespoons butter, melted
12 ounces semi-sweet chocolate
½   cup hot coffee
16 ounces cream cheese, softened
4   eggs
2   tablespoons vanilla

Raspberry glaze:
2   cups raspberries, divided
2   cups sugar
1   tablespoon lemon juice

Butter sides of 10-inch springform pan. Combine graham cracker crumbs, 1 tablespoon sugar, and butter. Mix well. Press onto bottom of springform.

In top of double boiler melt chocolate with coffee. Beat cream cheese until light and fluffy. Gradually beat in 1 cup sugar. Add eggs 1 at a time, beating well after each addition. Stir in vanilla. Add chocolate mixture. Mix just until blended.

Pour into springform. Bake in preheated 325°oven 55 minutes. Turn off heat, open oven door, and let torte cool 2 to 3 hours in oven.

While torte cools combine 1½ cups raspberries, sugar, and lemon juice in heavy saucepan. Cook over medium heat. As mixture heats, mash berries. Bring to boil, stirring frequently. Reduce heat and simmer until jelly coats spoon, about 20 minutes. Remove from heat. Skim foam from top. Strain mixture, which should measure approximately 1 cup. Cool. Spread over cooled torte.

Torte should be baked, glazed, and refrigerated 1 day before serving. On day of serving top with remaining berries.

See photo page 235.

CHOCOLATE APRICOT TORTE

Serves 10

2   ounces unsweetened chocolate
3   tablespoons vegetable oil
¼   teaspoon salt
½   cup strong coffee
1   cup sugar
1   egg
¼   cup buttermilk
1   teaspoon baking soda
1   teaspoon vanilla
1   cup flour
½   cup apricot preserves
2   tablespoons brandy

Frosting:
5   ounces semi-sweet baking chocolate
4   tablespoons margarine

In top of double boiler combine unsweetened chocolate, oil, salt, and coffee. Cook over simmering water, stirring until blended. Transfer to large bowl. Add sugar, egg, buttermilk, baking soda, and vanilla. Beat at medium speed until well blended. Add flour and continue beating 5 minutes. Pour into heavily greased and lightly floured 8-inch round cake pan.

Bake in preheated 350° oven 30 minutes or until cake begins to pull from sides of pan. Cool on rack. Remove from pan.

Cut cake in half horizontally to create 2 layers. Combine apricot preserves and brandy. Blend well and spread over bottom layer. Set top layer in place.

Combine semi-sweet chocolate and margarine in top of double boiler over simmering water. When melted stir well until mixture has shiny glaze. If it does not, add more margarine. Slowly pour frosting onto center of torte so it flows over entire surface. Using spatula, guide frosting over sides of torte to coat smoothly. Cool 30 minutes. Gently slide torte onto serving platter using wide spatula.

Cooled unfrosted torte may be wrapped and frozen for up to 1 week.

CHOCOLATE MOUSSE TORTE

Serves 8 to 10

Crust:
1½   cups chocolate wafer crumbs
6   tablespoons butter, melted

Filling:
12   ounces chocolate chips
5   egg yolks
3   tablespoons brandy
1½   cups whipping cream

Combine crumbs and butter. Mix well. Line bottom and sides of 9-inch springform pan with mixture. Chill.

In food processor or blender combine chips, yolks, and brandy. Bring whipping cream just to boil. With motor running slowly add cream to chips mixture. Blend 1 minute. Pour into crust. Chill at least 6 hours.

Variation:
Lemon or orange peel may be added to filling. Mint chocolate chips may be substituted for chocolate chips. Mint liqueur may be substituted for brandy.

FILBERT TORTE

Serves 12

12   eggs, separated
2   cups sugar
¼   cup flour
1   teaspoon grated lemon peel
1½   teaspoons vanilla
½   teaspoon salt
¼   teaspoon cinnamon
2   tablespoons lemon juice
3½   cups ground filberts

In large bowl combine egg yolks and sugar. Beat well. Gradually add all other ingredients except egg whites. Mix well. Beat egg whites until stiff peaks form. Fold into batter. Line bottom of removable bottom tube pan with wax paper. Pour batter into pan. Bake in preheated 325° oven 1 hour 10 minutes. Invert pan over rack and cool.

Torte may be iced with classic butter cream frosting or served plain with sifted confectioners sugar.

Prepare 1 or 2 days ahead of time for added firmness. Freezes well.

CINNAMON CHOCOLATE TORTE

Serves 12

1 egg
1 cup sugar
¼ pound plus 4 tablespoons butter or margarine, softened
1 tablespoon cinnamon
1⅓ cups flour, divided
2 cups whipping cream
⅓ cup cocoa
1 ounce semi-sweet chocolate, grated

Prepare nine 8-inch diameter circles of wax paper.

In large bowl, combine egg, sugar, butter, cinnamon, and 1 cup flour. Beat slowly to combine. Increase speed to medium and beat 3 minutes or until mixture is light and fluffy. Stir in remaining ⅓ cup flour. Dough will be soft.

With damp cloth moisten cookie sheets. Arrange wax paper circles on sheets. Place ¼ cup dough on center of each circle. With heel of hand, push from center to perimeter, until thin layer covers each circle.

Bake in preheated 375° oven 6 to 7 minutes or until lightly browned around edges.

Remove rounds, still on wax paper, to wire racks to cool. When cool, stack on flat plate. Do not remove wax paper. Cover with plastic wrap and store in cool dry place up to 3 days.

Assemble early on day of serving. Beat whipping cream with cocoa until soft peaks form. Carefully peel wax paper from 1 round. Place on flat plate. Cover with scant ½ cup whipped cream mixture. Repeat procedure, layering rounds with cream, ending with layer of whipped cream.

Refrigerate 2 to 3 hours after assembling to soften layers. Just before serving sprinkle with grated chocolate.

TURTLE TORTE

Serves 16

Crust:

¼   pound butter, softened
¼   cup sifted confectioners sugar
1   cup flour
2   ounces semi-sweet chocolate, melted

Filling:

6   cups pecan halves
3   cups sugar
⅓   cup light corn syrup
½   pound butter
1   cup whipping cream
3   ounces semi-sweet chocolate, melted

With electric mixer cream butter and sugar. At low speed, gradually add flour. Mix until just blended. Pat dough into bottom of greased 9-inch springform pan. Pierce dough with fork. Bake in preheated 350° oven 10 minutes. Reduce heat to 300° and bake until golden, about 20 to 25 minutes. Cool. Spread thin layer of melted chocolate over crust.

Toast pecans in single layer on cookie sheet in 325° oven 15 minutes or until crisp and brown. Watch carefully. Nuts burn easily.

In heavy pan caramelize sugar over low to moderate heat, stirring constantly until sugar is completely liquid with no lumps. Stir in corn syrup, butter, and cream. Cook over medium heat, stirring constantly, to 220° on candy thermometer, just shy of soft ball stage. Stir in pecans and immediately pour over prepared crust, pressing flat. Refrigerate until cold.

Drizzle melted chocolate over top of torte, allowing some to run down sides. Bring to room temperature. Cut in thin wedges with sharp knife.

SOUTHERN PECAN TORTE

Serves 8 to 10

This unusual pre-Civil War recipe is divinely rich.

Layers:
4 eggs
1 pound light brown sugar
1 cup flour
1½ teaspoons baking powder
½ pound pecan halves
1 teaspoon vanilla

Filling:
1 tablespoon butter
1 tablespoon flour
1 cup whipping cream
2 egg yolks, beaten
5 tablespoons confectioners sugar
5 ounces almonds, chopped

Frosting:
1 cup whipping cream, stiffly whipped
¼ pound pecan halves

Combine eggs and sugar. Beat well until light in color. Sift flour and baking powder together. Add to egg mixture. Stir in ½ pound pecans and vanilla. Pour into 2 well-greased 8-inch cake pans. Bake in preheated 375° oven 20 to 25 minutes. Cool.

Melt butter in saucepan. Add flour and mix well, eliminating lumps. Add cream to yolks. Mix well. Slowly blend with butter-flour mixture. Cook over low heat, stirring constantly until thickened. Remove from heat. Stir in confectioners sugar and almonds. Assemble cake with filling between layers.

Frost top and sides of cake with whipped cream. Decorate with pecans. Refrigerate until 1 hour before serving.

Cake may be made ahead and frozen. Filling and frosting should be prepared day of serving.

FRUIT TORTE

Serves 8 to 10

1 cup plus 2 tablespoons sugar, divided
¼ pound butter or margarine
1 cup sifted flour
1 teaspoon baking powder
  pinch salt
2 eggs
  Choice of 1 or combination of fruits in equivalent amounts:

  1 pint blueberries
  24 Italian plums, halved, pitted, skin side up
  2 cups peeled, cored, sliced Granny Smith apples
  2 cups peeled, pitted, sliced peaches
  2 cups soaked dried apricots
  2 cups frozen or canned fruits of choice, thawed, drained, rinsed

1 teaspoon cinnamon
1 tablespoon lemon juice
1 teaspoon grated lemon rind
1 pint whipping cream, whipped, or 1 quart vanilla ice cream

Cream 1 cup sugar and butter. Add flour, baking powder, salt, and eggs.
Mix well. Transfer to buttered 10-inch springform pan. Cover top with 1 or
combination of listed fruits. Combine 2 tablespoons sugar with cinnamon.
Sprinkle over fruit followed by lemon juice and rind. If fruit appears too juicy,
add 2 tablespoons flour to sugar-cinnamon mixture. Bake in preheated 350°
oven 1 hour. Serve warm with whipped cream or ice cream.

Torte freezes well. Thaw thoroughly and heat in 300° oven before serving.

MERINGUE LOAF WITH FRESH FRUIT

Serves 12

9 egg whites
¾ teaspoon cream of tartar
⅓ teaspoon salt
2¼ cups superfine sugar
1½ teaspoons vanilla
¼ teaspoon almond extract
1½ cups whipping cream, whipped
  fruit of choice, raspberries, strawberries, kiwi,
  or tangerine sections suggested

continued

336

Butter bottom only of 4½- by 16-inch loaf pan. In large bowl combine egg whites, cream of tartar, and salt. With electric mixer, beat at medium speed until foamy. Gradually add sugar, 2 tablespoons at a time, beating well after each addition. Add vanilla and almond extract. Continue beating until stiff glossy peaks form.

Spread mixture evenly in bottom of loaf pan. Place in preheated 450° oven. Turn heat off immediately. Leave in oven 8 hours or overnight. Use sharp knife to loosen loaf from pan. Invert onto serving platter. Frost with whipped cream. Garnish with fruit of choice.

Recipe may be reduced by one-third and baked in 9-inch tube pan.

SWEET MOUTHFUL (Boccone Dolce)

Serves 12 to 14

Meringue:
4 egg whites
  pinch salt
¼ teaspoon cream of tartar
1 cup sugar

Filling:
6 ounces semi-sweet chocolate chips
3 tablespoons water
3 cups whipping cream
⅓ cup sugar
1 pint strawberries, hulled, sliced (or fresh raspberries)

Beat egg whites until frothy. Add salt and cream of tartar. Beat until stiff peaks form. Gradually add sugar, continuing to beat until meringue is stiff and glossy.

Line 2 baking sheets with wax paper. Trace 3 circles 8 inches in diameter. Spread meringue evenly over circles. Bake in preheated 250° oven 20 to 25 minutes or until meringue is lightly colored but still pliable. Remove from oven. Carefully peel wax paper from bottom. Place meringues on rack to cool.

In top of double boiler melt chocolate chips with water. Whip cream until stiff peaks form. Gradually add sugar. Beat until very stiff peaks form.

Place 1 meringue layer on serving plate. Spread with thin layer of melted chocolate. Spread ¾-inch layer whipped cream over chocolate. Top with layer of fruit. Place second layer of meringue on top and repeat procedure. Top with third meringue layer. Frost sides and top with whipped cream. Decorate with fruit if desired. Refrigerate 2 hours before serving.

CHOCOLATE ANGEL FOOD CAKE

Serves 10 to 12

1¾ cups egg whites
¾ teaspoon salt
1½ teaspoons cream of tartar
1 teaspoon vanilla
¾ cup sugar
5 tablespoons cocoa
¾ cup sifted flour

Frosting:
½ pound unsalted butter
1 cup confectioners sugar
2 ounces unsweetened chocolate, melted
5 eggs, separated
1 teaspoon vanilla
½ pound slivered almonds
   whole blanched almonds

In large bowl beat egg whites with salt until foamy. Add cream of tartar. Beat until stiff but not dry. Add vanilla. Combine sugar and cocoa. Sift with flour 3 times. Fold dry ingredients into egg whites gradually, 2 tablespoons at a time. Pour into ungreased 10-inch tube pan. Bake in preheated 400° oven 35 minutes. Invert pan to cool.

Cream butter and sugar. Add chocolate. Add egg yolks 1 at a time, beating after each addition. Stir in vanilla. Beat egg whites until stiff peaks form. Fold into chocolate mixture. Blend in slivered almonds.

Cut cooled cake into 3 equal layers. Spread frosting between layers. Reassemble cake to frost top and sides. Garnish top with whole almonds.

For larger quantity of frosting increase ingredient amounts to ½ pound plus 4 tablespoons butter, 1¼ cups confectioners sugar, 2½ ounces chocolate, 6 eggs, 1 additional egg yolk, 1 teaspoon vanilla, and ½ pound slivered almonds.

Shortcut variation:
Add 3 tablespoons cocoa to 1 box angel food cake mix. Combine, bake, and cool according to package instructions. Cut, frost, and assemble as above.

MERINGUE CAKE WITH CARAMEL AND RASPBERRY SAUCE

Serves 12

superfine sugar

Meringue:
8   egg whites, room temperature
¼   teaspoon cream of tartar
⅛   teaspoon salt
1   cup superfine sugar
¼   teaspoon almond extract

Caramel:
2   tablespoons hot water
2   tablespoons light corn syrup
½   cup superfine sugar

Raspberry sauce:
20   ounces frozen raspberries, thawed
¼   cup superfine sugar
2   tablespoons framboise liqueur
     raspberries and/or strawberries

Sprinkle sugar in generously buttered 12-cup bundt pan. Tap out excess. Cut parchment paper to cover top of pan. Butter paper on 1 side.

In large bowl beat egg whites until frothy. Add cream of tartar and salt. Beat until soft peaks form. Gradually add sugar, beating until whites are stiff. Stir in almond extract. Carefully spoon mixture into bundt pan, smoothing surface. Cover with parchment, buttered side down.

Place bundt pan in deep roasting pan. Add enough boiling water to roasting pan to submerge bundt pan halfway. Bake in preheated 350° oven until top of meringue rises about 1 inch above edge of pan and is lightly colored, about 30 minutes. Remove bundt pan from roasting pan to rack. Cool thoroughly. (Meringue may be baked 2 days ahead, covered with plastic, and refrigerated.)

When meringue is cool remove parchment from top. Submerge bundt pan in warm water several seconds. Invert onto serving plate.

In small saucepan combine hot water and corn syrup. Add sugar. Cook over low heat, stirring occasionally, until sugar dissolves. Increase heat and boil until caramel colored. Remove from heat and cool until slightly thickened. Spread over meringue.

In food processor combine all sauce ingredients and purée. Strain and refrigerate.

Just before serving fill center of meringue with berries. Spoon raspberry sauce around meringue. Pass remaining berries and sauce separately.

GOLDEN WHEAT CHIFFON CAKE

Serves 12

A universally popular cake.

1½   cups sugar
1¼   cups unsifted cake flour
 ½   cup wheat germ
 3   teaspoons baking powder
 1   teaspoon salt
 ½   cup safflower oil
 5   egg yolks
 ¾   cup water
 2   teaspoons vanilla
7-8   (1 cup) egg whites
 ½   teaspoon cream of tartar

Optional glaze:
 2   cups confectioners sugar
 3   tablespoons Grand Marnier
 2   tablespoons melted butter
2-3   tablespoons water, to thin glaze to desired consistency

Combine sugar, flour, wheat germ, baking powder, and salt. Blend well. Add oil, egg yolks, water, and vanilla. Beat 2 minutes with electric mixer at medium speed, or 150 strokes by hand, until smooth.

In large bowl beat egg whites until foamy. Add cream of tartar and beat until very stiff peaks form. Fold sugar mixture into beaten egg whites very carefully with rubber spatula. Pour into ungreased 10-inch angel food cake pan. Bake in preheated 325° oven 55 minutes, then at 350° 10 to 15 minutes. Invert pan onto funnel to cool. When cool run knife around pan edges and remove cake carefully. Serve plain or glazed.

If glaze is desired, combine glaze ingredients. Stir until smooth. Drizzle over cake.

COCONUT PECAN RING CAKE

Serves 15 to 18

½ pound butter
2 cups sugar
6 eggs
12 ounces finely crushed vanilla wafers (3 cups)
½ cup milk
1 teaspoon vanilla
14 ounces flaked coconut
1 cup chopped pecans

Cream butter and sugar until light and fluffy. Add eggs, 1 at a time, beating well after each addition. Add wafer crumbs, milk, and vanilla. Mix well. Fold in coconut and pecans.

Pour into buttered 10-inch tube pan with removable sides. Bake in preheated 350° oven 1 hour 15 minutes or until inserted toothpick comes out clean. When cake is cool remove from pan, *not* turning upside down. This cake will not rise high. Serve thinly sliced.

Variation:
Brush warm, baked cake with Lemon Glaze, page 406 or 408.

BOURBON POUND CAKE

Serves 16 to 20

A rich pound cake, elegant served at Christmas garnished with glacéed cherries.

1 pound butter or margarine
3 cups sugar, divided
8 eggs, separated
3 cups flour, sifted
2 teaspoons vanilla
1 teaspoon almond extract
⅓ cup bourbon
½ cup chopped pecans
  confectioners sugar

Cream butter and 2 cups sugar until light and fluffy. Add egg yolks 1 at a time, beating after each addition. Add flour alternately with flavorings and bourbon in thirds, beating after each addition.

Beat egg whites until stiff, not dry. Gradually beat 1 cup sugar into egg whites. Fold into batter. Fold in nuts or place them on bottom of greased, floured tube pan or three 7- by 4-inch loaf pans. Pour batter into pan(s). Bake in preheated 350° oven 1 hour for tube pan, 40 minutes for loaf pans, or until inserted tester emerges clean. When cool remove from pan. Sprinkle with confectioners sugar.

SUNSHINE AND SNOW CAKE

Serves 10 to 12

2 tablespoons unflavored gelatin
⅓ cup cold water
1 cup boiling water
½ teaspoon salt
1 cup sugar
⅔ cup fresh orange juice
⅓ cup cream sherry or coconut rum
3 cups whipping cream, divided
1 10-inch orange chiffon cake, broken into medium pieces
3½ ounces flaked coconut
11 ounces canned mandarin oranges, drained
  green leaves

In large bowl soften gelatin in cold water. Add boiling water, salt, and sugar. Stir until dissolved. Add orange juice and sherry or rum. Mix well. Place bowl over ice water and stir until liquid is chilled.

Whip 2 cups cream. Fold into gelatin mixture with cake pieces. Pour into greased 12-cup bowl. Refrigerate 3 to 4 hours or until firm. Unmold onto serving platter.

Whip remaining cream and frost cake. Sprinkle coconut over frosting, pressing lightly. Decorate with orange sections to resemble flowers. Mound remaining oranges on green leaves around base of cake.

COCONUT CREAM POUND CAKE

Serves 10 to 12

1 cup flaked coconut
1 cup milk
12 tablespoons butter
2 cups sugar
3 eggs
1 teaspoon vanilla
2½ cups sifted flour
1 teaspoon baking powder
½ teaspoon salt
  confectioners sugar, optional

continued

Soak coconut in milk 10 minutes. In large bowl cream butter. Add sugar to butter gradually, beating well after each addition. Add eggs, 1 at a time, beating well. Stir in vanilla.

Sift together flour, baking powder, and salt. Add dry ingredients to butter mixture alternately with coconut-milk mixture. Pour into greased and floured standard 1 pound loaf pan. Bake in preheated 325° oven 1½ hours or until top is lightly browned and sides pull away from pan. Cool before removing from pan. Sprinkle with confectioners sugar if desired.

SAUERKRAUT SURPRISE CAKE

Serves 12

Cake:
¼   **pound butter or margarine**
1½   **cups sugar**
3   **eggs**
1   **teaspoon vanilla**
2   **cups sifted flour**
1   **teaspoon baking powder**
1   **teaspoon baking soda**
¼   **teaspoon salt**
½   **cup cocoa**
1   **cup water**
8   **ounces canned sauerkraut, drained, rinsed, chopped**

Frosting:
6   **ounces semi-sweet chocolate chips**
4   **tablespoons butter or margarine**
½   **cup sour cream**
1   **teaspoon vanilla**
¼   **teaspoon salt**
1   **pound confectioners sugar**

In large bowl cream butter and sugar until light. Beat in eggs 1 at a time. Add vanilla.

Sift together flour, baking powder, baking soda, salt, and cocoa. Add to creamed mixture alternately with water, beating after each addition. Stir in sauerkraut. Pour batter into greased 9- by 13-inch pan. Bake in preheated 350° oven 35 to 40 minutes.

In top of double boiler melt chocolate chips and butter. Remove from heat. Blend in sour cream, vanilla, and salt. Beating constantly, gradually add sugar until frosting reaches spreading consistency. Frost top of cooled cake.

SIX-LAYER CARROT CAKE

Serves 12

An impressive version of a favorite cake.

4 eggs
1½ cups sugar
1½ cups vegetable oil
2 cups flour
2 teaspoons cinnamon
2 teaspoons baking powder
2 teaspoons baking soda
1 teaspoon salt
3 cups grated carrots
½ cup raisins
½ cup chopped pecans

Frosting:
11 ounces cream cheese, room temperature
12 tablespoons butter, room temperature
2 cups confectioners sugar
1½ cups well-drained crushed pineapple
1½ teaspoons vanilla

In large bowl beat eggs until frothy. Add sugar gradually. Beat until light and lemon colored. Slowly add oil, beating until combined. Sift together flour, cinnamon, baking powder, baking soda, and salt. Fold dry ingredients by thirds into egg mixture. Add carrots, raisins, and pecans. Combine well.

Pour batter in equal quantities into 3 buttered and floured 8-inch round pans. Bake in preheated 350° oven 30 minutes or until tester comes out clean. When cake has completely cooled, cut each layer in half horizontally.

To make frosting beat cream cheese, butter, and confectioners sugar until creamy. Blend in pineapple and vanilla. Spread each layer with frosting, stacking evenly. Frost top and sides. Chill at least 1 hour before slicing.

Cake may also be baked in a well-greased tube pan in preheated 350° oven for 1 hour. Check after 50 minutes.

CARROT PINEAPPLE CAKE

Serves 10 to 12

Cake:
½ pound unsalted butter
2 cups sugar
3 eggs
2½ cups flour
½ teaspoon salt
2 teaspoons cinnamon
2 teaspoons baking soda
2 teaspoons vanilla
1 cup grated carrots
1 cup canned, drained, crushed pineapple
1 cup flaked coconut
1 cup coarsely chopped pecans

Sauce:
2 tablespoons unsalted butter
1 cup brown sugar
1 tablespoon light corn syrup
½ cup orange juice
1 teaspoon baking soda
½ cup sour cream
2 teaspoons orange liqueur, optional
½ cup chopped pecans, optional

Cream butter with sugar. Add eggs. Beat well. Sift together flour, salt, cinnamon, and baking soda. Gradually add to butter mixture, beating constantly. Add vanilla, carrots, pineapple, coconut, and pecans. Mix well. Pour into greased 9-inch angel food cake pan. Bake in preheated 325° oven 1 hour 15 minutes or until inserted toothpick comes out dry. Remove from oven. Cool 15 minutes.

In saucepan combine all sauce ingredients except sour cream, liqueur, and pecans. Stir over low heat until sugar is dissolved. Bring to boil and cook 5 minutes. Remove from heat and stir in sour cream and liqueur if desired.

Remove warm cake from pan to serving plate. With large fork poke holes over top. Pour hot sauce over cake. Sprinkle with chopped pecans if desired.

GHIRARDELLI ALMOND CAKE

Serves 6 to 8

A successful result hinges on the use of this special chocolate.

4   ounces Ghirardelli semi-sweet chocolate
2   tablespoons strong coffee
¼   pound unsalted butter
⅔   cup plus 1 tablespoon sugar, divided
3   eggs, separated
    pinch salt
⅓   cup finely ground almonds
1   tablespoon Amaretto or ¼ teaspoon almond extract
¾   cup sifted cake flour

Glaze:
2   ounces Ghirardelli semi-sweet chocolate
2   tablespoons strong coffee
6   tablespoons unsalted butter
    whole almonds, toasted

In top of double boiler melt chocolate with coffee over simmering water. Cream butter and ⅔ cup sugar until fluffy. Beat in egg yolks, blending well. Beat egg whites and salt until soft peaks form. Sprinkle 1 tablespoon sugar over whites. Beat until stiff peaks form.

Blend melted chocolate into butter-sugar mixture. Stir in ground almonds and Amaretto. Stir in a fourth of the egg whites. Fold in a third of the remaining whites, then a third of the flour. Alternate until all whites and flour are incorporated.

Pour batter into buttered, floured 8-inch round cake pan, smoothing top. Bake in middle of preheated 350° oven 25 minutes or until puffed. A straw inserted in edge of cake should come out clean (inserted in center of cake, straw will come out oily). Cool 10 minutes. Invert cake on rack and cool completely before glazing.

In top of double boiler over simmering water stir chocolate and coffee until creamy. Remove from heat. Beat in butter, 1 tablespoon at a time. Beat over cold water until mixture is cool and of spreading consistency. Spread over cooled cake at once. Decorate with whole almonds.

BLACK FOREST CHERRY CAKE

Serves 8 to 10

¼ pound butter, room temperature
½ cup plus 3 tablespoons sugar, divided
6 eggs, separated
½ teaspoon vanilla
¼ teaspoon almond extract
6 ounces semi-sweet chocolate, divided
pinch salt
¾ cup sifted cake flour
2 teaspoons baking powder
½ cup finely ground toasted almonds
6-8 tablespoons kirsch
16 ounces thick whole cherry preserves or jam
3 cups whipping cream, whipped
12 maraschino cherries with stems

In large bowl cream butter with ½ cup sugar until light and fluffy. Beat in egg yolks, vanilla, and almond extract. Blend well. Finely grate 4 ounces chocolate and fold into mixture.

In another large bowl beat egg whites until foamy. Gradually add 3 tablespoons sugar and salt. Beat until stiff peaks form. Stir 1 cup whites into chocolate mixture, blending well. Gently fold in remaining whites. Sift flour and baking powder together. Gently fold into batter a little at a time. Fold in almonds.

Spray vegetable coating on bottom of 9-inch springform pan. Pour batter into pan, smoothing top. Bake in preheated 325° oven 40 to 50 minutes until cake begins to pull away from sides of pan. Cool on rack 10 minutes. Run sharp knife around sides of pan. Remove sides of pan. Cool cake. Remove bottom of pan.

Three hours before serving slice cake horizontally into 3 equal layers. Place bottom layer on serving plate. Drizzle 2 to 3 tablespoons kirsch over layer. Spread with half of preserves. Top with one-sixth of whipped cream. Cover with second cake layer. Repeat filling. Place third layer on top. Drizzle with remaining kirsch. Frost cake with one-half whipped cream. Sprinkle tops and sides with 2 ounces grated chocolate. Spoon remaining one-sixth cream into pastry bag fitted with star tip. Pipe 12 rosettes around edge of top. Center cherry in each rosette. Let stand at cool room temperature 2 hours before serving or refrigerate.

YULE LOG

Serves 10

Cake:

6   eggs, separated, room temperature
¾   cup sugar, divided
⅓   cup cocoa
1½ teaspoons vanilla
     dash salt
½   cup confectioners sugar

Filling:

1½ cups whipping cream
½   cup confectioners sugar
¼   cup cocoa
2   teaspoons instant coffee crystals
1   teaspoon vanilla

Meringue Butter Cream:

3   egg whites
     pinch salt
¼   teaspoon cream of tartar
1⅓ cups sugar
⅓   cup water
2   cups semi-sweet chocolate chips
3   tablespoons coffee or rum
1   tablespoon vanilla
½   pound unsalted butter, softened

Grease jelly roll pan. Line with wax paper. Grease again. In large bowl beat egg whites at high speed until soft peaks form. Add ¼ cup sugar, 2 tablespoons at a time, beating until stiff peaks form.

In separate bowl beat yolks at high speed, adding remaining ½ cup sugar, 2 tablespoons at a time. Beat until mixture is very thick, about 4 minutes. Reduce speed to low. Add cocoa, vanilla, and salt. Mix well.

Gently fold chocolate mixture into egg whites. Spread evenly in pan. Bake in preheated 375° oven 15 minutes, until surface springs back when gently pressed. Sift ½ cup confectioners sugar in 10- by 15-inch rectangle on linen towel. Invert pan over sugar, lift off pan, peel off paper. Roll cake up. Place seam side down on rack. Cool 30 minutes.

In medium bowl combine all filling ingredients. Beat until thick. Refrigerate. Unroll cake and spread with filling. Roll again, placing seam side down on serving plate.

At medium speed beat egg whites until foamy. Add salt and cream of tartar. Beat on high until stiff peaks form. In saucepan combine sugar and water. Over high heat swirl, do not stir, until sugar is dissolved and liquid is clear. Cover and

continued

boil rapidly 30 seconds. Uncover pan and boil to 238°, measuring with candy thermometer. On low speed beat egg whites. Gradually add sugar syrup. Beat on high speed for 5 minutes or until mixture is cool.

Melt chocolate chips with coffee or rum. Add to meringue mixture. Add vanilla. Mix well. Gradually beat in butter. Chill until of spreading consistency.

Frost cake with meringue butter cream. To simulate a log, run fork lengthwise all around cake. Trim ends at an angle.

May be frozen.

If desired, cut out a 1- by 1½-inch oval from top of cake near an end. Into this shallow opening insert one of the ends trimmed when cutting cake at angle. This creates a "bump" on the log. Cake may be dusted lightly with confectioners sugar "snow" and decorated at ends with holly leaves or meringue mushrooms.

FRESH PLUM CAKE

Serves 4

A down-home dessert assembled at a moment's notice.

¼ pound margarine
1½ cups sugar, divided
2 teaspoons fresh lemon juice
2 eggs
1 cup flour
1 teaspoon baking powder
½ teaspoon salt
1 teaspoon cinnamon, divided
6 large purple plums, pitted, quartered

In medium bowl cream margarine and 1 cup sugar. Add lemon juice and eggs, 1 at a time, beating after each addition. Sift flour with baking powder, salt, and ½ teaspoon cinnamon. Add to batter mixture, combining well.

Pour batter into greased 9-inch pan with removable bottom, smoothing top. Arrange plum quarters closely in even circles, covering batter. Combine remaining sugar and cinnamon. Sprinkle evenly over plums.

Bake in preheated 350° oven 50 to 60 minutes, until tester comes out clean. Cool in pan. Loosen edges with sharp knife to remove pan sides before serving.

PRUNE CAKE

Serves 12

2 cups flour
1 teaspoon baking soda
¼ teaspoon salt
1 tablespoon nutmeg
1 tablespoon ground allspice
1 tablespoon cinnamon
1½ cups sugar
1 cup corn oil
3 eggs
1 teaspoon vanilla
1 cup buttermilk
1½ cups pitted, drained, cooked prunes
1 cup chopped walnuts

Buttermilk glaze:
1 cup sugar
½ cup buttermilk
¼ cup margarine
½ cup light corn syrup
½ teaspoon baking soda
½ teaspoon vanilla

whipped cream, optional

Sift together flour, baking soda, salt, and spices. Beat together sugar and oil. Add eggs 1 at a time, beating well after each addition. Stir in vanilla. Add sifted dry ingredients to sugar mixture alternately with buttermilk, a third at a time, blending well. Stir in prunes and nuts. Pour into buttered springform tube pan. Bake in preheated 350° oven 1 hour.

Fifteen minutes before cake has finished baking prepare glaze. In 3-quart saucepan over medium heat combine all glaze ingredients. Bring to full boil, stirring frequently. Boil 10 minutes or until sugar dissolves. Gently loosen side of springform pan. Pour glaze over hot cake. Let stand overnight. Serve with whipped cream if desired.

KILLER CAKE

Serves 20 to 24

Cake:
8 eggs, separated
1 cup sugar
¼ cup orange juice
2 tablespoons finely grated orange rind
1 cup sifted cake flour
½ teaspoon baking powder
¾ teaspoon cream of tartar

Filling:
½ pound chocolate-covered toffee, chilled
½ gallon premium vanilla ice cream

Frosting:
1½ pints whipping cream, whipped, or 1 quart
    frozen whipped topping, thawed
10 ounces grated coconut

    hot fudge sauce (page 438)
20 ounces frozen strawberries, thawed

Beat egg yolks well. Add sugar. Mix well. Continuing to beat, add orange juice and rind. Sift flour and baking powder together. Stir into yolk mixture. Beat egg whites until foamy. Add cream of tartar and beat until stiff peaks form. Carefully fold into batter. Pour batter into ungreased angel food cake pan. Bake in preheated 325° oven 30 minutes. Increase temperature to 350°. Bake 30 minutes. Invert and cool thoroughly.

One hour before beginning of meal slice cake in half horizontally. Place lower half on serving plate. In food processor or blender process toffee in small batches into small, not fine, pieces. Sprinkle layer of toffee on lower half of cake. Spread layer of ice cream over toffee. Repeat procedure until toffee and ice cream are used. Cover with top layer of cake.

Frost cake with whipped cream or whipped topping. Sprinkle coconut generously over entire cake. Transfer cake to freezer. It is important that cake is in freezer only short period. Cake portion should not freeze. This is just to hold ice cream.

Serve with choice of hot fudge sauce and/or strawberries.

Serves 12 to 14

Crust:
- ¼ pound unsalted butter, melted
- ⅔ pound graham crackers, finely crushed
- ½ cup walnuts, finely chopped
- 2 tablespoons cinnamon
- ¾ cup sugar

Filling:
- 1 pound cream cheese
- 1½ cups sugar, divided
- 1 cup whipping cream
- 1 pound small curd cottage cheese
- 8 eggs
- ¼ cup half and half
- 3 tablespoons vanilla
- 6 scant tablespoons flour
- 1 cup golden raisins or currants

Blend all crust ingredients, combining well. Reserving ½ cup crumbs, press mixture onto bottom and sides of 10-inch springform pan.

Have all filling ingredients at room temperature. Beat cream cheese with ¾ cup sugar and whipping cream. Add cottage cheese. Beat until smooth. Add 4 eggs, 1 at a time, beating after each addition.

Separate remaining 4 eggs. Beat yolks into cream cheese mixture. Add half and half, vanilla, flour, and remaining ¾ cup sugar. Mix well. Beat egg whites until stiff peaks form. Fold into cream cheese mixture with raisins or currants. Pour into prepared crust. Sprinkle top with reserved crumbs.

Bake in preheated 250° oven 2 to 2¼ hours. Soft center will firm later upon refrigeration. Let stand at room temperature 2 hours. Refrigerate at least 24 hours before serving.

STRAWBERRY CHEESECAKE

Serves 12 to 16

Crust:

2½ cups graham cracker crumbs
¾ cup melted butter or margarine
¼ cup sugar
1 teaspoon cinnamon

Filling:

4 extra large eggs, well beaten
1½ cups sugar
½ teaspoon salt
3 tablespoons lemon juice
36 ounces cream cheese, softened

Glaze:

12 ounces red raspberry jelly, divided
1 tablespoon cornstarch
¼ cup Cointreau or Grand Marnier
1 tablespoon water
1 quart medium to large strawberries, hulled

Combine all crust ingredients. Mix well. Press into buttered 10- or 12-inch springform pan, reserving 2 tablespoons for topping if no fruit topping is desired. If fruit topping is planned, do not reserve.

Combine eggs, sugar, salt, and lemon juice. Mix well. Beat cream cheese separately until smooth. Add egg mixture to cheese, blending well. Pour into crust. Bake in preheated 350° oven 30 minutes for 12-inch pan and 40 minutes for 10-inch pan.

If no fruit topping is desired, remove cake from oven. Increase temperature to 400°. After waiting 2 minutes, sprinkle reserved crumbs over top of cake. Return to oven and bake 15 minutes.

If fruit topping is desired, do not remove cake from oven. Increase temperature to 400° and bake 15 minutes. Cool. Refrigerate 3 hours.

In saucepan combine 2 ounces jelly with cornstarch. Mix well. Add remaining jelly, liqueur, and water. Stirring frequently, cook over medium heat until thickened and clear, about 10 minutes. Cool to lukewarm, stirring occasionally.

Arrange berries pointed end up over top of cake. Spoon glaze over berries, allowing some to drip down side of cake. Refrigerate until glaze is set.

AMARETTO CHEESECAKE

Serves 8 to 10

Crust:

1¼ cups vanilla wafer crumbs
¼-½ cup finely chopped blanched almonds (crumb consistency)
6 tablespoons unsalted butter, melted
¼ teaspoon almond extract

Filling:

24 ounces cream cheese, room temperature
⅛ teaspoon salt
1 cup sugar
½ teaspoon vanilla
½ teaspoon almond extract
1 cup sour cream
3 large eggs
¼-⅓ cup Amaretto to taste

Lightly butter sides only of 8-inch springform pan. In bowl combine all crust ingredients. Stir with fork until thoroughly mixed. Pour two-thirds of mixture into springform. Press crumbs partly up sides. Pour remaining mixture into bottom of pan and pat evenly. Crust must be firm. Bake in preheated 350° oven 6 to 8 minutes. Cool before filling.

Beat cheese until smooth. Add salt, sugar, vanilla, and almond extract. Beat well. Add sour cream. Beat 5 minutes. Add eggs 1 at a time, beating just until well mixed. Stir in Amaretto. Mix well. Pour filling into crust, smoothing top. Bake in preheated 350° oven 1 hour. Turn oven off, open oven door a few inches, and let cake cool thoroughly. Cover with foil. Refrigerate at least 4 hours, preferably overnight. Serve chilled.

May be refrigerated up to 1 week. The almond flavor becomes more pronounced each day.

DUBLIN CHEESECAKE

Serves 10 to 12   *An unusual cheesecake for sophisticated palates.*

Crust:
5½ tablespoons butter, melted
8½ ounces chocolate wafers, finely crushed

Filling:
24 ounces cream cheese, room temperature
1¼ cups firmly packed dark brown sugar
4 eggs
3 tablespoons Kahlúa
1 teaspoon vanilla
7 tablespoons Irish whiskey
6 teaspoons instant espresso coffee powder

Frosting:
1 teaspoon instant espresso coffee powder
2 tablespoons plus ½ teaspoon sugar, divided
1½ cups plus 1 tablespoon whipping cream, divided
    chocolate coffee beans

Combine butter and wafers; mix well. Press mixture in bottom and 1½ inches up sides of 9-inch springform pan.

Beat cream cheese with sugar. Add eggs 1 at a time, beating after each addition. Stir in Kahlúa and vanilla. Measure Irish whiskey into small bowl. Add espresso, stirring until dissolved. Blend coffee-whiskey mixture into cheese mixture, mixing well. Pour filling into prepared crust.

Bake in preheated 325° oven 45 minutes. Center will appear moist. Cracks may appear. Cool on rack at room temperature. Cover with plastic wrap. Refrigerate 1 day or more.

Three hours before serving blend espresso powder and ½ teaspoon sugar with 1 tablespoon whipping cream. Add remaining 2 tablespoons sugar to 1½ cups whipping cream. Beat until stiff peaks form. Fold in espresso mixture. Remove sides of pan from cake. Spread top with whipped cream mixture. Decorate with coffee beans.

LIME CHEESECAKE

Serves 6 to 8

An outstanding finale befitting a gala dinner.

Crust:

6 ounces crisp coconut cookies, finely crushed
1 teaspoon cinnamon
   pinch freshly ground nutmeg
6 tablespoons butter, melted
1 teaspoon grated lime rind

Filling:

24 ounces cream cheese, softened
⅛ teaspoon salt
1 cup sugar
1 teaspoon vanilla
1 cup sour cream
3 large eggs
⅓ cup lime juice
1 tablespoon grated lime rind

lime, very thinly sliced
chocolate curls or leaves (page 439)

Combine all crust ingredients. Mix well. Line bottom and sides of 8-inch springform pan with mixture.

Beat cream cheese until smooth. Add salt, sugar, and vanilla. Mix well. Add sour cream. Beat 5 to 6 minutes. Add eggs 1 at a time, until just incorporated. Stir in lime juice and rind. Pour filling into prepared crust. Bake in preheated 350° oven 1 hour. Turn off oven. Open oven door slightly and leave cake in oven until cooled to room temperature. Cover and chill at least 4 hours or overnight.

Before serving garnish with lime slices and/or chocolate curls or leaves.

See photo page 234.

CARDIOLOGISTS' CHEESECAKE

Serves 12

Crust:
2   cups graham cracker crumbs
1   tablespoon margarine, melted

Filling:
2   pounds creamed cottage cheese
4   eggs or equivalent egg substitute
1   cup sugar
2   tablespoons flour
1   teaspoon vanilla

Combine crumbs and margarine. Mix well. Spread on bottom and sides of 10-inch springform pan.

In food processor or blender combine all filling ingredients. Blend until smooth. Pour into crust. Bake in preheated 350° oven 45 to 60 minutes.

PECAN PIE

Serves 10

The combination of white sugar and dark corn syrup produces a clear filling that is not too sweet.

3   eggs
5½   tablespoons butter, melted, cooled
⅔   cup sugar
⅓   teaspoon salt
1   cup dark corn syrup
1   teaspoon vanilla
2   cups small pecan halves
1   9-inch unbaked pie shell

Beat eggs until foamy. Add remaining ingredients except pecans and pie shell. Beat until well blended. Stir in nuts. Pour into pie shell.

Bake in preheated 375° oven until set, about 40 to 50 minutes. Check closely toward end of baking time to avoid scorching filling. If pie crust appears to be baking too quickly, place foil collar around rim. Remove foil for last 10 minutes of baking. Serve at room temperature.

JAMAICAN PECAN FUDGE PIE

Serves 10

4	tablespoons unsalted butter
¾	cup brown sugar
3	eggs
12	ounces semi-sweet chocolate chips
2½	teaspoons instant coffee crystals
2	teaspoons boiling water
2	teaspoons Jamaican rum
¼	cup flour
1	cup coarsely chopped pecans
1	9-inch unbaked pie shell
½	cup pecan halves
1	cup whipping cream

In large bowl cream butter and sugar. Add eggs 1 at a time. Melt chocolate in top of double boiler. Add to butter mixture. Blend well.

Dissolve coffee crystals in boiling water. Combine with rum. Add to butter mixture. Gently stir in flour and chopped pecans. Mix well. Pour into pie shell. Decorate top with pecan halves. Bake in preheated 375° oven 25 minutes. Cool.

Before serving, whip cream. Pipe whipped cream along inner rim of crust, or spoon over each serving of pie.

CHOCOLATE VELVET MERINGUE PIE

Serves 8

Pie shell:

3	egg whites
⅛	teaspoon cream of tartar
	pinch salt
1	cup sugar
¾	cup chopped pecans
1	teaspoon vanilla

Filling:

8	ounces German sweet chocolate, in pieces
6	tablespoons strong coffee
2	teaspoons vanilla or 2 teaspoons brandy
2	cups whipping cream, whipped
	grated chocolate

continued

Beat egg whites until foamy. Add cream of tartar and salt. Beat until soft peaks form. Add sugar 1 teaspoon at a time. Beat until stiff peaks form. Fold in pecans and vanilla. Pour into buttered 9-inch pie pan. Bake in preheated 300° oven 1 hour. Turn off oven. Leave shell in oven to cool.

In top of double boiler melt chocolate with coffee over low heat. Add vanilla. Remove from heat. Cool. Fold in whipped cream. Pour into cooled shell and chill. To serve garnish with grated chocolate.

FROZEN FRENCH SILK CAKE

Serves 8

1 **cup flour**
½ **pound unsalted butter, divided**
½ **cup coarsely chopped pecans**
¼ **cup firmly packed dark brown sugar**
¾ **cup plus 2 tablespoons superfine sugar, divided**
2 **large eggs**
1 **ounce unsweetened chocolate**
1 **cup whipping cream**
2 **teaspoons crème de cacao**

Line 9-inch square baking pan with foil, leaving an overhang to serve as handle. Grease foil. In food processor, combine flour, ¼ pound butter in pieces, pecans, and brown sugar. Repeat on and off turns quickly until well blended. Press mixture in bottom of baking pan. Bake in preheated 350° oven 20 minutes or until lightly browned. Cool on rack.

Cream remaining ¼ pound butter. Add ¾ cup sugar gradually and beat until mixture is light and fluffy. Add eggs, 1 at a time, beating well after each addition. Melt and cool chocolate. Blend into mixture and beat 3 minutes. Spread on crust. Cover loosely and chill 2 hours.

Beat whipping cream until soft peaks form. Add 2 tablespoons sugar gradually, then crème de cacao. Beat until stiff peaks form.

Holding foil overhang, remove chocolate-covered crust from pan. Peel off foil. With sharp knife cut crust in half to form two 9- by 4½-inch rectangles. Place one half, crust side down, on serving plate. Spread top with half of cream mixture. Place other half over cream mixture. Cover top with remaining cream mixture. This may be done decoratively using pastry bag with fluted tip. Freeze dessert. Let stand 1 hour at room temperature before serving..

CHOCOLATE FREEZE

Serves 8 to 10

Crust:
1½ cups finely crushed chocolate wafers
6   tablespoons butter, melted

Filling:
8   ounces cream cheese
½   cup sugar, divided
1   teaspoon vanilla
2   eggs, separated
6   ounces semi-sweet chocolate chips, melted
1   cup whipping cream, whipped
½   cup chopped pecans

Combine crumbs with butter. Mix well. Press in bottom of 9-inch springform pan. Bake in preheated 325° oven 10 minutes.

Combine cheese, ¼ cup sugar, and vanilla. Mix well. Add yolks. Beat well. Stir in chocolate. Beat egg whites until soft peaks form. Slowly add remaining ¼ cup sugar, beating well until stiff peaks form. Fold into chocolate mixture. Then fold in whipped cream. Pour into springform over baked crumbs. Sprinkle with nuts. Cover with plastic wrap and freeze. Serve directly from freezer.

LEMON CHESS PIE

Serves 8

2   cups sugar
1   tablespoon flour
1   tablespoon cornmeal
4   large eggs
¼   cup milk
¼   pound butter, melted
2   tablespoons grated lemon rind
⅓   cup fresh lemon juice with pulp
1   9-inch unbaked pie crust (page 361)
    whipping cream, whipped, optional

In large bowl combine sugar, flour, and cornmeal. Blend well. Add eggs. Mix well. Add milk and blend. Stir in butter. Add lemon rind and juice. Mix well. Pour into crust. To prevent scorching of crust edge fold 3- by 3-inch strips of foil around edge of pie, taking care not to touch filling. Bake in center of preheated 375° oven 45 minutes, removing foil after 30 minutes.

Cool several hours before serving or refrigerating. If refrigerated overnight remove pie 3 hours before serving. If desired, garnish with whipped cream or serve whipped cream separately.

FOOD PROCESSOR CRUST

Yield: one
9-inch crust

1   cup flour
¼   pound plus 2 tablespoons unsalted butter
4   tablespoons ice water

In food processor, combine flour and butter. With steel blade process with quick on and off impulses until mixture resembles coarse cornmeal. Do not over-process. Add water with processor on. Process just until mixture forms ball.

With floured hands remove dough to wax paper. Press to form 1-inch flat pancake. Fold wax paper, enclosing dough, and refrigerate at least 1 hour.

Handling dough as little as possible, place on lightly floured surface. Dust dough lightly with flour. With chilled rolling pin roll dough to 10½-inch diameter. Gently transfer and press into 9-inch pie pan, folding overhang over edge of pan. Flute edges with floured fingers. Refrigerate until filled.

PUMPKIN CHIFFON PIE

Serves 10

1   tablespoon unflavored gelatin
½   cup milk
16   ounces canned pumpkin
¾   teaspoon cinnamon
⅛   teaspoon ground ginger
½   cup sugar
½   teaspoon salt
3   eggs, separated
¾   cup walnuts, finely chopped, divided
1   cup finely ground gingersnaps
6   tablespoons melted butter

In large saucepan sprinkle gelatin over milk. Cook over medium heat until dissolved. Add pumpkin, cinnamon, ginger, sugar, salt, and egg yolks. Stirring constantly, cook until thick, about 15 minutes. Cool in refrigerator.

Mix ½ cup walnuts, gingersnap crumbs, and butter. Press firmly in bottom and sides of 9-inch pie pan. Bake in preheated 375° oven 8 minutes. Cool thoroughly.

Beat egg whites unitl stiff peaks form. Carefully fold into cooled pumpkin mixture. Pour into cooled pie shell. Refrigerate at least 2 hours. Sprinkle remaining ¼ cup walnuts on top.

PEANUT BUTTER PIE

Serves 6 to 8

This southern recipe is adored by kids from 9 to 90.

¼ **pound butter, room temperature**
¾ **cup sugar**
¼ **cup creamy peanut butter**
1 **teaspoon vanilla**
2 **eggs**
1 **9-inch baked pie shell or graham cracker crust**
¼ **cup chopped peanuts**
  whipping cream, whipped, or hot fudge sauce (page 438)

Combine butter, sugar, peanut butter, and vanilla. Mix well. Add 1 egg. Beat 5 minutes. Add second egg. Beat 5 minutes. Pour mixture into pie shell and top with peanuts. Chill. Serve with whipped cream and/or hot fudge sauce.

LIME PIE

Serves 6

A tangy and refreshing version.

Crust:
1 **cup sifted flour**
½ **teaspoon salt**
⅓ **cup lard**
3 **tablespoons cold water**

Filling:
¼ **pound butter**
1 **cup sugar**
¼ **teaspoon grated lime rind**
½ **cup plus 1 tablespoon fresh lime juice**
4 **eggs, beaten**

Topping:
1 **cup whipping cream, whipped**

Sift flour and salt into bowl. Cut in lard. Sprinkle with water and mix lightly with fork. Press dough into ball. Wrap and refrigerate 30 minutes. Roll out to fit into 9-inch pie pan. Transfer gently to pan. Pierce bottom with fork. Bake in preheated 450° oven 15 minutes. Cool.

In top of double boiler combine butter, sugar, rind, and juice. Mix well. Add eggs. Stirring constantly, cook over boiling water until thick, about 10 minutes. Remove from heat and cool. Pour into baked crust. Cover and refrigerate 6 hours. Top with whipped cream.

BLENDER LEMON PIE

Serves 6 to 8

An unusual method of incorporating lemon.

1   9-inch unbaked pie shell
1   whole lemon
¼   pound butter, softened
1   cup sugar
4   egg yolks
½   pint whipping cream, whipped, optional

Meringue: optional
3   egg whites
¼   teaspoon cream of tartar
6   tablespoons sugar
½   teaspoon vanilla

Line 9-inch pie pan with shell. Pierce shell and bake in preheated 400° oven 5 minutes. Remove from oven and reduce temperature to 325°.

Slice ends from lemon and quarter. Remove seeds. In food processor or blender combine lemon, butter, sugar, and egg yolks. Process at high speed until liquid is blended. Pour into crust. Bake 35 minutes if using whipped cream for topping. Cool thoroughly. Frost with whipped cream.

If using meringue topping bake 25 minutes. While baking beat egg whites with cream of tartar until frothy. Gradually beat in sugar, continuing to beat until stiff and glossy. Top partially baked pie with meringue, making certain to cover edge of crust. Swirl points to create decorative top. Return to oven and bake 10 minutes longer. Cool thoroughly before serving.

PIE CRUST

Yield: two 9-inch crusts

2 cups flour
¾ teaspoon salt
½ cup vegetable oil
¼ cup milk

Combine flour and salt. Mix well. Mix oil and milk. Add to flour and salt. Stir lightly with fork to form a ball. Divide in half.

Form half the dough into smooth-edged "pancake" on 12- by 12-inch sheet of wax paper. Place equal-size wax paper on top. Roll out dough for pie pan. Remove top paper. Invert pastry carefully on pie pan and gently peel off paper.

Fill pie and repeat procedure for top crust or bake as 2 shells after piercing with fork to prevent bubbles.

For prebaked shells, bake in preheated 475° oven 8 to 10 minutes until brown.

SOUR CREAM APPLE PIE

Serves 10

Crust:
1 cup flour
3 ounces cream cheese, softened
¼ pound butter

Filling:
1⅔ cups sour cream
1 cup sugar
1 large egg
⅓ cup flour
2 teaspoons vanilla
½ teaspoon salt
6 large McIntosh apples, peeled, cored, sliced

Topping:
1 cup chopped walnuts
½ cup flour
¼ pound soft butter
⅓ cup sugar
⅓ cup brown sugar
1 tablespoon cinnamon
   pinch salt

continued

Combine crust ingredients. Blend well with pastry cutter. Press into 9-inch pie pan.

Combine sour cream, sugar, egg, flour, vanilla, and salt. Mix well. Stir in apples. Pour mixture into pie crust. Bake in preheated 450° oven 10 minutes. Reduce temperature to 350° and bake 35 minutes.

While pie is baking combine all topping ingredients. Mix well. Spoon over baked pie. Bake at 350° 15 minutes. Serve cold.

See photo page 234.

SUMMER BLUEBERRY PIE

Serves 6 to 8   *A unique recipe combining cooked and uncooked berries, with winning results.*

Crust:
3   ounces cream cheese, softened
1   cup flour
¼   pound butter or margarine

Filling:
1   cup sugar
½   teaspoon salt
5   tablespoons cornstarch
1⅓   cups water
6   cups blueberries, divided
3   tablespoons lemon juice
4   tablespoons butter
½   pint whipping cream
½   teaspoon vanilla
2   tablespoons confectioners sugar

Blend crust ingredients well. Press into 9-inch pie pan. Bake in preheated 325° oven until lightly browned.

In saucepan combine sugar, salt, cornstarch, and water. Mix well. Add 2 cups berries. Stirring constantly, cook until very thick. Bring to boil. Stir in lemon juice and butter. Remove from heat. When cool add 4 cups berries. Taking care not to break berries, mix thoroughly. Chill.

Beat whipping cream until thick. Blend in vanilla and confectioners sugar. Shortly before serving pour filling into crust and frost top with whipped cream. (This prevents crust from becoming soggy.) Pie is attractive with whole berries garnishing top.

GREEN TOMATO PIE

Serves 8

4 cups sliced green tomatoes
1¼ cups sugar
¼ teaspoon cinnamon
¼ teaspoon nutmeg
3 tablespoons flour
¼ teaspoon salt
1 9-inch unbaked pie shell (page 364)
1 tablespoon water
2 tablespoons lemon juice
3 tablespoons butter
  rind of 1 lemon, grated
1 unbaked top crust (page 364)

Soak tomatoes in boiling water 5 minutes. Drain. Combine sugar, cinnamon, nutmeg, flour, and salt. Mix well. Layer tomatoes and sugar mixture in pie shell. Sprinkle water and juice over top. Dot with butter and rind. Cover with top crust. Bake in preheated 450° oven 15 minutes. Reduce heat to 375° and bake 35 minutes. Serve warm or at room temperature.

POACHED PEACHES AMARETTO

Serves 8 to 10

Another way to enjoy the fresh bounty of summer.

2 cups water
4 thin slices lemon
8-10 large whole cling peaches, unpeeled
¼ teaspoon cinnamon
¼-½ cup sugar
⅓ cup Amaretto

In large kettle bring water and lemon slices to boil. Add peaches and cinnamon. Reduce heat at once. Cover and simmer until peaches are tender, approximately 20 minutes. Add sugar and Amaretto and continue simmering 3 more minutes. Remove from heat. Peach skins should be removed *after* cooking as they contribute to color and flavor. Chill peaches in syrup. Serve with whipped cream or crème fraîche.

POACHED PEACHES IN RASPBERRY SAUCE

Serves 5

5   large, firm peaches, unpeeled, halved, pitted
½   cup water
3   tablespoons sugar
1   pint raspberries, divided
     sour cream

In pan large enough for single layer of peach halves combine fruit with water, sugar, and ½ pint raspberries. Bring to slow boil. Cover and simmer 2 to 3 minutes, turning peaches to cook evenly. They should remain firm. Remove peaches from pan. Peel and place in glass dish. Continue to simmer liquid and raspberries in pan until thickened. Strain over peaches. Refrigerate, turning peaches occasionally. Before serving add remaining raspberries. Serve with dollop of sour cream.

POACHED PEACHES PRINCESS DI

Serves 4

A dazzling display and so simple.

4   ripe freestone peaches
1   vanilla bean
4   teaspoons strawberry jam
4   teaspoons currant jelly
4   teaspoons greengage plum or apricot preserves
8   tablespoons cognac
8   tablespoons kirsch
4   vanilla ice cream balls
½   cup toasted sliced almonds

In large saucepan combine peaches, vanilla bean, and water to cover. Bring to boil. Poach 2 minutes or until peach skins slip off easily. Return skinned peaches to water to prevent discoloration. Keep warm until served.

Combine jams in chafing dish. Heat well, stirring. Add drained peaches. Pour cognac and kirsch without stirring and flame. Place ice cream balls on individual serving plates. Add one peach to each plate. Ladle flaming sauce over peach and ice cream. Sprinkle with toasted almonds. Serve immediately.

NECTARINES IN LEMON-LIME SAUCE

Serves 8

1   cup sour cream
½   cup unflavored yogurt
4   tablespoons honey
1   teaspoon grated lime peel
1   teaspoon grated lemon peel
2   tablespoons lime juice
2   tablespoons lemon juice
    nectarines to serve 8, sliced

In medium bowl combine all ingredients except nectarines. Blend well and chill. Place sliced nectarines in individual serving dishes or into one large bowl. Pour sauce over fruit; stir once or twice.

Peaches may be substituted for nectarines.

SAUTÉED APPLES WITH RUM SAUCE

Serves 8

6   tablespoons butter
8   golden delicious apples, peeled, cored, sliced
¾   cup golden raisins
⅓   cup sugar
1   teaspoon lemon juice
½   teaspoon cinnamon

Rum sauce:
6   large egg yolks
1   cup whipping cream, warmed
1   cup milk, warmed
½   cup sugar
3   tablespoons rum
2   teaspoons vanilla

In top of double boiler combine all sauce ingredients except rum and vanilla. Cook slowly over simmering water for 20 minutes, stirring frequently. Remove from heat. Stir in rum and vanilla.

In large skillet melt butter. Add apples, raisins, sugar, lemon juice, and cinnamon. Sauté until apples are just tender, about 10 minutes.

To serve pour sauce on serving plate and spoon warm apples on top.

SWEDISH APPLES

Serves 4

½   cup finely ground almonds
½   cup plus 2 tablespoons sugar, divided
2   tablespoons water
4   medium tart apples, peeled
3   tablespoons butter, melted
5   tablespoons fine bread crumbs
10   ounces frozen raspberries, thawed
¼   teaspoon almond extract
    whole raspberries, optional

Combine almonds, ½ cup sugar, and water. Blend until soft paste forms.

Cut ⅓ inch from top of each apple. Core apples, leaving ⅓-inch base at bottom. Roll apples in butter and then in mixture of crumbs and 2 tablespoons sugar. Place apples upright in lightly buttered 8-inch square baking dish. Fill cavities with almond paste, mounding top and covering cut area. Bake in preheated 325° oven 30 to 35 minutes or until easily pierced with fork. Do not allow apples to become too soft.

In food processor or blender purée raspberries. Add extract and blend. Chill. To serve, ladle cold raspberry sauce on each serving plate. Place hot apple upright in center of plate. Decorate with several whole raspberries. Additional sauce may be passed.

Sabayon sauce (page 435) may be substituted for raspberry sauce.

PLUM BRÛLÉE

Serves 4

4   large plums, halved, pitted
¾   cup crème fraîche, preferred, or sour cream
1   tablespoon sugar
1   teaspoon orange liqueur or ¼ teaspoon grated fresh orange rind
¼   teaspoon vanilla
⅛   teaspoon nutmeg
¼   cup packed brown sugar

Arrange plums skin side down in single layer in small buttered baking dish. Combine crème fraîche or sour cream, sugar, orange liqueur or grated rind, vanilla, and nutmeg. Mix well. Spoon over plums. Sprinkle with brown sugar. Broil 6 inches from heat 5 minutes or until sugar melts. Serve warm.

Variation:
Follow above directions, eliminating crème fraîche from mixture. Broil. Serve crème fraîche (page 423) on side.

POACHED PEARS WITH RASPBERRY SAUCE

Serves 6

Simplicity in its most elegant form.

- 4 cups water
- 1½ cups sugar
- 1 vanilla bean
- 1 lemon, halved
- 6 Bartlett pears, peeled
- 1 pound frozen raspberries in syrup
- 1 cup raspberries, strawberries, or blueberries, optional
- 1 pint whipping cream
- 1 tablespoon confectioners sugar
- 2¼ ounces sliced almonds, lightly toasted

In large kettle combine water, sugar, and vanilla bean. Squeeze juice from lemon halves into sugar mixture. Add lemon halves. Trim bottoms of pears to stand upright. Add pears to syrup. Simmer until pears are soft enough to be pierced easily with sharp knife. Remove kettle from heat. Cool pears in syrup. Refrigerate.

In saucepan simmer frozen raspberries in syrup. Add fresh berries if desired. Simmer 30 minutes, stirring frequently. Cool. Purée in food processor or blender. Strain. Chill.

Shortly before serving, whip cream with confectioners sugar until stiff peaks form.

To serve, stand each cold poached pear in center of dessert plate. Pour raspberry sauce over pear. Using pastry bag, pipe whipped cream around pear. Sprinkle with almonds.

RASPBERRIES SABAYON

Serves 6 to 8

- 1 whole egg and 8 egg yolks
- 1 cup sugar
- 1½ cups dry white wine
- 2 tablespoons raspberry brandy
- 1 quart raspberries

With electric mixer beat egg, egg yolks, and sugar 8 minutes. Add white wine. Beat 2 minutes at high speed. Transfer mixture to top of double boiler. Cook over high heat, beating with wire whisk until thick. Add raspberry brandy. Whip 1 minute. Pour warm sauce into champagne glasses that have been filled with raspberries. Serve warm.

MELON IN RUM-LIME SAUCE

Serves 10

⅔ cup sugar
⅓ cup water
1 teaspoon grated lime rind
6 tablespoons lime juice
½ cup light rum
1 tablespoon chopped fresh mint, optional
1 cantaloupe
1 small honeydew melon
⅛ small watermelon
1 cup berries of choice

In small saucepan combine sugar and water. Bring to boil. Reduce heat and simmer 5 minutes. Add lime rind and cool. Stir in lime juice, rum, and mint if desired.

Cut melons into balls of different sizes. Combine with berries in large bowl. Pour sauce over fruit. Cover and chill several hours.

See photo page 226.

BANANAS GUADALUPE

Serves 4 to 6

Rich and cool; perfect for a Mexican fiesta.

4 large, firm bananas
6 tablespoons unsalted butter
½ cup sugar, divided
1 cup whipping cream
2-3 tablespoons white rum or to taste
¾ teaspoon vanilla
dash ground cloves or freshly ground nutmeg

Peel bananas and slice in half lengthwise. Gently sauté in butter until golden brown. Drain on paper towel. Place on shallow serving platter or in individual bowls. Cool. Sprinkle bananas with ¼ cup sugar.

Whip cream until stiff peaks form. Fold in ¼ cup sugar, rum, and vanilla. Completely cover bananas with mixture. Chill. Before serving sprinkle lightly with cloves or nutmeg.

BLUEBERRIES BAKED IN COINTREAU

Serves 4

1 tablespoon fresh lemon juice
3 tablespoons Cointreau
1 pint blueberries
½ cup sugar
1½ teaspoons arrowroot
⅛ teaspoon salt
2 tablespoons butter, melted
¼ teaspoon almond extract
  several grinds fresh nutmeg

Topping:
¼ cup flour
⅛ teaspoon salt
¼ cup brown sugar
2 tablespoons butter, softened
½ teaspoon cinnamon

vanilla ice cream or whipping cream, whipped with ½ teaspoon
  vanilla and 1 tablespoon confectioners sugar

In medium bowl pour lemon juice and Cointreau over berries. Let stand at least 30 minutes. Combine sugar, arrowroot, and salt. Mix well. Add to berries. Toss lightly. Stir in butter and almond extract. Spoon mixture evenly into 4 buttered 6-ounce custard cups. Grind a little nutmeg over top of each cup.

Combine flour, salt, and brown sugar. Mix well. Cut butter into mixture, blending well. Spread mixture evenly over custard cups. Sprinkle with cinnamon.

Place cups on baking sheet. Bake in preheated 375° oven 25 minutes or until bubbly and brown. Serve hot with vanilla ice cream or sweetened whipped cream.

RHUBARB BETTY

Serves 6 to 8

6 cups rhubarb, in ½-inch pieces
⅓ cup sugar
1 tablespoon lemon juice

Topping:
1 cup flour
1 cup sugar
¼ pound butter

whipping cream, whipped, or vanilla ice cream, optional

In top of double boiler, steam rhubarb a few minutes. Add small amount of sugar. Continue cooking, stirring frequently, gradually adding all sugar. When rhubarb is tender-crisp, after about 25 minutes, remove from heat. Add lemon juice. Transfer rhubarb to buttered 2-quart baking dish.

Combine flour and sugar. Mix well. Cut in butter until mixture is crumbly. Spread over rhubarb. Bake in preheated 350° oven 45 minutes. Serve warm or chilled with whipped cream or ice cream.

APPLE CRISP

Serves 8

4 cups peeled, cored, sliced apples, Granny Smith, Jonathan, or McIntosh
1 teaspoon cinnamon
½ teaspoon salt
¼ cup water
¾ cup flour, sifted
1 cup sugar
6 tablespoons butter
whipping cream, whipped, or vanilla ice cream, optional

Arrange apples in buttered 10- by 6- by 2-inch baking pan. Sprinkle with cinnamon, salt, and water. Combine flour, sugar, and butter with pastry cutter. Mix until consistency of coarse meal. Sprinkle mixture over apples. Bake in preheated 350° oven 40 minutes. Serve warm with whipped cream or ice cream if desired.

Variations:
For **Plum Crisp** substitute sliced purple plums for apples. Eliminate water.
For **Peach Crisp** substitute sliced peaches for apples.

CRANBERRY COBBLER

Serves 6

2¼ cups cranberries
¼ cup sugar
⅓ cup coarsely chopped pecans
6 tablespoons melted butter, divided
1 egg, beaten
½ teaspoon vanilla
½ cup sugar
½ cup flour
ice cream or whipped cream

Spread cranberries evenly over bottom of buttered 9-inch pie pan. Combine ¼ cup sugar, pecans, and 4 tablespoons butter. Pour over cranberries. Combine egg, vanilla, sugar, flour, and 2 tablespoons butter until flour is moistened. Spread evenly over cranberries. Bake in preheated 350° oven 45 minutes. Serve warm, topped with ice cream or whipped cream.

SOUFFLÉ GRAND MARNIER

Serves 6 to 8

1 cup sugar, divided
4 eggs, separated
4 teaspoons unflavored gelatin
¼ cup cold water
½ cup Grand Marnier
2 teaspoons lemon juice
1 cup whipping cream, whipped

Combine ½ cup sugar with egg yolks in top of double boiler. Stirring constantly, cook 5 minutes or until thickened. Cool slightly. Soften gelatin in cold water. Stir into egg yolk mixture. Add liqueur and lemon juice. Mix well. Beat egg whites with remaining ½ cup sugar. In separate large bowl whip cream stiffly. Pour egg whites over cream. Pour hot mixture over all. Gently fold together and spoon into soufflé dish or individual sherbet glasses. Chill at least 4 hours.

Recipe serves 6 in soufflé dish or 8 in sherbet glasses.

ALMOND SOUFFLÉ

Serves 4 to 6

⅓ cup plus 2 tablespoons superfine sugar, divided
3 tablespoons unsalted butter
3 tablespoons flour
¾ cup hot milk
3 tablespoons almond liqueur
5 eggs, separated
   pinch salt
   confectioners sugar

Almond sauce:
1 cup vanilla ice cream, softened
½ cup whipping cream, whipped
2 ounces Amaretto or 1 teaspoon almond extract

Butter 2-quart soufflé dish. Sprinkle with 2 tablespoons sugar to coat all sides. Tie foil around outside to form 4-inch collar.

In heavy saucepan melt butter. Add flour. Cook 2 minutes, stirring constantly. Gradually stir in milk. Continue to cook, stirring, until smooth and thickened. Stir in ⅓ cup sugar. Remove from heat and blend in liqueur. When slightly cooled stir in egg yolks. Mixture may be set aside, covered, for 1 hour.

Beat egg whites with 2 tablespoons sugar and salt until stiff but not dry. Fold gently into yolk mixture. Pour into soufflé dish. Bake in preheated 375° oven 30 minutes or until puffed and golden brown. Do not open oven door during baking. Remove from oven; detach collar. Sprinkle with confectioners sugar. Serve immediately.

Soufflé may remain in oven, with heat off, 5 to 10 minutes after baking if necessary.

Combine ice cream, whipped cream, and Amaretto or extract. Stir to blend well. Serve immediately.

Variation:
To make *Vanilla Sauce* substitute vanilla extract for almond extract.

COLD LEMON SOUFFLÉ

Serves 6 to 8

6   eggs, separated
1½   cups sugar
     grated rind of 2 lemons
1   tablespoon unflavored gelatin
     juice of 3 lemons
1   pint whipping cream
     chocolate leaves, optional

In top of double boiler combine egg yolks, sugar, and grated lemon rind. Mix well. Cook 15 minutes, stirring occasionally.

In small saucepan combine gelatin and juice. Cook over low heat until gelatin is dissolved. Add to yolk mixture. Cool.

Beat egg whites until stiff peaks form. Whip cream until stiff peaks form. Fold egg whites and cream into yolk mixture. Pour into oiled 6-cup melon mold. Refrigerate overnight.

May be prepared in advance and frozen. Thaw in refrigerator before serving.

Garnish with chocolate leaves (page 439) if desired.

APPLE SOUFFLÉ

Serves 4 to 6

6-7   Granny Smith apples, peeled, cored, thinly sliced
¼   pound butter, melted, divided
1   teaspoon lemon juice
3   eggs, separated
½   cup flour
½   cup milk
1   teaspoon salt
½   cup plus 1 tablespoon sugar, divided
1   teaspoon cinnamon

In skillet sauté apples in half the butter until glossy, about 4 minutes. Stir in lemon juice.

In large bowl beat egg yolks. Add flour, milk, salt, and 1 tablespoon sugar. Mix well. Stir in apples.

Beat egg whites until stiff peaks form. Fold into apple mixture. Pour into greased 1½-quart soufflé dish. Combine remaining butter with ½ cup sugar and cinnamon. Sprinkle over soufflé. Bake in preheated 450° oven 20 minutes. Reduce heat to 350° and bake 10 minutes. Serve immediately.

Accompany with lemon ice cream (page 391) if desired.

CHILLED COFFEE SOUFFLÉ

Serves 8

2 ounces semi-sweet chocolate
4 teaspoons instant coffee crystals
3 eggs
6 egg yolks
1 cup sugar
1 tablespoon unflavored gelatin
2 tablespoons water
2 cups whipping cream

Melt chocolate. Stir in coffee crystals. In top of double boiler combine and heat eggs, egg yolks, and sugar. Beat until light. Stir in chocolate mixture. Dissolve gelatin in water. Add to chocolate mixture. Beat 3 minutes. Remove top of double boiler from heat. Cool. Whip cream and fold into mixture. Pour into soufflé dish. Refrigerate.

Serve with vanilla sauce (page 375) flavored with brandy or Tia Maria.

MAPLE MOUSSE

Serves 6

Caramel brittle:
1 cup sugar

Mousse:
4 egg yolks
1 cup pure maple syrup
1 pint whipping cream, whipped

In heavy skillet melt sugar over low heat. Stir constantly until completely dissolved and nut brown in color. Pour into oiled pan. Let mixture cool and harden. Break into pieces. Transfer to towel and fold to form bag. Hammer bag until brittle is crushed into small bits.

In top of double boiler beat yolks until light. Add syrup. Place over simmering water. Cook 15 minutes stirring constantly. Transfer top of double boiler to large bowl filled with ice. Stir mixture until cool. Fold in whipped cream. Blend pulverized caramel brittle into mixture. Pour into 6-cup mold sprayed with vegetable oil. Cover top with plastic wrap. Freeze several hours.

A mold in shape of melon or other fruit makes a spectacular presentation.

May be prepared several days in advance.

MAPLE MARRON MOUSSE

Serves 8 to 10

Mousse:
3   egg yolks
    pinch salt
1   teaspoon dark rum or cognac
¾   cup premium quality maple syrup
15 ounces brandied marrons, drained, finely chopped
1   pint whipping cream

Garnish:
1   cup whipping cream
2   teaspoons superfine sugar
½   pint fresh blueberries
½   pint fresh raspberries

Mousse:
To be prepared day ahead.

In top of double boiler whisk egg yolks until light. Add salt and liquor. Cook over moderate heat. Gradually add syrup, stirring constantly. Cook until blended and thickened, 12 to 15 minutes. Cool to room temperature. Stir in marrons. Whip cream until stiff peaks form. Fold into syrup mixture. Rinse 6-cup ring mold in cold water and pour mixture into wet mold. Cover and freeze.

Garnish:
Thirty minutes before serving, transfer mousse in mold to refrigerator. Whip cream with sugar to moderately thick consistency. Do not overbeat. Invert mold on serving platter. Spoon cream in center and around sides of mold. Decorate cream border and center with blue and red berries.

Serves 6

1½ teaspoons unflavored gelatin
½ cup milk
6 ounces white chocolate
1 teaspoon vanilla
1 cup whipping cream
¼ teaspoon lemon juice
⅛ teaspoon salt
2 egg whites
  shaved chocolate curls, optional
  green leaves, optional

Sauce:
2 tablespoons unsalted butter
½ cup sugar
2 cups whipping cream, divided
½ cup Dutch cocoa

Soften gelatin in milk. When gelatin is dissolved, transfer to top of double boiler. Add chocolate. Stir over simmering water until melted. Remove from heat. Stir in vanilla. Transfer to large bowl. Cool. Beat whipping cream until soft peaks form. Carefully fold into chocolate mixture. Add lemon juice and salt to egg whites. Beat until stiff peaks form. Carefully fold into chocolate mixture. Chill.

In saucepan over medium heat melt butter. Add sugar and 1 cup cream, stirring. Add cocoa, whisking into mixture. Add remaining cream and bring just to simmer. Remove from heat. Strain. Place plastic wrap directly on surface to prevent skin from forming. Cool.

To serve, cover surface of individual serving plates with sauce. With heated spoon scoop 2 ovals of mousse over sauce. Garnish with chocolate curls and waxy green leaf, if desired.

SNOWFLAKE MOUSSE

Serves 12

2 tablespoons plain gelatin
½ cup cold water
⅓ cup boiling water
6 egg whites
¼ teaspoon salt
¾ cup sugar
1 pint whipping cream, whipped
1 teaspoon vanilla
3½ ounces flaked coconut
   whole strawberries

Strawberry kirsch sauce:
1 pint strawberries
4 ounces currant jelly
3 tablespoons kirsch

In small bowl soften gelatin in cold water. Add boiling water. Stir until dissolved. Cool. In large bowl beat egg whites with salt until frothy. Add sugar 1 teaspoon at a time. Beat until stiff peaks form. Add gelatin slowly. Beat. Combine vanilla and whipped cream. Gently fold into mixture.

Coat bottom and sides of buttered 9-inch springform with ½ cup coconut. Pour cream mixture into springform. Sprinkle top with remaining coconut. Refrigerate overnight.

Sauce:
Purée strawberries in blender or food processor. Strain through fine sieve. Melt currant jelly with kirsch. Mix with strawberry purée. Chill.

To serve, unmold mousse. Garnish with whole berries and serve with sauce.

CHOCOLATE BREAD PUDDING

Serves 8

10 slices white bread, crusts removed
1½ cups sugar
2 ounces unsweetened chocolate
1½ cups milk
2 eggs
¼ teaspoon vanilla
    crème fraîche, (see page 423) or whipping cream, whipped

In food processor or blender process bread to coarse, lumpy consistency, making 4 cups. Combine crumbs with sugar.

In saucepan melt chocolate in milk over low heat. Do not bring to boil. Cool and transfer to food processor or blender. Process with eggs. Transfer to top of double boiler. Add bread crumb-sugar mixture. Blend well. Cook uncovered over low heat 45 minutes, stirring occasionally. Add vanilla. Serve warm topped with crème fraîche or whipped cream.

FRENCH BREAD AND BUTTER PUDDING

Serves 6 to 8

⅔ cup golden raisins
    sherry
8 slices of French bread, ½-inch thick
    butter, softend
1 tablespoon cinnamon, divided
5 eggs
⅔ cup sugar
    pinch salt
3 cups scalded milk or 1 cup whipping cream and 2 cups milk
2 teaspoons vanilla
    whipping cream or half and half, optional

Soak raisins in sherry to cover 30 minutes. Trim bread crusts. Butter bread and cut into halves. Arrange half of bread slices in buttered 8-inch baking dish. Sprinkle with 1½ teaspoons cinnamon. Drain raisins and sprinkle over bread. Layer remaining bread over raisins. Sprinkle with remaining cinnamon.

Beat eggs with sugar and salt until pale yellow. Add milk gradually, stirring constantly. Add vanilla. Mix well. Strain mixture over bread slices. Let stand 15 minutes. Place baking dish in pan of hot water. Bake in preheated 375° oven 45 minutes or until knife inserted in center of pudding comes out clean. Serve warm, with cream if desired.

STEAMED CHOCOLATE PUDDING WITH CHERRY SAUCE

Serves 8 to 10

12 ounces semi-sweet chocolate chips
1/3 cup strong coffee
2 eggs
1 cup sugar
1 teaspoon vanilla
1¾ cups flour
½ teaspoon salt
½ teaspoon baking soda
¼ teaspoon cream of tartar
⅔ cup water

Cherry sauce:
16 ounces canned dark, sweet pitted cherries with syrup
¼ cup sugar
4 teaspoons cornstarch
½ teaspoon salt
1 tablespoon butter
2 tablespoons kirsch or 1 teaspoon vanilla

In top of double boiler over simmering water melt chocolate chips with coffee. Blend well. Beat eggs until foamy. Add sugar gradually. Beat on medium speed until thick and light colored. Blend chocolate mixture and vanilla with eggs. Sift together flour, salt, baking soda, and cream of tartar. With mixer on low speed add dry ingredients to chocolate-egg mixture alternately with water. Beat just until combined.

Pour into generously greased and sugared 5- to 6-cup pudding mold. Cover with wax paper and then with top of mold. Place on rack in large kettle. Pour water in kettle until mold is half submerged. Cover kettle and bring water to boil. Reduce to simmer and cook 2 hours. May be held in hot water until ready to serve.

Cherry sauce:
Drain cherries, reserving syrup. Measure syrup and add enough water for 1 cup liquid. In saucepan combine sugar, cornstarch, and salt. Gradually stir in syrup. Bring to boil over medium heat stirring constantly. Add cherries. Boil 1 minute. Remove from heat. Blend in butter and kirsch or vanilla.

Unmold pudding onto platter. Cut into wedges. Serve with cherry sauce.

PERSIMMON PUDDING

Serves 10 to 12

2 cups raisins, all dark or 1 cup golden and 1 cup dark
1 cup plus 1 tablespoon brandy, divided
2 cups chopped walnuts
2 cups puréed very ripe persimmon pulp
2 teaspoons vegetable oil
1 teaspoon vanilla
2 cups sugar
2 cups flour
⅛ teaspoon ground cloves
⅛ teaspoon ground nutmeg
2 teaspoons baking soda
2 teaspoons cinnamon
1 teaspoon salt
1 cup milk

Sauce:
2 cups whipping cream
2 tablespoons brandy
4 tablespoons sugar
  nutmeg to taste

Soak raisins in 1 cup brandy until soft. In large bowl combine walnuts, persimmon, oil, vanilla, 1 tablespoon brandy, and drained raisins. Mix well.

Sift together sugar, flour, cloves, nutmeg, soda, cinnamon, and salt. Add to persimmon mixture alternately with milk, a third at a time. Mix well.

Grease and flour 9-inch angel food cake pan. Line bottom with wax paper. Pour pudding into pan. Bake in preheated 325° oven 1½ hours. Pudding should shrink from sides slightly and be partially congealed in center. Remove from oven. When cool invert onto serving platter and remove from pan.

Whip cream until soft peaks form. Mix brandy and sugar with whipped cream. Season with nutmeg.

Serve pudding at room temperature with sauce on the side. For presentation, flame pudding with 100-proof brandy.

Pudding may be frozen after baking, then removed from freezer the night before serving. It may be served at room temperature or wrapped in foil and placed in preheated 300° oven 10 to 15 minutes.

APRICOT CURRANT DATE-NUT PUDDING

Serves 6

¼ pound butter or margarine
1 cup sugar
2 eggs, beaten
1 cup milk
1½ tablespoons flour
1½ teaspoons baking powder
½ cup chopped, dried apricots
⅓ cup chopped, pitted dates
¼ cup currants
1 cup chopped pecans
1 cup whipping cream, whipped

Cream butter. Add sugar and beat until fluffy. Add eggs, milk, flour, and baking powder. Mix well. Fold in fruits and nuts. Pour into buttered 1½ quart casserole. Bake in preheated 325° oven 1 hour or until set. Serve warm or at room temperature with dollop of whipped cream.

MOCHA POT DE CRÈME

Serves 8

12 ounces sweet dark chocolate
1½ cups strong coffee, divided
2 tablespoons sugar
⅛ teaspoon salt
2 eggs
2 teaspoons vanilla
½ pint whipping cream, whipped, optional
grated sweet chocolate, optional

In top of double boiler melt chocolate in ½ cup coffee. Stir until smooth. Remove from heat.

In food processor or blender combine sugar, salt, eggs, and vanilla. Bring remaining 1 cup coffee to boil and slowly add to ingredients in food processor. Add melted chocolate. Cover and blend 1 minute. Pour mixture into 8 pot de crème cups. Chill. If desired, top each cup with a dollop of whipped cream. Sprinkle with grated chocolate.

CHRISTMAS PUDDING WITH BRANDY SAUCE

Serves 8 to 10

2 cups whole cranberries
½ cup hot water
½ cup molasses
1½ cups flour
2 teaspoons baking soda
1 teaspoon baking powder
½ teaspoon cinnamon

Brandy sauce:
1 cup melted butter
1 cup whipping cream
2 cups sugar
⅓ cup brandy

In large bowl combine cranberries, water, and molasses. Sift together flour, soda, powder, and cinnamon. Add to cranberry mixture. Stir to combine well. Pour into oiled 6- to 8-cup mold.

Cover mold securely with wax paper or mold cover. Place on rack in deep kettle. Add water to level of rack. Bring water to boil, lower heat to maintain water at simmer, cover kettle and steam 3 hours. Add hot water as needed to keep it at rack level.

Remove from kettle, remove mold cover and place in preheated 350° oven 1 minute to dry top slightly. Remove from oven, loosen at one side to let in air, and turn out onto serving dish. Serve with warm brandy sauce.

Brandy sauce:
In medium saucepan combine all sauce ingredients. Stir to blend well. Heat.

LEMON CUPS

Serves 8

1 cup sugar
¼ cup sifted flour
2 tablespoons vegetable oil
¼ teaspoon salt
2 teaspoons grated lemon rind
⅓ cup lemon juice
3 eggs, separated
1½ cups milk, scalded
8 strawberries, optional

Combine sugar, flour, oil, and salt. Mix well. Add rind and juice. Beat egg yolks and stir into milk. Combine with sugar mixture.

Beat egg whites until stiff peaks form. Fold egg whites into sugar mixture. Fill 8 custard cups and set in pan. Fill pan with enough very hot water to submerge cups halfway. Bake in preheated 325° oven 40 minutes. Cool.

To serve, invert onto individual plates. Garnish with strawberry if desired.

MAPLE-COFFEE TRIFLE

Serves 6

An unusual make-ahead trifle. Ideal for leftover sponge or pound cake.

1 cup milk, scalded
3 egg yolks, well beaten
½ cup plus 1½ tablespoons maple syrup
¼ teaspoon salt
⅓-½ sponge or pound cake
½ cup strong coffee
½ cup whipping cream
1 teaspoon sugar
½ teaspoon vanilla
Brazil nuts or pecans

In top of double boiler combine milk and yolks. Stir gently until blended. Add ½ cup maple syrup and salt. Stirring, cook 10 minutes or until mixture becomes thick, smooth custard. Cool to room temperature.

Slice cake to fit bottom and sides of 1-quart dish. Combine coffee and 1½ tablespoons maple syrup. Pour over cake. Let stand 10 minutes. Pour cooled custard over cake. Refrigerate 2 hours. Whip cream. Add sugar and vanilla. Spread whipped cream over trifle. Garnish top with nuts.

Rum may be substituted for maple syrup.

CRÈME BRÛLÉE, THE PRINCE AND THE PAUPER

Serves 8

From Woodstock, Vermont, a favorite dessert.

8   egg yolks
1   cup sugar
1   teaspoon vanilla
1   quart whipping cream
    brown sugar

In large bowl combine yolks, sugar, and vanilla. Beat until light. Fold in cream. Pour into 8 greased small soufflé dishes or greased individual crème brûlée dishes. Place dishes in large pan filled with ½ inch hot water.

Bake in preheated 350° oven 45 to 50 minutes. Remove from water and cool. Before serving sprinkle liberally with brown sugar. Broil until sugar is carmelized.

Alternate carmelizing method:
Heat crème brûlée iron (available in specialty cookware stores) on stove burner until very hot. Gently "iron" topping until sugar is completely melted and carmelized, taking care not to burn sugar.

May be flavored with Kahlúa, Amaretto, or Grand Marnier if desired.

CLASSIC FLAN

Serves 10

2   cups sugar, divided
1   quart milk
5   eggs
1   teaspoon vanilla

Heat heavy pan over medium heat. Pour in 1 cup sugar. Cook until sugar begins to dissolve. Increase heat and stir until sugar becomes light or medium brown. (Caution: too brown will create a bitter taste.) Immediately pour cooked sugar into bottom of 6-cup solid bottom tube mold. Quickly rotate mold to cover outer sides halfway up. Spoon syrup onto inner wall. Cool.

In saucepan combine milk and 1 cup sugar. Bring to boil. Cool. Beat eggs well. Add cooled milk mixture gradually, beating briefly. Stir in vanilla. Strain into cooled, syrup-coated mold. Set mold in pan half filled with hot water. Bake in preheated 325° oven 2 hours. Remove from water and cool. Refrigerate until cold before serving.

To unmold run sharp knife along inner and outer walls of mold. Using serving plate with shallow sides to contain pool of extra syrup, invert flan to unmold. Spoon syrup over each serving.

EGGNOG MOLD WITH RASPBERRY SAUCE

Serves 12

5 cups dairy eggnog, divided
⅓ cup sugar
3 tablespoons unflavored gelatin
6 tablespoons cold water
½ teaspoon nutmeg
2 cups whipping cream, whipped
20 ounces frozen raspberries, thawed
2 tablespoons cornstarch
2 tablespoons brandy
1-2 pints raspberries, optional

Heat 1 cup eggnog. Stir in sugar. Blend gelatin into cold water. Stir into hot eggnog. Heat and stir until gelatin dissolves. Pour into large bowl. Stir in remaining 4 cups eggnog and nutmeg. Chill until slightly thickened. Fold in whipped cream. Pour into 8- to 9-cup ring mold. Chill until firm.

Drain thawed raspberries, reserving juice. In saucepan blend juice and cornstarch until clear. Heat to boil. Add brandy and drained raspberries.

Invert mold onto serving platter. Fill center with fresh raspberries if desired. Serve sauce hot or cold with mold.

Strawberries may be substituted for raspberries.

CHOCOLATE NUT CRUNCH

Serves 8 to 10

1 cup slivered almonds
½ pound plus 1 tablespoon butter, divided
    salt to taste
1⅓ cups graham cracker crumbs
4 cups confectioners sugar
1 cup cocoa
4 eggs
2 teaspoons vanilla
    kiwi or berries, optional

Sauté almonds in 1 tablespoon butter until lightly browned. Salt generously, taking care not to oversalt.

Spread half the graham cracker crumbs over bottom of buttered 13½- by 8¾- by 1¾-inch glass pan. Combine sugar, cocoa, softened ½ pound butter, eggs, and vanilla. Beat until smooth. Spread gently over graham cracker crumbs. Sprinkle almonds over top. Layer remaining graham cracker crumbs over all. Refrigerate until served. Cut into squares of desired size.

FRESH STRAWBERRY SORBET

Serves 8

A light, fresh summer dessert, cool as a Ravinia breeze.

3 pints strawberries, hulled
2 cups sugar
1½ cups fresh orange juice
½ cup fresh lemon juice
½ cup Grand Marnier
 whole strawberries
 mint leaves

In food processor or blender combine berries, sugar, and fruit juices. Blend until liquid. Stir in Grand Marnier. Pour into 2½-quart bowl. Freeze to sherbet consistency. With ice cream scoop form balls. Place balls in crystal bowl. Garnish with whole berries and mint leaves.

For smoother texture and longer storage period sorbet may be made in dasher-type ice cream maker.

See photo page 233.

FRESH RHUBARB SORBET

Yield:
approximately
1 quart

1½ pounds rhubarb, in 1-inch pieces
¾ cup sugar
1½ cups water
2 tablespoons fresh lemon juice

Place rhubarb in glass baking dish. Cover and bake in preheated 350° oven 25 minutes or until soft.

While rhubarb is baking combine sugar and water in small saucepan. Boil 5 minutes. Cool. In food processor or blender purée rhubarb and juice. Add sugar syrup and lemon juice. Mix well.

Pour into dasher-type ice cream maker. Process according to manufacturer's directions. Store in airtight freezer containers. Freeze until firm. Before serving thaw 30 minutes at room temperature or 1 hour in refrigerator.

FRESH ORANGE AND PAPAYA SORBET

Yield:
approximately
1 quart

2½ **pounds papaya, peeled, in large chunks**
½   **cup sugar**
1   **cup fresh orange juice**
¼   **cup fresh lemon juice**
1   **teaspoon grated lemon rind**
    whipping cream, whipped
    whole strawberries

In food processor combine papaya, sugar, orange juice, and lemon juice. Purée. Stir in lemon rind. Pour mixture into dasher-type ice cream maker. Process according to manufacturer's directions. To serve scoop into balls. Top with dollop of whipped cream and strawberry with hull.

See photo page 233.

PEAR SORBET WITH RIESLING

Yield:
approximately
1 quart

A delicate fresh pear flavor.

    rind of 1 lemon, finely grated
4   **tablespoons strained fresh lemon juice**
2   **pounds pears**
¾   **cup sugar**
1   **cup Riesling wine or champagne**

In large bowl combine lemon rind and lemon juice. Peel and core pears. Cut into chunks. To prevent discoloring, place pear chunks in bowl containing lemon and a sprinkling of sugar. When all pears are prepared, add remaining sugar. In food processor or blender purée pear, lemon, and sugar mixture until sugar has dissolved. Add wine and blend well.

Pour into dasher-type ice cream maker. Process according to manufacturer's directions. Sorbet will be white. Transfer to airtight container and freeze until firm. Before serving thaw 30 minutes at room temperature or 1 hour in refrigerator.

See photo page 233.

LEMON ICE CREAM

Yield: 1½ quarts   *Special equipment unnecessary. No fuss, no muss, no bother.*

3   **cups sugar**
1   **quart milk**
¾   **cup lemon juice**
    juice of 1 orange
1   **pint whipping cream, whipped**

In large bowl combine sugar and milk. Mix well. Stir in combined juices. Fold in whipped cream. Transfer to airtight container and freeze.

Serve with fresh blueberries, raspberries, or strawberries.

MOCHA CREAM

Serves 4 to 6

1   **quart premium chocolate ice cream**
2   **tablespoons Kahlúa**
2   **tablespoons dark rum**
½   **cup pulverized hard coffee candy**
½   **cup freeze-dried decaffeinated coffee crystals**

Soften ice cream. Stir in Kahlúa and rum. Mix well. Cover and freeze 4 to 6 hours. Spoon into brandy snifters or glass bowls. Pass candy and coffee in separate bowls to sprinkle in combination over ice cream.

FROZEN FRUIT YOGURT

Serves 4

16   **ounces fruit-flavored yogurt**
16   **ounces non-dairy whipped topping**
1   **cup fresh fruit garnish to match yogurt flavor**
8   **mint leaves**

In food processor or blender combine yogurt and whipped topping. Blend 2 minutes. Pour into 4 wide-mouthed glasses. Cover with plastic wrap and freeze 4 hours. Remove to refrigerator 1 hour before serving. Garnish with fresh fruit and mint leaves.

WHISKEY SOUR SLUSH IN ORANGE SHELLS

Yield: 2 cups

6   ounces frozen concentrated sweetened lemonade
6   ounces club soda
6   ounces bourbon
1   tablespoon sugar
    prepared orange shells
    mint leaves

Place all ingredients except orange shells and mint leaves in food processor or blender. Frappé quickly. Pour into metal freezer tray. Place in freezer overnight or until mixture reaches consistency of slush.

Serve in frosted sherbet glasses or frozen orange shells. Garnish with mint leaf.

Shells may be prepared, filled well in advance, and stored in freezer.

Variation:
To serve as beverage, prepare Whiskey Sour by combining lemonade, soda, bourbon and sugar. Frappé. Serve over ice.

PRALINE PUMPKIN ICE CREAM PIE

Serves 8 to 9

4   tablespoons butter
⅔   cup finely chopped pecans
⅔   cup brown sugar
1   9-inch baked pie crust (page 364)
1   quart premium vanilla ice cream, softened
1   cup mashed, cooked pumpkin, or 1 cup canned pumpkin
½   cup sugar
      pinch salt
½   teaspoon cinnamon
½   teaspoon ground ginger
¼   teaspoon nutmeg
½   pint whipping cream, whipped, optional

In small saucepan over low heat melt butter. Add pecans and brown sugar. Stirring frequently, cook until mixture begins to brown, 5 to 7 minutes. Spread on cookie sheet. Cool. Transfer to plastic bag or place between 2 sheets brown paper. Crumble with rolling pin. Sprinkle half of praline mixture into pie crust.

Combine ice cream with remaining ingredients except whipped cream. Mix well. Pour into pie crust. Top with remaining praline mixture.

Freeze until solid. Cover with plastic wrap. Remove from freezer and uncover 30 minutes before serving. Garnish with whipped cream if desired.

CHOCOLATE CRESCENDO ICE CREAM PIE

Serves 10

Ice Cream:
- 6 ounces unsweetened chocolate
- 2 tablespoons unsalted butter
- 1½ cups sugar
- ⅓ cup light corn syrup
- 2 cups half and half, divided
- 3 large eggs, beaten
- 2 cups whipping cream
- 2 teaspoons vanilla
- 12 ounces semi-sweet chocolate chips

Crust:
- 2 egg whites
- ¼ teaspoon cream of tartar
- ½ cup sugar
- ¾ cup mini chocolate chips

caramel or butterscotch sauce

In large saucepan melt chocolate and butter over low heat, stirring constantly. Add sugar, corn syrup, and ⅔ cup half and half. Over medium heat bring mixture to boil, stirring constantly. Simmer 4 minutes without stirring. Remove from heat and cool in pan.

In small bowl combine half the chocolate mixture with eggs. Mix well. Stir egg mixture into remaining chocolate mixture in pan. Stirring, cook 1 minute or until slightly thickened. Cool to lukewarm. Add whipping cream, vanilla, and remaining 1⅓ cups half and half.

Transfer to bowl. Cover and refrigerate overnight. Add chocolate chips. Process in electric ice cream machine according to manufacturer's directions. Store in freezer in airtight containers.

Beat egg whites until frothy. Gradually add cream of tartar and sugar, beating until stiff peaks form. Fold in chocolate chips. Spread onto bottom and sides of 9-inch oven-proof glass pie pan, building up ½ inch above rim. If desired sprinkle additional chocolate chips over top of rim.

Bake in preheated 275° oven 45 minutes. Turn off oven. Cool in closed oven 45 minutes. Remove from oven and cool thoroughly. Fill crust with ice cream, softened. Spread thin layer of sauce over top. Cover with plastic wrap and freeze.

Crust also may be filled with 1 quart commercial ice cream of choice, preferably rocky road.

ORANGE EGGNOG FRAPPÉ

Serves 4

1 pint vanilla ice cream
⅓ cup orange liqueur
3 tablespoons frozen orange juice concentrate, thawed
2 cups dairy eggnog
   nutmeg

Scoop ice cream into 4 tall glasses. In bowl combine liqueur, orange juice, and eggnog. Mix well. Pour over ice cream and stir lightly. Grate nutmeg over each serving. Serve immediately.

ALMOND BUTTER COOKIES

Yield: 5 to 6 dozen

½ pound butter
1 cup sugar
1 egg
1 teaspoon lemon juice
1 teaspoon vanilla
1¼-1½ cups flour
3-4 dozen slivered almonds, toasted

Cream butter and sugar. Add egg. Mix well. Stir in lemon juice and vanilla. Add flour. Mix well. Drop by ½ teaspoonsful on ungreased cookie sheets. Top with 1 slivered almond. Bake in preheated 350° oven 8 minutes or until edges are brown. Remove to rack. Cool and refrigerate. See photo page 236.

JELLY FILLED MELTAWAYS

Yield: 3 dozen

½ pound butter
½ cup sugar
1 egg yolk
2 cups presifted unbleached flour
   preserves of choice
   confectioners sugar

Cream butter. Add sugar and beat until fluffy. Add egg yolk and flour. Mix well. Form dough into small balls. Press onto unbuttered cookie sheet. Indent center of cookie and fill with preserves. Bake in preheated 350° oven 10 to 12 minutes. Cool 5 minutes. Sprinkle with confectioners sugar.

BUTTER PECAN COOKIES

Yield: 5 dozen

½   **pound butter**
½   **cup brown sugar**
2   **tablespoons sugar**
1   **egg yolk**
½   **teaspoon vanilla**
1¾   **cups flour**
3½   **ounces pecan halves**

Cream butter and sugars. Add egg yolk and vanilla. Gradually add flour, mixing well. Roll dough into balls ¾-inch in diameter. Place on cookie sheet. Press each ball with a pecan half. Bake in preheated 375° oven 10 to 12 minutes.

CHRISTMAS COOKIES

Yield: 4 dozen

¼   **pound butter**
1   **cup sugar**
1   **egg, beaten**
1   **teaspoon vanilla**
½   **teaspoon lemon zest, optional**
1½   **cups flour**
1   **teaspoon baking powder**
   pinch salt
   multicolored granulated sugar

Cream butter and sugar. Add egg, vanilla, and lemon zest if desired. Mix well. Sift together flour, baking powder, and salt. Blend into butter mixture. Roll out on floured board to ⅛-inch thickness. Cut into desired shapes with cookie cutters. Place on buttered cookie sheets. Sprinkle with multicolored granulated sugar. Bake in preheated 375° oven 10 to 15 minutes. Remove to rack until cool.

RASPBERRY ALMOND WREATHS

Yield: 2 dozen

½ **pound butter**
½ **cup confectioners sugar**
2 **tablespoons milk**
2 **teaspoons vanilla**
2¼ **cups flour**
½ **teaspoon salt**
¼ **teaspoon baking powder**
1 **egg white, lightly beaten**
⅔ **cup sliced almonds, toasted**
½ **cup seedless red raspberry preserves**

In large bowl cream butter and sugar until light and fluffy. Stir in milk and vanilla. Sift together flour, salt, and baking powder. Add to butter mixture, beating until well blended. Cover and chill at least 1 hour.

On lightly floured board roll dough to ⅛-inch thickness. Cut into 48 2-inch rounds. Cut 1-inch hole from center of 24 rounds to form rings. Brush rings with egg white. Sprinkle with almonds. Place rounds and rings on lightly greased cookie sheets.

Bake in preheated 350° oven 10 minutes or until golden brown. Carefully transfer to rack. When cool spread 1 teaspoon preserves on each round. Cover with rings. Work gently as cookies are fragile.

May be frozen.

See photo page 236.

NURSERY SCHOOL COOKIES

Yield: 3 dozen

Teachers like them, too.

1 **egg, beaten**
1 **cup creamy peanut butter**
1 **cup sugar**
36 **chocolate kisses**

Combine egg, peanut butter, and sugar. Mix well. Form into small balls. Place 2 inches apart on greased cookie sheet. Bake in preheated 350° oven 10 minutes. Remove from oven. Place chocolate kiss in center of each cookie. Dough will crack. Bake additional 1 minute. Cool on rack.

SWEDISH COOKIES

Yield: 4 dozen

¼   **pound butter**
¾   **cup sugar**
1   **egg yolk**
1¼ **cups flour**
1   **scant teaspoon baking ammonia powder (ammonium carbonate*)**
1   **teaspoon vanilla**

In food processor with plastic blade or with electric mixer combine all ingredients. Process until well mixed. Roll dough into small balls. Place 2 inches apart on greased cookie sheet. With tip of finger or spoon, press slightly on each. Bake in preheated 350° oven 10 to 12 minutes. Cool.

*Available in pharmacies

LEMON DROP COOKIES

Yield: 50 to 60

Cookie:
½   **pound butter**
½   **cup confectioners sugar**
2   **cups flour**

Lemon curd:
1   **egg, beaten**
¾   **cup sugar**
1½ **tablespoons butter**
3   **tablespoons lemon juice**
     rind of 1 lemon, grated

     confectioners sugar

Combine butter, confectioners sugar, and flour. Mix well. Roll into small balls. Flatten and dent centers. Place on greased cookie sheets. Bake in preheated 350° oven 10 to 12 minutes. Remove to rack and cool.

In saucepan combine all curd ingredients. Cook, stirring, until thick. Cool. Spoon curd into dent of each cookie. Sprinkle with confectioners sugar.

This curd may also be used as ice cream topping, spread for toast, or combined with fresh pineapple, oranges, and coconut.

See photo page 236.

ALMOND TRIANGLES

½   **pound butter or margarine**
1   **cup sugar, divided**
2   **cups flour**
½   **teaspoon vanilla**
½   **teaspoon almond extract**
½   **cup chopped almonds**

Cream butter and ½ cup sugar. Add remaining ingredients. Mix well. Pat or roll on sugared board into large rectangle. Slice into small triangles. Arrange on ungreased cookie sheet. Bake in preheated 350° oven 8 to 10 minutes. While hot coat each side with remaining ½ cup sugar.

CINNAMON BREAKAPARTS

Yield: 9 huge cookies

1   **egg**
1   **cup sugar**
¼   **pound plus 4 tablespoons butter or margarine, softened**
1   **tablespoon cinnamon**
1⅓   **cups flour, divided**

Prepare nine 8-inch diameter circles of wax paper.

In large bowl, combine egg, sugar, butter, cinnamon, and 1 cup flour. Beat slowly to combine. Increase speed to medium. Beat 3 minutes or until mixture is light and fluffy. Stir in remaining ⅓ cup flour. Dough will be soft.

With damp cloth moisten cookie sheets. Arrange wax paper circles on sheets. Using ¼-cup measure, divide dough among circles, placing each portion in center of each circle. With heel of hand push dough from center to perimeter until thin layer covers each circle.

Bake in preheated 375° oven 6 to 7 minutes or until lightly browned. Cool on wire racks. Do not remove wax paper until cool. If not used immediately, store without removing paper in cool dry place.

A torte may be made using these cookies as layers. See Cinnamon Chocolate Torte, page 333.

SOUTHERN SPICE COOKIES

Yield: 4 to 5 dozen

¼ pound plus 4 tablespoons butter
2 cups sugar, divided
1 egg
¼ cup molasses
2 cups flour
1½ teaspoons baking powder
1 teaspoon cinnamon
1 teaspoon ground cloves
1 teaspoon ground ginger
1 teaspoon baking soda

In large bowl cream butter and 1 cup sugar. Add egg. Mix well. Blend in molasses. Sift together remaining ingredients. Add to sugar mixutre. Mix well. Chill. Roll dough into small balls. Then roll balls in remaining sugar. Place 2 inches apart on ungreased cookie sheet. Bake in preheated 350° oven 8 to 10 minutes or until golden brown. Remove to rack to cool.

CRUNCHY CHOCOLATE OATMEAL COOKIES

Yield: 4½ dozen

2½ cups packed brown sugar
½ pound butter
2 eggs
1 teaspoon vanilla
3½ cups uncooked quick rolled oats
1½ cups flour
1 teaspoon baking soda
6 ounces semi-sweet chocolate chips

In large bowl cream sugar and butter. Add eggs and vanilla. Beat until fluffy. In separate bowl combine oats, flour, and baking soda. Mix well. Combine with creamed mixture. Stir in chocolate chips. Batter will be thick. Drop by rounded teaspoonsful onto greased cookie sheets. Bake in preheated 375° oven 12 to 14 minutes. Place on rack to cool.

OLD-FASHIONED MOLASSES OATMEAL COOKIES

Yield: 18 to 20 very large cookies

1¼ cups unbleached flour
¾ teaspoon baking soda
½ teaspoon baking powder
½ teaspoon salt
1½ teaspoons cinnamon
1 teaspoon ground ginger
½ cup vegetable shortening
¾ cup brown sugar
½ cup molasses
2 extra large eggs
1½ cups uncooked quick rolled oats
1 cup raisins
1 cup chopped pecans

In food processor with steel knife combine flour, baking soda, baking powder, salt, cinnamon, and ginger. Blend with quick on and off pulses. Add shortening, sugar, molasses, eggs, and oats. Repeat quick on and off pulses until blended. Stir in raisins and nuts with fork.

With long-handled ¼ cup measure scoop out dough onto ungreased cookie sheet, 2 to a row. Bake in preheated 350° oven 15 minutes. Transfer to cooling racks with spatula.

Recipe should not be doubled.

CHOCOLATE PECAN MACAROONS

Yield: 5 dozen

2 ounces unsweetened chocolate
14 ounces sweetened condensed milk
2 cups flaked coconut
1 cup chopped pecans
1 tablespoon strong coffee
1 teaspoon almond extract
salt to taste

In large, heavy saucepan combine chocolate and condensed milk. Cook, stirring constantly, until chocolate melts and mixture is thick, smooth, and glossy. Remove from heat. Stir in remaining ingredients. Blend well. Drop by teaspoonsful onto greased cookie sheets. Bake in preheated 350° oven 10 minutes or until bottoms are just set. Remove immediately to wax paper.

SWEDISH GINGERSNAPS (Peppar Kakor)

Yield: 5 dozen

¼ pound plus 4 tablespoons butter
2 cups sugar, divided
1 medium egg
4 tablespoons molasses
1 teaspoon cinnamon
1 teaspoon ground cloves
1 teaspoon ground ginger
2 teaspoons baking soda
1 teaspoon salt
2¼ cups sifted flour
½ cup slivered almonds

Frosting, optional
2 cups confectioners sugar
1 egg white
1 teaspoon lemon juice

Cream butter and 1 cup sugar. Add egg, molasses, spices, soda, salt, and flour. Mix well.

Roll dough into small balls and dip in sugar. Flatten with small glass which has been greased and dipped in sugar. Press almond sliver into each cookie. Bake in preheated 375° oven 10 minutes. Cool.

Blend confectioners sugar, egg white, and lemon juice. Cream until smooth. Fit cake decorating tube with fine point tip. Fill with beaten frosting ingredients and decorate cookies if desired.

BRYN MAWR COOKIES

Yield: 3 dozen

3 cups firmly packed confectioners sugar
7 tablespoons cocoa
2 tablespoons flour
4 egg whites
2 cups finely chopped pecans
   parchment paper

In medium bowl combine sugar, cocoa, and flour. Add egg whites. Beat with electric mixer on high speed 1 minute. Stir in nuts.

Using 1½ tablespoons for each, drop cookies 2 inches apart on cookie sheets lined with parchment paper. Press tops of cookies lightly with back of spoon. Bake in preheated 350° oven 12 minutes. Cool on parchment before removing.

FESTIVE FRUITCAKE COOKIES

Yield: 3 dozen

Attractive addition to a holiday cookie tray.

- ¼ cup butter or margarine
- ½ cup dark brown sugar
- 2 eggs
- ½ cup premium bourbon or apricot nectar
- 1½ cups flour, divided
- 1½ teaspoons baking soda
- 1 teaspoon cinnamon
- 1 teaspoon ground allspice
- ¼ pound pitted dates, chopped
- ½ pound candied pineapple chunks
- ½ pound candied cherries
- ½ pound raisins
- ¾ pound pecans or walnuts, coarsely chopped

Cream butter and sugar. Add eggs, 1 at a time, beating after each addition. Stir in bourbon or nectar. Let stand 5 minutes.

Sift together 1 cup flour, baking soda, cinnamon, and allspice. Add to butter mixture. Mix well.

In large bowl combine dates, pineapple, cherries, and raisins. Sift ½ cup flour on fruit. Mix gently to coat. Add nuts and butter mixture. Mix well.

Drop by tablespoonsful onto lightly greased cookie sheets. Bake in preheated 300° oven 25 minutes. Cool and store in tightly covered tin with piece of cheesecloth soaked in bourbon.

See photo page 236.

MYSTERY BAR COOKIES

Yield: 3 dozen

- ¼ pound butter
- ½ teaspoon salt
- 1½ cups brown sugar, divided
- 1 cup plus 2 tablespoons flour, divided
- 2 eggs
- 1 teaspoon vanilla
- ½ teaspoon baking powder
- 1 cup chopped nuts
- ½ cup flaked coconut

Combine butter, salt, and ½ cup brown sugar. Mix well. Blend in 1 cup flour. Press into 8- by 12-inch baking pan. Bake in preheated 325° oven 20 minutes.

While mixture is baking combine eggs, 1 cup brown sugar, and vanilla. Beat until thick. Add 2 tablespoons flour, baking powder, nuts, and coconut. Spread over baked mixture. Bake 25 minutes. Cool. Cut into small bars.

SINFUL CHOCOLATE LAYER COOKIES

Yield: 3 dozen

¾   **pound plus 4 tablespoons butter, divided**
¼   **cup sugar**
⅓   **cup cocoa**
1   **teaspoon vanilla**
1   **egg, lightly beaten**
2   **cups graham cracker crumbs**
1   **cup flaked coconut**
½   **cup chopped nuts**
6   **tablespoons milk**
4   **tablespoons instant vanilla pudding mix**
4   **cups sifted confectioners sugar**
8   **ounces semi-sweet chocolate chips**

In large saucepan combine ¼ pound butter, sugar, cocoa, and vanilla. Stir over medium heat until blended. Add egg and cook 5 minutes, stirring constantly. Remove from heat. Blend in crumbs, coconut, and nuts. Press into 9- by 13-inch pan. Let stand 15 minutes.

Cream ½ pound butter until light and fluffy. Mix milk with pudding mix. Add to creamed butter and beat well. Add confectioners sugar gradually, beating until smooth after each addition. Spread over mixture in pan. Refrigerate 1 hour.

Melt chocolate with 4 tablespoons butter. Spread over top layer in pan. Chill. Cut into very small bars.

Yield: 16

Brownie:
1/4 pound butter
2 ounces unsweetened chocolate
1 cup sugar
2 eggs
1/2 cup flour
1 teaspoon vanilla

Filling:
1 cup confectioners sugar
2 tablespoons butter, softened
1 tablespoon milk
1/2 teaspoon vanilla
1 ounce unsweetened chocolate, melted

Glaze:
1 ounce unsweetened chocolate
1 tablespoon unsalted butter

In top of double boiler combine and melt butter and chocolate. In bowl thoroughly combine sugar, eggs, flour, and vanilla. Add to chocolate mixture. Blend well. Pour into greased 8-inch square pan. Bake in preheated 350° oven 20 minutes. Cool in pan on rack.

Combine filling ingredients. Beat until smooth. Spread evenly over cooled brownies. Chill.

In small saucepan over low heat melt chocolate and butter, stirring until smooth. Drizzle over filling. Tilt pan back and forth until glaze completely covers filling. Chill.

To serve slice into 2-inch squares.

Variations:
1. Brownie layer may be used alone with a sprinkling of confectioners sugar.

2. For *Double Chocolate Brownie* fold 1 cup chocolate chips into brownie batter.

3. For *Mint Brownie* substitute 1 tablespoon green crème de menthe liqueur or desired amount for spreading consistency for vanilla in filling. Omit chocolate and milk from filling. See photo page 236.

4. For *Orange Brownie* substitute 1 tablespoon orange liqueur for vanilla in filling. Add 1/2 teaspoon finely grated orange rind. Omit milk and chocolate from filling.

5. For a richer brownie add 20 large marshmallows to top of double boiler when melting butter and chocolate. Stir until smooth. Proceed with remaining brownie, filling, and glaze instructions.

CARAMEL CHOCOLATE FINALES

Yield: 20

1 cup plus 3 tablespoons flour, divided
1 cup quick rolled oats
¾ cup packed brown sugar
½ teaspoon baking soda
¼ teaspoon salt
¼ pound plus 4 tablespoons butter, melted
6 ounces semi-sweet chocolate chips
½ cup chopped pecans
¾ cup caramel ice cream topping or peanut butter caramel topping

Combine 1 cup flour, oats, sugar, baking soda, salt, and butter. Blend until mixture resembles crumbs. Press half the mixture into bottom of 11- by 7-inch baking pan. Bake in preheated 350° oven 10 minutes.

Keeping oven on, remove pan and sprinkle chocolate chips and pecans over crust. Blend caramel topping with remaining 3 tablespoons flour. Pour over chips and nuts. Sprinkle remaining crumb mixture over top. Bake in 350° oven 20 minutes. Cool and chill. Slice in squares to serve.

Best made day ahead.

MACAROON CUPCAKES

Yield: 1 dozen

4 egg whites
  pinch salt
¾ cup superfine sugar, divided
1½ cups flaked coconut
½ cup ground blanched almonds
2 tablespoons flour
1 teaspoon grated lemon rind

Beat egg whites with salt until soft peaks form. Slowly add ½ cup sugar beating until stiff, shiny peaks form. In separate bowl combine coconut, ¼ cup sugar, almonds, flour, and rind. Mix well. Fold coconut mixture into egg whites. Spoon into 12 paper-lined muffin tins. Bake in preheated 350° oven 25 minutes or until a little crusty. Cool on rack.

GINGERBREAD WITH LEMON GLAZE

Serves 9

1⅔ cups flour
1½ teaspoons baking soda
1½ teaspoons ground ginger
¾ teaspoon cinnamon
¾ teaspoon salt
1 egg, lightly beaten
½ cup sugar
½ cup light molasses
½ cup boiling water
½ cup vegetable oil

Glaze:
⅔ cup confectioners sugar, sifted
3 tablespoons fresh lemon juice

Sift together flour, baking soda, ginger, cinnamon, and salt. Add egg, sugar, and molasses. Mix well. Stir in water and oil until smooth. Pour into greased 9-inch square pan. Bake in preheated 350° oven 35 to 40 minutes.

Combine glaze ingredients. Pour over hot cake.

"SHORT" APRICOT BARS

Yield: 2 dozen

Filling:
¾ cup finely chopped dried apricots
½ cup water
⅓ cup sugar
½ teaspoon vanilla

Dough:
1 cup sugar
½ pound butter
2 egg yolks
2 cups sifted flour
1 cup chopped pecans or walnuts, optional
½ teaspoon salt or to taste

continued

406

In saucepan combine apricots and water. Cover and cook 20 minutes over medium heat. Add sugar. Cook uncovered until thickened. Remove from heat. Cool slightly. Stir in vanilla. Cool completely.

Cream sugar and butter until light and fluffy. Blend in egg yolks. Add flour, nuts, and salt. Mix well. Spread half the dough in greased 9-inch square pan. Cover with apricot filling. Spread remaining dough over filling. Bake in preheated 325° oven 45 minutes. Slice into bars when cool.

Raspberry jam or pineapple preserves may be substituted for apricot filling.

CARAMEL TEA SQUARES

Yield: 12 to 16

Cake:
4 tablespoons melted butter
1 cup dark brown sugar
1 egg
½ teaspoon salt
¾ cup flour
1 teaspoon baking powder
½ teaspoon vanilla
¼ cup flaked coconut
¾ cup chopped pecans

Icing:
½ cup butter
½ cup dark brown sugar
¼ cup milk
2 cups confectioners sugar
1 teaspoon vanilla
¼ teaspoon salt

16 pecan halves

In large bowl combine all cake ingredients. Mix well. Spread batter in lightly greased 8-inch square pan. Bake in preheated 350° oven 25 minutes. Cool.

Melt butter until lightly browned. Add brown sugar and stir until completely dissolved. Stir in milk. Remove from heat to cool. Add confectioners sugar, vanilla, and salt. Beat until of thick spreading consistency. Frost cooled cake and cut into small squares. Top each square with pecan half.

LITTLE LEBKUCHEN

Yield: 10 dozen

A spicy German bar cookie.

1   egg
¾   cup brown sugar
½   cup honey
½   cup dark molasses
3   cups sifted flour
1¼   teaspoons nutmeg
1¼   teaspoons cinnamon
½   teaspoon ground cloves
½   teaspoon ground allspice
½   teaspoon salt
½   teaspoon soda
½   cup slivered, blanched almonds
½   cup chopped mixed candied fruits

Glaze:
1   egg white, lightly beaten
1   tablespoon lemon juice
½   teaspoon grated lemon rind
1¾   cups confectioners sugar

In large bowl beat egg. Add sugar and beat until fluffy. Stir in honey and molasses. Sift together flour, nutmeg, cinnamon, cloves, allspice, salt, and soda. Blend into egg mixture. Stir in almonds and fruits. Refrigerate 3 hours. Pat mixture into 2 greased 9- by 13-inch metal pans. Bake in preheated 350° oven 15 minutes. Cool 12 minutes. Remove from pans and cut into 1-inch squares. Cool thoroughly.

Combine all glaze ingredients. Invert cookies and brush with glaze.

These keep best in a tightly covered container.

See photo page 236.

MADELEINES

Yield: 3 dozen

¼ **pound plus 4 tablespoons unsalted butter**
1¼ **cups flour**
1½ **teaspoons baking powder**
¼ **teaspoon salt**
3 **eggs**
1 **teaspoon vanilla**
2 **teaspoons grated lemon rind**
⅔ **cup sugar**
½ **cup confectioners sugar**

Melt butter and cool. Sift flour, baking powder, and salt together. Beat eggs well. Stir vanilla and lemon rind into eggs. Add sugar, 1 tablespoon at a time, mixing well after each addition. Add 1 cup flour mixture gradually, mixing well after each addition. While still mixing add butter, a small amount at a time, and finish with ¼ cup flour mixture. Butter and flour madeleine tins well. Fill each section two-thirds full. Bake in preheated 350° oven 12 minutes. Cool. Sprinkle with confectioners sugar.

MINIATURE PECAN TARTS

Yield: 2 dozen

Crust:
3 **ounces cream cheese, softened**
¼ **pound butter or margarine**
1 **cup flour**

Filling:
¾ **cup brown sugar**
1 **egg, beaten**
½ **cup chopped pecans**
1½ **tablespoons melted butter or margarine**
½ **cup confectioners sugar**

Blend crust ingredients with pastry blender, mixing well. Chill several hours or overnight. Line 24 miniature (1¾-inch) muffin tins with mixture.

Combine sugar, egg, pecans, and butter. Fill pastry-lined tins. Bake in preheated 350° oven 25 to 30 minutes. Cool several minutes. Dust with confectioners sugar.

CANDIED ORANGE PEEL

Yield:
approximately
40 strips

4   medium oranges, peeled, quartered
1½   cups water, divided
2   cups sugar, divided

In small saucepan combine peel and 1 cup cold water. Bring to boil. Reduce heat and simmer until peel is soft. Drain peel. Scrape gently with spoon to remove white inner layer. Slice into thin strips.

In small saucepan combine 1½ cups sugar and ½ cup water. Boil to 232° (measure with candy thermometer) or until syrup "threads". Add orange strips. Cook over low heat 5 minutes. Drain strips. Sprinkle remaining ½ cup sugar on wax paper. Roll strips in sugar until lightly coated. Let strips dry.

PEANUT BRITTLE

Yield: 2½ to 3
pounds

½   cup cold water
2   cups sugar
1   cup light corn syrup
2   tablespoons unsalted butter
2   cups raw peanuts, walnuts, cashews, almonds or
       Spanish peanuts
2   teaspoons baking soda
     salt

Arrange 1 cookie sheet overlapping another by 3 inches. Cover both with heavy foil, tucking sides under pans.

In copper, copper-bottomed or heavy pan combine water, sugar, syrup, and butter. Stirring constantly, cook over low heat until candy thermometer measures 250°. Add nuts. Continue stirring until thermometer measures 300°. Immediately stir in soda. Stir quickly, blending well.

Pour mixture onto prepared pans. Tip pans to spread candy evenly. Let harden. Salt brittle lightly. When candy is room temperature break into pieces of desired size.

See photo page 236.

BUTTER WALNUT TOFFEE

Yield: 2 to
2½ pounds

½   **pound unsalted butter**
1   **cup sugar**
⅓   **cup brown sugar**
2   **tablespoons water**
6   **ounces semi-sweet chocolate, chips or bar, melted**
½   **cup walnuts, coarsely chopped**

Cover large cookie sheet with heavy foil. Tuck sides under pan and butter foil lightly.

In heavy saucepan melt butter. Add sugars and water. Mix well. Bring to boil, stirring constantly. When candy thermometer measures 300° remove mixture from heat.

Quickly and carefully pour mixture over foil. As candy cools, spread with knife to form even layer. Spread melted chocolate over toffee and smooth evenly over top. Sprinkle nuts over chocolate. Refrigerate until candy is set. Break into pieces of desired size.

CARAMEL PECAN "TURTLES"

Yield: 3 dozen

108   **pecan halves**
36   **caramel cubes**
1   **tablespoon butter**
1   **ounce unsweetened chocolate**
1   **cup confectioners sugar**
2   **tablespoons hot milk**
1   **teaspoon vanilla**

On teflon cookie sheet place pecans in groups of 3. Place 1 caramel over each grouping, making sure some of caramel overlaps each nut. Bake in preheated 350° oven 6 minutes. Remove from oven. Flatten caramels slightly with finger or spoon to form small "bowl". Cool slightly. Remove to wax paper or rack.

Melt butter and chocolate together. Add remaining ingredients. Mix until smooth. Fill caramel "bowls" with chocolate mixture.

PEANUT BUTTER CHOCOLATE BALLS

Yield: 75 to 80

¼ pound butter, melted
2 cups confectioners sugar
2 cups creamy peanut butter
2 cups crushed Rice Krispies
½ cup finely chopped pecans or peanuts
1 pound semi-sweet chocolate chips or dipping chocolate

In large bowl combine all ingredients except chocolate. Stir and knead until well blended. Chill at least 1 hour. Roll into 1-inch balls. Place on baking sheet and chill until firm, about 1 hour.

Melt chocolate in top of double boiler. Water should not touch bottom of pan. Using candy dipper or wooden skewer, dip each ball into melted chocolate. Place on wax paper. Chill until firm. Store in airtight container in refrigerator.

CHOCOLATE AMARETTI TRUFFLES

Yield: 44

8 ounces sweet or semi-sweet baking chocolate
¼ cup Amaretto
2 tablespoons strong coffee
¼ pound unsalted butter
1 tablespoon vanilla
¾ cup pulverized cookies, amarettis (Italian macaroons),
     or vanilla wafers
½ cup cocoa
½ cup pulverized instant coffee crystals

In top of double boiler over simmering water, melt chocolate with Amaretto and coffee. Stir until smooth. Slice butter into pieces and whisk into mixture 1 at a time. Add vanilla and pulverized cookies. Mix well.

Set top of double boiler in bowl of ice and water. Beat mixture to chill. When congealed and firm form mixture into teaspoon-size balls.

In small bowl combine cocoa and instant coffee crystals. Mix well. Roll balls in mixture. Place in miniature paper cups. Cover and refrigerate until served.

Rum, applejack, or Grand Marnier may be substituted for Amaretto.

May be frozen.

BOURBON BALLS

Yield: 3 to 4 pounds

36 ounces vanilla wafers
2   cups chopped walnuts
2   cups confectioners sugar
2   cups bourbon or to taste
4   teaspoons cocoa
1   cup superfine sugar

In food processor or blender combine wafers and walnuts. Process until finely ground. Add remaining ingredients except superfine sugar. Blend well.

Roll into small balls and dip into sugar, coating well. Cover and refrigerate until served.

See photo page 236.

WHITE CHOCOLATE MACADAMIA BARK

Yield: 1 ½ pounds

1   pound white chocolate
6   ounces macadamia nuts

In top of double boiler melt chocolate over very low simmering water. Arrange nuts evenly in 8-inch square pan. Pour chocolate over nuts. With knife smooth chocolate decoratively, making sure nuts are well covered. Refrigerate until chocolate has hardened. Cut into desired size pieces.

Alternate method: On sheet of wax paper group 3 nuts together. Spoon melted chocolate over each group using half the chocolate. When cool and set, turn each group over and spread remaining chocolate over bottom. Refrigerate until set.

See photo page 236.

MAPLE FUDGE

Yield: 1¼ pounds

2¼ cups maple syrup
½ cup milk
1 tablespoon flour
3 tablespoons unsalted butter

In medium copper or copper-bottom saucepan combine all ingredients. Stirring constantly, cook over low heat until candy thermometer registers 234°. Remove from heat. Stir until mixture thickens. Pour into 4-by 7-by 1½-inch pan. Cool and cut into small pieces.

HOLIDAY NUT "CANDY"

*Yield: 2½ to
3 pounds*

2 cups walnuts
2 cups pecans
2 egg whites
   dash salt
1 cup sugar
1 teaspoon cinnamon, optional
¼ pound butter, melted

Toast nuts until lightly browned. Beat egg whites until foamy. Add salt and sugar in small amounts, beating after each addition. Beat until stiff and shiny. Stir in cinnamon if desired. Fold nuts into meringue. Pour into shallow baking pan filled with melted butter. Spread evenly into single layer. Bake in preheated 325° oven 30 minutes, stirring and turning nuts every 10 minutes to coat thoroughly. Cool.

ALSO NOTEWORTHY

Ravinia Notes

James Levine was appointed Ravinia's Music Director in 1973, a post which he still holds. The legendary Maestro Levine is Music Director of the Metropolitan Opera, a regular guest at the Bayreuth and Salzburg Festivals, as well as major orchestras around the world. He has been described as "a brilliant conductor of both opera and symphony, a fine pianist, a skilled chamber musician, and a highly successful administrator." These accomplishments are very evident during his residence at Ravinia where he is a genial, familiar figure, admired for his rapport with orchestra and audience, his boundless energy, and his inspired talent. Maestro Levine and Executive Director Edward Gordon, having built Ravinia into a world-class festival, look ahead to fresh and innovative goals for tomorrow.

The construction of Ravinia's long-desired Young Artists Institute is under way. The Institute's lofty aim is to offer career-oriented training for exceptional young musicians, assuring them a special performance at the Festival. In an atmosphere charged with creativity, forty to fifty students will spend the summer studying and performing at Ravinia. This unique and challenging project will contribute to the vitality and future growth of the Festival.

Truly, there will be "nothing like it under the stars."

TOMATO FLIP

Yield: 6 pints

7 **pounds ripe tomatoes, peeled, quartered**
1-2 **quarts vinegar**
4 **pounds sugar**
½ **teaspoon ground cloves**

In crock or enamel bowl (not aluminum) soak tomatoes completely covered with vinegar overnight. Drain 10 minutes.

In large kettle combine tomatoes with sugar and cloves. Cook slowly until mixture thickens and reaches consistency of jam, about 1 hour, stirring frequently. Pour tomatoes into clean canning jars and seal. In large kettle submerge jars in boiling water 1-inch over lids. Simmer 15 minutes. Remove and cool.

A condiment to be served with poultry and meats. Especially good with chicken or lamb.

TOMATO MARMALADE

Yield: 2 pints

3 **pounds (about 10 large) red tomatoes, peeled**
1 **large navel orange, very thinly sliced**
  juice of 1 lemon
3½ **cups sugar**
½ **teaspoon uniodized salt**
½ **teaspoon ground ginger**
½ **teaspoon ground nutmeg**
1 **cinnamon stick**

Chop tomatoes into ¼- to ½-inch pieces to make 7½ cups. Cut orange slices into fourths. Combine tomatoes and orange sections in 6-quart kettle.

Cook over low heat until juice of tomatoes runs freely. Increase heat. Boil uncovered until orange peel is fork tender, about 15 to 20 minutes. Add lemon juice, sugar, salt, and spices. Boil rapidly, stirring frequently, until mixture thickens to marmalade consistency. Ladle into sterilized jars. Cover and refrigerate. Use canning process to store indefinitely.

See photo page 229.

GREEN OR RED PEPPER JELLY

Yield: 4 to 5 cups

¾ cup seeded, deveined, minced green or red sweet pepper
¼ cup seeded, deveined, minced jalapeño pepper
1½ cups cider vinegar, divided
5½ cups sugar
1 package Certo
paraffin

In food processor or blender process peppers and ½ cup vinegar. Transfer to large saucepan. Add remaining 1 cup vinegar and sugar. Bring to full boil. Add Certo. Mix well. Pour into hot sterilized jars. Seal with paraffin.

Serve with cream cheese and crackers.

Beautiful colors; excellent gift.

See photo page 229.

ONION CONSERVE

Yield: 3 cups

2 pounds yellow onions, thinly sliced
½ cup sugar
½ teaspoon salt
pinch pepper
½ cup dry red wine
¼ cup red wine vinegar
2 tablespoons lemon juice
¼ cup currants
¼ teaspoon thyme

In heavy enamel saucepan combine onions, sugar, salt, and pepper. Cook covered over very low heat 40 minutes. Blend in wine, vinegar, and lemon juice. Bring to boil. Reduce heat. Add currants and thyme. Simmer uncovered 25 to 35 minutes, stirring occasionally. Mixture will be reduced and thickened. Cool and refrigerate.

A good accompaniment to meat.

CRANBERRY CHUTNEY

Serves 10

12 ounces fresh cranberries
1 cup sugar
½ cup packed brown sugar
½ cup golden raisins
1 teaspoon cinnamon
1 teaspoon ground ginger
½ teaspoon ground cloves
¼ teaspoon ground allspice
1 cup water
1 cup chopped onion
1 cup peeled, chopped baking apples
½ cup chopped celery

Combine cranberries, sugars, raisins, spices, and water in uncovered 2-quart saucepan. Cook over medium heat until cranberries pop. Reduce heat. Stir in onion, apples, and celery. Simmer uncovered 30 minutes, stirring occasionally. Chill.

Serve as accompaniment to meat or poultry.

To use as appetizer, spoon over cream cheese.

May be refrigerated for up to 2 weeks.

MRS. POPE'S ENGLISH CHUTNEY

Yield: approximately 6 pounds

An old family recipe from Stratford-upon-Avon, England.

3 large onions, sliced
1 tablespoon pickling spice, in muslin bag
1½ pints cider vinegar
4 pounds green tomatoes, diced
1½ pounds apples, peeled, cored, diced
½ pound raisins or sultanas
1 tablespoon salt or to taste
1½ teaspoons ground ginger
1 pound dark brown sugar

In large kettle combine onion, pickling spice in bag, and vinegar. Boil vigorously 20 minutes. Add tomatoes, apples, raisins, salt, ginger, and sugar. Mix well and boil gently 2 hours, stirring every few minutes. Cool and store in preserve jars.

PEACH CHUTNEY

Yield: 6 quarts

1 quart cider vinegar
5 pounds sugar
1 pound cucumbers, peeled, in small chunks
1 pound lemons, quartered, ground, seeded
1 pound onions, chopped
2 pounds green peppers, chopped
6 pounds peaches, peeled, pitted, sliced
20 ounces canned tomatoes
2 tablespoons ground allspice
2 tablespoons curry powder
2 tablespoons ground ginger
1½ tablespoons turmeric
1 pound crystallized ginger
5 ounces slivered almonds
1 pound golden raisins
10 ounces green tomato relish

In 12-quart kettle combine vinegar and sugar. Bring to boil. Add cucumbers, lemons, onions, green peppers, peaches, tomatoes, allspice, curry, ground ginger, and turmeric. Mix well. Return to boil. Reduce heat and simmer uncovered 3 hours, stirring occasionally. Add crystallized ginger, nuts, raisins, and relish. Cook 30 minutes, stirring frequently to prevent mixture from sticking. Remove from heat. Pour into 12 sterilized pint jars with double lids and seal.

PUNGENT GIVE-AWAY SAUCE

Yield: 8 cups

An always-welcome hostess gift.

17 ounces mango chutney
5 ounces pickled walnuts, optional
14 ounces ketchup
12 ounces chili sauce
10 ounces steak sauce
10 ounces Worcestershire sauce
Tabasco to taste

In food processor or blender blend chutney and walnuts if desired. Transfer to large bowl. Add remaining ingredients. Mix well. Serve with beef or cold lamb.

May be stored in sterilized jars.

PRESERVATION HALL FIG CHUTNEY

Yield: 1½ to 2 cups

4   cups whole fresh or dried figs
1   lemon, unpeeled, seeded, in small pieces
¼   teaspoon ground ginger
¼   teaspoon ground allspice
¼   teaspoon cinnamon
¼   teaspoon ground cloves
⅓   cup sugar
⅓   cup water

In large saucepan combine all ingredients. If using dried figs use 1½ cups water. Bring to boil over medium heat, stirring constantly. Reduce heat. Simmer 40 to 60 minutes or until figs are soft and well blended. Cool.

If using fresh figs cook 5 minutes or until thick brown syrup forms. Cool.

CANTALOUPE PICKLES

Yield: 4 pints

2   firm, ripe cantaloupes, about 2 pounds each
1   quart cold water
4   tablespoons salt
1½   cups cider vinegar
4   cups sugar
3   sticks cinnamon, 2 inches long
1   tablespoon whole cloves
½   teaspoon nutmeg
2½   cups boiling water

Halve cantaloupes. Remove seeds, peel, and cut into 1-inch squares. Mix cold water and salt. Pour over melon and let stand 3 hours. Drain.

Combine vinegar, sugar, and spices with boiling water. Stir until sugar is dissolved. Add cantaloupe and boil 10 minutes. Cool. Cover and let stand 10 to 12 hours. Remove cantaloupe with slotted spoon. Boil syrup 10 minutes. Add melon and simmer 40 to 50 minutes or until melon is transparent.

Pour mixture into hot pint jars with 2-piece screw tops, filling to within ⅛-inch of top. Wipe rims of jars and cover with lids. Put on screw bands and tighten as much as possible. Place jars in large kettle. Add enough boiling water to cover jars by 1 inch. Boil 10 minutes. Cool on rack. Recipe may be doubled.

See photo page 229.

QUICK SWEET ZUCCHINI PICKLES

Yield: 5 pints

4 quarts thinly sliced small zucchini
6 white onions, sliced
2 medium green peppers, diced
2 cloves garlic, minced
½ cup salt
5 cups sugar
1½ teaspoons turmeric
2 tablespoons mustard seed
1½ teaspoons celery seed
3 cups cider vinegar

In large enamel or stainless steel pan combine zucchini, onions, green peppers, garlic, and salt. Fill plastic food storage bag with ice cubes, secure the opening, and place on top of mixture. Cover and let stand 3 hours.

In separate pan combine sugar, turmeric, mustard and celery seed, and vinegar. Bring to boil, making sure sugar is dissolved. Remove from heat. Drain and rinse zucchini mixture. Return to pan and blend in sugar mixture. Bring to boil. Pour into hot, sterilized jars and seal. May substitute cucumbers for the zucchini.

See photo page 229.

QUICK MAYONNAISE

Yield: 1¼ cups

1 egg
1 egg yolk
½ teaspoon Dijon mustard, or to taste
 salt to taste
1½ teaspoons *fresh* lemon juice
½ teaspoon white wine vinegar
½ cup extra virgin olive oil
½ cup peanut or safflower oil
 white pepper to taste

In blender or food processor combine egg, egg yolk, mustard, and salt. Process 25 seconds. Add lemon juice and vinegar. Process 30 seconds. With motor running, add oils in slow steady stream. Check for seasoning. Blend in pepper and additional juice, vinegar, or mustard if desired.

Variations:
Add 1 of following to mayonnaise and use as cold meat accompaniment or filling for hard-boiled eggs: ¼ cup chutney, ½ cup spinach pesto (page 70), or ¼ cup horseradish plus 1 tablespoon lemon juice.

FRIGIES

Yield: 5 pints

A garden relish.

8   cups thinly sliced cucumber pickles
1   cup diagonally sliced celery
1   green pepper, seeded, diced
1   red pepper, seeded, diced
1   Spanish onion, thinly sliced
2   teaspoons coarse salt
1   cup distilled white vinegar
1   teaspoon mustard seed
½   teaspoon celery seed
1¾   cups sugar, or to taste

In large bowl combine pickles, celery, peppers, and onion. Mix well. Sprinkle with salt. Place in colander; weight with plate. Set aside to drain for at least 1 hour.

In small saucepan combine vinegar, mustard and celery seed, and sugar. Bring to boil over medium heat. Stir until sugar is dissolved and mixture becomes syrupy. Remove from heat. Cool. Place drained vegetables in bowl. Pour vinegar mixture over vegetables. Stir. Spoon into sterilized pint jars. Store in refrigerator.

CRÈME FRAÎCHE

Yield: 2 cups

Traditional version:
1   cup whipping cream
1   cup sour cream

Sweeter version:
1⅓   cups whipping cream
⅔   cup sour cream

In separate bowls beat whipping cream and sour cream 1 minute each. Combine creams and beat 2 minutes. Cover loosely with plastic wrap and leave at room temperature overnight. Refrigerate at least 4 hours. Crème fraîche thickens as it sits.

Stir dollop of traditional version into cooked vegetables or hot sauces. Spoon sweeter version over fresh fruits or hot fruit desserts.

May be refrigerated up to 2 weeks.

DRIED HERBS

Clean fresh herbs. Hang upside down in bundles in a dry place. Do not put in direct sunlight. Let hang from 2 to 5 days. When dry, remove leaves from stems and crumble onto a piece of wax paper which can be used as a funnel for putting herbs into jars.

Alternative:
Place leaves only between a double thickness of paper toweling. Place in microwave. Microwave 30 seconds. Turn. Repeat until dry, approximately 2 minutes. Crumble and store in small tightly-covered jars.

INGRID'S HOT-SWEET MUSTARD

Yield: 1 cup

A fabulous mustard not available commercially.

- ½ cup dry mustard
- ½ cup dark brown sugar
- ¼ cup white vinegar
- ½ cup olive oil

Combine mustard, sugar, and vinegar. Mix well. Stir in olive oil. Beat at high speed until thick.

Delicious with ham or cold tenderloin.

MUSTARD SAUCE

Yield: 1 cup

- 1 tablespoon water
- 2 teaspoons dry mustard
- 1 cup mayonnaise
- ¼ cup prepared mustard
- 2 teaspoons dry white wine
- 2 teaspoons lemon juice
- 3 drops Tabasco
  Worcestershire sauce to taste
  salt to taste
  pepper to taste

Mix water and dry mustard. Combine with remaining ingredients. Mix until smooth. Chill. Serve with crab or smoked meat.

FIVE-HERB VINEGAR

Yield: 1 gallon

peel from 2 lemons, in 1-inch pieces
1 cup mint leaves, clean, dry
1 cup basil leaves
10 tarragon sprigs
10 thyme sprigs, leaves only
3 oregano sprigs
4 large cloves garlic, slivered
4 quarts white wine vinegar

Scald 1-gallon glass jug or jar with hot water. Drain and dry. Combine peel, herbs, and garlic in jug. Heat vinegar to boiling point and add to jug. Cover tightly. Store in dark place 2 weeks, inverting jug occasionally to redistribute herbs. Pour vinegar through paper-lined filter into small bottles. Cork tightly and store at room temperature.

See photo page 229.

BARBECUE SAUCE

Yield: 5 cups

1 cup commercial barbecue sauce, regular flavor
1 cup tangy chili sauce
1 cup ruby port
½ cup ketchup
½ cup white vinegar
½ cup water
½ cup mango chutney, chopped or sieved
½ cup dark brown sugar or to taste
½ cup strong coffee, cooled
2 cloves garlic, crushed
3 tablespoons Worcestershire sauce
½ teaspoon Liquid Smoke
¼ teaspoon Tabasco
onion powder to taste
black pepper to taste

In large saucepan combine all ingredients. Bring slowly to boil. Reduce heat and simmer uncovered 10 minutes exactly. Remove from heat and stir with nonmetallic spoon. When sauce is room temperature pour into canning jars. Refrigerate.

Aging improves taste of sauce when it is reheated. Bring sauce to room temperature before reheating.

3 HAPPINESS SAUCE

Yield: ¾ cup

2   shallots, minced
2   cloves garlic, minced
3   tablespoons vegetable oil
4   tablespoons soy sauce
2   tablespoons honey
½   teaspoon finely grated ginger root
¼   teaspoon cayenne pepper
3   drops Tabasco or to taste or hot pepper
    flakes to taste

Sauté shallots and garlic in oil until golden. Add remaining ingredients and bring to boil. Serve over cold chicken or as an accompaniment to sliced steak.

MUSHROOM SAUCE

Yield: 2 cups

3   cloves garlic, minced
1   bunch parsley, minced
3   tablespoons vegetable oil
½   pound dried Italian mushrooms
8   ounces tomato sauce
1   chicken bouillon cube
    salt to taste
    pepper to taste

Soak mushrooms in warm water to cover 5 minutes. Drain. Chop coarsely. In large saucepan sauté garlic and parsley in oil. Add remaining ingredients. Cook 30 minutes. Serve over polenta, rice, or pasta.

MINT SAUCE

Yield: 1 cup

Packed in small cruets, this makes a welcome gift.

1   cup cider vinegar
1   cup superfine sugar
½   cup packed, finely snipped, small, tender mint leaves
    (or more if stronger flavor is desired)

In saucepan combine vinegar and sugar. Cook over low heat until sugar is dissolved. Cool. Stir in mint leaves. Serve with hot or cold lamb. Sauce may be stored in refrigerator for up to 1 year.

SOUR CHERRY SAUCE

Yield: 3 cups

3   cups pitted sour cherries, divided
1   cup plus 3 tablespoons sugar, divided
½   teaspoon chopped crystallized ginger
1   tablespoon orange juice
1   tablespoon lemon juice
    rind of 1 orange, finely grated
1-2   tablespoons cherry liqueur

In saucepan combine 2 cups cherries, 1 cup sugar, ginger, and orange juice. Bring to boil over low heat. Reduce heat and simmer 10 minutes. Add lemon juice, zested orange rind, liqueur, and remaining 3 tablespoons sugar. Stirring constantly, continue to simmer until slightly thickened. Add remaining 1 cup cherries. Remove from heat. Serve warm with poultry or ham.

POULTRY SAUCE

Yield: 2 cups

4   tablespoons butter
1   cup fresh orange juice
    juice of 1 large lemon
¼   cup honey
¼   cup soy sauce
¼   cup chopped parsley
1   tablespoon dry mustard
2   medium cloves garlic, mashed

In saucepan combine all ingredients. Mix well. Bring to boil and stir. Use as basting and accompanying sauce for turkey, chicken, or Cornish hens.

May be made 2 days in advance.

SUMMER TOMATO SAUCE

Yield: 1½ quarts

¼ cup finely chopped onion
¼ cup finely chopped celery
¼ cup finely chopped green pepper
2 tablespoons safflower oil or 1 tablespoon margarine plus
    1 tablespoon vegetable oil
1 cup chopped fresh tomatoes
4 parsley sprigs, stems removed
⅛ teaspoon garlic powder
⅛ teaspoon ground ginger
⅛ teaspoon cinnamon
1 teaspoon oregano
1 teaspoon basil
1 teaspoon crushed rosemary
1 bay leaf
28 ounces canned puréed tomatoes
¼ teaspoon freshly ground pepper
1 cup unsalted chicken broth
½ cup decaffeinated coffee, cooled

In large skillet sauté onion, celery, and green pepper in oil until vegetables are limp. Stir in fresh tomatoes and parsley. Cook 5 minutes over medium heat.

Add garlic powder, ginger, cinnamon, oregano, basil, rosemary, and bay leaf. Blend well. Simmer 5 minutes. Add puréed tomatoes and ground pepper. Cover and simmer gently 1 hour. Stir in chicken broth and coffee. Simmer covered 1 hour, stirring occasionally. Transfer to bowl. Remove bay leaf. Cool. Cover tightly and refrigerate.

Freezes well.

HOLLANDAISE SAUCE

Yield: 1 cup

4 cold egg yolks
  juice of 1 lemon
12 tablespoons cold butter
  salt to taste
  cayenne pepper to taste

In small saucepan combine egg yolks and lemon juice. Cook over low heat, adding butter 1 tablespoon at a time. Stir constantly with wire whisk until sauce thickens, 3 to 5 minutes. When desired consistency is reached, remove from heat. Add salt and cayenne.

POPEYE'S POTATO TOPPING

Yield: 2 cups

4 ounces cream cheese, softened
1 tablespoon minced scallions
¼ teaspoon garlic salt
¼ teaspoon pepper
5 ounces frozen chopped spinach, thawed, drained
3 ounces cooked ham, cubed
½ cup sour cream
6 tablespoons chopped pecans

In medium saucepan combine all ingredients. Mix well. Over medium heat, stirring constantly, cook 5 minutes or until very hot. Serve as topping for baked potato.

JELLIED ORANGE SLICES

Yield: 15 to 20 wedges

A decorative accompaniment to turkey or ham.

6 large navel oranges
 juice of 1 lemon
2 tablespoons sugar
1½ teaspoons unflavored gelatin

Cut oranges in half lengthwise. Juice oranges; reserve juice. Remove pulp from 6 orange halves, leaving cups clean. To steady cups, place in standard size muffin tins.

In saucepan combine 1 cup orange juice, lemon juice, sugar, and gelatin. Bring mixture to boil, stirring. Reserving small amount, pour juice mixture into orange cups. Let stand 10 minutes. Some of mixture will be absorbed into shells. Using reserved juice mixture refill cups to top level.

Refrigerate several hours or overnight, until firm. When ready to serve slice cups into 3 or 4 wedges. Garnish platter with wedges and serve.

APPLE-RAISIN POULTRY DRESSING

Yield: 10 cups

½   **pound butter, divided**
3   **medium onions, chopped**
2   **cups chopped celery**
½   **pound mushrooms, thinly sliced**
16   **ounces double strength chicken broth**
¾   **cup dry white wine**
1   **pound Pepperidge Farm herb dressing**
3   **Granny Smith apples, peeled, cored, in large chunks**
1   **cup golden raisins**
1   **tablespoon crystallized ginger, finely chopped**
    salt to taste
    pepper to taste
    chopped giblets, optional
    chopped liver, optional

In large skillet melt ¼ pound butter. Add onions and sauté until soft, about 3 minutes. Add celery and cook 3 to 5 minutes, stirring frequently. Add mushrooms and cook 4 to 5 minutes or until lightly browned. Remove from heat and set aside.

In medium saucepan combine chicken broth, wine, and remaining ¼ pound butter. Heat until butter melts.

In large bowl combine herb dressing with three-fourths chicken broth mixture. Stir. Add onion mixture. Combine well. Stir in apples, raisins, and ginger. Add more broth mixture if a more moist dressing is desired. Season to taste. Stir in giblets and liver if desired.

Stuff poultry. Leftover dressing may be baked separately. Use any remaining broth mixture to baste poultry.

Recipe may be doubled. Bake portion not used as stuffing in lightly buttered, uncovered 3-quart casserole in preheated 350° oven 40 minutes.

CRANBERRIES GRAND MARNIER

Yield: 4 cups

2 cups plus 3 tablespoons superfine sugar, divided
1¼ cups water
¾ cup orange juice
1 pound fresh cranberries
¼ cup Grand Marnier or Cointreau
rind of 2 oranges, grated
2 tablespoons lemon juice

In medium saucepan combine 2 cups sugar, water, and orange juice. Boil 4 minutes. Add cranberries and continue boiling. After berries pop boil 5 minutes. Mixture should be nearly jelled. Remove from heat. Stir in liqueur, rind, lemon juice, and remaining 3 tablespoons sugar. Chill.

A festive accompaniment for turkey or ham.

PINEAPPLE PUDDING

Serves 8 to 10

A mock soufflé from Richmond, Virginia

¼ pound plus 6 tablespoons butter, melted
10 slices white bread, crusts removed, cubed
4 eggs, beaten
½ cup sugar
2 tablespoons flour
¼ teaspoon salt
¼ teaspoon pepper
40 ounces canned unsweetened crushed pineapple, drained
2 tablespoons juice from crushed pineapple
2 teaspoons grated lemon peel

In large bowl combine all ingredients. Mix well. Pour into buttered 2½- to 3-quart casserole. Bake in preheated 325° oven 1 hour.

Excellent with ham or poultry.

SCALLOPED OYSTERS

Serves 4 to 6

1   cup cracker crumbs
6   tablespoons melted butter
1   pint fresh oysters, divided
    salt to taste
    pepper to taste
4   tablespoons oyster liquid, divided
2   tablespoons milk or cream, divided
½   teaspoon Worcestershire sauce, divided
    dash cayenne

Combine crumbs and butter. Mix well. Spread a third of the mixture over bottom of shallow buttered baking dish. Cover with half the oysters. Season with salt and pepper. Add half the oyster liquid and 1 tablespoon milk or cream mixed with ¼ teaspoon Worcestershire sauce and cayenne. Repeat procedure ending with crumbs. Bake in preheated 350° oven 30 minutes.

Do not make more than 2 layers.

Excellent with roast turkey.

CURRY RING MOLD

Serves 4

½   cup cold water
2   envelopes unflavored gelatin
⅔   cup hot vinegar
4   eggs
3   tablespoons sugar
2   tablespoons curry powder
½   cup mango chutney
1   cup whipping cream
    salt to taste
    pepper to taste

In food processor or blender, pour water. Sprinkle with gelatin. Let soak 10 minutes. Add vinegar. Blend until gelatin is dissolved. Add eggs, sugar, curry powder, chutney, whipping cream, and salt and pepper to taste. Blend well.

Pour into lightly oiled 4-cup decorative mold. Refrigerate until firm.

Unmold onto center of platter. Surround with thinly sliced cold pink lamb, pork, or chicken. Place wedges of melon and grapes in center of mold.

An unusual mold; a change-of-pace luncheon or supper dish. Doubles well.

MUSTARD MOUSSE

Serves 10 to 12

2   **tablespoons unflavored gelatin**
¼   **cup cold water**
2   **cups imported whole grain hot mustard**
1½   **cups mayonnaise**
¾   **cup whipping cream, whipped**
     watercress or parsley

In small saucepan soften gelatin in water. Place over very low heat and stir until dissolved. Cool until thick and syrupy.

In medium bowl mix mustard and mayonnaise. Stir in gelatin. Fold in whipped cream. Pour into lightly oiled 6-cup mold. Cover and refrigerate 2 hours or until firm.

Loosen edges with sharp knife. Invert onto platter. Garnish with watercress or parsley. Serve in thin slices.

Delicious with cold meats, ham, and poached or cold fish.

Leftover mold can be stirred and served at room temperature as a dip with raw vegetables.

CUCUMBER SORBET

Yield: 1 quart

Refreshing, unusual, and cool.

2   **cups water**
1½   **cups sugar**
2   **cups peeled, seeded, puréed cucumber**
½   **cup calvados (apple brandy)**
     cucumber peel

In medium saucepan combine water and sugar. Bring to boil. Cook uncovered until candy thermometer registers 222°. Cool slightly. Stir cucumber purée and calvados into cooled sugar syrup. Cook again until candy thermometer registers 210°. Cool to room temperature. Freeze mixture in ice cream maker. Garnish with cucumber peel when serving.

CROÛTE FOR SOUP

Serves 4

1   sheet frozen puff pastry, thawed
4   cups soup, chowder, or bisque of choice, room temperature
1   egg white, slightly beaten
4   teaspoons sour cream or sour half and half
2   teaspoons black caviar

Roll out puff pastry on floured surface with floured rolling pin to about half original thickness. Place individual oven-proof soup containers (4 ½-inch custard cups may be used) upside down on pastry. Cut around bowls ¼ to ½-inch larger than perimeter. Reserve pastry rounds.

Fill bowls with soup to within ¾-inch of top. Rub egg white around outside top edge of each bowl and cover with pastry round. Pinch pastry down around top, pressing into egg white. Pierce center twice.

Bake in preheated 375° oven 15 to 20 minutes or until pastry is browned and puffy. Remove from oven. Cut into each center and drop 1 teaspoon sour cream into soup. Top sour cream with ½ teaspoon caviar. Serve immediately.

OPEN FACE BLT

Serves 4

1   cup grated Cheddar cheese
1½   ounces cream cheese
½   teaspoon Worcestershire sauce
3   tablespoons mayonnaise
2   teaspoons prepared mustard
2   tablespoons chopped scallions
½   loaf French bread
5   slices tomato or as needed
10   slices bacon, cooked, drained

In bowl combine Cheddar cheese, cream cheese, Worcestershire sauce, mayonnaise, mustard, and scallions. Mix well. Slice bread lengthwise and spread mixture on each half. Cover with tomato and crisscross bacon over top. Wrap loosely in foil, leaving top open. Bake in preheated 350° oven 25 to 30 minutes. Cut each piece in half. Serve immediately.

MUSHROOM BUBBLE

Serves 8

1   pound mushrooms, sliced
6   tablespoons butter, divided
2   tablespoons flour
½   teaspoon salt
¼   teaspoon pepper
¾   cup milk
1   tablespoon half and half
1   teaspoon cognac
¼   pound Gruyère cheese, grated, divided
8   slices toast

Sauté mushrooms in 4 tablespoons butter. Set aside.

Melt remaining 2 tablespoons butter in heavy pan. Blend in flour, salt, and pepper. Add milk. Cook, stirring constantly, until mixture is very thick and smooth. Add mushrooms, half and half, cognac, and half of Gruyère. Mix well. Spread on toast. Sprinkle with remaining Gruyère. Broil until bubbly and delicately browned.

An excellent savory luncheon dish or, with toast points, an entrée accompaniment.

SABAYON SAUCE

Yield: 2 cups

3   egg yolks
⅔   cup sugar
½   cup Marsala or cream sherry
1   cup whipping cream, whipped
1   square semi-sweet chocolate

Beat egg yolks well. Gradually add sugar, beating constantly. Stir in Marsala or sherry. Transfer to top of double boiler. Over simmering water cook until thickened, stirring constantly. Remove from heat. Chill thoroughly. Fold whipped cream into cooled mixture.

Using potato peeler, shave chocolate curls for garnish.

May be combined with or served over peaches, berries, or grapes.

BRANDIED CHERRY SAUCE

Serves 8

2 cups dry red wine
1 cup superfine sugar
3 cups sweet dark pitted cherries, fresh or canned, drained
1 tablespoon cornstarch
3 tablespoons lemon juice
¼ cup kirsch
¼ cup brandy
   homemade or best quality vanilla or cherry ice cream

In saucepan bring wine to boil. Reduce heat to moderate. Add sugar and stir until totally dissolved, about 5 minutes. Add cherries. Cook until tender if fresh or heated through if canned. Transfer cherries with slotted spoon to separate bowl.

Over high heat cook liquid in saucepan until reduced by a third. Mix cornstarch with lemon juice. Add to saucepan. Stirring constantly, cook until slightly thickened. Add kirsch and cherries. Mix well. Add brandy. Ignite and shake pan until flames go out. Serve warm or chilled over ice cream.

LEMON SAUCE

Yield: 3 cups

4   egg yolks
⅔   cup sugar
¼   pound plus 3 tablespoons butter, melted
4   tablespoons lemon juice
2½ tablespoons grated lemon rind
⅔   cup whipping cream, whipped

Beat egg yolks until thick. Add sugar a little at a time, beating well after each addition. Add butter, juice, and rind. Mix gently. Fold in whipped cream. Refrigerate. Serve chilled with fruit or cake.

DEVONSHIRE CREAM

Yield: ¾ cup

3 ounces cream cheese, regular or low-calorie, softened
½ cup whipping cream
¼ teaspoon vanilla
   confectioners sugar to taste
   fresh fruit of choice

In small bowl beat cheese. Gradually add cream. Beat until smooth. Blend in vanilla and sugar to taste. Serve with fresh strawberries, pineapple chunks, apple slices, orange segments, grapes, sliced bananas, or any other fruit desired.

May also be served with scones, pages 310 and 311.

PRALINE SAUCE

Yield: 2 cups

¾ cup light corn syrup
1½ cups light brown sugar, lightly packed
4 tablespoons butter (do not use margarine)
5 ounces evaporated milk
¾ cup chopped pecans

In saucepan combine corn syrup, sugar, and butter. Stirring frequently, heat to boiling. Cool. Stir in evaporated milk and pecans.

Serve over vanilla ice cream.

May be stored several weeks in refrigerator.

For **Praline Ice Cream,** combine sauce with softened vanilla ice cream. Stir to "marble". Refreeze.

APRICOT SAUCE

Yield: 1 cup

10 ounces apricot preserves
1 tablespoon fresh orange juice
4 teaspoons fresh lemon juice
1 teaspoon grated orange rind

In small saucepan over low heat melt preserves. Stir in remaining ingredients. Serve warm or at room temperature over ice cream, on toast, or spooned over cream cheese accompanied by crackers.

HOT FUDGE SAUCE

Yield: 4 cups

¼   **pound butter**
2   **cups sugar**
14   **ounces sweetened condensed milk**
4   **ounces unsweetened chocolate**
16   **large marshmallows**

In top of double boiler over medium heat combine butter, sugar, milk, and chocolate. Melt completely and mix well. Add marshmallows. Heat until melted. Mix well and serve hot. May be stored in refrigerator for weeks.

CHOCOLATE SAUCE

Yield: 3 cups

4   **ounces unsweetened chocolate**
¼   **pound butter or margarine**
⅓   **cup cocoa**
1½   **cups sugar**
1   **cup whipping cream**
2   **teaspoons vanilla**

Melt chocolate in top of double boiler. Add butter, cocoa, and sugar. Cook 45 minutes, stirring frequently. Add cream and cook 10 minutes longer, stirring constantly. Slowly add vanilla.

If sauce appears to curdle when cream is added, do not be alarmed. It will become smooth.

Especially good served hot over peppermint ice cream. May be stored in refrigerator several weeks.

CARAMEL SAUCE

Yield: 1½ cups

¼   **pound butter**
½   **cup whipping cream**
1   **pound brown sugar**
2   **teaspoons vanilla**

In large saucepan combine butter, cream, and sugar. Simmer until thick and smooth, stirring frequently. Remove from heat. Add vanilla.

May be stored in refrigerator several weeks.

HOT FRUIT SAUCE FOR CHEESECAKE

Yield: 1 cup

A rosy addition to an unadorned cheesecake.

10   **ounces frozen raspberries, thawed, or fruit of choice**
1   **tablespoon cornstarch**
2   **tablespoons Cointreau or orange juice**

In saucepan heat berries over medium heat. In small bowl dissolve cornstarch in Cointreau or juice. Stir cornstarch mixture into simmering berries. Cook, stirring constantly, until thickened. Pour into serving bowl. Pass with cheesecake.

CHOCOLATE LEAVES

Yield: approximately 20-25

½   **ounce Hershey's all natural unsweetened baking chocolate**
2   **ounces semi-sweet chocolate bits**
    silk leaves or fresh green leaves, 2 to 3 inches in length

In top of double boiler or in heavy copper pan, melt chocolate. Stir until smooth. Remove from heat. Using pastry brush, spread chocolate on lightly oiled backs of leaves. Refrigerate until set. Carefully peel chocolate from leaves. Use leaves to decorate cake, ice cream, sorbet, or dessert of choice.

See photo page 234.

SPIRITED EGGNOG

Yield: 4 quarts

3   **quarts dairy eggnog**
3⅓   **cups rye whiskey**
½   **cup Jamaican rum**
¼   **cup cognac**
1   **pint whipping cream**
    nutmeg to taste

Combine eggnog and liquors. Mix well. Refrigerate several hours or overnight.

Whip cream until soft peaks form. Transfer eggnog to punch bowl. Stir in 1 cup whipped cream. Place remaining whipped cream in bowl next to punch bowl. Place dollop of cream and sprinkle of nutmeg on each serving.

WHITE SANGRÍA

Yield: 4 quarts

3   quarts Rhine or Chablis wine
¾   cup Curaçao
½   cup brandy
10 ounces frozen strawberries, thawed
10 ounces frozen mixed fruit, thawed
2   oranges, quartered
1   lime, quartered
1   lemon, quartered
    sugar to taste
    fresh fruit of choice, optional

Combine all ingredients except fresh fruit. Stir until sugar dissolves. Refrigerate 24 hours. Garnish with fresh fruit.

See photo page 227.

BRANDY SLUSH

Serves 12

9   cups water, divided
2   cups sugar
4   tea bags
12 ounces frozen orange juice concentrate
12 ounces frozen lemonade concentrate
2   cups brandy
1   quart 7-Up or ginger ale

In large saucepan combine 7 cups water and sugar. Boil 10 minutes. Cool.

In separate saucepan boil remaining 2 cups water. Remove from heat. Add tea bags and let stand 20 minutes. Remove tea bags and cool.

When both liquids are cool, mix together. Add undiluted orange juice and lemonade. Mix well. Stir in brandy. Pour into 2 or 3 plastic containers. Cover and freeze. To serve do not defrost. Place entire frozen mixture in punch bowl. Add 7-Up or ginger ale. Stir quickly and serve immediately.

To serve as dessert, place several scoops frozen mixture in individual footed glasses, add ¼ to ⅓ cup ginger ale or 7-Up, and serve immediately.

Marvelous summertime drink or dessert. Keep in freezer ready to serve at a moment's notice.

LO-CAL FRUIT SHAKE

Yield: 1 tall glass

½   cup orange juice
½   ripe banana
½   peach, ½ apple, or 5 strawberries
1   tablespoon plain yogurt
¼   teaspoon cinnamon
1   teaspoon honey or 1 package sugar substitute
4-5   ice cubes

In food processor or blender combine all ingredients. Blend on high 20 to 30 seconds. Start and stop machine a few times to settle ice. Blend until ice lumps disappear. Serve immediately.

Any ripe fruit may be substituted for fruits listed.

HOT CRANBERRY BREW

Yield: 4 quarts

Wonderful aroma.

1   cup brown sugar
1½   teaspoons whole cloves
4   cinnamon sticks
2   quarts cranberry juice
46   ounces pineapple juice
4½   cups water

Place sugar and spices in 30-cup electric coffee pot basket. Add juices and water. Cycle as for coffee. Serve hot, directly from coffee pot.

ACKNOWLEDGMENTS

NOTEWORTHY would like to thank those who contributed, tested, and proofread the recipes in this book. It is their diligence and commitment that have assured its high quality.

Area Testing Chairmen

Chicago:
Heather Bilandic, Gloria Gottlieb, Norma Harris

Glencoe:
Muriel Fulton

Highland Park:
Ilo Harris

Hinsdale/Oak Brook:
Phyllis Forward, Betty Harvey, Parsla Mason

Lake Forest:
Mary Beth Donnelley, Joan Lydy, Pat Sikorovsky

Northbrook/Bannockburn:
Charlotte Hadley, Barbara Marshall, Lois Steans

Oak Park/River Forest:
Ellen Gignilliat, Martha Tardy

Winnetka/Kenilworth:
Sandy Crown, Margy Eberhardt, Jeannie James, Sallie Scott

Abbado, Claudio
Abrahamson, Sonya
Ackerberg, Carol
Adler, Joan
Akos, Marion
Allen, Pat
Allyn, Margaret
Alsdorf, Marilyn
Anderson, Kathie
Anderson, Mary
Anderson, Ruth
Anderson, Trisha
Anthony, Catherine
Antley, Mills
Arena, Alice
Arenberg, Joan
Arthur, Marianne
Ault, Valerie
Aurandt, Tanya
Avery, Jean
Bachner, Margaret
Baird, Julie
Baker, Ann
Baker, Beverly
Baker, Louise
Bartlett, Janice
Bash, Flora
Baskin, Judith
Baty, David
Bauer, Carol
Bay, Karen

Beals, Alice
Beattie, Mary
Beatty, Frances
Beautyman, Daphne
Beers, Jane
Bender, Muriel
Bendix, Gretchen
Benstein, Julie
Berghoff, Jean
Bertolli, Louise
Bertolli, Paul
Bertolli, Tom
Biggs, Ruth
Bilandic, Heather
Binzel, Betty
Blankshain, Ruth
Blatchford, Irma
Bloom, Katie
Bodeen, Nancy
Boreisha, Ludmilla
Botti, Sheila
Bottum, Joyce
Bourn, Jane
Bradley, Marilyn
Bramson, Mary Liz
Brandon, Joyce
Bransky, Beverly
Brecher, Anita
Bredrup, Elizabeth
Brennan, Frances
Breuer, Alyson

Brodwin, Carol
Brody, Clark
Bronner, Elaine
Brown, Barbara
Brown, Jean
Brown, Judy
Bunta, Muriel
Burnham, Alice
Busch, Barbara
Butler, Mary Jane
Cagen, Lila
Cain, Talbot
Calhoun, Shirley
Camino, Lanie
Campbell, Heather
Campbell, Jane
Canovi, Claudia
Carton, Ann
Carton, Jean
Cartright, Lenora
Castonguay, Cathy
Chaffetz, Sara
Chalmers, Georganne
Chanen, Doralu
Chauner, Diane
Christopherson, Myrna
Cirzan, Andy
Cirzan, Ruth
Cleveland, Candy
Clevenger, Dale
Cline, Richard

Cobey, Mitchell
Cole, Sharon
Colman, Jane
Collins, Carolyn
Corzatt, Susan
Coven, Ludmilla
Crown, Sandy
Daly, Martha
D'Ancona, Terri
Darby, Nettie
Darrow, Anita
Dart, Susan
David, Joan
David, Pam
Davis, Jill
Davis, Merri
DeGroot, Helen
DeWitt, Eleanor
Dickes, Sue
Dixon, Sharon
Donnelley, Mary Beth
Douglas, Bunny
Downey, Chris
Dubinsky, Sherrie
Duffy, Bea
Duncan, Deuel
Durand, Jacqueline
Eberhardt, Margy
Edvenson, Claire
Edwards, Nancy
Egan, Maureen

Egan, Michael
Elman, Joan
Engelman, Mary
Epkins, Carol
Erickson, Jeanne
Eyerman, Mary Kay
Falls, Carol
Felsenthal, Geoff
Felton-Elkins, Nancy
Fick, Cindy
Field, Mindy
Fishbein, Ann
Fitzgerald, Patricia
Flair, JoAnn
Florsheim, Nancy
Foreman, Hinda
Forward, Phyllis
Frankel, Adrienne
Freehling, Joan
Freeto, Betty
Freivogel, Caroline
Frey, Mary
Friedler, Kit
Friedman, Marilyn
Fulton, Muriel
Ganzer, Anne
Ganzer, Theresa
Garvy, Addie
Garvey, Kristen
Garza, Marge
Georgis, Bill

Gerdom, Ann
Gibbs, Jean
Gidwitz, Jane
Giesen, Jeannine
Gignilliat, Ellen
Gignilliat, Suzanne
Gilbert, Connie
Gilhooly, Mary Ann
Gillel, Connie
Gillette, Karla
Gingiss, Helene
Gingiss, Rosalie
Glazer, Marilyn
Gleason, Kathy
Glick, Nancy
Glickman, Sarita
Golden, Marian
Gomez, Estella
Gonzalez, Elaine
Good, Alison
Goodman, Mary
Goodman, Valerie
Gordon, Edward
Gordon, Judy
Gore, Sandra
Gottlieb, Donna
Gottlieb, Gloria
Govert, Mary
Gramm, Annemie
Grebe, Ann
Greenebaum, Helen

Grisemer, Jan
Grube, Ann
Grunther, Alma Gene
Gunn, Ann
Gunn, Betty
Guthman, Patricia
Guthrie, Lou
Haarlow, Lynne
Haber, Dorothy
Haber, Robin
Hadley, Charlotte
Harris, Ilo
Harris, Margaret
Harris, Meredith
Harris, Nancy
Harris, Nicki
Harris, Norma
Harrison, Kathy
Hart, Talley
Hartman, Betsy
Harvey, Betty
Harvey, Lynne
Healy, Jeannie
Hegwood, Janet
Hergott, Renée
Hey, Joan
Heymann, Pat
Hicks, Mary Jane
Hilden, Marjorie
Hill, Ann
Hiller, Dora
Hirsh, Harriet
Hirte, Karen
Hodgkins, Bondy
Hollander, Lois
Hotchkiss, Sue
Horcher, Florence
Hornick, Danielle
Hungerford, Sally
Hunt, Julia
Hunter, Maxine
Innes, Ernestine
Irvine, Dodie
Irwin, Katie
Isserman, Barbara
James, Jeannie
Jester, Pat
Johnson, Arlene
Johnson, Eileen
Jones, Darlene
Jones, Dollie
Jorndt, Pat
Kadet, Juell
Kammerer, Mia
Kaplan, Kathy
Karzas, Dianne
Kates, Diane
Kates, Linda
Katris, Helen
Kay, Jean
Keare, Miriam
Keefe, Kika
Keim, Alice
Kelley, Janet

Kerth, Dawn
Kijac, Maria
Kindsvater, Connie
King, Sue
Kirkland, Mary
Kirkwood, Ann
Kneibler, Maycat
Kohn, Helene
Kolb, Judith
Korff, Shirley
Kostrubala, Ingrid
Kovach, Marilyn
Kovas, Kathy
Krauss, Anne
Kravitt, Beverly
Kravitt, Shirley
Kroeschell, Susan
Kroha, Nona Jane
Lackritz, Therese
Landreth, Helen
Langbein, Kirsti
Law, Ruth
Lawton, Mary
Lee, Lois
Leonard, Vivita
Levine, Helen
Levy, Carolyn
Levy, Lois
Lind, Carla
Lind, Nancy
Linhart, Barbara
Lins, Louise
Lipsig, Joan
Lipsky, Nancy
Lloyd, Marion
Locke, Lou
Lockett, Maggie
Lovett, Danny
Lowinsky, Bonnie
Lubin, Amy
Luke, Ceil
Lydy, Joan
Lyman, Anne
Lynch, Dolores
Lynch, Maureen
McClevey, Lupie
McClory, Doris
McClure, Margaret
McCormick, Mari
McDermott, Ann
McDonough, Elke
McGreevy, Marilyn
McNally, Carolynn
MacIntire, Joan
Mackenzie, Betty
Mackey, Winnie
Mackler, Natalie
MacLeod, Martha
Madoff, Shenah
Magill, Jeanette
Magoun, Patti
Manilow, Susan
Mann, Sada
Marber, Vicki

Marovitz, James
Marr, Ruth
Marshal, Kristen
Marshall, Barbara
Martin, Sally
Martynenko, Justyna
Mason, Anabel
Mason, Christopher
Mason, Julie
Mason, Parsla
Mathews, Elaine
Meador, Emily
Melamed, Dorothe
Metz, Maryanne
Metzger, Jan
Millmon, Lucy
Minor, Lucy
Minow, Jo
Missimer, Jane
Moriarty, Meredith
Moser, Diana
Muehrcke, Gail
Muehrcke, JoAnn
Mueller, Marge
Mueller, Martha
Muir, Patti
Mulroy, Dorothy
Murphy, Breege
Nath, Ruth
Nathan, Boots
Nathan, Peggy
Nathan, Lou
Nathanson, Evalyn
Neibury, Diane
Nelson, Beverly
Nelson, Kay
Nerad, Ann
Newberry, Diane
Nicholson, Anne
Noah, Dorie
Norman, Jessye
Noyes, Ginny
O'Connor, Ellen
Oelman, Sue
Olson, Joan
Olson, Katie
Olson, Mary
Ostrander, Mimi
Palombi, Maureen
Papa, Rebecca
Pappas, Bette
Parsons, Margaret
Patterson, Connie
Pearsall, Jane
Pedersen, Boots
Perutz, Gerald
Peterson, Clarka
Petyson, Nina
Pfaelzer, Alice
Pick, Sue
Pieracci, Wilma
Pikas, Joan
Piskorsky, Mary
Plum, Betty

Powell, Ruth
Pratt, Marilyn
Preservation Hall
Presman, Helen
Pritzker, Cindy
Quaid, Mary
Rabert, Bonnie
Randolph, Patricia
Rapp, Helen
Ratcliff, Patti
Razor, Sharon
Reed, Judith
Reskin, Merle
Reyes, Lepida
Reynolds, Eileen
Richland, Lucy
Rieger, Nancy
Rieger, Pearl
Rinella, Gloria
Ritter, Mary
Robb, Christine
Robinson, Dorothy
Robson, Margaret
Rohan, Ruth
Rohlen, Carolyn
Rohr, Jimmy
Rome, Topsy
Roob, Barbara
Rose, Ann
Rosenberg, Madeline
Rosensweig, Betsy
Rothschild, Babette
Rusnak, Sallyan
Ruwitch, Shirley
Sakar, Rita
St. Germaine, Georgia
Salem, Nancy
Salzman, Janis
Sands, Barbara
Savage, Muriel
Schatz, Peggy
Schmidt, Sally
Schmidt, Mary Jane
Schofield, Nancy
Schram, Natalie
Schubert, Carol
Schultz, Barbara
Scott, Connie
Scott, Sallie
Scoville, Peggy
Segal, Diane
Seweloh, Kathleen
Shapiro, Kate
Shapiro, Louis
Shean, Lyn
Shein, Jane
Sherman, Marge
Shevick, Shirley
Shorney, Erika
Shriver, Ione
Shrock, Phyllis
Sickle, Valerie
Sideman, Barbara
Siegel, Patricia

Siglin, Shirley
Sikorovsky, Pat
Silverstein, Marcy
Slaughter, Florence
Slivers, Gottchen
Smith, Muriel
Smith, Patricia
Solano, Pat
Solomon, Shirley
Sooy, Jane
Sparks, Esther
Spears, Susan
Spiegel, Audrey
Spitz, Barbara
Spooner, Mia
Steans, Heather
Steans, Jennifer
Steans, Lois
Steans, Robin
Stein, Florence
Stein, Ruth
Stern, Florence
Sternberg, Doris
Stevens, Dorothy
Stevens, Louise
Stocker, Gage
Stoltz, Mary
Stone, Barbara
Stone, Susan
Stotler, Lori
Stromberg, Sue
Strubel, Ella
Stucka, Kay
Svoboda, Carol
Svoboda, Marion
Swan, Sue
Swift, Peggy
Swingle, Mary
Taich, Sarah
Tardy, Martha
Tarochione, Jeannine
Taylor, Ann
Taylor, Betty
Test, Betty
Tetzloff, Marian
Thaviu, Ellie
Ther, Terry
Thomas, Helen
Thompson, Alejandra
Tomaras, Terry
Treskon, Bea
Trienens, Paula
Tyler, Marian
Uhlmann, Karen
Uhlmann, Ginger
Ullman, Ann
Vail, Peggy
Valach, Marion
Vale, Virginia
Vance, Melinda
Vanderaa, Audrey
Van der Kieft, Carol
Van Gorkom, Betty
Van Verst, Mary

Vasterling, Dorothy
Vignocchi, Mary
Von Schlegell, Abbie
Von Schlegell, Fran
Voyvodic, Peg
Wagner, Marcia
Walken, Naomi
Wallenstein, Betty
Walters, Janet
Walters, Suzie
Walton, Karen
Walton, Rheda
Wanic, Paul
Ward, Jeann
Warrington, Lenore
Watson, Martha
Webb, Pat
Webber, Clarine
Webber, Myra
Weeden, Jane
Weidner, Debi
Weil, Angela
Weil, Frederick
Weil, Jan
Weil, Jane
Weil, Susan
Weinberg, Nina
Weinstein, Mary
Weiss, Flo
Weissler, Suzanne
Wellman, Barbara
Wessel, Nancy
White, Kitten
White, Patti
Whitsell, Janice
Wierun, Jean
Wilder, Caryl
Wiley, Sally
Wilheim, Lois
Williams, Barbara
Williams, Janet
Williams, Lynn
Willner, Maddie
Wineman, Pat
Woldenberg, Jane
Wolff, Gail
Wood, Pat
Woulfe, Nancy
Wurzberg, Minna
York, William
Young, Sandra
Zapffe, Sandy
Zimmer, Barbara
Zobel, Claudette

NOTES

To Reorder

Please send _____ copies $15.95 each _____

Add shipping and handling 2.75 each _____

Add gift wrap 1.00 each _____

For books to be sent to an
Illinois address add 7%
sales tax 1.05 each _____

Total _____

Please print carefully

☐ Check payable to NOTEWORTHY enclosed or
Please charge to: ☐ MasterCard ☐ VISA
Card Number
☐☐☐☐ ☐☐☐☐ ☐☐☐☐ ☐☐☐☐

Expiration Date ☐☐ ☐☐

NOTEWORTHY
1575 Oakwood Avenue, Highland Park, Illinois 60035
Telephone 708/433-8800

Signature _____

Name _____

Address _____

City _____

State _____ Zip _____

Daytime Telephone _____

Please allow three weeks for delivery
If you wish cookbooks mailed to other addresses please enclose
additional names and addresses on a separate piece of paper. If you
wish to enclose personal gift cards, please write name of recipient
on outside of envelope and enclose with your order.

All proceeds from the sale of NOTEWORTHY will be used to
benefit the Young Artists Institute of the Ravinia Festival
Association.

Thank you for your order

To Reorder

Please send _____ copies $15.95 each _____

Add shipping and handling 2.75 each _____

Add gift wrap 1.00 each _____

For books to be sent to an
Illinois address add 7%
sales tax 1.05 each _____

Total _____

Please print carefully

☐ Check payable to NOTEWORTHY enclosed or
Please charge to: ☐ MasterCard ☐ VISA
Card Number
☐☐☐☐ ☐☐☐☐ ☐☐☐☐ ☐☐☐☐

Expiration Date ☐☐ ☐☐

NOTEWORTHY
1575 Oakwood Avenue, Highland Park, Illinois 60035
Telephone 708/433-8800

Signature _____

Name _____

Address _____

City _____

State _____ Zip _____

Daytime Telephone _____

Please allow three weeks for delivery
If you wish cookbooks mailed to other addresses please enclose
additional names and addresses on a separate piece of paper. If you
wish to enclose personal gift cards, please write name of recipient
on outside of envelope and enclose with your order.

All proceeds from the sale of NOTEWORTHY will be used to
benefit the Young Artists Institute of the Ravinia Festival
Association.

Thank you for your order

cut on dotted lines